BEYOND FOUR WALLS

BEYOND FOUR WALLS

The Origins and Development
of Canadian Museums

Archie F. Key

MCCLELLAND AND STEWART LIMITED

Contents

Preface

Originally this book was to have been an official report of a three years' survey of Canadian museums' resources commissioned by the Canadian Museums' Association on grants from the Department of the Secretary of State of Canada and which involved 52,000 miles of automobile travel over Canadian highways. A temporary cutback in funds saw the final phase of this project cancelled, but the C.M.A. Council granted me permission to have access to all material. Obviously it is impossible to list all those who responded at varying times to my insistent requests for information and I can only hope that each one will enjoy a sense of satisfaction in the role he has played.

Many former colleagues, government officials and friends have played their respective roles as correspondents and advisers and have given graciously of their time and knowledge, while others have sent me books and periodicals without which my manuscript would have suffered. To all these people and to that generation of pioneers who, in face of frustrations, public apathy, and discouragement, made their individual contributions to keep the Canadian museum movement alive, this book is dedicated.

I also wish to acknowledge assistance in the form of travel grants from The Canada Council and its special grant to the publishers; the services of my wife Marjorie as amanuensis and editor, with a special word of gratitude to Jack McClelland who, when asking for first option on the manuscript, wrote "It is the sort of thing which should be supported even if we don't make money." I would like to hope that he is right on his first premise and wrong on the second one.

A.F.K.

Introduction

Until the mid-1960's, Canadian museums functioned in a grey area within the body politic. Over the years, the word "museum" gradually fell into disfavour, eventually presenting an image of a morgue designed to collect, identify and preserve inanimate objects for an undefined posterity. There is a measure of truth in such a definition. Until recently, sometimes to the detriment of the public, the major role of the larger museums was in the field of scholarly research, a function now more and more being transferred to the university campus.

Despite both public and private apathy, lack of funds, and appropriate buildings, the dedicated men and women involved in the museum movement persisted in the belief that Canadians eventually would find an awareness in the significance of their history and achieve with it a cultural maturity.

The first half of the nineteenth century saw the genesis of Canadian museums. In the Atlantic provinces they made important contributions to adult education, while in Quebec museums served as annexes to scholastic institutions dedicated to the philosophy of classical education. But governments at all levels were reluctant to provide fiscal aid to institutions which they viewed as esoteric, failing to recognize their educational value, and, more important, their economic importance as showcases for the display of the flora, fauna, and economic geology of a young colony rich with natural resources overdue for exploitation.

Throughout the years the occasional glimmer of light filtered through, but events, national and international, conspired to douse the flame. World War I saw money and manpower diverted to the war effort; the disastrous fire on Parliament Hill in 1916 resulted in a virtual closing down of the National Museums complex for five years during a critical period in Canada's cultural growth. Ambitious programs were launched during the brief period of affluence in the late 1920's only to be shattered following the stock market collapse, and in 1939 once again manpower and monies were diverted to a second war effort.

The next faint flutterings of museum resurgence appeared in the 1940's as Canadians became more conscious of a national identity. The Canadian Arts Council was founded in 1945 to serve as a political voice. Two years later the American Association of Museums, as a fraternal gesture to its Canadian colleagues, held its annual meeting in Quebec. Twenty-four hours later the Canadian Museums Association was organized, and within a few weeks it had linked itself with the International Council of Museums. That same year, the American Geological Society staged its annual meeting in Ottawa to celebrate, somewhat belatedly, the centenary of the founding of the Geological Survey of Canada, and, incidentally, that of Canada's National Museum of Science.

The flutter turned to ferment in the next decade but not until the one thousand days before centennial year did the reverberations of the museum explosion hit public consciousness.

There were factors other than the centennial which contributed to this spectacular development. Paved highways from coast to coast and a proliferation of automobile travel closely followed by the jet age exposed Canadians to new scenes and old cultures. The museum fraternity was beginning to move out of the philosophy (and techniques) of the morgue to a level of activity more closely resembling a beehive, with here and there some experimental cross-fertilization.

No apologies are offered for taking the reader on an extensive detour in time and space for a tabloid picture of the compulsions of man to create, collect, and communicate to his fellow man, or the prevailing gods. Too many people view the museum as a static institution confined within four walls. That museums have functioned and still are functioning under many nomenclatures is relatively unrecognized: the names extend through the alphabet from archives to zoos.

In the course of this history one finds parallels, landmarks and motivations applicable to Canada's museum scene, and as we laugh at the foibles, speculations, superstitions, and rationalizations of our forbears we nevertheless discover that museums throughout the years have responded to the challenge of changing social orders. It is also well to remember that two hundred, or perhaps twenty thousand years from now our descendants may have their lively chuckles at our expense.

ARCHIE F. KEY

BEYOND FOUR WALLS

I

From Lascaux to Darwin

*A few random definitions
followed by the story of
museum origins, changing
philosophies and techniques*

1

Historians date the origin of museums to the edifice of Ptolemy Sotor, concerning themselves more with the origin of the word than with the compulsions of primitive man to create and display visual objects as educational instruments. More often than not such artifacts may have been used to appease the spirits or the prevalent gods, to reinforce the ego, or as seems to be the case with our contemporary Eskimo, as a form of entertainment to relieve the boredom of long winter nights with an occasional moral lesson added.

The twentieth century definition of what constitutes a museum was established in Paris at the first Congress of the International Council of Museums in 1947: "The word 'museum' shall include all collections, open to the public, of artistic, technical, scientific, historical or archaeological material, including zoos, botanical gardens, but excluding libraries except insofar as they maintain permanent exhibition rooms." In this definition, there is an acceptance of the premise that museums are not necessarily confined to four walls, as for instance, the restored military fortifications, ghost towns, aboriginal agricultural lands, and the long buried communities of early history such as Pompeii and Troy.

Accepting this premise, the Lascaux Grottoes, in south-western France, could well form the oldest museum complex known to twentieth-century man. The wash drawings and rock engravings on the walls and roofs of these intercommunicating subterranean galleries depict the animal life of the palaeolithic period, thus spelling out the story of the thought processes of the Aurignacio-Perigorden tribes.

Annette Lamming, in her definitive work on Lascaux, refers to this palaeolithic sanctuary as providing "the first testimony of any human activity unconnected with immediate material needs." And she continues, "On the emotional plane the paintings seem to bear witness to a sense of religious awe, of harmony and beauty which brings these remote ancestors closer to us; on the technical plane to

14

show a capacity to create magnificent works of art; and on the intellectual plane to make the first step toward conceptual art and writing itself."

The Lascaux Grottoes were opened to the public shortly after the end of World War II, attendance being limited to five hundred in any one day. However, the grottoes have been closed since 1960, when conservationists discovered a form of green mould insidiously destroying paintings which had survived "thousands of years of solitude and darkness," and have only recently been reopened on a highly restricted basis.

While the story of Lascaux has many unique features, it has parallels in the cave drawings of Altamira in Northern Spain. Other important cave museums may be seen at Tassili, Rhodesia, and more recently, in the still-to-be-completed excavation and restoration at Catal Huyuk, the oldest known organized agricultural community of the early neolithic (c.6600-5800 B.C.) period on the Konya Plains of Turkey. The latter site has revealed multi-coloured murals of human figures participating in ritual dancing and dramatic hunting scenes, as well as many shrines whose walls are covered with totemic symbols. An interesting sidelight of the Catal-Huyuk exploration is the involvement of Toronto's Royal Ontario Museum in this archaeological project.

On this continent, the ancient Mexican pyramids easily come to mind as another such discovery. Canada has a few small but increasingly significant twentieth-century "caves" as seen in the Tom Thomson shack recently salvaged from a Toronto junkyard and re-established at the McMichael Conservation Collection of Art at Kleinburg, Ontario, and the Group of Seven summer camp brought from the Algonquins which has been reassembled in the National Gallery.

Possibly the most significant "cave" has only recently been discovered by the art world, a fragile two-storey frame dwelling at 669 rue Tache in Chicoutimi, Quebec, where M. Arthur Villeneuve, *"barbier-peintre,"* has virtually covered every inch of wall-space in his Musée de l'Artiste with *"peintures représentant des scènes folkloriques."* It is to be hoped that this dwelling will be declared an important historic site before urban renewal engineers move into the district.

Total historical involvement has extended into entire communities since the beginning of this century, Williamsburg, Virginia, representing the ultimate. In Mexico, the city of Taxco is another such community museum.

In recent years attempts have been made in Canada to conserve communities in whole or in part for posterity with Niagara-on-the-Lake, Ontario, as one such example, and the ghost town of

Barkerville in northern British Columbia as another. Canada's Centennial Commission in the two or three years prior to Confederation celebrations sought to persuade citizens in many communities to undertake major restoration programs and met with some success in Perth and Niagara Falls, Ontario.

Historic reconstructions have met with a modicum of success in Canada largely due to the National Historic Sites Service, its major project being the restoration of Fort Louisbourg on Cape Breton Island.

André Malraux, in his *Voices of Silence* speaks of "museums without walls," putting forward the premise that objects removed from their environment lose much of their significance. Just as a phrase taken out of context is frequently subjected to misinterpretation, so an object displaced from its original setting can take on a new and at times spurious character.

A recent and notorious example is that of London Bridge, now dismantled for reassembling "with dignity and respect, in the form that it has been known to generations of world travellers" as advertised by Creative Enterprises Inc. of Lake Havasu City in Arizona. The McCulloch Oil Corp. views the bridge reconstruction as an attraction which could bring more than two and a quarter million tourists during its first year in operation. It is conceded that there were segments of the bridge left over, the stones from which have been used for fireplace mantels or sold as souvenirs. An expatriate Canadian, one Ken Buck, is quoted by *Canadian Magazine* of June 20, 1970 as saying "There's going to be money in the pockets of those tourists." However, the bridge itself can now be viewed as an alien and lonely structure divorced from the historic setting around which its legends had blossomed.

Malraux gives an apt parallel to this callous exploitation when he speaks of art galleries which "have tended to transform even portraits into pictures. . ." What do we care who the "Man with the Helmet" or the "Man with the Glove" may have been in real life? For us their names are Rembrandt and Titian. The men who sat for these portraits have sunk into oblivion.

This philosophy is not advanced to debase the functions of museums in general, but rather to emphasise the fact that another museum technique, that of interpretation, is all important. The two paintings just mentioned have had their historical content subordinated to their qualities as fine art, which is, after all, somewhat better than being cut up and used as a jig-saw puzzle for the people of Lake Havasu City.

It is only within recent years that museums have developed techniques to simulate total environment, such as the diorama type of display usually associated with natural history, the reconstruction of pioneer rooms in the museums of human history, and emphasis on thematic display. One notable example of such techniques is to be seen at The Cloisters, the late medieval castle which serves as an annex to New York's Metropolitan Museum of Fine Art, and made possible through the generous financing of the Rockefeller family. The success of the Cloisters is due almost wholly to the fact that the building serves as a frame within which objects reflecting the social mores of one specific era have been assembled.

"The story of Greece is the first chapter in the political and intellectual life of Europe," said George Brown Goode, for many years Assistant Secretary of the Smithsonian Institution and first Director of the National Museum in Washington, D.C., when addressing the American Historical Association on December 26th, 1888. He spoke of the era of Alexander the Great and Aristotle, a period of conquest, enquiry and exploration. It was a pagan civilization whose people worshipped at the shrine of the muses, mythological figures symbolising what we refer to now as the humanities, including history and astronomy. "Around the altar they sang of the origin of the world, of gods and men, of the glorious deeds of Zeus; they also honored the great legendary heroes in song, dance, drama and poetry."

The Alexandrian library and a complex of other buildings which comprised what we would call today a university were then aptly named *mouseion* as a tribute to the nine goddesses. By the end of the fourth century A.D., the word fell into temporary disuse, only to be revived eleven centuries later in the early 1600's by Paolo Giovo, historian and Bishop of Como, who latinized it to *musaeum,* describing it as a "place of study." Giovo, an avid collector, was reported as having several hundred works of art "ranging from Aristotle to Leonardo which he displayed in what was known as *guarderoba* or *studiolo.*" Later, *musaeum* was again to be translated into more contemporary Italian as *museo,* adapted by France as *musée,* and eventually anglicised about the beginning of the seventeenth century when it was applied to the Ashmolean Museum at Oxford, England.

Other designations were also in vogue during the age of learning when collectors vied with each other to establish areas for display, such terms being used as *arca rerum fossilium, chambre de raretés, galeries d'antiquités,* still later in the German states, *Kunstkammer,* and at this same period in other European countries, *cabinet de curiosités.* It is possible that Dr. Samuel Johnson gave to "museum" its first authoritative function when he wrote that it represented "a repository of learned curiosities."

A picture gallery is reported as having been a popular gathering place in Sicyon toward the end of the fourth century B.C. where local artists exhibited. During the next century, the sanctuaries of Olympia and Samos employed guides to lecture on the many pieces of sculpture they possessed. Reproductions of these works became the prototypes of the mass-produced replicas of later centuries.

At about this same time, an art museum dedicated to the display of works of earlier centuries existed in Athens. Pausanias, the Greek geographer of the second century B.C., speaks of a *pinacothece* in Athens, an edifice adjacent to the Propylaea where pictures "which time has not effaced" were shown. The term *pinacotheca* was commonly used by the Romans to define a gallery containing pictures, statues, and other works of art, the name being immortalized much later in Munich where two art museums, the Alta Pinakothek and the Neu Pinakothek, have existed for more than a century.

In his saga of eleven years of war, conquest, and exploration taking him from the Mediterranean to the borders of China, Alexander the Great travelled with a retinue of 30,000 infantry, 5,000 cavalry and a vast company of artists, poets, philosophers, historians, surveyors, engineers, geographers, hydrographers, geologists, botanists and other scientists for the purpose of studying the phenomena of Asia.

Alexander also granted to Aristotle, his illustrious teacher, a large sum of money for use in his scientific researches; sent him natural history collections from conquered lands and put at his service more men to collect specimens upon which he, Aristotle, based his work on natural history. Emily Hahn, in an article entitled "Days at the Zoo" published in *The New Yorker* of September 2 and 9, 1972 and later published in book form, adds to this by remarking that "Greeks generally preferred wild birds to mammals as pets, but Alexander maintained stables of both South African and Indian elephants, and kept bears, monkeys and other strange animals he received in tribute from the peoples his army vanquished, thus being the first man in history to turn his menagerie to scientific use, enjoining his tutor, Aristotle, 'to study natural history by means of captive animals.' "

The first zoological gardens of which there are any records were founded in China in the twelfth century B.C..

Between the third and the thirteenth centuries throughout the known occidental world human values underwent radical change. As Christian and Mohammedan philosophies and faiths took root, man's conduct was moulded to conform to new patterns of social organization. However, through this period there was still extensive creative activity, the church itself assuming the functions of the museum by displaying religious symbols on walls, in addition to stained glass windows, statuary, and relics dedicated to "the glory of God" and on occasion to the prevailing Pope or patron. Such decor served to augment the spoken word uttered by the clergy to their predominantly illiterate congregations.

Although the museum had vanished, the collector in church or state still remained. Travellers to distant lands invariably returned with souvenirs for display or distribution to friends or patrons. Relics, many of which were believed capable of invoking supernatural influence, were kept in cabinets, or for more personal reasons contained in a reliquary specifically designed for easy transportation. A writer in 1888 emphasizes this fact by declaring the reliquary as "the most precious ornament in the Lady's chamber, in the Knight's armoury, in the King's hall of state, as well as in that of the Bishop or the Pope." At this time religious relics – the hair of the prophet, wood from the true cross, bones of the saints – were also used and displayed as instruments for the performance of miracles, a practice still extant. This urge to collect in a highly specialized field became a major activity of the priest. David Murray, in his work *Museums, Their History and Use* published in 1904, tells of relics, such as "the shift of the Virgin, the thumbs of St. Sergius and of St. Bartholemew being carried and exposed to counteract all manner of danger, tempest and lightning."

It was both logical and expedient for the individual church to collect, preserve and display such relics and "curiosities" credited with miraculous powers even though the relationship between the object and the divine authority was somewhat tenuous. Thus one could find in many churches such articles as the egg of an ostrich, claws of the mythical griffin, the "thunderbolt" horn of the unicorn (of which there were many), giants' bones, some measuring several feet in length, the rib of a whale, and similar oddities. Boccaccio records that "in the church of the Annunciation in Trapini, Sicily, three teeth weighing a hundred ounces of an enormous giant of 200 cubits in height were hung on a wire." And in the church of St. Vulgran, a cayman (presumably a giant alligator) was "suspended on the wall near the north-east door."

King David of Scotland presented to "the Abbey" two walrus or hippopotamus tusks, while in the treasury of St. Mark's Cathedral in Venice "they show you likewise a lilly, offer'd by Henry III of France to the Most Serene Republic, and a surprising pearl, call'd mother-pearl, and several things of that nature."

The many centuries from the disintegration of Greece and through the rise and fall of the Roman Empire saw what appears to have been a deliberate desire to wipe out every last vestige of pagan culture, although historians are inclined to disagree. John Thomas Shotwell, writing in the 11th edition (1910-1911) of the *Encyclo-*

pedia Britannica states that "in the realm of art the 'middle ages' had already set in before Constantine II (in the 4th century) robbed the arch of Titus to decorate his own (arch) and before those museums of antiquity, the temples, were plundered by christian mobs."

From the fourth to the twelfth centuries ecclesiastical authorities, while in agreement that all traces of pagan culture should be destroyed, were in conflict concerning visual interpretation of the Christian doctrine, the iconoclasts requiring the removal of all sacred images, while the Germans and other barbarians were sacking and destroying the monuments of Greek civilization. At the end of the sixth century, Pope Gregory I voiced his argument, later to become an edict of the church, that "it is one thing to worship a picture and another to learn from the language of a picture that which ought to be worshipped. What those who can read learn by means of writing, that do the uneducated learn by looking at a picture . . . that, therefore, ought not to have been destroyed which had been placed in churches not for worship, but solely for instructing the minds of the ignorant."

The use of churches and temples as proselytizing art galleries was not always popular, for in the crusading epoch the Cathers and Paulicians carried all over Europe the old iconoclastic spirit and helped to transmit it to the English reformer, John Wycliffe and his disciple John Huss. Conybeare writes that "not the least racy clause in a document compiled about 1389 by the Wycliffites in defence of their defunct teacher is the following – 'Hit seemes that this offrynge ymages is a sotile cast of Antichriste and his clerkis for to draw almes fro pore men. . . . certis, these ymages of hemself may do nouther gode nor yvel to mennis soules, but thai myghten warme a man's body in colde, if thai were sette upon a fire.' "

In 1563 the Heidelberg Catechism emphatically declared that images were not to be tolerated in churches, but by this time the revival of learning had seen also a revival of the philosophy upon which contemporary museums were founded. John Addington Symonds, the great nineteenth-century historian of the Italian Renaissance, describes this transition in phrases akin to poetry, an art in which he was renowned: "To this task (the rediscovery of the classic past) Boccaccio addressed himself and was followed by numerous Italian citizens who visited Byzantium before its fall, as the sacred city of a new revelation. The next step was to collect MSS, to hunt out, copy and preserve the precious relics of the past. Learning was then no mere pursuit of a special and recluse class. It was fashionable and it was passionate, pervading all society with a fervour of romance. . . . It was the resurrection of the mightiest spirits of the past. The men who followed it knew they were restor-

20

ing humanity to its birthright after the expatriation of ten centuries. When Greek had been acquired, MSS accumulated, libraries and museums formed, came the age of printers and expositors. . . . Scholarship became the surest path of advancement to ecclesiastical and political honours. Italy was one great school of the new learning at the moment when the German, French and Spanish nations were invited to the feast."

Not only the church but the secular arm, as exemplified by the royal courts and their satellites, showed a consciousness of history and the need to preserve the story of heroic feats. The Bayeux tapestry, detailing the events of the Norman invasion and conquest of England in cartoon form, is one of the few such antiquities to survive and which today constitute a museum in their own right. Originally hung in the Cathedral of Bayeux, the tapestry is now housed behind glass in the former Bishop's Palace, complete with electronic docents which relate the tale of "1066 and All That" to viewers as they absorb the visual interpretation of the designer, Queen Matilda.

2

The transition from the Middle Ages to the Renaissance saw a slow but continuing emergence from ecclesiastical and feudal despotism leading to the revival of learning and to a measure of intellectual emancipation. In turn, this encouraged the study of classical antiquity and a more realistic interpretation of natural phenomena. The collecting of curiosities as such was still popular but was slowly being replaced by the amassing of objects with historical or scientific interest.

Morris Bishop, author of *The Middle Ages,* suggests that John the Good (1319-1364) and his four sons, Charles V of France, Jean Duc de Berry, Louis Duc d'Anjou, and Philip the Bold, were among the first royalty to become patrons of the arts and avid collectors. John, in the face of having been impounded for debts and being classified as "the worst of the medieval kings," acquired two hundred and thirty-five tapestries, and even while held prisoner in Windsor Castle retained his court painter, Gérard d'Orléans, to serve on his staff.

Between 1450 and 1500, excavations exposed thousands of antiquities helping historians to reconstruct the story of earlier civilizations. In Rome itself it was estimated that between 60,000 and 170,000 statues were unearthed. Merchant princes and their descendants assumed the role of patrons of the arts and sciences, encouraging and employing scholars to collect on their behalf. Prominent among them was Cosimo de Medici, Florentine banker and ruler of the republic; his grandson, Lorenzo the Magnificent, continued the role, building up collections which eventually became the nuclei for both the Vatican and Lateran museums with many other objects finding their way into the museums of Vienna, Dresden, Munich, Paris, St. Petersburg, and London. It was Lorenzo who created a "Garden of Antiquities" to display his acquisitions, which included paintings, sculptures, and plaster studies by Donatello in addition to cases filled with cameos, jewels, and gems, some of which are now in the British Museum.

Included among such patrons were the houses of Gonzaga of Mantua, Este of Ferrara, and Montefeltro of Urbino, some of whom designed halls, corridors, and rooms in which to house and display their treasures. The Grand Tour of Europe was considered incomplete if such collections had not been viewed. We are told that Giovanni Grimani, nephew of the Doge of Venice, had a collection so extensive that when Alfonso, Duke of Ferrara and Henry III of France visited Venice in 1547 "it took them a whole day to look over it."

Thomas Howard, the second Earl of Arundel, founded the first "galleria" in England in the early seventeenth century. His collection, now known as the Marlborough Gems, is housed in the British Museum, while his manuscript collection, the "Marmora Arundelian," can be seen at Oxford University. A partial list of this collection included 37 statues, 250 inscriptions and part of a sarcophagus, in addition to a vast quantity of intaglios and cameos.

The rise to power of the merchant princes in the fifteenth and sixteenth centuries, which has its parallel in the United States toward the end of the nineteenth century, had a profound sociological effect on society as the nouveau riche established their own cultural values and developed an intellectual curiosity concerning earlier civilizations.

Heterogeneous collections ranging through all areas of science, history and art were assembled, smaller objects being placed in "cabinets" while larger accessions were displayed in areas designed for viewing and discourse. In Italy such areas eventually were named *Museo*, but elsewhere, as in France, the term *cabinet de curiosités* continued to be used.

It was in the sixteenth century that the "art gallery" made its debut. In fact, museum architecture had its genesis when lengthy corridors were expressly designed to serve the dual purpose of display for the decorative arts while providing exercise during inclement weather. The Ufizzi Palace built by Bernardo Buontalenti around 1580 is one of the few such buildings which still function as a museum. Originally the loggias were exposed to the elements but as accessions increased lantern windows were built in. Toward the end of the sixteenth century, the architect Vincenzo Scamozzi, whose designs are representative of the transition from Renaissance architecture to Baroque, wrote a treatise on architectural theory in which he designated a north light for such galleries.

In France, a *cabinet de curiosités* was founded at Fontainebleau by Francis I in the mid-fifteenth century and the same name was given to the Luxembourg collection more than half a century later by Gaston, Duc d'Orleans. It was in the Luxembourg Palace in the mid-eighteenth century that the first "*galerie des refusés*" or "non-museum" was created when servants of the court of Louis XV displayed works of art classed as "antiques," along with works of the Italian Renaissance "which the king disliked."

The royal courts of Europe, not to be outdone by the wealthy commoners, added men knowledgeable in the arts to their retinues of servitors to commission and purchase paintings and sculptures and gather for their further entertainment antiquities and natural curiosities. Philip II of Spain included in the Escorial a library and other areas capable of housing a rapidly growing collection of paintings which at one time exceeded one thousand, the emphasis being on the Spanish Masters, but also including representative works from the Netherlands and Italy. At the suggestion of a member of his entourage, Philip agreed to make his collection available to "people of artistic sensibility," and we are told that "there passed through the Escorial not only foreign ambassadors and travellers of high rank, but also artists and other humble visitors."

Throughout this era, naturalists were encouraged to study natural phenomena and build up collections for further research. Two of these immortals are Henry Cornelius Agrippa von Nettesheim, author of, among other works, *The Vanity of Sciences and Arts*, and Georg Agricola, born at Glauchau, Saxony in 1494, who at an early age devoted himself to "the new learning" and at twenty was appointed "rector extraordinarius" of Greek at the Great School of Zwickau. His all-consuming interest was that of mineralogy despite the fact that he had mastered philology, philosophy, medicine, physics and chemistry. Agricola's studies and authorship in this field were climaxed with the publication of his *De Re Metallica*, earning him the title of the father of mineralogy. Equally important was the fact that throughout his lifetime he had built up a collection of geological and mineral specimens which prompted the Elector of Saxony, Augustus, to establish the Kunst und Naturalien Kammer upon which the various museums of Dresden have been built.

Also of this period was Konrad Gessner (1516-1565), a Swiss naturalist called "the German Pliny," who founded his private museum with collections of animals, plants, gems, metals, and fossils. Like Agricola, Gessner studied physics and medicine but primarily he was a botanist. A prolific writer whose works cover a wide range of subjects, his *Historia Animalium* is today viewed as the foundation upon which modern zoology has developed.

Von Holst in his work on collectors and connoisseurs interposes a commentary on the German Kunstkammer: "an expression which conjures up the image of a faustian universality in collections, something peculiar to that sombrely reflective age of the late sixteenth century," adding that "at the time Shakespeare wrote Hamlet his contemporaries were assembling all kinds of objects in a Theatrum

24

Mundi. Here there were early scientific and pre-scientific stirrings and, with a rare appreciation of spiritual values, an attempt was made to catalogue the entire field of knowledge including the artifacts of alchemy, such as the bezoars which were the gallstones of a camel reputed to banish melancholy; adders' tongues and fossilized shark with which to detect poisons. . . . In these surroundings the belief in the magic of precious stones was still alive. One of the Habsburgs saw in the crystal revelations of the power of the Almighty even the reflection of the Godhead himself. In certain unusual older works of art, the Gemma Augustea for instance, the key to secret astronomical knowledge was discovered."

In Mantua the Galleria della Nostra displayed *rarita naturali* along with works of art, while in Bavaria Maximilian, grandson of the art-collecting Albert IV, built a *galleria* based on Scamozzi's plans which emphasized the north light.

Initial steps toward the organization and classification of collections occupying the *cabinets de curiosités* and *guardaroba* of the sixteenth century were taken by Cardinal Albert (1490-1545) of Brandenburg, whose collection of religious relics was displayed in elegant glass cases at the Halle Stiftskirche and the Mainz Cathedral. Each object was meticulously labelled and, in addition, recorded in an illustrated catalogue, the first such document in museum history. Albert, who served as Archbishop of Magdeburg and Mainz, while building up his extensive cabinets and displaying them in elaborate settings also acquired many major paintings. One such painting, a work of Dürer, was bequeathed to the Mainz Cathedral for installation in the chapel of St. Michael, "or where it will receive the best light." Lacey Baldwin Smith expresses the view that Albert had a pecuniary incentive in protecting and cataloguing "one of the most spectacular collections of relics to be found in Europe" which included "four hairs from the Virgin's head, fourteen scraps of her clothing, a wisp of straw from the manger, a strand of Christ's beard, a nail from the cross and some nineteen thousand bones, the whole of which, if venerated in the proper spirit and accompanied by a small monetary token could cut 1,902,202 years and 270 days from the pains of purgatory."

Another early museum catalogue, in a format which found immediate favour among museum curators, was published by Samuel von Quiccheberg, a physician of Antwerp, who also included as a preface a plan for arranging antiquarian and ethnological collections by systematic classification of subject matter. The publication, despite its somewhat lengthy title of *Inscriptiones von tituli Theatri amplissimi complectentis rerum universitatis singulas materias et imagines eximias,* served as a valid technical document on museum practices for the next hundred years.

However, the first comprehensive bibliography of museums and their practices did not make an appearance until 1727 when Casper Friedrich Neickelius published his *Von dem Ursprung der Kunst-und-Naturalien-Kammern* in which were listed all the then known museums of Natural History, including Noah's Ark which he cited as the most complete museum known to mankind. Also included were King Solomon's collection of curiosities and the museum of King Hezekiah, in which were to be found "precious things of silver and gold, spices and precious oils."

The most meticulous and certainly the best documented publication on museums is undoubtedly the three-volume publication from the pen of Dr. Arthur Murray, who spent seven years, from 1897 to 1904, of travel and research to produce his *Museums, Their History and Use*, an authoritative history which covers twenty-two centuries and provides fascinating reading. Volume One, comprising 340 pages, is supported by two further volumes listing institutions throughout Europe and on the North American continent in what Dr. Murray calls "a bibliography of bibliographies," insofar as the book and directory give only those institutions which have published catalogues or scientific papers.

The author indicates that in the sixteenth and seventeenth centuries Royal collections, later to become national museums, existed in Rome, Florence, Vienna, Dresden, Munich, Berlin, Brussels, and Paris. England's royal collection was and still is one exception, never having left the custody and control of the reigning royal family.

There were other private collections which not only served as monuments of industry and learning but which eventually found their way into public institutions. Such was the collection of naturalist Ulisse Aldrovandi (1527-1605) whose all-consuming ambition was "to describe and illustrate all external nature," and who employed a painter for two hundred crowns a year, sparing no expense in obtaining the services of the finest artists of the day. The collection was undoubtedly significant. The research undertaken by Aldrovandi resulted in the compilation of thirteen folio volumes extensively illustrated, in addition to between two and three hundred manuscripts. One of the works, *Musaeum Metallicum*, describes rocks, earths, minerals, metals, fossil plants, shells, fish, and "such artificial productions as stone axes and flint arrowheads." An anonymous Scottish scientist entreated a friend to "buy me Aldrovandus' works, which are 13 or 14 tomes in Folio; you may buy them in sheets and have them packt up in your own things for Venice, where you will not fail to meet with frequent occasions of sending them to London."

At least two other Bologna residents, Giacomo Asnoni (1615-

26

1682), a botanist, and Gioseppi Bucemi, a chemist, likewise had collections which attracted wide attention, Bucemi having "the bononian stone known as Lapis phosphurus, which if exposed a while to the illuminated air, will imbibe the light, so that withdrawn into a dark room, and there look'd upon, it will appear like a burning coal; but in a short time gradually loses its shining."

The *musaeum* of the Duke of Modena contained a representative selection of curiosities treasured at that time, including "a choice of natural rareties, jewels, ancient and modern coins and medals, ancient and modern entaglias, curious turn's works, dried plants pasted upon smooth boards whiten'd with ceruss, which may be put in frames and hung about a room like pictures; and a great collection of designs of the best painters. Among other things a human head petrified; a hen's egg having on one side the signature of the sun, which I rather noted, because some years before Sir Thomas of Norwich sent me the picture of one, having the perfect signature of a duck swimming upon it, which he assured me was natural. Moss, included in a piece of chrystal, silver in another. A fly plainly discernable in a piece of amber. A Chinese calendar written on wooden leaves."

Still another museum at Verona, belonging to one Mapheus Casanus, an apothecary, contained "many ancient Aegyptian idols, taken out of mummies, divers sorts of petrified shells, petrified cheese, cinnamon, spunge and mushrooms, . . . stones having upon them the perfect impression or signature of the ribs and whole spines of fishes, . . . and a stone called Oculus mundi, which when dry shows cloudy and opake, but when put into water, grows clear and transparent."

In 1564 at Innsbruck, Archduke Ferdinand II brought together "a rich collection of books and manuscripts, works of art, weapons, antiquities and curiosities, which attracted sightseers from every part of Europe," much of the collection eventually going to the university of that city, with the armour, art and other valuable objects now forming the Ambras collection in the British Museum.

Murray lists what is undoubtedly one of the pioneer museums in technology and applied science, quoting Addison to the effect that "Canon Settala's cabinet is always shown to a stranger among the curiosities of Milan. Here we observed several sorts of machine contriv'd for finding out the perpetual motion, looking-glasses of all sorts, dials, musical instruments, both ancient and modern, some of which were invented by Settala himself, in addition to a great piece of cloth made of the stone Amianthus; and without engaging further in those tedious enumerations I promis'd to avoid, all the most rare and curious productions of art and nature, not forgetting Monsters."

Athanasius Kircher (1601-1680) German mathematician, prolific author on philology, mathematics, natural history and physics and also an inventor, was frequently visited by Sir Robert Southwell, who described this Jesuit Father as "a person of great parts and of great industry, . . . one of the most naked and good men that I have seen," but who was somewhat credulous and apt to put into print "any strange, if plausible story, that is brought to him." Kircher likewise devoted himself to inventing mechanical devices. Sir Andrew Balfour, visiting Rome in about 1655 wrote of the "famous shop and Laboratories for Pharmacie" and also alluded to a garden. Later John Ray described Father Kircher's Cabinet in the Roman College as one of the most curious in Europe, "but it has been mangl'd and dismember'd; yet there remains a considerable collection of natural rareties, with several mechanical engines." Another visitor remarking on his visit wrote that Kircher "with Dutch patience shew'd us his perpetual motions, catoptrics, magnetical experiments, modells, and a thousand other crochets and devices."

France was keeping pace with the rest of Europe in the zest for collecting natural curiosities and fine art, and creating the nuclei for major museums in later years. Fabri de Peiresc (1580-1611) a scholar and antiquary occupied "his lifetime in study, in travelling, corresponding with scholars of Europe," in addition to gathering antiquities and natural curiosities which "he bestowed with munificent liberality." Peiresc had agents throughout the world, one of whom unearthed the Arundel marbles, later acquired by Thomas Howard, second earl of Arundel and presented to Oxford University in 1667 by his grandson Henry, Sixth Duke of Norfolk. It was Peiresc who exposed the myth concerning skeletal remains of giants by declaring that some objects so labelled were in actual fact the teeth and bones of elephants. Science was coming into its own.

Scientific explanation for the profusion of horns of the mythical unicorn had to wait for another century. Unicorn horns, possibly because of their phallic resemblance, were in great demand, crushed to a powder and served as an aphrodisiac. The horn had other legendary qualities as a softening influence of love upon the fiercest of men and as a symbol of purity. It was also considered an antidote for poison although the Royal Society, after experiments, dismissed the legend as superstition.

Catherine Beatrice Philips of Bedford College, London, writing on this subject in 1900, describes this non-existent phenomenon as having been viewed as "a fabulous beast, usually having the head and body of a horse, the hind legs of an antelope, the tail of a lion (sometimes a horse's tail) with a beard of a goat, its chief feature being a long, sharp, twisted horn similar to the narwhal's tusk, set in the middle of its forehead." In legend, the creature resembled the wild asses of India "having on the forehead a horn a cubit and a

28

half in length, coloured white, red or black."

Robert Wallace, writing about the same time, indicates that a breed of sheep existed in Nepal or Tibet whose rams have two horns which are completely welded together while Von Holst in 1969, in reporting on the demands by collectors for such objects, writes of "unicorns whose origin from the walrus was still unknown and which was supposed to have the power for transmitting harmful materials." One of the unresolved mysteries relating to the unicorn is the sudden disappearance of these horns once the myth had been exploded.

While the Tradescants are credited with being the first museum operators to charge admissions, Felix Plater of Basle (1535-1614), whose museum contained some of the collections of Conrad Gessner, was not adverse to encouraging donations from the interested public, it being recorded by the English botanist John Ray that he had visited the Plater museum in "the company of Skippon, the doctor's son, who showed us them, brought us a book wherein we wrote our names, and then gave a golden ducat, it being covetously expected of us."

Archaeology entered the museum field as an emerging science in the mid-seventeenth century. Olaf (Ole) Worm, a Danish physician having specialized in prehistoric archaeology, opened the Museaum Wormianum in Copenhagen but his major achievement was the writing and publication of a text book on this subject which "is a practical exposition of the scope and aims of the museology of the seventeenth century and is still valuable as a summary of the scientific opinion of the times." His collection was more highly specialized than others of that period and his contribution to archaeology and to museum classification cannot be overlooked. Dr. Worm attracted many eminent scholars and scientists. It is evident that one of his visitors was Alexander Pope, the English poet and satirist who immortalized the eminent Danish doctor by writing:

> But who is he, in closet close y-pent,
> Of sober face, with learned dust besprent?
> Right well mine eyes arede the myster wight,
> On parchment scraps y-fed and Wormisu hight.
> To future ages may thy dulness last,
> As thou preserv'st the dulness of the past.

3

In general terms the proliferating museums of the fifteenth and six-teenth centuries were founded largely for the sake of prestige, or from acquisitive compulsions lacking any fundamental philosophy. The relatively few collectors who were dedicated to one basic science undoubtedly had evolved programs requiring much study and an advancement of the particular discipline, while the church had finally rationalized its role as custodian of religious art and relics.

As Europe entered the seventeenth century there were those seek-ing new answers to age-old subjects relating to natural phenomena. Francis Bacon, Baron Verulam, Viscount St. Albans (1561-1626) was one such person. A prolific writer of philosophical essays, Bacon questioned man's sovereignty over nature as a myth so long as "vain notions and blind experiments" continued.

In his treatise *The Advancement of Learning* Bacon contended that up to this period of history the means for intellectual progress had been used for amusement and teaching and not for the augmen-tation of science. In *The New Atlantis,* published posthumously one year after his death, he visualized a national museum of science and art, explaining that: "It is not to be esteemed a small matter that by the voyages and travels of these later times, so much more of nature has been discovered than was known at any former period. It would, indeed, be disgraceful to mankind, if, after such tracts of the material world have been laid open which were unknown in former times – so many seas traversed – so many countries explored – so many stars discovered – philosophy, or the intelligible world, should be circumscribed by the same boundaries as before."

Dr. William J. Holland of the Carnegie Institute wrote in 1911 that Bacon was "the first person to elaborate and present to modern minds the thought of an institution which should assemble within its walls the things which men want to see and study."

Bacon's many essays were provocative and controversial but the rigid barriers which had been long established by the theologians

30

were being broken down. Indeed it was Bacon who relegated theological questions, which had tortured the minds of generations, from the province of reason to that of faith. Bacon's influence was far-reaching. Many of his works had been written in Latin, making for wider circulation of his views and encouraging correspondence between savants throughout Europe. Such discussions undoubtedly led to an expansion of collections for scholarly research.

How far Baconian philosophy served to stimulate the founding of university museums is difficult to determine. There is ample evidence that objects drawn from the various fields of natural history were extensively used as teaching aids, but organized planning of repositories designed for research and preservation was spasmodic.

One of the first campus museums to have survived the centuries is the Ashmolean at Oxford, England, founded through the generosity of Elias Ashmole in 1677 on the condition that a suitable building be provided to house the collection of the Tradescants. The museum was officially opened in 1683.

The Tradescants, John the father who died in 1637 and son John, sometimes described as "gardeners in the employ of the Duke of Buckingham," were essentially keen botanists. They travelled widely and had an insatiable scientific curiosity which took them into many other fields. Originally they were in the employ of Charles I who, it is recorded, directed letters to be written to the merchants of New Guinea asking that the Tradescants be accommodated with natural curiosities to include all manner of flesh, fowl and "flying and sucking fishes, all sorts of serpants, dried fruits and shining stones." In that same year Tradescant senior addressed himself to Nicolas, the then Duke of Bedford, advising that he was prepared to deal with all merchants on the Duke's behalf in all places, but especially in Virginia, Bermuda, Newfoundland, Guinea, the Amazons, and the East Indies. It is obvious that father and son built up for themselves a vast personal collection while fulfilling other assignments. The two men established their Closet of Curiosities, which they named "Tradescantium," shortly before the death of the father. An anonymous critic described the institution as "an arch of novelties," but Lord Balchares disagreed, two hundred and fifty years later calling it "an aimless collection of curiosities, bric-a-brac, brought together without method or system. . . and a miscellany without didactic value [contributing] nothing to the advancement of art, its arrangement being unscientific, the public gaining little or no advantage from its existence."

Apparently Ashmole and the university authorities at Oxford had other ideas. The entire collection comprised twelve carloads, Ashmole entering in his diary on January 17, 1683, that "the last load of my rareties was sent by barge [for conveyance to Oxford] and this afternoon I relapsed into the gout."

31

The collection had been subjected to extensive litigation, the widow of Tradescant junior presenting a will which gave her full control over the collection during her lifetime, with the Lord Chancellor eventually giving judgement in favour of Ashmole. The University invited James, Duke of York, and his consort to view the museum on May 21,1683, doctors and masters of the faculty getting their preview three days later. One vitriolic critic, apparently irked at the Lord Chancellor's ruling, wrote that "the name of Tradescant has been unjustly sunk in that of Ashmole."

Sidelights of the peripatetic Tradescants indicate that they made valuable contributions in the field of botany, two plant species being named after them. It is also on record that John the younger returned from Malaysia in 1656 with "a material with plastic property which can be softened in warm water, reshaped and returned to its hardness when cold" and which he christened "masor" but which is known to us as gutta-percha. The findings were published in one of the many papers which the two gardeners of the Duke wrote during their respective lifetimes.

While Agricola is called "the father of mineralogy," Sir John Woodward (1665-1728) can be credited with having initiated the first museum (as distinct from a collection) for the earth sciences. The Ashmole gift to Oxford has overshadowed Woodward's significant contribution to museum development in the universities insofar as he catalogued his collection of fossils and geological specimens and later bequeathed it to Cambridge University. Woodward had immersed himself in natural history at an early age, his major interest being geology. Between 1695 and his death he wrote many essays on the subject in addition to delivering lectures before the Fellows of the Royal Society; one such lecture on experiments with vegetation prompted one writer to designate Woodward as "the founder of experimental plant physiology." Woodward was the subject of much ridicule and satire during his lifetime, being "of a somewhat jealous and petulant temperament" with one critic alluding to him as "the greatest curiosity in the whole collection."

In addition to the collection, Woodward willed his entire estate to the University as an endowment to perpetuate the institution and directed that land of the yearly value of one hundred and fifty pounds be purchased and conveyed (in the legal sense) to the University and that a lecturer, who also would serve as curator, be engaged at a stipend of one hundred pounds annually, whose responsibility it would be to read at least four lectures each year on some one or another of the subjects appearing in Woodward's *Natural History of the Earth*. Thus did Woodward add two new dimensions to museum operations, an endowment for administration, and lectures.

The museum opened in Cockerell's building shortly after the death of the benefactor. The Woodwardian, one of a complex of campus museums, was replaced in 1904 by the Sedgwick Geological Museum, named to commemorate the contributions made by Adam Sedgwick (1785-1873). Sedgwick had a distinguished career as geologist, served as Woodwardian professor, and continued the lecture program until a year before his death.

4

On April 6, 1660, Hans Sloane was born in County Down, Ireland. Six months later the Royal Society for Improving Natural Knowledge was founded at Gresham College, London, following a lecture delivered by the English architect Christopher Wren. Sloane, while still a child, developed an insatiable curiosity in natural history but he gravitated into medicine while still studying his first love as an avocation.

The Royal Society, oldest scientific society in England and one of the oldest in the world, devoted much of its time and energies to the examination and discussion of "Physico-Mathematical Experimental Learning." Members of the Society had undoubtedly been influenced by Francis Bacon and his writings, and it could well be that the idea to found a museum at Gresham College was the result of Bacon's advocacy of such an institution. Within four years the Society had purchased the collection of one Mr. Hubbard, or was it Hubert or perhaps Forges, who had given public exhibitions of his rareties in The Musik House at the Miter near St. Paul's church. The museum soon became a major attraction and Sir Andrew Balfour advised all and sundry to "inquire at Gresham College for Dr. Pope that by his means you may see a verie fine collection of naturall rareties kept in the Colledge."

Sir Thomas Gresham had bequeathed his home and virtually all his estate to the corporation of London and the Mercers' Company "for the purpose of instituting a college in which seven professors should read lectures – one each day of the week – on astronomy, geometry, physics, law, divinity, rhetoric and music." Several years before he died he had arranged the marriage of his illegitimate daughter Anne to Sir Nathaniel Bacon, brother of Francis.

The Royal Society museum continued to receive additions, some of which emerged out of the lectures, discussions, and experiments conducted by various members. A catalogue prepared by one Nehemiah Grew listed "the horns of a hare" (so inscribed), the leg of a dodo, the leg and egg of a cassowary, and a giant's thigh-bone

34

more than four feet in length which the sceptical cataloguer inferred "could well be the leg of an elephant."

In 1683 Hans Sloane had attained his Medical Doctorate at the University of Orange, returning to England that same year with a considerable collection of plants and other botanical objects. In 1687 he was elected a Fellow of the Royal Society, an honour conferred on not more than fifteen candidates in any one year. He also became a Fellow of the Royal College of Physicians and was shortly thereafter attached to the retinue of the Duke of Albermarle as personal physician when the Duke journeyed to Jamaica to fill the post of Governor. Albermarle died shortly after his arrival in the colony but Sloane remained there for fifteen months exploring the local plant life. On his return to England he brought with him 800 newly discovered species of flora. This was his first large addition to a collection which by the year 1725 contained "5497 specimens of earth, bitumens, metals, minerals, stones and fossils; 804 corals; 8226 vegetable substances; 200 large volumes of dried plants; 3824 insects; 3753 shells; 1939 extinct crustacae, fishes and the like; 658 birds and 185 eggs; 1194 quadropeds and their parts; 345 vipers and serpents; 507 humana; 1169 miscellaneous objects both natural and artificial; 300 things relating to customs of ancient times such as antiquities, urns, instruments, etc; 81 large (metal) seals; 319 pictures; 54 mathematical instruments; 10,228 coins and medals; 136 books in miniature; 580 books of prints; 2666 volumes of manuscripts; a total of 53,018 specimens which by the year 1733 had increased to 69,352."

By this time Sloane had been created a hereditary baronet and had succeeded Sir Isaac Newton, the philosopher and mathematician, as president of the Royal Society, a post he held until 1740. Sir Hans died in 1753 at the age of ninety-seven. He bequeathed his extensive collection to the British nation on condition that twenty thousand pounds be paid to his family, "desiring very much that these things, tending many ways to the manifestation of the glory of God, the confutation of atheism and its consequences, the use and improvement of the arts and sciences, and benefit of mankind, may remain together and not be separated."

While the Sloane bequest is generally credited with the founding of the British Museum, Henry C. Shelley, author of *The British Museum; Its History and Treasures* (1911), suggests that the bequest served only to speed up legislation for a national repository to house the complete library of Sir Robert Cotton, a collection which interestingly enough, had formerly been sequestered by the Crown on the suspicion that manuscripts of a seditious nature had been deliberately placed there by its owner. Also, the decision at this same time of the Countess of Oxford to sell to the government the library and antiquities of Robert Harley, first Earl of Oxford, for "the nominal sum of thirty thousand pounds" helped to hasten parliament in passing the necessary legislation, and authorizing monies to be raised for capital and administrative costs by means of a lottery which brought into the treasury ninety-five thousand pounds. On January 15, 1759, the British Museum was officially opened to the public in Montague House. In 1781 the Royal Society turned over its entire museum collection to the trustees of the British Museum.

The stipulation that the British Museum should be thrown open to the public, this in the mid-eighteenth century, requires elucidation. The Luddites had still to be heard from, but the squalor and degradation among the poor were paving the way for an uprising. The government of the day actually saw to it that only the desirable public should be admitted to the museum. The story is delightfully told by Mr. Shelley who writes of this situation with an initial suggestion that the term "thrown open to the public" had a number of mental reservations. "Today," he wrote in 1911, "the building is open throughout the year save on Good Friday and Christmas Day; even on Sunday afternoons the visitors are welcomed; and, save for the special students' rooms, every nook and corner of the vast treasure house may be freely explored. . . . Difficult indeed, would it be to name a public institution where the highest officials to the lowest are more unfailing in courtesy and helpfulness . . .but a century and a half ago it needed a small pamphlet to contain the regulations thought necessary by the trustees.

"At the outset it demanded something like a mathematical calculation to determine when the building was and was not open. . . . For example, 'except Saturday and Sunday in each week; likewise except Christmas Day and one week after . . . also except the week after Easter and the week after Whit Sunday and except Good Friday and all days which are now, or shall hereafter be specially appointed Thanksgivings or fasts by public authority.' Then followed a further reminder that 'Between the months of September and April inclusive, from Monday to Friday the museum be opened, from nine o'clock till three and likewise at the same hours on Tuesday, Wednesday and Thursday in May, June, July and August but on Monday and Friday only from four o'clock to eight in the afternoon.' "

After reading the time-table the eager visitor was advised that not more than ten people could be accommodated at any one time; that they would be escorted in groups for a tour which generally lasted not more than thirty minutes (keeping in mind that the Sloane collection alone numbered close to 70,000 items). To get on such a tour, personal application was made to the porter at his lodge who

36

inscribed in the register the name, condition (drunk, sober, clean, dirty, seemingly of means or otherwise) after which the librarian or his understudy decided whether the applicant was "proper" for admission, "and until . . . the solution being in the affirmative . . . either of those officials issued an invitation, the prospective visitor had no more chance of getting inside the museum than Satan has of eluding the vigilance of St. Peter."

Two visits were required to obtain a ticket, and a third visit actually to gain admission. "Even then he might have to wait several hours for his turn, for the visitors were escorted around in little parties." There were other restrictions also, such as "that the coins and medals, except such as the standing committee shall order, from time to time, to be placed in glass cases, be not exposed to view, but by leave of the trustees, in general meeting, or of the principal librarians; that they be shown between the hours of one and three in the afternoon, by one of the officials, who have the custody of them; that no more than two persons be admitted at any one time unless by particular leave of the principal librarian." It should be noted that at no time were children, even when accompanied by parents, allowed to enter the sacred portals.

In 1761 regulations had been relaxed but only slightly; a guidebook published that year provided for fifteen persons "in one company" being permitted to take a two-hour tour of the institution, but the procedure of making application still prevailed, a footnote stating that tickets were not transferable and "it is remarked that the fewer Names there are in a list, the sooner they are likely to be admitted to see it."

In 1776 people who had applied for admission in April were still waiting in August. In 1882 one disillusioned visitor who had obtained his ticket in two weeks sadly noted that "it was the room, the glass cases, the shelves which I saw; not the museum itself, so rapidly were we hurried through the departments. . . In about thirty minutes we finished our silent journey through this princely mansion, which would have well taken thirty days. I went out much about as wise as I went in, but with the severe reflection that, for fear of losing my chance, I had that morning abruptly torn myself from three gentlemen with whom I was engaged in an interesting conversation, had lost my breakfast, got wet to the skin, spent half a crown in coach, paid two shillings for a ticket, and had been hackneyed through the rooms with violence."

In 1883 the reformer William Cobbett opposed a grant of sixteen thousand pounds for the upkeep of the institution remarking that "those who lounged in it and made it a place of amusement should pay for its support (as it was) intended only for the amusement of the curious and rich and not for the benefit or for the instruction of the poor. If the aristocracy wanted the museum, let them pay for it."

It is to be regretted that there still are a few public institutions in Europe, on the North American continent, and even in Canada which make little or no provision for mass attendance of visitors; which rarely open in the evening hours; which always close on all public holidays and which actively discourage children. One curator, when asked by a visitor for a report on juvenile attendance replied "we don't keep count, kids are a damned nuisance." Happily such institutions are a dying breed.

Despite the discouraging report on the early operations of the British Museum, a more liberal policy was introduced in the last half of the nineteenth century, one which continues to be geared to sociological changes. It was one of the first museums to recognize the need for curatorial departments. It moved its natural science collections into new premises in South Kensington in the years 1881-1885 and in 1925 reorganized that branch for the interpretation of science as history while retaining the Bloomsbury edifice for its library and other branches.

Over the years it has attracted scholars with international reputations to serve in various capacities. They have pioneered in research programs; conducted archaeological and botanical exploration; encouraged satellite museums throughout Great Britain and Ireland and encouraged benefactors to turn over important collections for safe-keeping and use. Today it continues to administer a geological museum, the botanical gardens at Kew, and the Royal College of Surgeons anatomical museum.

The publicity given to the Hans Sloane bequest, along with the prestige it engendered, encouraged other collectors to offer their acquisitions to the nation and resulted in a concentration of curiosities (natural and unnatural), libraries, and art treasures in London at the expense of other cities. The private collection as an "attraction for the idle hour" was on its way out to be replaced by publicly endowed or administered institutions, but from 1753 until the end of that century only five such museums were opened in other areas of the British Isles, these being the National Museum of Antiquities in Edinburgh, the Museum of Anatomy and Zoology and that of the Royal college of Surgeons on Trinity College campus in Dublin, the Museum of the Society of Natural Science in Perth, and the Museum of the Royal Irish Academy, later to become the National Museum of Eire.

In one short clause in the will of Hans Sloane the Apothecaries' Company was given the botanical and physic garden which the benefactor had cultivated early in his adult life and which later had been rented to the apothecaries, a garden which came into being due to the interest shown in the recently opened Kew Gardens (1670).

Princess Augusta of Saxe-Gothe was the instigator of the Kew project, having interested herself in the encouragement of scientific study of herbs for medicinal purposes. However, physic gardens had been in existence since 1500 B.C., when such a garden was recorded at Karnak, Egypt. The first museum dedicated to the study of living plant life had its genesis in Padua in 1545. In Pisa, one year later, Andrea Cesalpino, a professor of materia medica widely known for his works on the vascular system, established a herbarium, and in his role of naturalist outlined the principle of Linnaean classification in his *De Plantis* published in 1583, one hundred and seventy years before the author of modern systemized botany wrote his *Philosophia Botanica* and *Species Plantarum*. Linneaus, in his works, gave full credit to Cesalpino.

Other such gardens came into being in Italy, in Leiden (1577) and Leipzig (1579), and a very large number were founded in every corner of Europe in the seventeenth century. A botanical garden was established in Oxford in 1632, while a physic garden created specifically for the study and development of plants for medical needs was administered by the University of Edinburgh at about the same time.

Gaston, Duc d'Orléans, who had interested himself in natural history, established at Blois a botanical garden and museum in the first half of the seventeenth century which later was named as the great "cabinet du roi." The Jardin des Plantes, founded in Paris in 1783, launched as a pharmaceutical garden, gradually expanded its interests to embrace other forms of plant life and by the early nineteenth century had developed a zoological garden. From its beginnings, it was accorded the distinction of being not only a museum but a University of Science, with its large collections of flora and fauna, vast experimental gardens and laboratories, and full academic courses were given. The grounds were also opened to the general public following a policy initiated in 1750 when the Luxembourg Palace had opened its doors at restricted hours "for the entertainment of citizens."

Collecting art for art's sake, or on occasion for the prestige which art attracts, became the vogue among royalty and their courts with Charles VIII of France setting the trend after his invasion of Italy. He returned to Fontainebleau in 1494 not only with paintings but with a rare collection of Italian painters. This policy continued into the sixteenth century with Francis I who induced Leonardo to join his court in 1516, to be followed two years later by Raphael and a steady flow of other Florentines.

Rarely was there rhyme or reason associated with display, paintings being hung cheek by jowl, floor to ceiling in badly illuminated rooms and corridors and with little or no regard save for quantity. Peter the Great of Russia, observing the collecting tendencies of other monarchs, notably Philip II of Spain, sought to build an art collection "larger than ever before"; Catherine II continued the program, building The Hermitage as an annex to the Winter Palace in which to display her acquisitions.

In Dresden, Augustus the Strong remodelled a former Catholic chapel during the first years of the eighteenth century to serve as an art gallery which, we are told, "gave great pleasure to the court and was much admired by visitors." In 1749, Augustus II, who inherited his father's treasures, built what can be viewed as the first gallery expressly designed as a public institution.

In Vienna, in the 1770's Joseph II announced that his collection of paintings and sculpture would be placed on public view free of charge, thus arousing violent antagonism from the court artists who declared that "waiters' helpers and the lowest type of women would disturb the silent contemplation of the works." Joseph, it was felt, was carrying regal paternalism a little too far. Naked goddesses and nymphs might be viewed by the aristocracy and even the educated classes of a somewhat lower order, but such works would undoubtedly undermine the morals of the *hoi polloi*. This tendency to safeguard morality among the lower orders had extended to Madrid where "pictures of nude figures were gathered together in a few rooms to which artists and foreign travellers were admitted." One anonymous puritan of that period declared that "whereas in the majority of rooms everything was decently draped, people found in the secret rooms only flesh, colour and sensuality."

The obsession to collect posed many problems. Housing needs were resolved by creating art galleries and employing knowledgeable advisers and trained keepers. This eventually resulted in more discriminating buyers, more ordered arrangement, and a system of classification.

Such an innovation occured in Vienna in 1781 when Christian von Mechel, director of the state art collection, launched a program involving the chronological arrangement of paintings by schools and the establishment of distinct areas, specifically planned, to display prints or artists' proofs, from which was formed the Albertina collection. Von Mechel likewise rejected the ornate frames which were the fashion of the day in favour of frames designed to enhance the individual work of art, and to this end he spent 70,000 guilders. The discarded frames, he claimed, had reduced the paintings to secondary importance in the minds of visitors as they walked through the Stallberg gallery.

The metamorphosis of royal collections into state-owned museums gained currency at the time of the French Revolution. In the period when the Emperor Joseph was encouraging public participation in Vienna, royal collections elsewhere were jealously guarded from profane encroachment, although public exhibitions outside the Court were gaining in popularity. In Paris, the Musée de la République was opened in 1793 and a few years later the Palais du Louvre became known as the Musée National with the contemporary paintings by Academicians being described as "ouvrages appartenant à la nation." In 1803, the Louvre was re-christened, somewhat briefly and for obvious reasons as the Musée Napoléon, but what with one thing and another, including a plethora of acquisitions which poured into the edifice, it was somewhat downgraded by at least one caustic critic who referred to it as "a warehouse containing the plunder of a usurper."

National museums opened in Brussels in 1795, Munich in 1800, the Hague in 1804, and in Amsterdam four years later, the latter being reorganized and rechristened as the Rijksmuseum in 1815. In the same year, in Madrid, the Museo del Prado which had been founded to house a mammoth *cabinet de curiosités* of natural history and antiquities in 1785 became the repository for the royal art collection. In London, a national art gallery had been proposed as early as 1792 by the American artist Benjamin West, but not until 1824 was the National Gallery opened in Trafalgar Square, one of the few national institutions functioning "without royal participation."

Gradually museums and galleries extended their influence to embrace all segments of the body politic, with collections being displayed "not only as a source of pleasure but much rather as a source of instruction" and to promote the moral conduct of life.

5

Adult education as a way of life had its origins in England. The end of the eighteenth century saw Great Britain entering into the steam age. The perfection of the steam engine by James Watt was coincident with other inventions which helped materially to initiate the age of industrial expansion. The industrial revolution had a disruptive influence on British society, with the new capitalists asserting themselves socially and politically while the worker, pitchforked almost overnight from the security of his particular craft into unemployment and penury, turned to violent and primitive methods to voice his unrest.

It was a time of social upheaval, the Chartists demanding political democracy and the Luddites venting their spleen on machinery. The Luddite movement originated in Nottingham, the centre of the lace industry, and it was in that city that Dr. George Birkbeck, whose name is memorialized at the Birkbeck College in London, launched a school for artisans who wished to improve their skills in the new mechanized society.

George Birkbeck was born in Yorkshire in 1776 of moderately wealthy parents and from childhood he became aware of the unrest among the mill workers without having been involved himself. As a youngster he had developed an interest in the natural sciences, later graduating as a medical doctor, and in 1799 he joined the faculty of the Andersonian Institute in Glasgow as a lecturer in the department of natural philosophy. The following year he announced a series of free lectures of a scientific nature directed at artisans, and such was the popularity of the program that he continued the project over a period of years. Birkbeck was thus the founder of a program of adult education out of which grew the Mechanics Institute movement.

Birkbeck's philosophy found immediate acceptance among workers, and, aided by his active leadership, Mechanics Institutes blossomed throughout the industrial north. Originally designed for lecture courses, the Institutes took the form of workmen's clubs

42

where the educational programs were expanded and social activities encouraged. The vast majority of artisans and tradesmen of the early nineteenth century were at best only semi-literate. Birkbeck recognized that access to technical books and visual aids was essential; consequently and in short order the Institutes developed their library-reading-room facilities and almost simultaneously areas were set aside for museum objects which could be related to the educational programs. The museums, some of which anticipated the museums of applied science, were eventually used to raise finances for the overall operations through admission charges. The Manchester exhibition of 1838, for instance, displayed "models, drawings and specimens illustrating science, statics and hydrodynamics, pneumatics, heat, light, electricity, astronomy, geodesy, and chemistry; the fine arts (architecture, sculpture, and painting); the useful arts (building, engineering and various manufactures); and natural history."

It was obvious, therefore, that some of the more ambitious Institutes, operating as independent units, should found permanent museums to serve the dual purpose of providing lecturers with visual aids and members with facilities for research and experimentation.

Ten years prior to the Manchester exibition the first such museum came into being at Preston, Lancashire at the Institute for the Diffusion of Useful Knowledge (1826), and within a few years had amassed over 800 items. In 1845, a Museums' Act was passed by the British Parliament, making possible the merging of museums with public libraries under the administration of the municipal authority and resulting in the abandonment of the Institute library-museums, which inevitably faced fiscal problems, in favour of municipally- financed institutions.

The influence of Birkbeck and the Institutes had already been extended to the New World, while its impact in the British Isles was reflected in the Saint George's project launched by John Ruskin in 1871. Mechanics Institutes were in full bloom at the time of the Great (Crystal Palace) Exhibition of 1851, but by 1875 the movement had virtually died out, replaced by the government-sponsored technical institute.

Another aftermath of the Industrial Revolution was the growing awareness of standards in design. The Society of Arts, later to become the Royal Society for the Encouragement of Arts, Manufactures and Commerce (not to be confused with The Royal Society whose Fellows were concerned solely with the scientific disciplines) began to agitate for the establishment of an Academy of Arts as one of its initial projects. The Society of Arts was founded in 1754 by a group of notable burghers of London which included Viscount Folkstone, the portraitist George Romney, Dr. Steven Hales, Jr., and William Shipley. Informal meetings had been held at Rawthmell's Coffee House in London's Covent Garden and it was here that the proposal for such an Academy was first broached. That same year the newly fledged society offered prizes for paintings and drawings; four years later the program was extended to include awards for industrial design as distinct from what was known in those days as "the Polite Arts." The first art exhibition in Britain open to the public was sponsored by this Society and within a few years it included architectural design in the competitive classes.

While the Society of Arts did not become actively involved in museums until well into the nineteenth century, it is recorded that one William Bailey, registrar, wrote in 1772 an authoritative work on *The Advancement of Art, Manufactures and Commerce, or Descriptions of the useful Machines and Models contained in the Repository of the Society*, a repository, incidentally, which might well have been the prototype for technological museums eighty years later when the Society had linked up the many Mechanics Institutes in a Union of Institutions "to encourage the formation of local collections of a practical and educational value in connection with them," and had introduced a new philosophical approach to museums by proclaiming that "A museum, properly considered, is not a collection of curiosities, monstrosities, antiquities and artistic works grouped together in glass cases in a species of native confusion, but, if it deserves the name, is a place in which instruction is to be gained, and consequently in which order, arrangement and method is evident throughout."

Twenty-eight Mechanics Institute museums were listed in the appendix to this document. The most recent history of the Society, published in 1954, cites three examples: at Bacup, Lancashire, which had "illustrations of the various stages of the cotton manufacture, from the raw materials to the finished article, and collections in illustration of the geology of the district"; at Bridgewater, Somerset, which "showed specimens of the entire series of rock formations of the country, with selection of organic remains, and specimens illustrating the manufacture of Bath Brick and Scouring brick."; and at Newbury, Berkshire, where there were displayed "samples of wool selected so as to show the various qualities and the points of chief importance in connection with the wool trade."

The Royal Society of Arts also concerned itself with political reforms affecting museums, proposing that the control of the proliferating institutions be placed under a Minister of the Crown, that objects from the national collections be made available to local institutions, and also that hours of opening be extended for the benefit of the working classes. Supporting this latter demand, John Ruskin

44

gave evidence in 1860 before a Select Committee on Public Instruction, proposing that business establishments close early to enable workers, who at that time worked twelve to fourteen hours daily, six days a week, to visit museums and galleries. During this period Ruskin also produced plans for a proposed museum in which provision would be made for active participation of visitors, "particularly artisans."

In 1871 Ruskin founded the Saint George's Guild, a utopian enterprise which its founder visualized as becoming a self-contained community working toward a new communal society. While his dream of the Guild fell by the wayside, the Saint George's Museum, later to be called the Ruskin Museum, was opened by him at Walkley near Sheffield, a diminutive building housing a collection of objects carefully selected by its founder and run by a curator whose functions included encouraging artisans to study design in relation to industrial production.

In his biography of Ruskin, E. T. Cook quotes him as saying of the South Kensington Institution, "I lost myself in a Cretan labyrinth of military ironmongery, advertisements of spring-blinds, model fish-farming and plaster bathing nymphs with a year's smut on all noses of them; and had to put myself in charge of a policeman to get out again."

In his own museum "there were few things to see, but everything was co-ordinated in an intelligible scheme of artistic education. And in the second place, whatever there was, was beautiful and good of its kind so that every visitor saw the interest and value of things collected in its single room." The first curator, Mr. Harold Swan, wrote in 1888 that "the museum contains specimens, copies, casts, etc., selected by John Ruskin, of the truly greatest of human art of the times [and] of the highest development in each brand."

The curator served as an exciting and always available guide, one of his major functions being to involve actively all visitors. On the periodic visits of the founder, Swan would organize informal evening meetings for workers where Ruskin would expound his philosophy while also conducting classes in drawing and painting, "utilizing things in natural history or in legend" as points of departure, a program which exerted a profound influence with sponsors of the adult educational and technical training programs of Victorian England.

William Morris, a contemporary of Ruskin, came under his influence in early manhood. Both men were idealists and utopians. They were friends of the pre-Raphaelites although Ruskin became the defender of J.M.W. Turner's revolutionary painting techniques. It could be suggested that, while the two men never had a collaborating relationship, Morris adopted the Ruskin philosophy and became the activist in seeking to popularize the aesthetic principles of art nouveau. Morris, born in 1819, was fifteen years younger than Ruskin. He died in 1896, Ruskin outliving him by four years. Art nouveau was already becoming *passe* and it required another half century for the significance of this short-lived art movement to be recognized.

Jacques de Vaucanson (1709-1782), French engineer, inventor and somewhat of a showman, has all but been forgotten. Yet this master of many trades can be viewed as the founder of one of the first, if not the first, museum devoted exclusively to the physical sciences and technology.

Vaucanson's name, and indeed his reputation as an inventor, was overshadowed by that of Cartwright and Jacquard. Yet it was Vaucanson along with Bouchon and Falcon who developed the principles of the "Jacquard machine" in 1745, with Jacquard being called upon in 1801 only to correct certain defects in the mechanism. One biographer suggests that Jacquard at the age of fifteen could have been the inventor of the swivel-loom used for the weaving of ribbons and tapes, but the subject remains in doubt; however, he is credited with inventing the first milling machine, used at a gun factory in Connecticut in 1818.

The versatile Vaucanson created the first automaton, and this invention in all probability was responsible for the founding of the Conservatoire des Arts et Métiers in 1775 which opened in the Priory of Saint-Martin-des-Champs in Paris where "this celebrated mechanician exhibited three admirable figures – the flute player, the tambourine player and the duck, which was capable of eating, drinking and imitating exactly the natural voice of the fowl."

The museum, however, served also as a technical school and had a major collection of machinery and working models. Early in its checkered career, in 1784, the institution was taken over by the state, and the word "National" added to its name. Despite the fact that admission was charged, it proved to be a popular source of education and entertainment, but in later years the museum became static, its collection suffered from neglect, and the area in which it was located became the victim of urban decay.

In 1967, Alexis Blanc, instructor at the Centres d'entrainment aux méthodes d'éducation, writing in *Museum* described the Conservatoire as "the oldest and one of the richest technological museums in the world [but] the victim of a deep-rooted prejudice on the part of the French public, especially the Parisian public, for whom it conjures up ideas of decrepitude, disuse and boredom . . . due to the relative state of neglect in which its collections were left for more than half a century. . . . The quarter in which it is situated, and which in the nineteenth century was a popular centre of social activity, has gradually been taken over by wholesale business establishments. Nevertheless," M. Blanc informed his readers, "the efforts that have been made over a period of years to make the best possible use of the valuable collections are beginning to make an impression on the general public, teachers, school parties and young people in general.

M. Blanc, in the same article announced that "the Musée du Conservatoire National des Arts et Métiers, which has become the Musée des Techniques, is emerging from a long period of lethargy and beginning once again to play an active role," adding that "plans for the establishment of a modern scientific and technological museum are being studied . . . which would bring together in the same building, situated in the centre of a green zone, the Palais de la Découverte and the Musée des Techniques."

Without wishing to dispute the claim of M. Blanc, the honour of being the oldest technological museum in the world could be argued by the Stora Kopparbergwerks Museum at Salun, Sweden, which owes its existence to the oldest public industrial company still extant. The company, founded by, a Fellowship of Master Miners in the eleventh century, organized a "museum" over two hundred years ago in which to house artifacts relating to the technological advancement of mining and containing models dating from 1740. However, the museum was only opened to the general public in 1922. The company in later years expanded its interests to include forestry, pulp and paper, and associated industries, all which are represented in its recently expanded display areas which occupy over 20,000 square feet of floor space.

Aina Stenklo, the administrative officer in charge of the museum, points to the fact that the early collection of models and minerals was for pedagogical purposes, and over the years has been used "as a tool of introduction for the employees, giving them detailed information on the activities they are involved in. Its educational department gives lessons to school groups in history, sociology and geology. Its guides are tri-lingual."

London's Science Museum also lays claim to having pioneered in the field of applied science. Originally opening its doors in 1857 as an indirect satellite of the Great Exhibition of 1851, it was at first associated with the Victoria and Albert Museum, moving to South Kensington in 1877 under the aegis of the London Board of Education, and eventually achieving its own independence in 1909. Today the museum has a floor space of over 300,000 square feet to house displays and perform its museum functions in twenty-seven scientific and forty-one engineering fields.

The Osterrichisches Museum fur Kunst und Industrie was founded in Vienna in 1893 and ten years later in Munich the Deutsches

Museum broke through the traditional concepts to become the first institution to bring a new and revolutionary policy and program into being, that of visitor involvement and projection into the future.

In later chapters, the origins and development of museums in the fields of applied science and technology on the North American continent will be dealt with, but two new European institutions deserve mention, one in England, the other in Holland. Both are classified as company museums and have been opened in very recent years.

The Pilkington Glass Museum at Saint Helens, England, opened in 1964 and concentrates largely on the history of glass-making from antiquity to contemporary industrial processes. And at Eindhoven in the Netherlands the Evoluon was officially opened as a science centre in September 1966. This museum is revolutionary in its design, being mushroom-shaped and supported by twelve V-shaped columns, with a diameter of about 250 feet. The main building contains three concentric ring-shaped floors, the largest about 700 feet long and as wide as a main highway. It is a museum for active participation both by children and adults, but more important is the fact that the displays and programs are designed to illustrate the sociological involvement of man in this technological era.

Public museums in many instances have grown either out of the inspiration and dedication of one individual, or alternatively by a series of events in the form of trail blazing which have led inevitably to the founding of such an institution. London's Victoria and Albert Museum represents both of these factors.

The Royal Society of Arts had, almost from its inception, initiated and encouraged exhibitions of art and industry. Francis Whishaw, who served as secretary to the Society from 1843 to 1845 had offered from his own private purse various prizes amounting in all to three hunded pounds for different types of painting and useful inventions, later proposing a national exhibition of industrial products. The proposal was eagerly seized upon by Prince Albert, the President of the Society, who in the face of violent opposition from sources outside the Society persuaded Parliament to vote funds for an exhibition international in scope, and now immortalized as The Great Exhibition of 1851. Contrary to the moanings of the pessimists, the exhibition closed with a healthy financial surplus, part of which was used for the establishment of the Victoria and Albert museum which opened its doors to the public in 1857. The balance of the surplus was set up as an endowment trust for the continued operation of the institution.

The International Exhibition of 1855 held in Paris saw the erection of the Palais d'Industrie which remained in operation as a museum until torn down and replaced by the Palais des Beaux Arts for the exhibition of 1900.

Thus a pattern was established for the retention of major pavilions on International Exposition sites later to be converted into permanent galleries and museums. This pattern has made its impact both in the United States and Canada in more recent years and is dealt with in a succeeding chapter.

The Victoria and Albert, originally known as the Department of Practical Art, sought to perpetuate the philosophy of the 1851 exhibition by concentrating its efforts on "the illustration of art applied to industry." However, over the years it has received gifts, loans and bequests outside its purview, including books, prints, manuscripts and drawings, and the royal collection of Raphael cartoons. In 1884, it inherited the collection of the Patent Office, and at one time had as "dependencies" the Dublin and Edinburgh museums. This institution also pioneered in the areas of extension and loan services to scholastic bodies in addition to encouraging research for the elevation of standards. It was one of the first museums to initiate a specific theme, that of encouraging sound industrial design.

While archaeology and the associated disciplines of anthropology, pre-history and ethnology were being increasingly introduced into the museum field throughout the eighteenth century, human history as an all-embracing subject associated with sociological trends was a comparative late-comer. The Musée National d'Histoire de France was one such institution which opened in 1837 with a collection consisting mainly of paintings.

Hamburg had its Hamburgisches Museum fur Volkerkunde in 1850 which, as its title suggests, devoted itself largely to ethnology and folk-lore. But the Germanisches National Museum at Nuremberg deserves citing as a pioneer in the historic field and as the brainchild of Hans von Aufsess who, in 1852, conceived a program calling for the collection of objects directly relating to German culture as it emerged after the decline of Roman influence. This institution in later years strayed somewhat from the philosophy of its founder, but not before museums in other countries in Europe had received the message. Among these were the Rijksmuseum in Amsterdam (1855), the Croatian National Museum in Zagreb (1880) and what is now called the State Historical Museum in Moscow, which was founded in 1873.

Closely related to the human history museum is the institution generally referred to as archives, dating back to antiquity but taking on new meaning and new techniques after the French Revolution with the establishment of the Archives Nationales in Paris in 1789.

Archives are generally concerned with the preservation, documentation, and co-ordination of public records, manuscripts, books and papers, but many archivists go further afield by housing three-dimensional objects related to the historic growth of the area embraced under the archives' terms of reference. While their most important function is to aid scholarly research, there is a growing tendency for archives to include display areas open to the general public. Collins, in his work on Canada's National Museum written in 1926, refers to the Public Archives of Canada as "a separate museum of history."

6

In earlier chapters a tabloid history of museum origins and growth has dealt with significant techniques introduced to meet changing social norms. The French Revolution saw the take-over of royal collections and the establishment of national museums and galleries. Parallels are to be found in Mexico following the revolution of 1910 and the Russian Revolution of 1917. In earlier social changes, from the downfall of the Greek Republic to the Reformation, the conquering forces had preferred wilfully to obliterate all evidence of earlier civilizations as being subversive. By the early nineteenth century, museums had developed a common philosophy of supposition rather than discovery. Bacon had written in his *Advancement of Learning* that the foundation of all learning was to discover what nature does or may be made to do. Science was not a belief to be held but a thing to do. He also relegated theological questions, "which tortured the minds of generations," from the province of reason to that of faith.

While individual scientists were making marked advances in the study of natural phenomena divorced from the Book of Genesis, universities for the most part continued to conform to the classical philosophies and seek to turn out "gentlemen" whose function would be to prolong the status quo. Not until the mid-nineteenth century was the world to see the final break-through of the Baconian philosophy, with the publication in 1859 of Charles Darwin's *Origin of Species by Means of Natural Selection or the Preservation of Races in the Struggle for Life.*

Charles Robert Darwin was born at Shrewsbury, England on February 12, 1809, and as a young boy became engrossed in natural history. He had been destined to study first for the medical profession and later for the ministry, but in 1831 he was invited to join a geodesic expedition in the Pacific, a voyage of five years during which time he made copious notes and collected hundreds of specimens for later study. From his notes came first his *Origin of Species,* a highly controversial work, and in 1871 his second major work, *The Descent of Man or the Preservation of Races in the Struggle for Life.*

Alfred Russel Wallace, born in 1825, had arrived at similar conclusions, and in 1858 sent Darwin his theories on "the idea of the survival of the fittest," which Darwin described as the same ideas which he had penned in his notebook in 1842 and which resulted in close collaboration between the two.

Coincidentally, William Henry Flower, later to be knighted, and at that time Curator of the Hunterian Museum of the Royal College of Surgeons, was devising a new and radical philosophy for the museum world. There is no evidence to show that he had embraced the Darwinian theories other than the fact that in his essays on mammoths and mammals Flower speaks of possible relationships between mammals and the lower vertebrates. However, it is certain that he envisioned a new and significant role for museums as institutions for research and a continuing program of discriminatory collecting. "He insisted on the importance of distinguishing between collections intended for the use of specialists and those designed for the instruction of the general public, pointing out that it was as futile to present to the former a number of merely typical forms as to provide the latter with a long series of specimens differing only in the most minute details." His essays on museums and other subjects, along with his article in the ninth edition of the *Encyclopedia Britannica* published in 1889 are still viewed as basic principles for the contemporary museum. Sir William, in one of his essays, summed up his philosophy by writing, "A museum is like a living organism; it requires continued and tender care; it must grow or it will perish."

Within a few years of these two events, the Darwinian doctrines and Flower's new directions, the "curiosities," including bones of giants, unicorn horns, dodo skeletons and other accessions to which were attributed supernatural powers disappeared from the walls and glass cases of the major institutions both in Europe and on the North American continent, although even today one may still find, without too much searching, a few such antiquities in the more isolated community museums.

In 1911, Lord Bacarres, one-time trustee of the British National Portrait Gallery, summarized Sir William's "new museum idea first enunciated in 1870 [and] which is now beginning to receive general support," as follows:

"The first aim of public collections shall be education, and their second recreation. To be of teaching value, museum arrangement and classification must be carefully studied. Acquisitions must be added to their proper sections; random purchase of 'curios' must be avoided. Attention must be given to the proper display and cataloguing of the exhibits, to their housing and preservation, to the lighting, comfort and ventilation of the galleries. Furthermore, facilities must be allowed to those who wish to make a special study of the objects on view."

Despite the agitation of the Royal Society of Arts and of John Ruskin and his friends for reduced hours for workers, the twelve-hour day or longer was still in effect as the Victorian era drew to a close. A few years later, music hall comedians were to satirize the impossible dream of "the eight hour day," but in the meantime the agitation had produced tangible results in which a further dimension was added to museum operation. Derek Hudson and Kenneth W. Luckhurst, co-authors of a recent history of the Royal Society of Arts, elaboraté on this subject. "The Society," they write, "also concerned itself with advocating the evening opening of museums, a step which it considered of vital importance because without it, working people were in so many cases unable to visit these places." Most of the small museums associated with the local institutions (such as Mechanics' Institutes) were already open in the evenings, and so were the Geological Museum and the South Kensington Museum, but in 1859, when further buildings were added to the South Kensington Museum to house the Vernon and Turner collections belonging to the National Gallery, no provision was made for their lighting and they were closed in the evening, although the rest of the building remained open.

After unsuccessful correspondence with the Trustees of the National Gallery, the Society persuaded Lord Shaftsbury in the House of Lords, and the Rt. Hon. Mr. Cowper in the House of Commons, to move for copies of the correspondence, with the result that a Select Committee of the House of Commons was appointed to inquire into the matter. Lord Overton, on behalf of the Trustees, had previously raised in the House of Lords the question of the effect of gaslight on paintings, and accordingly a commission of scientists, including Michael Faraday (the eminent authority on illumination and power), was appointed to inquire into this aspect. They reported that, with suitable precautions, the use of gaslight would not be deleterious to the pictures, citing the Sheepshanks Gallery at South Kensington Museum which, being under different control, had been illuminated at night when the Vernon and Turner galleries were closed.

"The House of Commons Committee then inquired into the general principles and concluded that institutions such as the British

Museum and National Gallery ought to be open on weekday evenings to the public. The British Museum Trustees accordingly made careful inquiry, but found that in their case there were many special risks in the use of gas and decided only to open on summer evenings when no artificial light was necessary.

"The National Gallery Trustees also agreed to open the Vernon and Turner collections three evenings a week, and thus the Society's original point was won, but no action at all appears to have been taken with regard to the National Gallery in Trafalgar Square. The Society can now claim, however, to have been the first to make the evening openings of museums and galleries a public issue."

It could further be added that the same controversy made an important contribution to the subject of environmental security, relating both to fire hazards and deterioration of fine art through exposure to artificial light.

Sir William Flower credits John Hunter (1728-1793) with having founded what he described as "the modern museum" whose distinguishing features were specialization and classification. Certainly the distinguished anatomist effectively used his collection for research and instruction; the collection was originally put on display at the Museum of the Royal College of Surgeons in Lincoln's Inn Fields in 1800.

The contributions of museums to the advancement of human knowledge are frequently overshadowed by the undue, and for the most part unwarranted emphasis on the social aspects of such institutions. Dr. Murray, writing of archaeology, cites "the great museum of Copenhagen," originally founded in the seventeenth century, as being directly responsible for creating this science during the first half of the nineteenth century. Through classification and arrangement, the theories expounded but not necessarily originated by Christian Thomsen, known as the three-age system, served as bedrock for archaeology.

One of the major museum techniques, that of scientific conservation and restoration, was a spasmodic one at best until 1900 when F. Rathgen established the first museum laboratory at the Staatlichen Museum in Berlin, where systematic methods of conservation were developed in the fields of art and archaeology. In 1905 Rathgen wrote the first definitive textbook, *Die Konservierung von Altertumsfunden.*

Murray summed up his exhaustive study of the European museum climate in 1904 by saying "In a general sense a museum is a popular educator. It provides recreation and instruction for all classes and for all ages. Its doors are open to all alike, and each visitor gets profit or pleasure by viewing its gallery. The modern museum however has more definite aims. A museum has now be-

54

come a recognized and necessary instrument of research; it plays an important part in university and technical instruction, and it should be adopted as an aid in elementary and secondary education." Here Dr. Murray pointed to Denmark and Sweden as having taken the lead in using the museum as an annex to the primary and secondary classrooms. He emphasized the growing list of publications emerging from these institutions; loan exhibits and other extension services had also been developed. The author visualized a developing role for the museum "conducive to the improvement of the trade and industry of its community through improved techniques and design." His peroration ended on an optimistic note as he indicated that Great Britain "is slowly awakening to the necessity for an adequate and regulated training in every field of culture and every department of industry," adding, "one of the most potent engines by which this is to be secured is the museum."

In his definitive three-volume work, Murray listed 517 museums and related institutions in Great Britain and Europe, 30 in London alone, with 159 throughout the English provinces, 30 in Scotland and 8 in Wales. The remaining 277 were on the continent. "Many of these," the author related, "are lending valuable assistance to the advancement and appreciation of art and science. A large number however are still content to be mere holiday resorts. [The criticism is equally valid on the North American continent seventy years later.] All, even the best, must advance, and for this end enlightened and sympathetic administration and a liberal income are required. The museum of 1897 is far in advance of the museum of 1847, but it in turn will be old-fashioned by the end of twenty years and when the coming century is half-way through, its methods and arrangements will probably be wholly superseded by something better. We are ever moving onwards, but we do not reach the goal.

"And men through novel spheres of thought,
Still moving after truth long sought,
Will learn new things when I am not.
. . . .
Thou hast not gained a real height,
Nor art thou nearer to the light,
Because the scale is infinite."

If the two stanzas are somewhat deficient in rhyme, they do contain a simple truth.

II

The
American
Scene

*The Learned Societies, the
James Smithson Legacy, and
a Covey of Robber Barons*

7

The early colonization of the United States saw the Dutch, French, Spanish, Swedish, and British explorers and Gentlemen Adventurers making bids for exclusive possession of the territories. By the end of the seventeenth century all but a few isolated regions had come under British control. The British colonists, usually wealthy individuals or syndicates, functioned under royal charter which provided for the building of ships, engaging or impressing and transporting retinues of seamen and artisans to the New World for the development of trade, and the settling of lands. The beneficiaries, in return for this largesse, were called on to continue their allegiance to the British Crown.

So strong was the British tradition that even at the height of the Revolution statements were issued to the effect that there was yet no quarrel with British royalty in general, but rather with the current reigning monarch. In fact, so well entrenched was the monarchy that proposals were made to have George Washington proclaimed as king and given the powers accorded to the British Throne.

The early organization of urban communities was also carried out under provisions of the Royal Charter. Expatriate members of the aristocracy often served as governors and created cultural and social patterns including the establishment of academies, colleges, and other educational institutions. For the edification of their friends and associates, they also launched various societies for intellectual stimulation out of which developed many of the major museums still in existence today.

One of the first and certainly most publicized urban developments after Jamestown was Philadelphia, originally a tract of land both fertile and rich in minerals, which was deeded to William Penn after much shrewd bargaining by Charles II. While Penn was for the most part a governor in absentia, he encouraged members of the Quaker sect to establish settlements. Despite Penn's violent opposition to the established church he was elected a Fellow of The Royal

58

Society prior to his first visit to the New World in 1681. He brought with him, and was followed by, members of the Quaker faith adhering to a humanistic philosophy and eventually Learned Societies were founded which were dedicated not only to science but to the arts and humanities.

It is not surprising that Philadelphia in the seventeenth century was viewed as the centre for cultural expression. Its predominantly British citizens pioneered in the organization of academies later to become museums, some of which still flourish. But of course there were other motivating forces at work in the New World, such as the urge to titillate rather than stimulate – a fine distinction in anybody's vocabulary – or the desire to capitalize on the avocation of collecting. Thus "a curious collection of insects and birds" was displayed in Norwalk, Connecticut, in 1656 by a man named Arnold, which vanished much later when British forces razed the settlement in 1779.

In 1773 a museum of natural history was launched in Charleston, South Carolina, by the local library society following extensive scientific studies of the flora and fauna of the region. Here again, the original contents and building were destroyed by fire. A second collection found a new home in 1792 making it the oldest continuing natural history museum in the United States. Incorporated as a civic museum in 1907, its collection now concentrates on period furniture and state and city history, with an annex devoted to natural history. In addition, the museum administers the Heyward-Washington House, built in 1770, and the Joseph Manigault mansion of the same period.

Nine years after the Charleston project got underway, Pierre Eugène du Simitière, a native of Geneva, Switzerland, opened at Philadelphia what was advertised as a Curio Cabinet. Two years later du Simitière died, and his collection was scattered. His short-lived career as museum entrepreneur overshadowed the significant contribution made by him in the final years of his life when he amassed documents and artifacts relating to the War of Independence, thus laying the foundation for the first military archives on the continent.

Among other firsts in museum chronicles is the name of Charles Wilson Peale, who is given credit by some historians as the founder of the first museum "dedicated to the dissemination of knowledge and open to the general public." Peale was a portrait painter of note and his dedication to this craft is indicated by the fact that his three sons, all of whom became successful portrait painters in their own right, bore the names of Raphael, Rembrandt, and Titian Ramsay. Peale had portrayed many distinguished figures associated with the War of Independence, including George Washington. The museum first opened in his Philadelphia home, with portraits filling the walls and tables crowded with natural history specimens scattered through the halls. In 1785, one entranced visitor stated that "to wander through the rooms, play upon the organ, examine the rude electrical machine and have a profile drawn by the physiognomitian, were pleasures from which no stranger to the city refrained." Among other exhibits were a mammoth's tooth, a woman's shoe from Canton along with a Chinese fan and nests of a kind to make soup of, in addition to wampum belts, stuffed birds and feathers from Friendly Indians, scalps and tomahawks (presumably from unfriendly tribes) and, some time later, a mastodon skeleton which Peale himself had excavated on the Ohio and about which he delighted to give lectures.

In 1794 the collection had grown so large that it was now difficult to live with. There were now approximately three hundred portraits in addition to still further accessions including skeletons of members of the Wabash tribe, an ant-eater, an armadillo and other stuffed creatures. The Philosophical Society offered space in their new hall, complete with living quarters for the Peale household, which was gratefully accepted. Due to still further acquisitions the collection was moved in 1802 to the State House, now known as Independence Hall. The Lewis and Clark expedition turned over much of its collections of Indian artifacts and natural history to Peale. After Peale's death in 1827, his eldest son Raphael continued to administer the museum, later moving the collection to still another and larger building on monies borrowed from the United States Bank. The ambitious plans collapsed, however, when the bank failed.

Rembrandt had acquired many of the exhibits, taking them to Baltimore where he opened a museum in that city in 1817, continuing its operation until 1830. Brother Raphael sought to establish still another branch in New York, only to fail in 1837 and see the balance of the collections seized and sold to help pay his debts.

Peale's Baltimore Museum building was finally taken over to house the Municipal Museum, which eventually changed its name to honour the founder. A memorial show was held in 1956, at which time the atmosphere of the original institution was re-created. In 1968, a further wing, christened The Kirk Gallery, was added to the building in order to house a permanent collection of antique silver donated by Samuel Kirk and Son.

In 1790, the Tammany Society of New York voted to set aside one room in the City Hall, which its political machine controlled, to house a collection of Indian relics at the instigation of John Pintard and Gardiner Baker. Had the word Ethnology been coined at that time, this collection could have been so described. Unfortunately, as in the case of a vast majority of neophyte museums even in this enlightened age, donations of other miscellaneous artifacts soon arrived, making the premises too small to accommodate the accessions. While an admission fee of two shillings was charged for the general public (members of the Tammany Society naturally were admitted without charge) the museum ran into fiscal difficulties. In 1795 the museum was turned over to Mr. Baker, who forthwith changed the policy and exhibits, which now included freaks of nature. In later years Pintard was to found The New York Historical Society.

The museum moved to other quarters toward 1801, coming under the ownership of a Mr. Savage who engaged John Scudder, a taxidermist, as his assistant. Nine years later Scudder had bought out his employer and launched his American Museum, this time in the Alms House adjacent to City Hall, sharing the building with the Academy of Fine Arts and the Historical Society. Scudder died in 1821 but his family continued operating until 1839 at which time it had acquired over one hundred and fifty thousand items. These served as background for vaudeville performances and attracted the attention of P. T. Barnum.

Phineas Taylor Barnum, the immortalized circus entrepreneur, had a brief sortie which could have had a profound influence on museum philosophy and techniques. Born in 1810, Barnum had a somewhat checkered career as store keeper in Bethel, Connecticut, became involved in lotteries, and published in 1829 a weekly paper called *The Herald of Freedom* which brought him a short term in jail for libel. He then moved to New York where he exhibited a coloured woman, Joyce Heth, who had reputedly served as nurse to George Washington. Had this been true it would have made her one hundred and sixty years old. Four years later he purchased Scudder's Museum, introducing sensational publicity techniques. Under Barnum's direction the museum attracted nationally known figures such as Henry Ward Beecher, William Cullen Bryant, and Horace Greeley.

Bryant, a poet, publisher and philosopher who should have known better, is reported to have approached President Andrew Johnson during his term of office (1865-1869) to have Barnum recommended to Congress as Director of the then proposed National Museum. Johnson did submit Barnum's name to Congress only to see it rejected, not because Congressmen were opposed to Barnum, but because they were opposed to Johnson. In any event, before further overtures could be made Barnum's Great American Museum was totally destroyed by fire on March 3, 1868, and the indomitable P.T. turned his attention to "The Greatest Show on Earth," the Barnum and Bailey Circus.

While Barnum's career was meteoric in the museum field, the

contributions he made, good and bad, are worth recording. Most certainly he popularized the technique leading to active participation of the spectator and undoubtedly he can be considered the first man on the North American continent to create what today is called "the tourist attraction," frequently operating under the guise of a museum.

It was Barnum who blended the side show of natural and unnatural phenomena with the circus which has a very personal posthumous association with one bona fide institution, the Ringling Circus Museum at Sarasota, Florida. He is also remembered in Bridgeport, Connecticut, where he took up residence in 1842 and briefly served as mayor. Naturally there is a Barnum Museum in that city administered by the Bridgeport Science and Historical Society.

The museums of Peale, Scudder, and Barnum represent the demise of the *cabinet de curiosités*. The collections generally lacked authenticity and were accepted at face value. There was little or no research and any restoration carried out was dubious. Most certainly the Peale family and the founders of the Tammany museum were sincere in their desire to collect, preserve and display, but lacking the philosophy which was even then developing, and which saw the museum as a significant educational instrument, they serve today only as a footnote to museum history.

This footnote would be incomplete without reporting that Congress eventually appointed Joseph Henry, a physicist, as Secretary and Director of the Smithsonian Institution in 1846, being followed by Spencer Fullerton Baird, a zoologist, in 1850. When the controversial and much delayed National Museum building was completed in 1881, Dr. Baird placed George Brown Goode in complete charge of the newly-launched institution. It was in this same year that Barnum linked careers with James Anthony Bailey. The museum philosophy of P. T. Barnum, as exemplified today in the alligator farm-service station complexes masquerading under the name "museum," had taken to the road.

George Brown Goode, having absorbed the philosophy of Sir Henry Flower, provided the impetus for the growth and development of the contemporary museum movement throughout the North American continent. In an address delivered to the American Historical Association of December 26, 1888, Dr. Goode described what he termed "the museum of the future" as being adapted to the needs of the mechanic, the factory operator, the day labourer, the salesman, and the clerk (here echoing the philosophy of Dr. George Birkbeck) as much as those of the professional man and the man of leisure. "It is proper that there be laboratories and professional libraries for the development of the experts who are to organize, arrange and explain the museums," he noted, adding that, "no museum can do good and be respected which does not each year give additional proofs of its claims to be considered a centre of learning. On the other hand, the public has a right to ask that much shall be done directly in their interest. They will gladly allow the museum officer to use part of his time in study and experiment. They will take pride in the possession by the museum of tens of thousands of specimens, interesting only to the specialist, hidden away perpetually from public view, but necessary for proper scientific research. They are the foundations of the intellectual superstructure which gives to the institution its proper standing."

Five years after the Peale museum was opened in 1790, the first population census in the United States indicated that approximately four million people were living in the then known and explored regions, extending as far west as Wisconsin, Illinois, and Mississippi. An attempt had been made to include Indian bands but it is doubtful if anything more than a cursory estimate was made of these aborigines or the Negro slaves who had been imported to Virginia and neighbouring regions since 1620.

The same census disclosed that ninety per cent of the population were of British origin or directly descended from British stock, indicating that cultural patterns and philosophies emanated from this one source. German and other European immigrations reached their flood only in the 1840's and infiltration from Ireland attained its peak between 1871 and 1895. Beginning at the time of the potato famine of 1846, almost one and a half million people, representing thirteen per cent of the population of the United States, crossed the Atlantic from Ireland.

While the Mechanics' Institute movement launched by Dr. George Birkbeck played a significant role in the museum program of Canada's Atlantic Provinces, there is little to indicate that this had an appreciable effect on early museums in the United States, although such Institutes did appear where there was a concentration of English and Scottish artisans. One such Institute was established in Cincinnati in 1825, and as late as 1907 was reported to have had an active membership of over one thousand, yet there is nothing to indicate that it influenced in any way the museum growth of that city.

On the other hand, Learned Societies were flourishing. The Pennsylvania Academy of Fine Arts was founded in Philadelphia in 1805 and almost immediately faced criticism for allegedly inflicting European art on the public at the expense of the home-grown product. The problem was resolved apparently by 1810, and today it ranks high on the list of major art galleries on the North American continent.

In 1812, the Academy of Natural Sciences came into existence in the same city. It too was born under a cloud, being suspect of having atheistic tendencies despite the fact that its founder and some members of the Board were staunch Quakers. In 1815, a member named Jacob Gilliams erected a building at his own expense, but due to a proliferation of collections and activities during the ensuing years the Academy was compelled to move into a vacated church, and in 1876 participated in the Centennial Exposition where it found a permanent home.

Benjamin Franklin established his "Junto Club" in 1727, which sixteen years later became the American Philosophical Society. Although born in Boston, Franklin was an early member of the British Royal Society of Arts; appointed its corresponding Fellow in 1755, he attended his first meeting in London in 1759 and remained active in the society throughout his five-year tenure as representative of the Pennsylvania Assembly.

Franklin's wide range of interests made its impact in areas other than literature and philosophy. The Franklin Institute founded in Philadelphia in 1824, initially provided space for the Peale Collection but exhibited many of the inventions created by the author of *Poor Richard's Almanack*.

The Society for the Promotion of Agriculture, Arts and Manufacturing, undoubtedly inspired by Franklin, was incorporated in Albany, New York, in 1791, changing its name in 1796 to the Society for the Promotion of Useful Arts, and still later merging with the Albany Lyceum. Out of this merger came the Institute of History and Art, which continues to administer a museum concentrating on American painting of the eighteenth to twentieth centuries.

Throughout the New England states during the first quarter of the nineteenth century there was a proliferation of such societies, dedicated to science, the fine and useful arts and history, many almost overnight building collections from which, in later years, museums developed.

In Boston the Linnaeum Society of New England was founded in 1816, the precursor of the Boston Society of Natural Science. Nineteen years prior to its founding a natural history museum had opened its doors in that city for its collections of curiosities, with a special display area devoted to wax figures. After a series of fires what remained of the collection was sold to the New England Museum, an offshoot of the Linnaeum Society, which eventually underwent another metamorphosis to become the Boston Society of Natural Science. We are told by the authors of *Museums U.S.A.* that included in the exhibits were "The great elephant Horatio and a Vampyre of the Ocean weighing five tons . . . along with the Musical Androides, a mechanical panarama, a musical clock, stone

64

sarcophagus and curious mirrors, also a marine room (in which were displayed) a great variety of fishes, monsters and curiosities from the sea," all in addition to birds, heathen gods, Indian implements, antiquities with also "a mermaid, monkeys, domestic fowl, wild ducks and Chinese punishments." There was also a large painting in an elegant frame painted by, of all people, Rembrandt Peale, Esq. of Philadelphia.

The paintings by Charles Wilson Peale which led a peripatetic existence from 1785 to 1837 could be viewed as America's first art gallery. Undoubtedly the entire Peale family took pride in the collection but surrounded as they were by miscellaneous curiosities and memorabilia, the emphasis on the paintings was somewhat diverted from aesthetics to history and the sciences.

As research techniques developed it was natural that museum collections were encouraged as teaching aids but generally little or no attention was paid to this fact of educational life. In 1808, a small anatomical museum was founded at the University of Pittsburg by Casper Wister of the medical faculty. Nine years later the first full-fledged campus museum in the United States was built to house a conglomeration of artifacts and objects now lost to posterity. Williams College is reported to have started a geology collection in 1816. Vail Coleman, in his definitive book *The American Museum Movement*, also reports that "James Bowdoin left a lot of pictures to Bowdoin College in 1811, and they were in the way for decades," adding "the teaching of art in college was not yet."

Continuing his survey of art and the universities, Coleman cites the Trumbull Gallery at Yale, built in 1832, as the first campus art gallery, but not until the 1850's were there further developments in this area of education when the University of Michigan purchased casts of sculpture, suggesting that anatomical drawing had been inaugurated.

Unlike the art museums, many of which bear the names of their benefactors, the science and historical museums had their origins in two separate environments. The universities, naturally, had to concern themselves with the artifacts and objects for teaching aids. Scholars found it necessary to make field trips in order to gather data for the preparation of theses, resulting in accumulations of accessions which, more often than not, found their way into the basements and boiler rooms of these institutions. It is to be regretted that even today many campuses still function under these conditions, but some of the world's most important museums are to be found on the campus, many of which, like Topsy "just growed." Benefactors have emerged from time to time, for example George Peabody, the Massachusetts banker, who in the 1890's not only endowed the museum of the East India Marine Society, but left much of his fortune to the universities of Harvard and Yale for the specific purpose of founding campus museums.

Peabody's junior partner in the investment field was Junius S. Morgan. How far one had influenced the other in the field of museum endowments could make an interesting story even if conjecture were to be the sole source. Junius Morgan, founder of the clan, and father of the legendary John Pierpont, was one of the early benefactors of the American Museum of Natural History, later making substantial contributions to the Metropolitan Museum of Fine Arts. Peabody, on the other hand, devoted the major portion of his energies and money to the establishment of educational institutions and charitable foundations geared to the pursuit of science. The Peabody Museum of Natural History on the campus of Yale University is one example, while Harvard perpetuates the name of its early benefactor in its Museum of Archaeology and Ethnology.

It was at Harvard that battle lines were drawn around the Darwinian hypothesis. Louis Agassiz, professor of zoology and geology, challenged what were described as the atheistic writings of this British upstart by voicing his belief that the first book of Genesis was not to be questioned. The disputation was to be waged in the United States over the next half century, culminating in the Scopes trial of 1925 in Dayton, Tennessee.

Agassiz gathered a large retinue of avid supporters to his cause but simultaneously many of his Harvard colleagues and protégés turned their backs on their former idol. One of these was Albert S. Bickmore who was to become the moving spirit in the founding in 1869 of New York's American Museum of Natural History.

Throughout the first half of the nineteenth century, educational institutions had little regard for human history, but in the areas of the natural sciences the need for economic exploitation of natural resources became a political reality. Many States launched their own surveys, and the extensive collections gathered by the survey teams were usually turned over to the universities. The State of Massachusetts gave such material to Amherst, with Connecticut turning over its collections to Yale in 1835. The University of Michigan established a Cabinet for similar accessions in 1837, and Amherst, after receiving a second windfall, built its first edifice in which to house a science museum in 1846. Ann Arbor entered the zoological field at an early date. Its collection also included botanical accessions.

In addition to sponsoring and nurturing American museums, the societies and academies devoted to studies in science, history, and art made possible a more liberal climate for research and acceptance in the several fields of interest in the face of Puritan philosophy with its witch hunts and persecutions reminiscent of the Inquisition. The Baconian philosophy emphasizing the need to investigate the laws of nature, coupled with the new concepts spelled out in *The Origin of Species* and *The Descent of Man* had an almost overnight effect on museum policies.

Original speculation on the part of any one individual tended to produce negative results. As one writer explained, "The practical scientists knew no logic, while the logicians with their conservative devotion to syllogisms, knew no science." It was here that the societies generally provided a forum for discussion and made possible a radical transition in museum policies and techniques. Henceforth, the bona fide museum would reject the curiosities, freaks, and other conversation pieces, turning to scholarly research and the authentication of its accessions "with reference to their value to investigators or their possibilities for public enlightenment." This new role called for staffs of qualified scientists, historians or art experts whose functions were to build up systematic collections, serve as interpreters, and provide the necessary facilities for research in depth by scholars and students, functions which in the mid-twentieth century are now largely undertaken by university faculties.

8

The story of the Smithsonian Institution and the United States National Museum bridges a period of seventy years from the first proposal by Joel Barlow, poet, politician and enthusiastic Francophile, who, in 1800, advocated that the United States Congress turn its attention to the organization of a national scientific institution. At the same time, M. Dupont de Nemours corresponded with President Jefferson on much the same subject.

In Washington, D.C. the Columbian Institute for the Promotion of Arts and Sciences was founded in 1812, and early in its history started "to collect, cultivate and examine . . . vegetable productions, the various mineral productions and natural curiosities of the United States." It persistently lobbied for financial assistance and land to establish a museum and botanical garden and had been hopeful of action until the advent of Andrew Jackson as President when "science languished," and the institute dropped out of existence.

It may have also been coincidental that James Smithson, the British chemist and mineralogist, spent much of his time in France during that same period and could have met both Barlow and de Nemours. It was Smithson who wrote a will in 1826 bequeathing his entire fortune to his nephew Henry J. Hungerford with the proviso that if the beneficiary died without issue the balance of his inheritance, including his collection of rocks, minerals and fossils and his many papers, should go to the U.S. Government "to found at Washington, under the name of the Smithsonian Institution, an establishment for the increase and diffusion of knowledge among men."

James Smithson was born in France in 1765, the illegitimate son of Sir Hugh Smithson, first Duke of Northumberland and a direct descendent of the House of Percy whose ancestry dates back to William the Conqueror. The child James was given his mother's surname of Macie who was a grand-daughter of Sir George Hungerford of Studley. Bastardy carried no stigma in the period of the Georges, provided only that class barriers had been respected; consequently the economic future of the child was ensured, enabling him to concentrate on studies in chemistry and mineralogy, in addition to having ample funds for travel. He also indulged in authorship. James Macie eventually took the name of his father although as late as 1795 he was referred to as M. de Mecies of London by the author of *Travels in England, Scotland and the Hebrides.*

Smithson had found it expedient to live abroad, possibly because of the domestic relationship of his parents but there is no evidence to indicate that he ever travelled further than Europe or had associated with American citizens to any extent. However, a history of Smithson written by W.J. Rhees includes a reference to a copy of *Travels through North America* by Isaac Weld, secretary of the Royal Society, in which Weld had prophetically described the City of Washington as "likely some time to become the intellectual and political centre of one of the greatest nations in the world." Smithson had developed a reputation as scientist and author at an early age and had been elected a Fellow of the Royal Society at the age of twenty-two. Undoubtedly he received a copy of this paper.

To would-be benefactors who wish to pave their path to paradise, achieve immortality through good deeds, or simply find ways and means to escape death duties, the terms of the Smithson bequest deserve analysis. Smithson in his will had specified "an establishment for the increase and diffusion of knowledge among men." In 1753, Sir Hans Sloane had instructed his executors to obtain "sufficient and effectual powers for the preserving and continuing my said collection in such manner as they shall think most likely to answer the public benefit by me intended." Both The Royal Society and the Royal Society of Arts had been advocating for many years the founding of public museums and only one interpretation was possible when the Sloane bequest was read.

The word "Museum" to the average American conjured up an image of Peale or Barnum so it is not surprising that, in addition to political gerrymandering there was widespread disputation when Congress sought to implement the terms of the bequest. Had the bequest been given to the British Government or even to France, the interpretation would have been obvious insofar as, in addition to his money there were "Two large boxes, eight cases and one trunk," which among other effects contained "a choice and beautiful collection of Minerals, comprising probably ten thousand specimens . . . [which,] though generally small, are extremely perfect, and constitute a very complete Geological and Mineralogical series embracing the finest varieties of crystallization; rendered more valuable by accompanying figures and descriptions by Mr. Smithson, and in his own handwriting." The benefactors were also advised that "The cabinet also contains a valuable suite of meteoric stones, which appear to be specimens of most of the meteorites which have fallen in Europe during several centuries."

In September 1838 the clipper *Mediator* sailed up the Delaware to deposit one hundred and four thousand nine hundred and sixty gold sovereigns to the Philadelphia mint, "where it was recoined into American money." Later in the year it was invested, if that is the word, in bonds of the State of Arkansas, which by 1841 had become worthless. However, although controversy had already started as to whether to accept the bequest or to reject it offhand, Congress as official trustee voted an appropriation to cover the loss.

That same year the Smithson collection, which had been placed in storage, was turned over to the custody of the National Institute, a scientific quasi-governmental society which had been founded in 1840 to supersede the Columbian Institute, but lacking any display or other suitable storage area the collection remained until 1858 more or less,in limbo.

Congressional confrontations were lengthy and controversial. While the National Institute had theoretical possession of the Smithson collection, the cases were in the custody of the Director of the Patent Office, an official who was jealous of his rights and functions. George Brown Goode, in a footnote to his *The Genesis of the United States National Museum* reports that "one enlightened Commissioner of Patents, in power between 1830 and 1860, was annoyed by the presence of a collection of fossil vertebrates in one of the rooms of his building, and without consulting anyone sent them to a bone mill in Georgetown, where they were transformed into commercial fertilisers – once for thought, they now became food for the farmers' crops."

A proposal to found a Smithsonian Institution was placed before Congress in 1836 but the passage of the measure was delayed for ten years. In 1837 a start was made on a building in which to house staff, documents, and collections owned by the Federal Government but this was not completed until 1855 at which time one large area on the ground floor was designated for display, once funds were made available, for glass cases and other furnishings, and it was only in 1859 that a temporary National Museum, with an appropriate sign above the door, was finally opened.

In 1865 a disastrous fire swept through the premises destroying, among other things, the entire Smithson collection. It required the Columbian Exposition of 1867 in Philadelphia to awaken the politicians to the need for a permanent museum building, but even this had an element of chance. Reluctantly, Congress had been persuaded to extend a loan of several million dollars to finance the Exposition. Members of the Appropriations Committee half-jokingly stated that if the loan were ever repaid a grant for the National Museum building would be forthcoming. While the Exposition was a financial debacle, Philadelphia merchants raised funds with which to repay the loan, whereupon the grant was made, "a sum, pitiably small if compared with the money devoted by most civilized nations to housing their national museums." By a lucky chance, an unparallelled depression in the iron trade enabled contracts to be made to the great advantage of the government. A building was finally put up, without architectural pretensions but giving light and floor space at a lower cost than in any other permanent structure of equal size ever erected by the United States, and a new organization effected. At last the National Museum possessed a habitation and a name.

John Caldwell Calhoun, one time U.S. vice president but serving as Senator during the Smithsonian controversy, had led the campaign for the rejection of the bequest but by this time he had long since (in 1850) gone to his reward. Andrew Johnson, who had sought to make P. T. Barnum the Director, had faced impeachment, been acquitted and died a few months before the final vote.

Throughout the years of controversy, various bills had been placed before Congress calling for the monies to be used for an observatory; for a university; to place funds at the disposal of the American Institution for the Promotion of Literature and Science; for the establishment of an institution for the promotion of agriculture; for an astronomical school; for "an institution which should occupy the space between the close of a collegiate education and a professional school"; and for a number of schools associated with various scientific disciplines. It required eight sessions to sift through the various proposals and formally establish the Smithsonian Institution and mark the bequest as an endowment fund. The congressman who drafted the legislation for the founding of the Smithsonian was Robert Dale Owen, eldest son of the English radical, social reformer and founder of the British co-operative movement, Robert Owen.

Interestingly enough, one Canadian, Alexander Graham Bell, served as a Regent of the Smithsonian from 1898 until his death in 1922. An excerpt from a biographical memoir presented to the National Academy of Sciences in the early 1920's states that "in 1890 a generous gift by Mr. Bell helped start the Astrophysical Observatory of the Institution." In 1894 Mr. Bell journeyed to Genoa and brought the body of Mr. Smithson to Washington for reinterment in the Smithsonian grounds.

More fascinating is an excerpt from the biography of Alexander Graham Bell written by Catherine Mackenzie, who served as Mr. Bell's secretary from 1914 to 1922: "When Mr. Charles Freer offered his valuable art treasures to the Smithsonian Institution in

1904, Bell was named one of a committee of four officials to visit Mr. Freer in Chicago and inspect the collection. He took his daughter Marian along. The other members of the committee were mature gentlemen of scientific tastes with very much Bell's point of view on what, for want of a better word, may be called art. Politely and gloomily the four surveyed the 950 pieces of pottery from the Far East and Central Asia; the priceless group of ancient Chinese and Japanese bronzes and the ceramics so rare that they were still unidentified. Not even the one hundred framed paintings of James McNeill Whistler and the entire decorations of the Peacock Room could move them to any enthusiasm for this 'dingy array,' valued at more than half a million dollars. They looked to Bell like 'a lot of old pots' and his distinguished confreres thought so too. It was Marian Bell's insistence, Bell always said – with delightful chuckles – that saved the Freer collection for the nation."

A much better account of the Freer collection and its eventual disposition is told by Dr. David Fairchild, world renowned agronomist who married Miss Bell in 1904. In his book, *The World was my Garden*, published in 1908, Dr. Fairchild wrote: "Early in November 1903, I received an invitation from Mrs. Gilbert H. Groosvienor asking me to dinner. It was a small party and I found myself seated next to Miss Marian Bell, who had recently returned from New York where she had been working in the studio of Gutzon Borglund [the sculptor]. . . . In commenting on the Freer incident, Miss Bell had said that her father did not pretend to have a knowledge of such things as Oriental porcelain so had asked his daughter to accompany him. She had been keen to go as she realized this particular committee would probably fail to appreciate the value of the collection. The account Marian gave us was both humorous and pathetic. Mr. Freer proved to be courtly, sensitive and a gentle man, his life completely centered in his beautiful art treasures while his three [*sic*] distinguished visitors were entirely out of their element. The scientists sat wearily hour after hour as each picture or objet-d'art was brought out and displayed separately, Japanese fashion, for their inspection. The opinions of all three regarding the priceless examples of ancient Chinese art were expressed in a remark of Senator Henderson that 'The things were all very well of their kind – but damn the kind.' Marian proudly treasures a telegram which Mr. Freer sent her indicating his appreciation of her influence in bringing about the decision of the committee to accept his collection, which is now housed in a beautiful marble building on the Mall."

Between the announcement of the Smithson bequest to the formal opening of the United States National Museum, twelve major institutions were established all of which are still functioning. They include the Museum of the University of Michigan, Ann Arbor (1837); the Wadsworth Athenium in Hartford, Connecticut (1842); the Essex Museum at Salem, Massachusetts (1867); the American Museum of Natural History (1869) and the Metropolitan Museum of Fine Arts (1870), both in New York; the Boston Museum of Fine Arts (1870); and the Farnsworth Art Museum at Wellesley, Massachusetts (1875).

In the nation's capital, the Corcoran Gallery of Art had been given to the nation by William Wilson Corcoran with what one critic described as "a collection of minor importance." Corcoran had started to build the gallery in 1859, but the Civil War caused suspension of the work, the gallery being completed in 1869 but formally opened in 1871. In the meantime a portion of an uncompleted gallery was used by the Smithsonian in which to store and display a small art collection of its own saved from the fire of 1865. Corcoran served as prototype for "robber-baron-philanthropists" who were to spread their benefactions from coast to coast during the ensuing fifty years.

The Smithsonian, parallelling the diversified program of the British Museum, subsequently established curatorial divisions in the fields of the fine and decorative arts, history, and natural and applied sciences. In 1890, its astrophysical observatory was opened along with the National Zoological Park while a few years later its aerodynamics division was launched under Samuel P. Langley. In 1893, the Smithsonian was pioneering in "research and investigation of atmospheric air in connection with the welfare of mankind." Today the Smithsonian controls and administers the largest museum complex in the world, including the Freer Gallery; the National Gallery of Art; the most recent Hirshhorn collection; the National Air and Space Museum; the United States National Museum, including the Museum of History and Technology; the Museum of Natural History; and the Zoological Park.

9

At the time of James Smithson's death, William Wilson Corcoran was thirty-one and Meyer Guggenheim was one year old.

When Congress had voted funds for the National Museum (1876), a host of future philanthrophists were amassing vast reservoirs of wealth through the sometimes ruthless exploitation of natural and human resources, which in later years would be dispersed in endowments and other forms of gifts to the museums and galleries of the United States.

Possibly the philanthrophists were not all robber barons. There were some who through inheritance or other good fortune had devoted their life and energies to studying the cultural needs of a nation. As time progressed, from the nineteenth and into the twentieth century, the sons and grandsons of some of the empire-builders assumed the responsibilities which great wealth should require.

From the opening of the Corcoran gallery in 1871 until World War II, the monies, buildings, and acquisitions of virtually every major museum and gallery in the United States came from one or a small group of wealthy patrons. Some such benefactions continued into the 1950's and here and there the odd benefactor continues his support.

The Belmont Report presented in 1968 to the United States Federal Council on the Arts and Humanities makes reference to a serious decline when it points to the fact that in 1967 "Private foundations and business firms have . . . substantially increased their contributions to colleges and universities but have yet to do so for museums," adding that in that year the major foundations, most of them bearing the names of nineteenth-century capitalists and financiers, had limited their contributions to museums (and bear in mind this includes all institutions from aquaria to zoos) to less than two per cent of their grants.

It seems to be relevant to insert in parentheses the comparable picture as it relates to Canadian museums. The Dominion Bureau of

Statistics in 1937 reported that gifts and endowments constituted only one-tenth of operating revenues in that year. In its 1966 report, the same Federal agency gave a breakdown of gross expenditures for the year 1964 as a little over $300,000 for operations from gifts and endowments, out of a total expenditure of just under $9,500,000 and just under $250,000 for capital gifts out of a gross of slightly more than $2,000,000, a decline of around five per cent since 1937.

If this work had been designed as a definitive history of museum proliferation, the next few chapters would be scarely enough to present in detail the many endowments and gifts which were responsible for the origin and early development of American institutions. In 1954 close to five hundred United States museums and galleries were receiving revenues from endowments, a commentary serving as footnote to this particular statistic stating that "endowment, once considered a major item, has shrunk to a source involving less than a quarter of the museums." The same report, which included Canadian museums, disclosed that out of 162 Canadian institutions replying to this particular question only twelve, or approximately seven per-cent, drew revenue from endowments and of that number half of them got ten per cent or less of their finances from such a source.

One of the first major benefactions in the United States was that of Daniel Wadsworth of Hartford, Connecticut, which provided funds for the building of a library and art gallery in his native city. In 1844, the Wadsworth Atheneum was formally opened with great fanfare when visitors were entertained with five scenes of the Revolution from the brushes of Colonel John Trumbell. Four years later the benefactor died, bequeathing his personal collecton of paintings by Trumbell and the Hudson River artist Thomas Cole.

This building was gutted by fire at the turn of the century and a few years later a second gallery suffered a similar fate. The Board of Trustees persisted, however, by erecting not one but two galleries, both of which have survived and expanded. The latest annex opened in 1968, at which time the Athenium director announced somewhat modestly that "this is no longer a small museum" as he guided visitors through fifteen galleries, occupying two hundred thousand square feet of floor space, filled with accessions which included gifts from John Pierpont Morgan, Wallace Nutting, Philip Hammerslough, and many other prominent figures.

A review of some of the early American benefactions provides interesting reading. The Guggenheim fortune, amassed by Meyer (1828-1905), was the source for the Guggenheim Foundation, launched by Meyer's son David in 1924, which has contributed heavily to the advancement of art galleries and artists since that time. The

Samuel R. Guggenheim Museum, the only museum institution to perpetuate the name, was opened in 1959 to memorialize Meyer's fourth son.

Andrew Carnegie is remembered for his contributions to the public library development on the North American continent, but two of his major endowments created the Carnegie Museum of Natural History and the Museum of Art in Pittsburg, Pennsylvania, which were opened in 1901 with an endowment of $2,000,000. The Natural History Museum has for many years administered a training program for museum curators and technicians open to candidates throughout the world which provides an all-expense program extending over twelve months.

Carnegie, the son of a rabble-rousing Scottish street-corner orator and political dissenter, came to the United States from Dumferline at the impressionable age of thirteen after his father had become a fugitive from justice because of his activities in the Chartist movement. The library-museum program of Dr. Birkbeck which was part of the Mechanics' Institute movement and which had reached Glasgow in the first years of the nineteenth century can be viewed as a major factor in determining the pattern of the Carnegie benefactions.

Andrew Carnegie died the same year as his former industrial associate, Henry Clay Frick. A few years prior to his death Carnegie had established a charitable foundation with a capital fund of $125,000,000 whose benefactions are too extensive and well known to be recorded here.

Frick, who had built a mansion on New York's Fifth Avenue in which to store his vast fine art collection ranging from fourteenth-century tapestries to eighteenth-century European Masters, established his own foundation to endow in perpetuity the mansion, the art treasures, and an extensive art reference library on the adjacent property. The complex known as the Frick Collection is protected by its own corps of uniformed armed guards stationed in every room and corridor, and also has its own organist who presents recitals each Sunday afternoon. In 1948 the Foundation published the most expensive catalogue ever to be printed; the estimated cost exceeding one million dollars for an edition numbering not more than one or two hundred which was distributed to the national museums throughout the world.

John Pierpont Morgan (1837-1913) continued his father's benefactions to the Metropolitan Museum of Fine Art, served as its president, made important contributions in cash and accessions also to the New York Public Library (which has its own extensive museum collection), and helped finance the building of the Wadsworth Athenium, this institution being further financed by John Pierpont

Junior. To the Metropolitan, J. P. Senior gave over 6,000 objects of fine and decorative arts from 1869 to 1877. He was also a heavy contributor of money to the American Museum of Natural History in New York, though somewhat reluctantly at a time when his interests were in other directions.

Carnegie and Rockefeller Foundation grants were available to cultural and educational institutions in Canada for specific projects until the advent of the Canada Council. The National Gallery of Canada was one such institution which received grants from both these agencies. It is also noted that a grant of $30,000 from the Carnegie Corporation circa 1930 – obtained by the late E.A. Corbett, at that time Director of Extension Services at the University of Alberta – launched a summer school of drama at Banff, the original cornerstone upon which the Banff School of Fine Arts was built.

The benefactions of the Rockefeller family have been widely publicized. John D. Senior, progenitor of the clan, whose most notorious idiosyncrasy was limiting his gratuities for services rendered to ten cents, created four multi-million dollar foundations following his retirement from the oil industry in 1911. Two of these, the Rockefeller Foundation and the Laura Spellman Rockefeller Memorial, have both made many significant contributions to the endowment and support of museums not only in the United States but throughout the world. It remained for his sons, and still later his grandsons, to become personally involved in the continuing development of the museum programs in the United States, starting with a grant from the Laura Spellman Foundation to the American Association of Museums to develop what is now called a "trailside" museum at Yosemite Park, and shortly thereafter to erect a similar museum in the Yellowstone National Park, this due to the interest of John D. Rockefeller Junior.

In the period from 1922 to 1930, the Rockefeller interests, again inspired by John Davidson II, planned, created and endowed The Cloisters at Fort Tryon Park, New York as a museum dedicated to the conservation and interpretation of medieval art and architecture which, during its formative development, was presented to the Metropolitan Museum of Fine Art. In other areas of the fine and decorative arts, the Museum of Modern Art on New York's Fifty-third Street has been largely financed and provided with endowment funds by the Rockefeller family, while John D. Rockefeller III made possible Asia House in New York, a museum devoted to organizing travelling exhibitions of the decorative arts of the Far East. Adjacent to this museum is the Museum of Primitive Art, founded by Nelson Rockefeller and containing most of his collection of primitive arts. These contributions to the museum field encouraged the development of a complex of highly specialized institutions in the immediate area, including the Museum of Early American Folk Arts and the museum of Contemporary Crafts.

Two more families linked by marriage have also made contributions to the museum world, the Whitneys and the Vanderbilts. Gertrude Vanderbilt had established herself as both artist and patron at the time of her marriage at nineteen to Harry Payne Whitney. An early resident of New York's Greenwich Village, Mrs. Whitney gave encouragement through patronage to the younger schools of American painters when she opened a MacDougall Alley studio as a focal point for informal displays, and she made what proved to be highly discriminating purchases from the then unknowns. In 1929 she offered her collection to the Metropolitan Museum of Fine Art only to have it rejected. As a result the first Whitney museum opened in the Village in 1931. Subsequent developments saw the Whitney move to a location adjacent to the Museum of Modern Art in 1954, and in 1966 it moved once again to Madison Avenue and 57th Street into a building designed by architect Marcel Breuer.

The Vanderbilt interests moved in another direction, but Cornelius Junior, son of the colourful Commodore (1794-1887), presented the Metropolitan Museum with a Rosa Bonheur painting, later bequeathing his summer mansion, "The Breakers" at Newport, as a historic example of American-Baroque of the late nineteenth century. William K. Junior also made his Long Island summer home available as a museum to display, among other things, his extensive collection of ship models, shells, and curios.

An interesting parallel is to be found between the social aspirations of the great European families of the sixteenth century and those of the financial overlords, merchant princes, and robber barons of the second half of the nineteenth century in the free enterprise society of the United States.

The vast accumulation of wealth in the hands of comparatively few individuals created problems among the recipients. Investments and speculation caused a momentum in profits which was all but uncontrollable, requiring bizarre methods of expenditure, such as building elaborate and generally ornate mansions to serve as winter residences, summer homes with way stations en route, or, in the manner of Commodore Vanderbilt, fleets of sailing vessels, or again, as with the Whitney family, lavish racing stables.

In a Europe undergoing great social change, the rich art collections of the now declining aristocracy began appearing on the market at a most opportune time. As early as 1830, Luman Reed had been acquiring American paintings for a collection which eventually became the nucleus for the New York Gallery of Fine Arts. At the century's half-way mark one Thomas Bryan returned from Europe with his collection of "Christian Art" (the emphasis being on subject matter rather than aesthetics), which was shortly turned over to the New York Historical Society. In 1860, James Jackson Jarves had raided European art salons to bring to the United States a collection of 119 paintings by Italian Masters, major and minor, covering a period of five centuries. His motive was purely altruistic, but interestingly enough this doughty and determined benefactor spent the ensuing decade attempting to persuade the newly-opened Metropolitan Museum of Fine Art in New York and later the Boston Museum of Fine Art, which opened its doors at about the same time as its New York contemporary, to accept the collection at a price. Mr. Jarves eventually persuaded a more far-sighted body of trustees at Yale University to purchase the paintings for display in the recently opened Peabody Museum, this in 1871.

Thus, in the last quarter of the nineteenth century, a pattern of collecting and benefactions was taking form. Paradoxically it should be noted that such benefactions and endowments related almost wholly to the areas of fine and decorative arts. While a few of the *nouveau riche* of that period developed active interests in the various scientific disciplines, the natural science museum as a general rule emerged from the cocoon of locally or regionally organized natural history societies which involved primarily individuals of moderate wealth and/or members of the university science faculties. As in Europe, the development of museums dedicated to human history had to wait for a historical perspective.

The delayed interest on the part of benefactors in the areas of natural history was due largely to the recently publicized Darwinian works with Louis Agassiz leading the fundamentalist forces and actively dissuading any financial support to the dissenters. After all, had not Sir Hans Sloane made it explicit in his will that his gift to the British nation was made, among other reasons, "for the confusion of atheistic tendencies"?

Joseph Duveen, later to become Lord Duveen of Milbank, is frequently credited with initiating massive gifts and endowments by the most affluent members of an affluent society, but the trend was well under way long before Duveen had established a firm foothold in the American art milieu. Duveen provided new impetus to this trend through his super-salesmanship, with assists from Knoedler and other members of a new breed of traders, the owners of the commercial art gallery.

In the meantime the tycoons, along with the occasional aesthete, had taken matters into their own hands by raiding the European markets for objets d'art, paintings, sculpture pieces including plaster casts, and anything else associated with the fine and decorative arts.

Niels von Holst, in his *Creators, Collectors and Connoisseurs*, gives a highly descriptive picture of the tastes of some of the first collectors: "In accordance with the prevailing Anglo-Saxon views, nudes were not yet permitted to be exported to the United States; however, (William H.) Vanderbilt favored precise drawing and anecdotal themes. The principal apartments of his house were entered through a bronze portal. Next came an atrium in French Renaissance. The chief gallery was filled with contemporary genre works and other paintings by the fashionable French and English artists in rows of three, but the ordinary public was not admitted to this fairyland palace."

Laurence Vail Coleman, in his *History,* quotes James Jackson Jarves as having remarked in 1864 that "It has become the mode to have a taste. Private galleries in New York and Boston are becoming almost as common as private stables." Unfortunately much of the taste was reflected in quantity rather than quality, the dealers of the day also concentrating on selling authentications at greatly enhanced prices, whether they were genuine or spurious.

The taste noted by Mr. Jarves was limited to the Italian Renaissance painters, French academicians, the schools of the fin-de-siècle and art nouveau. Here and there one could find more discerning collectors but they were viewed as a queer lot, for instance the Freer collection of works by James McNeill Whistler which, but for a happy fluke, would have been rejected by the Smithsonian trustees. In Baltimore, two eccentric spinsters, Claribel and Etta Cone, spent considerable time in Europe picking up canvases of the younger French painters around the turn of the century.

As in the case of Commodore Vanderbilt, so with other collectors of the late nineteenth century. It was not enough to purchase paintings in wholesale quantities but a special environment had to be created in which to house the collections. Thus Mrs. Isabella Stewart Gardiner, an extrovert member of Boston Society, who in the first years of the twentieth century found herself at odds with the United States Treasury Department on a matter of fair values for imports of works of art, had her husband purchase a Venetian palace which when reassembled in Boston housed both her family and the entire collection of art, extending from early Spanish through to Degas, Manet, and Matisse. "Fenway Court," the name given to the palazzo, was bequeathed to the City of Boston, but with rigid restrictions imposed. The endowment fund still provides for the employment of gardeners and other staff members "to provide flowers and music."

The greatest extravaganza in the United States, if not in the entire world, is the San Simeon estate of the late William Randolph Hearst who in his later years spent four million dollars annually to accumulate art treasures, castles and cloisters, curiosities and bric-a-brac, a sampling of which is on display daily in what is still the most inaccessible public institution on the continent – an instance where the finest works of art serve only as a reminder of one man's ostentation and vulgarity.

The most erudite of institutions founded by this first generation of North American art patrons is the J. Pierpont Morgan Library on New York's East 36th Street. Morgan's tastes were relatively catholic but his all-consuming interest became channelled into the field of incunabula. By the time Morgan died he had acquired art works and other associated accessions valued at over $60,000,000. To house those objects which he considered of supreme importance he built a repository reflecting the Italian Renaissance of the quatrocento and in complete harmony with its contents of manuscripts, early illuminations, books, engravings, and old master drawings. Here the librarian, archivist, and museologist found a common meeting ground. Used primarily for scholarly research since its founding shortly before Morgan's death, it has gradually extended its hours and rearranged displays to encourage the general public to view the rare objects.

The metamorphosis of this institution "neither library nor museum but a combination of the two" as described by a former director, was spelled out recently by *Time* magazine upon the appointment of its third director in 1969. Until Morgan's death in 1913 the enormous collection of incunabula, objects relating to the very beginnings of the printed word, had been jealously guarded by its owner who showed his treasures only to his closest friends. In 1924 the building was open to the public but only scholars and students were encouraged to conduct research projects, and only today are the doors freely opened to all and sundry to view art treasures which can truthfully be described as priceless and irreplaceable.

While the Cone sisters were building up their collection of the modern French schools, William Walters, Baltimore merchant turned railroad tycoon, was pouring his surplus wealth into amassing what can only be described as decorative antiquities which soon required a special building in which to house them. The range of acquisitions embraced Oriental objets-d'art, French sculpture, paintings by traditionalists of the region, and, in fact, anything and everything which, for the moment, delighted the eye of this impetuous patron. It was natural, therefore, for him to build a Florentine palazzo to serve the dual function of home and gallery which in 1931 was presented to the city of Baltimore. His son Henry developed a more discriminating taste, picking up for the endowed institution one of the finest collections of early illuminated manuscripts in the northern hemisphere dating from the ninth century.

Edward D. Libbey, whose name is still associated with the glass industry, was responsible for the founding of the Toledo Museum of Art in 1901. In doing so he demanded that, for his continued support of the institution, the community, at that time numbering less than 150,000 souls, should demonstrate their interest through financial support and attendance. When its doors opened it was a museum sans exhibits, seemingly destined to develop as another *cabinet de curiosités.* However, Libbey's major interest was in the field of fine art so from time to time he encouraged citizens to make contributions to funds which he augmented. This policy of giving continued as the museum required more space, a dollar for dollar fiscal program being initiated. At his death, however, his personal collection, together with a trust fund of $4,000,000 and an estate valued at over $13,000,000 was willed to the city to endow the institution. The name Toledo Museum of Art is something of a misnomer, insofar as it serves also as a historical museum, and was the earliest institution in the United States to devote areas to the history and processing of glass products. Its founder also deserves recognition for encouraging active community participation as an indication that the benefactions to come would be well deserved.

The pattern of gifts and endowments was not restricted to eastern states, although such benefactions elsewhere did not start until the last decade of the last century. Tourists now travelling in the eastern, southern, and mid-western states discover a chain of museums memorializing their benefactors and usually dedicated to fine and decorative arts.

The Albrecht-Knox Art Gallery of Buffalo, New York, pays tribute to two native sons who, in addition to donating works of art paid handsomely for a building and sculpture garden to house them. The names of Mastbaum, Taft, Thomas Barlow, Walker, Pillsbury, and Phillips are emblazoned on the portals of art museums or gallery areas in Philadelphia, Cincinnati, Minneapolis, and Andover, also in St. Louis, Kansas City, Louisville, New Orleans, Atlanta, and on the west coast, San Marino, Los Angeles, La Jolla, Fresno, San Francisco. In fact, virtually every major city of the United States can point to extensive benefactions in the arts.

The most spectacular and certainly the most notorious gift was that of Andrew A. Mellon who, while involved in the Teapot Dome Oil scandal and being sued by the United States government for outstanding taxes amounting to over $3,000,000, announced at about the time of the court hearing that he had organized a charitable trust which, within the next few years would give to the people of the United States his collection of works of art numbering 150, together with a building in which to house them, a gift which eventually totalled $50,000,000.

As late as 1968, Joseph Hirshhorn, international entrepreneur,

82

who amassed much of his fortune through the exploitation of Canadian uranium mines and whose home base for many years was in Eastern Canada, presented to the United States government a collection of over 6,000 art works valued in multiples of millions on the condition that a suitable gallery would be built in Washington, D.C. in which to house it. The fifteen million dollar circular building and adjacent sunken sculpture garden was opened in 1971. Hirshhorn had been a consistent patron of contemporary Canadian artists and it had been anticipated that all or part of the collection would have been left in Canada. Cynics on the fringe of the Canadian art world suggest that had the Canadian government made the appropriate gesture for tax write-off with an assurance that a contemporary gallery would be built, Ottawa now might have two National Galleries instead of one.

Another history-making gift to the art museums of the United States is that of Samuel H. Kress, chain store magnate, who in the early years of this century began to acquire, largely through the Duveen agencies, Old Master paintings, many of which were given to the National Gallery in Washington. The collection became so extensive in the Kress residence and in Washington that other means for disposal and dispersal were involved. A formal statement from the Director of the National Gallery in 1956 stated that Mr. Kress, through his Foundation, "wished to make some return to certain cities for all they have done for the Kress Company." Eighteen cities in all received enough Old Masters to require the construction of major annexes in which to house them.

Since the National Gallery in Washington was opened it has been the recipient of thousands of other art works from individuals, corporations, and foundations. An isolated example is the collection of P. A. B. Widener which embraces medieval tapestries, Chinese objets d'art, 18th century French furnishings, and "more than one hundred Dutch and Italian masters." Another collection, that of Chester Dale, currently on indefinite loan but which is eventually destined to become an outright gift, favours the French Impressionist school, while the Lessing J. Rosenwald collection of etchings, drawings, illuminated manuscripts, and water colors exceeds 20,000 individual items.

Over the years since the founding of the Smithsonian, that Institution and its gallery subsidiaries have received many more extensive gifts which for one reason or another have been diverted to the custody of other areas within its complex. It can be taken for granted that this largesse from well publicized or anonymous benefactors has added billions of dollars in real assets to the American economy, assets which, it should be pointed out, steadily continue to appreciate in value.

The museums devoted to science and history were somewhat less fortunate than the art museums insofar as it was difficult to wax ecstatic over a caseful of impaled insects, a collection of geological specimens, or even replicas of the log cabin in which a president had been born. There were too many log cabins still being occupied by the hoi polloi, generally under decidedly unsanitary conditions, to distinguish one from the other.

While an appreciation of fine art was, and still is in some circles, considered akin to sexual deviation, the cash value of such works in a society attuned to monetary judgements is what counts. Duveen had seen to that. Undoubtedly among the wealthy purchasers there were men and women with discrimination and good intent. More often, however, the primary motive was due more to an embarrassment of riches which if not utilized in one form or another would be pre-empted by government. Anything was better than being mulcted for taxes. A story is told which may be apocryphal, of a false exhaust pipe being installed in an automobile to conceal Van Dyke paintings which had been removed from their frames. In this way they were smuggled into the country to be added to the collection of P. A. B. Widener and later to be given to the nation.

An analysis of benefactions over the past three quarters of a century shows that the vast amount of gifts took the form of accessions donated, with funds for capital development coming second, and endowments for administrative purposes being a poor third in the tabulation. The endowment funds of half a century ago which at the time appeared to be more than adequate to provide for all administrative costs have steadily shrunk as the value of the dollar has declined, and not too many people of the free enterprise society in this or earlier eras seek to be remembered by posterity for having kept the washrooms clean in the museums of the nation.

That benefactors still exist and are continuing to make important contributions to museums is illustrated in a short news item in *Museum News* of November 1969, which stated that to celebrate the centennial of New York's Metropolitan Museum, a dinner honouring one hundred and three living benefactors was held. A footnote also announced a gift of 3,000 items of the late Robert Lehman, long a trustee of the Metropolitan.

In this same issue it was reported that a new million dollar addition to the Huntington Galleries, West Virginia, had been made possible by a gift from the Doherty Charitable Foundation, and one cannot overlook the Huntington Hartford Gallery of Modern Art on Columbus Circle in New York City, dedicated to one man's taste and belief that "there is a valid alternative to the present day dominance of abstract art," created, fashioned, administered, financed, and named after Mr. Hartford as an antidote to mid-twentieth century modernism. However, in late 1970 Mr. Hartford had withdrawn his collection and instructed Parke-Bernet Galleries to auction individual items as "we could use a little extra cash these days", adding that 'I've done pretty well with art from a business point of view."

In contrast to Mr. Hartford's so-called Indian-giving propensities, the Museum of Modern Art, founded in 1929, stands as a monument to dedicated and intelligent planning with dollar values subordinated to public enlightenment. Its launching was in many respects a protest against the ultra-conservative policies prevailing in the first four decades of the twentieth century. Here again, the Rockefeller interests became involved following the death of John Quinn, a collector whose contemporary works had been snubbed by the Metropolitan.

Certainly worth noting as a historical happening, the germ grew out of the 1913 Armoury Show and was nurtured by a three-woman team at a time when women were fighting for emancipation. Mrs. Cornelius Sullivan, in company with Miss Lille P. Bliss and Mrs. Abby Aldrich Rockefeller, decided to do "something about." In 1929 the Museum of Modern Art took possession of rented quarters in a mid-town office building. Ten years later it had acquired a site, again donated by the Rockefeller family, on New York's 53rd Street, where it continues to expand in size and services. The museum is still subsidized largely with funds raised by the Rockefellers and their friends.

10

As the implications of the new evolutionary theory made their impact, and the furore continued to rage in American academic circles, museum personnel were similarly confronted with violent controversy.

George Brown Goode was eight years old when Darwin published his book on the origin of species. Goode's appointment as assistant secretary of the Smithsonian Institution and first director of the National Museum was confirmed by Congress in 1877. In England, Sir William Henry Flower had voiced new and revolutionary thoughts on the need for museums to play a more significant role in scientific education and interpretation which were echoed in Washington by the twenty-six year old ichthyologist turned museum director.

A prolific author during his brief lifetime, Dr. Goode published more than one hundred and sixty essays and technical papers, collaborated on fifty-eight others, and was a popular lecturer. In an address delivered before the Brooklyn Institute in 1889 Goode reviewed the state of American museums and announced that the United States had "two or three centres of great activity in museum work but there have been few new ones established within twenty years, and many of the old ones are in a state of torpor."

"The museum of the past," he continued "must be set aside, reconstructed, transformed from a cemetery of bric-à-brac into a nursery of living thought," adding, "the museum of today is no longer a chance assemblage of curiosities, but rather a series of objects selected with reference to their value to investigators, or their possibilities for public enlightenment." In this same speech Dr. Goode noted that new classifications for the disparate disciplines were still not clearly defined. A grey area existed which failed to provide for "the natural history of civilization, of man and his ideas and achievements," adding, "the museums of science and art have not yet learned to partition the territory."

The new museum philosophy called for laboratories and scientists to devote time to research and for two areas in which to house

86

collections, those for public display and a much vaster quantity for scholarly study. The role of the museum was changing from a place of entertainment to an institution which could educate while entertaining. The philosophy also included new techniques in collecting, authenticating, and interpretation.

A little known aspect of the scientific value of museums is outlined in their book *Museums U.S.A.* by Herbert and Marjorie Katz, who while writing about the early development of science museums in the United States, argue that "The flowering of anthropology in America is directly attributable to our museums. As Western civilization pressed on across the continent, inevitably altering and frequently obliterating the indigenous life in its path, Indian handicrafts – from weapons to wearing apparel, from cooking vessels to ritual paraphernalia – began accumulating in museums, where their availability piqued the curiosity of staff members trained in the natural sciences. Applying a familiar technique, museum men made field trips to accumulate more artifacts, and returned with extensive collections of data as well as arrowheads. These natural scientists whose previous areas of specialization may have been geology or biology became engrossed in studies of the ethnological material, and turned into the first generation of anthropologists. A parallel of this is spelled out in a subsequent chapter.

An unfortunate result of the new emphasis on research and the development of new scientific disciplines within the museum was a tendency on the part of the new breed of curator-scientists to perpetuate the ivory tower philosophy of the university campus to the detriment of the lay visitor. This was the era of static displays and restricted visiting hours. The display technician and public relations officer had still to be invented.

Another change in museum philosophy and techniques also brought about radical departures from the norm. The specialization of museum disciplines tended to develop isolation and the subsequent loss of association of ideas. The sociologist, whose philosophy emerged as a vital force in museum techniques, had still to find his own highly specialized niche in the structure.

Exhibitions and expositions dedicated to the display of man's progress in the arts, sciences, and manufactures have also had a profound but little publicized effect on museum development throughout the United States.

The 1851 (Great) Exhibition at Earls Court, London, initiated a program of expositions, thirty-four of them sponsored by national governments with official recognition from an international commission. There were also many others organized by the lower branches of government.

The Philadelphia Exposition of 1876, in addition to being indirectly responsible for the building of the National Museum of the United States, saw one of its temporary buildings converted into a more permanent structure to house the collections of the art academy and later to be known as the Pennsylvania Museum of Art. Later the art museum moved into still larger quarters with the original Memorial Hall continuing as the first museum in the United States devoted to the industrial arts.

The Art Institute of Chicago, founded in 1879, raised close to $650,000 to erect a building on the site of the "World's Columbian Exposition" of 1893 in which to display its ever increasing collection. Over the years the building has expanded to become one of the largest such institutions in the world.

The Art Institute at that period in its history attracted its share of benefactors. Prominent among them were Martin A. Ryerson, and Charles L. Hutchinson who, we are told, "spent $200,000 on thirteen old master paintings" for the initial opening, while Mrs. Potter Palmer, wife of the owner of the famous Palmer House hostelry, made generous donations from her collection of French Impressionists, thereby providing the nucleus of one of the most important collections of French paintings outside France.

The same Exposition saw the founding of the Chicago Natural History Museum. Its original benefactor, Marshall Field, department store magnate, subscribed $1,000,000 for a building for many of the exhibits in the areas of anthropology, botany, and geology which had been brought to the Fair from other parts of the world. Upon his death, Field bequeathed a further $8,500,000 as an endowment fund for what today is the Chicago Natural History Museum.

The Louisiana Purchase Exposition held in St. Louis, Missouri in 1904, saw the building of a permanent art gallery, originally called the Palace of Art, on the Forest Park site and which today is the St. Louis Museum of Fine Art. While this museum has a lengthy list of donors and benefactors, it is one of a relatively few civic institutions which derives its administrative funds from a property tax of "one mill on the dollar." Balboa Park in San Diego, the site of the 1915 World's Fair, now provides areas for its Zoological Gardens, Fine Art Gallery, Museum of Man, and Natural History Museum, in addition to buildings devoted to arts and crafts activities and the replica of the Globe Theatre.

Michael H. de Young, publisher of the San Francisco Chronicle, was largely responsible for initiating the California Mid-winter Exposition of 1893-94 in San Francisco. It was due to his enthusiasm and generous contributions that the M.H. de Young Memorial Museum was founded in the Golden Gate Park, site of the exposition. In addition to its large collections of fine and decorative arts it more recently received the Avery Brundage collection of Oriental art for which the city built an annex at a cost of $2,750,000. This gallery was one of the eighteen fortunate recipients of accessions from the Kress collection. Also holding forth on the Exposition site are the California Academy of Science, originally founded in 1853, and the Strybing Arboretum and Botanical Garden. Perpetuating the whim of sugar baron Adolph B. Spreckels and his wife, who were inspired by a plaster model of the Palais de la Légion d'Honneur displayed at this same fair, a replica was erected, christened the California Palace of the Legion of Honor, and filled with major European works of art.

The City of Seattle launched its "Century 21" World's Fair in 1962, with one of its major themes dedicated to the advance of science and technology. The relatively small fair site, within one mile of the city centre, has its Pacific Science Center, a complex of five buildings on the perimeter of what is described as "a water garden, a Museum of Flight and a pavilion to house temporary art exhibitions administered by the Seattle Art Museum." This latter institution, incidentally founded, administered, directed, and financed by one family, opened in 1933. Richard Eugene Fuller, son of the founder has built up, among other things, one of the most extensive collections of Oriental art in the Occidental world.

Even the disastrous New York World's Fair of 1964-65 saw a science education center as one of its more popular pavilions. Herbert and Marjorie Katz write of this "multi-million dollar Hall of Science, located on city-owned land at Flushing Meadows" as having the largest parking facilities of any museum in New York.

A developing consciousness in pioneer history encouraged the growth of historical societies frequently working within the framework of natural history groups. Universities quite naturally were creating within their historical departments specialized disciplines relating to ethnology with professors becoming involved in burgeoning community organizations.

The first society dedicated to the historical study of regional events was born in Boston in 1791. It concerned itself with compiling a history of Massachusetts as expressed in the society's constitution which outlined its function as "the preservation of books, pamphlets, manuscripts and records containing gustorical facts, biographical anecdotes, temporary projects and beneficial speculation (the activities of which) conduces to mark the genius, delineate the manners and trace the progress of society in the United States." The Massachusetts Historical Society continues to operate as an archival institution in addition to having its own museum.

Similar historical societies were organized in the New England and other states, including New York, Maine, Rhode Island, and

Pennsylvania with a spread westward in the second half of the nineteenth century to Wisconsin, Ohio, Nebraska, and Kansas.

One of the early historical societies was at Plymouth, Massachusetts where a representative group of citizens founded the Plymouth Society in 1820 to celebrate the bicentennial of the arrival of the *Mayflower*. Its immediate program was "to perpetuate the character and virtues of our ancestors to posterity."

The Chicago Historical Society, founded in 1856, had its own quarters twenty years later after having passed "into the 3rd lustrum of its existence," a building which was destroyed in the fire of 1871 but was rebuilt a few years later. This Society initiated the first project on this continent relating to the documenting of historic buildings in the early 1900's when members were taken on a tour of the city by one Ossian Guthrie who personally recounted the history of the city starting with Marquette's camp of 1674. Society members not only recorded the stories told by their mentor but took photographs and placed markers at the various sites. The Chicago Society continues to administer its museum, one of the outstanding of its kind in the mid-west. In its formative years it had been denied access to the personal papers of Abraham Lincoln (which eventually found their way to the Library of Congress) but this institution persisted in its intention to establish a significant collection of Lincoln memorabilia. About 1920 the Society purchased from the estate of Charles Frederick Gunther for $250,000 the most complete collection of Lincoln relics, previously offered to the City of Chicago as a gift but which was rejected by the city fathers, a negative gesture typical of the political species even today.

11

In 1874, speaking at Birmingham, England, Sir Henry Cole, an active member of the Royal Society of Arts and at one period policy advisor for the Victoria and Albert Museum, stated that "If you wish your schools of science and art to be effective, your health, your air, and your food to be wholesome, your life to be long, your manufactures to improve, your trade to increase, and your people to be civilized, you must have museums . . . to illustrate the principles of life, health, science, art and beauty." Dr. Goode, this time addressing members of the American Historical Association on December 26, 1888, quoted Sir Henry as a preface to his philosophy by describing "The people's (community) museum as a house full of ideas, arranged with the strictest attention to system . . . . Like the library it should be under the constant supervision of one or more men, well informed, scholarly, and withal practical, and fitted by tastes and training to aid in the educational work . . . . The museum of the future," he continued, "should be adapted to the needs of the mechanic, the factory operator, the day laborer, the salesman, the clerk, as much as to those of the professional man and the man of leisure . . . . The museum must, in order to perform its proper functions, contribute to the advancement of learning through the increase as well as the diffusion of knowledge."

Dr. Goode freely admitted that, while museums of natural sciences had evolved both philosophies and techniques in recent years making provision both for scholarly study of stored collections and attractive displays for the general public, the known historical museums in the United States "contain as a rule, chance accumulations." Contemporary archaeology, anthropology, and ethnology were relatively new words woven into the university calendars. Sociology, a word first coined in 1837, had still to be authentically defined with Spencer, Wallace, Huxley, and others searching for a tenable definition.

Unfortunately Dr. Goode was addressing academics who quite readily understood and agreed with his philosophy but had no communication with the dedicated amateurs at the local level. Even at this point of time the amateurs were becoming increasingly conscious of their pioneer heritage. Whereas the academics were discriminating scientists sifting out the significant from historical debris, the amateur grass roots historian was generally an indiscriminate romantic whose inductive reasoning was reflected in the accumulations of inconsequential artifacts having no relationship to the historical theme upon which the local museum had been founded.

The line of communication from the National Museum in Washington where Dr. Goode presided, extended to the university campus and generally to the museums established by the various states. The local Historical Society Museums had yet to find a method of communication which could effectively change their haphazard policies. While museum specialization had become an accepted fact of life as the nation was entering into the twentieth century, the relationship between aesthetics, human history, and applied sciences with the natural sciences had still to make its impact on the existing professionals other than a few individuals such as Dr. Goode.

The first museum directory to be published in the United States appeared in 1903 under the auspices of the New York State Museum at Albany but was limited only to Museums of Natural History. In 1906 the American Association of Museums was organized, its constitution giving recognition to various disciplines previously neglected, and in 1910 the Buffalo Society of Natural Sciences in association with the Museums' Association commissioned Paul Marshall Rea to compile a new directory. Yet interestingly enough, neither art galleries nor the museums of the historical societies appear in the index of two hundred and sixty-three institutions. In fact all, with one exception, were museums related to the scientific disciplines or technology.

A breakdown of this listing points to two significant factors in the field of museum origins and the development of a nation's economy. Sixteen geological surveys were administered by state governments while twenty-five states had established and were financing museums in the state capitals. Here one finds the emphasis on agriculture with six institutions devoted solely to this subject, five others dividing their interests between agriculture and what was known as the Mechanic Arts, three concentrating on mining, with eleven others of a general nature.

Equally significant is the fact that ninety-three universities administered natural history and science museums along with a further ninety-four other scholastic institutions ranging from high schools to colleges and with only thirty-five under the jurisdiction of privately financed scientific societies.

The first historic restoration noted in all works on this subject

92

was the George Washington headquarters at Newburgh in New York state which was formally opened in 1851. The second such restoration, the birth place of Washington was completed in 1860, this being the first such project undertaken by a voluntary (Mount Vernon Ladies') association who raised $200,000 for the project.

Four years later the Gettysburg Memorial Association initiated a project for the restoration of fortifications but it required twenty-one years of lobbying before the United States government declared the battlefield, with its 600 monuments, 1000 markers, cannon, observation towers, and other objects as a National Historic Park.

In 1905 the U.S. government passed an Antiquities Act for the protection and preservation of significant artifacts on government lands and in 1935 the Historic Sites Act gave further momentum for the acquisition and development of significant sites and buildings. There were still hundreds of houses of historical note awaiting authentication many of which had housed America's heroes or the occasional villain; the antebellum homes of gracious living and Negro exploitation in the deep south; the log huts of pioneers and such homes as the Harrison Gray Otis residence in Boston; the Robert E. Lee House at Richmond; the Letitia Street mansion and early Quaker meeting houses; taverns and roadside inns. A few years later the Spanish Missions of the south-west would be attracting the attention of conservationists.

In the first quarter of the twentieth century the preservation or reconstruction of entire communities brought into being as historical museums *in situ* Old Deerfield; Sturbridge; Cooperstown; Shaker and Amish settlements; the Richardson restoration on New York's Staten Island; and still later, Greenfield Village at Dearborn centered around the friendship of Henry Ford and Thomas Edison and which offers a tip of the hat to other illustrious personalities. Towering over them all is the Williamsburg, Virginia, restoration.

The vast majority of historic restorations in the United States interpret faithfully the taste and fashion, and sometimes the privations, within their own particular environment. The Historical Society (community) Museum on the other hand, by virtue of the fact that beyond preserving the artifacts of pioneers its members rarely had a clear sense of direction, took on the flavour of a repository for anything and everything which was "too good to throw away but too bad to sell." The major problem, as in Canada, was isolation from the main stream of America's historical authority and cultural development. Many such museums were reminiscent of the *cabinets de curiosités* of the eighteenth century, with articles placed in cramped and crowded disarray with no regard to subject matter, each item bearing the label of the donor but little else.

Dillon Ripley, current Secretary of the Smithsonian Institution, in

93

his book of essays titled *The Sacred Grove* (1969), depicts the changing museum techniques in the latter half of the nineteenth and first half of the twentieth centuries where he suggests that museums "drifted into two positions which gradually became separate, almost polarized. On the one hand certain museums came to exist purely as storehouses, as catch-alls, elegant as they might have been. The average historical society was a good, though often inelegant example. . . . Many art galleries in our cities suffered the same fate. Either the curator hoped for more and better quality in future by being nice to the Joneses in their hour of need or he simply didn't know how to say no. Paintings and decorative objects poured in, usually without a coherent plan, and the common attic-for-all image was the result." The author even pointed to The Smithsonian as having "come to be thought of not as a sponsor of basic research, but as the 'Nation's Attic,' "although he qualifies this statement by adding that "The Institution has somehow never received that credit that was its due."

It is only in recent years that museums and galleries have endeavoured to face up to the problem of educating the would-be benefactor by creating first a museum philosophy followed by clear terms of reference defining its specific areas of interest.

In the half century prior to 1920 there were only approximately 1200 museums from coast to coast in the United States. A developing social consciousness has resulted in an accelerated expansion of museums which by 1964 had 4595 institutions listed in *The Museums Directory of the United States and Canada.* An analysis of these institutions, as published in *The Belmont Report* submitted to former U.S. President Lyndon B. Johnson a few days before he relinquished office, disclosed that by 1968 museum growth was accelerating. For a 1972 survey, ten thousand questionnaires were sent out in preparation for a directory published in January 1973. This directory listed only those institutions which responded, reporting a decrease of 1,762 from the 7,000 found to be in operation in 1970 by an earlier survey.

In the first half of the present century museums were listed under no more than five or six distinct disciplines. The Belmont Report points to the fact that today the directories have a breakdown of eighty-four categories embracing art, history, and science, "which account for forty-three of the eighty-four categories. The remaining forty-one are specialized museums, proceeding alphabetically from agriculture and animal farms to whaling and woodcarving, and along the way listing circus museums, a crime museum, lock, numismatics, transportation and (even) wax museums." This diversification now makes possible more disciplined collecting programs with unwanted gifts being loaned indefinitely or in perpetuity to more appropriate institutions.

More important is the growth in attendance. The report points to the fact that "Thirty years ago attendance at museums was in the neighbourhood of 50 million visits a year." Fifteen years ago attendance exceeded 100 million visits a year. By 1962 the United States total had reached 200 million, and by 1969 total attendance exceeded 300 million.

One of the lesser known American societies associated with history and historical museums deserves something more than a footnote for its somewhat unobtrusive contributions to the historical consciousness of North Americans. The American Association for State and Local History emerged out of a succession of conferences with a burgeoning list of regional and national associations. At its initial 1940 conference, Christopher Crittenden, the chairman, noted that there were more than a thousand historical organizations in the United States and Canada, indicating that the young Association was having an immediate impact on American regional and local societies. A project was launched in 1949 in the field of publications and the Association became the precursor of what is now the commercially produced *American Heritage Series.* In this area it has consistently commissioned and published technical leaflets and bulletins on such diverse subjects as genealogy, historical research, and the complex questions facing administrators of the small historical museums and restorations, which are used as valuable text books on the North American continent. More recently it has established an advisory service for historical museums at the community level financed through a grant from the Smithsonian Institution which parallels the government funded advisory services recently adopted at the provincial level in Canada.

In 1967, in paying tribute to Canada's centenary, the Association held its twenty-seventh annual conference in Toronto. Four years later, it launched a study in depth of Canada's centennial programs on a grant from the United States National Endowment for the Humanities, "to help us understand better what is possible for our (1976) Bicentennial."

Continuing this study, and at the same time paying tribute to its affiliation with many of Canada's smaller museums, the Association held its thirty-first annual convention in Edmonton, Alberta in the fall of 1973.

III

Colonialism in Canada - A One-Way Street

*Mechanics' Institutes,
the Jesuits, and Early
Canadian Learned Societies*

12

The outline of museum growth in the United States will now allow the reader to compare and contrast the social mores of that country and of Canada. While the great majority of American museums prospered from infancy, Canadian museums faced close to one hundred and fifty years of frustrations, poverty, and governmental apathy while dedicated individuals and idealistic societies sought to serve as guardians of Canada's heritage.

The United States and Canada were conceived almost simultaneously. In 1604, Pierre de Guast was given the right in the name of France to explore and take possession of all lands in the new world lying between the 40th and 46th parallels. Two years later James I of England granted charters to two trading companies to colonize the territory christened Virginia and in 1607 a settlement was established at Jamestown. Only one year later, Champlain gave the name Quebec to a community of two families on the St. Lawrence which served as stopping place for fur traders. De Guast and Champlain had already created seigniories at Port Royal and St. Croix, while to the south the English planters were building their self-contained communities. The more benign climate, along with the discovery of tobacco and extensive cotton-growing lands, provided the incentive for permanency there, whereas in the north a more rugged wilderness environment combined with extensive cod resources off the Atlantic coast and the abundance of fur-bearing animals inland made for a more transient population. This latter was responsible also for the organization of co-operative entities. The Company of New France was given a monopoly of trade in the St. Lawrence watershed in 1627, while thirty-one years later Charles II of England granted a charter to the Company of Gentlemen Adventurers thus initiating a rivalry for possession of lands and monopoly of trading rights which continued for the next century and a half.

Religion also played a major role in the developing social structure of the two regions. To the south the Quakers and other reli-

98

gious dissenters immigrated to the New World bringing with them a humanistic philosophy which at times was at variance with a non-conformist puritanism, whereas to the north all settlements established during the French regime saw the church as the focal point of all phases of community life.

The wars between French and English following the Acadian expulsion of 1613 had a debilitating effect on the body politic. While the aftermath of the Treaty of Paris signed in 1763, as expounded by historian George Robert Parkin, may be open to question, there is an element of truth in his statement that "The first English settlers in the (now conquered) country were chiefly petty traders not of a character to lead in social or public affairs." And of course the settlers to the south were divesting themselves of colonial status, making possible a diversion of taxes previously paid to the British Crown for use to finance their immediate domestic needs.

In 1790 the United States had a population of approximately four million, density being 9.6 per square mile, which by 1880 had increased to 24 million with a density of 16.1. The first Canadian census of 1881 disclosed a population of less than four and a half million, density even twenty years later being only 1.8 per square mile. It is not surprising, therefore, that all activity beyond the essential needs for survival by Canadian settlers would be slow to mature.

The absence of authentic records makes it difficult to name the first museum in Canada. Religious institutions in Quebec and the predominantly French communities in the Maritimes had natural history collections in the eighteenth century for use as visual aids by priest-educators, and at the same time religious relics were also being accumulated. Such relics associated with reported miracles can be seen at Ste Anne de Beaupré and at the Musée Kateri Tekakwitha in Caughnawaga which pre-date the formal opening of their respective museums. The first authentic documentation indicates that Laval University had a geology and mineralogy collection in the last decade of the eighteenth century but a museum as such was not formally organized until 1852.

In Pictou, Nova Scotia, the Rev. Thomas McCullough opened a grammar school in 1811, one of three protestant secondary institutions in the Atlantic region, and by 1816 had succeeded in having it upgraded to that of an Academy. Sir Henry Miers and S.F. Markham, in their 1932 report of Canadian museums, state that a natural history collection had been in existence since the founding of the Academy but qualify this by adding "or so it would seem." A further comment states that "in contrast (to Quebec), the school museums of the Maritime provinces, organized in the early 19th century. . . have fallen into disuse and neglect." This blanket criticism was directed equally to Pictou, Dalhousie, and Acadia Colleges.

Other slender threads of circumstantial evidence have been brought to light with Dr. C. Bruce Fergusson, Nova Scotia's Provincial Archivist quoting T.C. Haliburton as reporting in 1829 that Pictou Academy had "the most extensive collection of zoology in the country" referring to "the birds, which were finely preserved and made a beautiful appearance." Dr. Fergusson added his comments, "I can substantiate the fact that there was a collection of insects there as early as 1822, and I suppose it would be fair to say as at least one writer did, that from the beginning of the Academy there was a collection of birds, mammals, reptiles and minerals. At the turn of the (19th-20th) century the collection filled an area of 500 square feet."

Just how far the original collection has been preserved is even more debatable. R.H. Sherwood of Pictou, a historical devotee of the Pictou region, has tracked down a number of natural history items which had been abused, "some mischief having been wrought by students on the stuffed animals and birds," also stating that when the Academy was preparing to celebrate its 150th anniversary, plans for restoration of the collection were discussed "but lacking technical guidance, the project proved abortive." George MacLaren, Chief Curator of History for the Nova Scotia Museum, however, points to the fact that the original museum was discontinued for a period when "Mr. McCullough sold his original collection of birds in London through the agency of John James Audubon, with McCullough's son launching a second collection, remnants of which are currently in the custody of the Academy Board and the Town of Pictou."

Mr. McCullough has earned another footnote in history by being the first educationalist in Canada to advocate interdenominational education, only to find his efforts blocked when the Legislative Council amended the bill of incorporation of his Academy to exclude all but Presbyterians and members of the Church of England as members of the Board, or of the teaching staff at his Academy.

The proliferation of the community museum in nineteenth century Canada can be directly traced to the influence of Birkbeck and his Mechanics' Institute movement. Scotch and north country miners, sailors, fishermen, and industrial workers, in addition to the small merchant class who immigrated to the colonies during political and industrial upheavals had undoubtedly been exposed to Dr. Birkbeck's philosophy when the Mechanics' Institute movement was in its formative stage, but by 1823, when the first Institute was founded, his program had already received wide acceptance and had been communicated overseas.

100

The most persistent advocates for the establishment of Institutes in the Maritimes were the newspapers. Dr. Fergusson, in his *Mechanics' Institutes in Nova Scotia*, writes that "proposals were put forward by the editors of the *Colonial Patriot,* the *Nova Scotian* and the *Acadian Recorder*, Jotham Blanchard describing the advantages to be derived from associations for mutual improvement in an editorial on January 11, 1828. Joseph Howe, who had written of this subject one year earlier, supported this agitation while P.J. Holland (another editor) gave the proposal his blessing in 1831. With the support of these and others, the movement gathered momentum, and action was soon taken in Halifax."

In Newfoundland, Nova Scotia, and New Brunswick, Mechanics' Institutes were founded in quick succession, all of which sponsored lectures on diverse subjects relating to natural science, industry, and manufacture. An important part of the program was the development of library facilities while at the same time amassing haphazard objects covering the entire gamut of curiosities.

A list of such accessions owned by the Halifax Institute included such articles as "a set of minerals; . . . a wheel and axle; a large map of North America; insects; South Sea curiosities; a colossal bust of Napoleon; specimens of West Indian woods; a planetarium; war spear; letters of marque; spear heads; a young turtle and three silver pennies." Later acquisitions included the sword of a swordfish, together with a collection of portraits including significantly one of Dr. Birkbeck. There were also elephants' teeth, an armadillo's skin, paintings of wild flowers, in addition to models of a fire-escape and a sailing vessel, along with some sand from Sable Island, gunlocks used at the Battle of Trafalgar, a stuffed deer, two dolphins, "and a great many other objects and books." We are also told that, in addition to this mixed bag, the Institute possessed models and apparatuses used for illustration and demonstration at lectures "and for other educational purposes."

At a formal meeting on December 24, 1831, a Mechanics' Institute Museum was founded in Halifax and R. Lawson was appointed curator of models and apparatus, but as early as 1829 a Mechanics' Institute library had functioned; "for a time, but only for a time, the books of the library and the models, apparatus and museum. . . were accommodated in the lower floor of Mrs. Grovis' boarding house on Hollis Street."

In October 1833, the Museum was given quarters on the Dalhousie College grounds where it remained until the creation of the Provincial Museum. Government grants were forthcoming from 1833 to 1835 out of which Titus Smith received fifteen pounds "to assist him in making a collection of specimens of geology, botany, and mineralogy for the museum." But as such societies grew in number, with increasing demands made on the public purse, the Legislature apparently felt that the pursuit of culture and technology was getting out of bounds and voted to discontinue such support.

Institute lectures, held in association with the museum covered a wide range of subjects "from cart-making to architecture and from music to mechanics." A collection of minerals, birds, fossils, and plants was sent to the London International Exposition in 1862 giving encouragement to the Legislature to found its own Museum of Science. Eight years later, when the Institute museum was discontinued, its collections, quite naturally, were turned over to the provincial repository.

Passing reference is made to the fact that the first zoo north of Mexico City was opened at the North-east Arm in Halifax harbour by Andrew Downs in 1847.

Throughout Nova Scotia, Mechanics' Institutes, many with libraries and lecture halls, proliferated during the 1830's most of which acquired illustrative material. At Antigonish, one such society was organized in 1840 and two years later had "procured an electrical machine and apparatus from Halifax." Lectures that season included "a discourse on the pre-eminence of poetry over painting and music; an historical account on manners and customs of the Moors; lectures on mechanical power, geology, dramatic poetry, and atmosphere together with a periscope of ancient and modern arts and sciences."

In Liverpool, Nova Scotia, an Institute was launched in 1841 "for the advancement of human knowledge," its members petitioning the Legislature for assistance in getting "philosophical apparatus for the promotion of same." Similar societies cropped up in Windsor and Dartmouth while at Guysborough in 1843, when presenting a list of lectures covering economics, the arts, astronomy, mechanics, electronics, chemistry, naval architecture, magnetism, and agriculture, the president announced that "an electrical and chemical apparatus had been procured and Stewart Campbell delivered a lecture on the pleasures and advantages of science." Two museums, described only as collections but which are still on display, were the Des Brisay collection at Bridgeport and the Gordon Cameron Edwards collection at Wolfville dating from 1860 and 1884 respectively.

In 1868, the miscellaneous collections garnered from the Mechanics Institutes, together with two collections which had been exhibited at The Paris Exposition and in London, were displayed in one room designated for museum purposes in the government building. Later these moved to the provincial science library. In 1878 the museum had a more permanent home in the technical institute, its one staff member having a budget of twenty-six hundred dollars.

By 1932 the curator had been given "a messenger" but the museum remained financially starved despite its increasing activities and collections including a pioneer museum which was located in the cavernous barracks within the partially restored Citadel. By 1937 the average daily attendance at the two institutions was given as thirty-two.

A provincial archives was formally founded in 1929 although the archival office dated back to approximately one hundred years before. The new archives was the focal point for many three dimensional objects normally associated with historical museums including paintings and ships' models. Its historical counterpart in the Citadel concentrated on native manufactures and domestic Canadiana.

It was in Nova Scotia that the federal government first paid token recognition to the need to preserve historical sites and buildings. In 1917, what was then the National Parks administration formally took over responsibility for Fort Anne, outgrowth of two French fortifications with both English and French connotations, but it was not until 1935 that the building whose cornerstone was laid by Edward, Duke of Kent in 1797 was completely restored and established as a museum. Three years later, the Habitation at Port Royal was re-constructed and in the meantime Fort Beausejour at Aulac, New Brunswick, had also come under federal jurisdiction. Thus was established what today is a chain of restored fortifications extending from coast to coast.

At St. John's Newfoundland, in the early 1800's, a Cabinet of Curiosities was placed on public view in the Merchant's Club on Water Street, named after Valentine Merchant, owner of the building. The exact date of this event has been lost to posterity as, according to regional historians, the Colonial administration showed little or no interest in cultural growth or historical documentation. Enough circumstantial evidence exists to suggest that Mr. Merchant had been acquiring antiquities and curiosities for a number of years and his store gradually became the focal point for fellow businessmen interested in intellectual speculation and stimulation.

The Club with its continuing flow of accessions was a natural outcome of such an atmosphere. In 1849, a joint committee of The Mechanics' Institute, whose founding date has also been lost, and the St. John's Library Board found a more suitable environment for the collection. A museum committee was formed with a set of rules and regulations which, among other things, prohibited "discussions of religious and political topics." Rule 13 served as instruction to the curator, so named, to "keep the premises in good order and to keep a list of articles on display." The new society concerned itself primarily with the natural history of the island and the museum was open to the public on Mondays, Wednesdays, and Fridays from 11 a.m. to 3 p.m. Included in the catalogue were two polar bears; native birds; specimens of minerals and implements of the aborigines, Indians of the Beothuk tribe who had been hunted down and slaughtered.

The last member of the Beothuk tribe, a woman, died in 1829 after being held in captivity for a number of years. A story, which could be apocryphal, is told of a humanitarian Newfoundlander who believed that the Beothuk race should be continued and had deliberately kept the woman captive hoping that she would give birth to children. But "despite his best efforts" it was all to no avail.

The St. John's Museum Society won three prizes for an exhibit at the New York Exhibition of 1855 for "its quality of artifacts." In March 1861 the Society merged with the Library Board, the Young Men's Institute, and the Mechanics' Institute, a merger which eventually in 1878 embraced the Athenaeum Club. This club, patterned after the London club of the same name, had been brought into being by Sir Walter Scott and the Irish poet, Thomas Moore, "for the association of individuals known for their scientific and literary attainments." The St. John's museum was transferred to the Athenaeum building and remained there until 1892 when the building and contents were destroyed by fire.

The Museums' Bulletin No. 62 published in 1903 by the New York State Museum at Albany lists the Geological Survey of Newfoundland as having a museum whose director was James P. Howley. The collection consisted in part of "1173 specimens of paleontology; 500 of mineralogy and 1,659 zoological items, together with bones and other remains of the Beothucs [sic] being the Indians of the colony, stone and iron implements, ornaments, drawings, etc. A good set of fishery products, . . . models of fishing vessels and implements, . . . and a number of historical relics and many others from foreign sources."

A second listing, this time in a museums' directory compiled by the Buffalo Society of Natural Sciences in 1910, mentions exhibits of "250 native and 500 foreign shells, a few native and many foreign insects, 50 native and 502 foreign fishes, 150 native and 165 foreign birds and 30 native and 12 Australian mammals."

When the Gosling Library and Museum opened in 1917, the accessions of the survey served as the nucleus upon which a substantial collection could be built, but in 1934, when depression hit the colony, the museum was pronounced an unnecessary expense and the contents were stored in various buildings including The Smoke House at the Cold Storage Plant. Many other artifacts were piled in the laundry building of the Sanatorium and "but for the alertness of the workmen, these specimens would have been shovelled into the concrete mixer." A number of accessions, however, went to Memorial University and the Historical Society but much of the original collection was lost. Peter J. Cashin, in an article on Newfoundland's emergence from colonialism, speaks of the museum dismantling as "another outrage for which the Commission must accept the guilty verdict" adding "nothing was sacred to these incompetent and vicious Commissioners."

There is no record, at least in the reports of national surveys, of any museum developments on Prince Edward Island until the founding of the Robert Harris Memorial Art Gallery in Charlottetown's Regional Library building in 1928, with Mr. James Harris, son of the now immortalized Canadian painter, serving as curator. While the provincial building in Charlottetown has now received recognition for its historical role in the story of Confederation, it was matter-of-factly viewed only as the seat of government and office building housing the civil service hierarchy until early in the second half of the twentieth century.

As early as 1904 an art society had functioned in Charlottetown and in the desultory manner of many other such societies, devoted its energies to the Saturday painter with an annual exhibition serving as incentive for more creative work. The Canadian artist, Robert Harris, who had lived on the island and whose paintings, his portraits in particular, had gained him recognition on the Canadian mainland, was resurrected from temporary oblivion in 1928 when the Harris family sought a permanent home for the large collection of paintings in their possession. The creation of space in the library resulted with both city and province guaranteeing funds for its continuance. The gallery area, it is reported, occupied 1400 square feet of the second floor of the library. In 1952, it was proving to be a popular attraction having been visited that year by 2,000 adults and children.

In New Brunswick, interest in museums was first generated by Dr. Abraham Gesner, native of Nova Scotia and medical practitioner who also was a keen student of geology. His avocation led to his appointment as provincial geologist in 1838, two years before William Logan received a similar appointment in Montreal. At this time, Gesner had expanded his interests to embrace the animal and bird life of the Atlantic regions. While in Nova Scotia, Gesner had been actively collecting rock specimens. He added still further specimens when he moved to New Brunswick and found it necessary to rent space on the top floor of a building on Prince William Street in Saint John which he used as an exhibition area in 1840-41.

Although the Legislative Assembly had been agreeable to having Gesner as their official geologist, they balked when he sought funds for the opening of a museum. As a result, he appealed to the Mechanics' Institute of the city for the use of a room in their new building on Carleton Street. In his History of the New Brunswick Museum, Dr. W. Austin Squires mentions that the collection was then housed in six glassed cases containing marine animals and plants; fishes; reptiles; birds; mammals; Indian relics; minerals, rocks and fossils.

Coincident with the opening on April 5, 1842, a catalogue titled *Synopsis of the Contents of Gesner's Museum of Natural History* was published. Its 48 pages gave 2,173 items, two thirds of which were associated with the earth sciences including fossil fish and plants, corals and crustacea. Two sections were devoted to birds and mammals and a miscellaneous section listed 63 curiosities, one of which was a Perpetual Motion "as invented by Mr. Richard McFarlan" and quite naturally donated by the same gentleman. There was also "a Horn of the Sea Unicorn, a Book of Surgery dated 1684, a Timber head of the Royal George and a Singular substance found on the snow after a fire at Gagetown." On the back page was an appeal for further specimens "belonging to the Animal, Vegetable and Mineral Kingdoms, Fossils, Relics, Works of Art, Ancient Books and Papers, Models, Inventions, Domestic Manufactures and Curiosities of all kinds," donors being promised suitable recognition and free admissions to the museum "according to their value." Twelve months later an appendix was published listing an additional 315 specimens. "Complete sets of the Minerals of Nova Scotia, of sixty specimens each" arranged were offered for sale at the price of six pounds per set.

Not only was Gesner rebuffed when he asked for funds with which to develop the museum but that same year he was refused any further grant for his work as provincial geologist. Finding himself financially embarrassed the dedicated doctor negotiated a loan and later offered his collections for sale. In return for monies borrowed from Mr. Justice Chipman and His Honour Judge Parker, Gesner gave them shares in his museum which ultimately were turned over to the Mechanics' Institute. After submitting his fifth report to the Lieutenant-Governor on January 1st, 1843 and still being refused compensation for his services, the embittered doctor resigned and returned to his native Nova Scotia to resume his medical practice at Cornwallis.

Gesner's contribution to the economic development of the North-American continent was climaxed following his meeting with Lord Dundonald who had been commissioned by British interests to investigate the possibilities of producing fertilizer from bitumen deposits. Gesner joined in the research and while so doing discovered a new source for illumination and invented a retort for its production. Commenting on this discovery, Dr. Squires records that "later, he obtained illuminating oil from coal and other bituminous sub-

106

stances which he patented in 1854. . . and (which) led to the subsequent extraction of kerosene from petroleum and the development of the enormous oil industry of the present day."

By 1846 ownership of the Gesner Museum was in the name of the Saint John Mechanics' Institute under whose administration it continued to draw an increasing audience until 1870, a period which saw the decline of all such Institutes. In 1890 the Natural History Society which had been organized in 1862 purchased the collection, its showcases and papers for a nominal sum, more as a token gesture than anything else as the Society had been adding to the collection over the years. The museum was then transferred to 72 Union Street, along with a library, where it remained until 1932. In that year the provincial Legislature, having at long last recognized its responsibilities, voted funds for the erection of the present building on Douglas Avenue. This edifice was designed to accommodate the natural sciences, decorative arts, Canadian history, a military hall, and marine gallery and also included a children's museum, first in Canada and one of the first in North America.

Mention is made in early survey reports that one or possibly two campus museums existed in Fredericton around 1860. One is described as "The Library Museum" containing historical documents and artifacts in the realm of pioneer history, while in the same report mention is made of a Biological Museum occupying 3,000 square feet of floor space where "birds (also skins and eggs), mammals and invertebrate types" were exhibited. The curator, undoubtedly serving in an honorary capacity, was C.W. Argue.

The Miramichi Museum of Natural History, described in the same report as housed in a wooden structure and "a veritable firetrap," is one of the oldest such repositories in New Brunswick. Founded in 1897 for the purpose of collecting natural history material in the four northern counties, it provided lectures and instruction for adults and school children. In 1908, the museum had its own building through a money raising campaign which produced $2,400 and received an annual grant of $200 from the province and $50 from the county. It was open to the public each Tuesday evening from January 1st to June 1st. In more recent years, the museum expanded into the field of pioneer history, and was one of the few community institutions which had departmentalized its collections.

As New Brunswick entered the twentieth century, about twenty per cent of its 300,000 inhabitants were French-speaking. The classical colleges of the Roman Catholic Church, which had played a major educational role in the province of Quebec had quite naturally overflowed into the Maritimes. One such institution, l'Ecole Supérieure de St-Basile, originally a convent school for girls, obtained college status in the first years of the century and a few years later merged with St. Louis College. Natural history collections of the two institutions were brought together to provide faculty and students with a well-stocked museum which continued throughout the first half of this century. Another such museum was founded at St. Joseph's College and functioned until it became an affiliate of the University of Moncton in 1963. The public school system in Moncton likewise had natural history collections which were distributed in various schools of the immediate region as did the Saint John system.

The collection and preservation of historical documents and artifacts relating to pioneer life in the Maritimes followed a spasmodic road until well into the twentieth century. A Historical Society, as distinguished from the Mechanics' Institutes, was functioning in Nova Scotia at some time prior to 1838 for a Mechanics' Institute award for an essay on the Society's collections was awarded to T.B. Atkins in that year. Atkins, who was to be appointed Archivist of Nova Scotia some years later, had done considerable research on the origins of the province and had been associated with Thomas Chandler Haliburton, who in 1837 had published *The Sayings and Doings of Sam Slick,* and six years later his *Life in a Colony.*

The first serious attempt to write a comprehensive history of the young Canada came from the pen of François Xavier Garneau whose *Histoire du Canada* was published in 1845-48. However, this work has been overshadowed by the writings of Francis Parkman, the American historian who wrote a series of books from 1851 until one year before his death in 1893 on the military and political struggles in Canada's history.

A few painters, notably Cornelius Krieghoff and Paul Kane, interpreted the Canadian scene in many of their genre paintings, while somewhat later came the drawings of C.W. Jeffrey.

The few public archives in the latter half of the nineteenth century were mainly concerned with the custody of state documents, but as the terms of reference were generally not too clearly defined individual archivists saw fit to collect other material. As a result, some of these institutions served a subsidiary role as historical museums.

13

In the province of Quebec a different situation prevailed in the museum field. Scholastic institutions were under the direct control of the church. Seminaries and academies had clerics trained in the classical tradition for teachers and teaching techniques called for visual aids, a practice discussed in an earlier chapter. For three centuries the Jesuit order had required novitiates to devote five years to a formal arts education and then to serve as teachers for a further five to six years.

The first museum in the Province of Quebec, Le Musée del Vecchio, was founded by an Italian entrepreneur in 1824 in Montreal. The collection was made up of "mounted animals and other natural reproductions, in addition to figures in wax and works of art," and while it was short-lived, it attracted considerable attention as a place to spend the idle hour. Two years later, in Quebec City, one Pierre Chasseur, "sculptor and gilder," opened a museum at 4 rue Sainte-Hélène. His entire collection was purchased in 1836 by the Government of Quebec for $2,000 and thus became the first museum publicly owned and administered in Canada. An area in the provincial legislative building was provided but the disastrous fire of 1854 saw premises and collection completely destroyed. In 1880, the province authorized a "Museum of Public Instruction" to house a miscellaneous collection of botany, geology, palaeontology, and zoology, in addition to "95 Deyrolle's tableaux on natural history and industry," while in another room were coins and medals and other items all of which had been accumulated by Abbe D.N. Saint-Cyr. Originally accommodated in the old legislative palace, the collection was moved nine years later to a more spacious area of 5,000 square feet and at that time an annual grant of $600 was voted for its maintenance. In 1932, the present museum and archives building on the Plains of Abraham was opened and much of the earlier collections was eventually dispersed or placed in storage.

The Literary and Historical Society of Quebec, oldest chartered institute in Canada, had assembled cabinets of mineralogical and geological specimens as early as 1824. In that same year, it received a large botanical collection from the Countess of Dalhousie whose husband was then serving as Governor of the British Colonies, His Excellency having been elected a member and first patron of the Society.

At almost the same time the Natural History Society of Montreal came into being. By 1903, it had a well-filled cabinet which contained, among other exhibits, "the C. U. Shepherd collection of minerals of 4000 specimens presented by Dr. Holmes." In his *Museums: Their History and Use* (1904), Dr. David Murray lists a publication dated 1826 headed "Instructions for Preserving Objects of Natural History, respectfully addressed by the Natural History Society of Montreal to persons willing to assist its labours and add to the museum." This Society, in collaboration with the Literary and Historical Society of Quebec, petitioned members of Canada's first united parliament in 1841 for the creation of a Geological Survey, a petition which was eventually answered and out of which grew Canada's National Museum.

There is considerable evidence pointing to many cabinets de curiosités assembled by members of religious orders, primarily the Jesuits, who were given the responsibility of founding settlements under the aegis of The Company of New France. Other religious communities, for example the Ursulines and Augustines, preserved significant artifacts relating both to the religious and humanitarian programs for use as instructional aids to novices entering Orders. And, of course, the parish priest frequently established his own reliquary to provide visual evidence of miracles performed by the saint to which his community was dedicated.

A national census of "museums and collections" conducted by the Dominion Bureau of Statistics in 1937 lists one hundred and sixteen museum collections in the educational institutions of the province of Quebec as opposed to only sixty-four similar collections in the remaining eight provinces (Newfoundland was still to enter Confederation). Of this impressive number only two of the Quebec listings were classified as "religious." Twelve were in the areas of anthropology, archaeology and pioneer history, two were completely devoted to the decorative arts, and an even one hundred fell under the heading of natural sciences. The province, in an earlier survey, listed fifty-five schools and colleges administering museums, "the nature of whose contents embraced anthropology, botany, geology, mineralogy, numismatics, palaeontology, and zoology."

Unfortunately, data covering the founding of these collections is sketchy or non-existent. A 7500 mile tour of the province in search of such material points eloquently to the fact that many of them were conceived in the late eighteenth century and were established as recognized teaching collections in the early nineteenth century. The dedicated priests who had garnered and nurtured them relin-' quished their responsibilities to equally dedicated juniors thus ensuring continued care and development. Four examples are noted: the St. Hyacinthe Seminary (1854); an agricultural museum at Kamouraska (1859); Longeuil College (1867); and the Collège Bourget (1880) at Rigaud.

Antonio Drolet, chief librarian of the Quebec Archives, writing of the religious museums of the province, points to the proliferation of paintings and sculpture which, while serving primarily as votive symbols were appreciated for their decorative qualities. Some of the examples he cites are: "the ancient church of Ste-Anne-de-Beaupré in the town of that name east of Quebec City, and within the city walls are, le Séminaire de Québec, l'Hôtel-Dieu de Québec, la Cathédrale de Québec, l'Hôpital Général, le couvent des Ursulines, and l'Église Notre-Dame des Victoires." He adds that "these were not art galleries as we know them but the public were, and still are, admitted to the buildings to see the works of art."

Laval University, originally founded as a seminary for the education of priests by the first Bishop of Quebec to whom it is dedicated, received its charter as an institution of higher learning in 1852 and in that year, it established a museum complex to house its several collections. Two of these, geology and mineralogy, had been presented to the seminary by the Grand Vicaire of 1795-1805 and were described as having been gathered and arranged by Abbé Hauy. At the same time collections in other scientific disciplines received extensive additions.

In 1876 the Musée du Séminaire de Québec, an affiliate of Laval, opened its doors to students and the general public to view European Old Masters as well as a large numismatic display. The museum, at 6 rue de l'Université in the hub of Quebec City, was built in 1852 at a cost of one million francs and provided 50,000 square feet of floor space for display areas and an additional 5,000 square feet for museum offices and workrooms. Its art accessions were long viewed as being "the best private collection in America." Also in the latter half of the nineteenth century, various departments at Laval established individual collections, medicine being one such example, but except for displays at the Musée du Séminaire all other campus exhibits were, and still are, restricted to the university community.

The Peter Redpath museum building on the McGill University campus in Montreal was the first such edifice expressly designed for museum purposes and more specifically to house the vast palaeontology collection of Sir William Dawson. Erected in 1882 the two and a half storey structure was described some fifty years

111

later by Sir Cyril Fox, Director of the National Museum of Wales, as being "the most scholarly (neo-classic), the most distinguished, the most beautiful building in the University, in a finely chosen position which gives an air of Athenian dignity to the campus," adding that, "it is an historic document marking a phase in cultural evolution as expressed in architecture, as well as being a thing of beauty."

The main floor comprised a lobby, making possible the initial reception of large classes, with showcases in the corridor leading to a tiered lecture hall. The second floor, its display areas circling the main rotunda, had curatorial laboratories and storage facilities. In the original planning, space had been provided for natural history accessions but shortly after 1900 the entire collection of the Literary and Natural History Society was presented to the university resulting in drastic overcrowding. In 1910, however, by dint of much juggling, the museum was showing "archaeological and ethnological collections from the Queen Charlotte Islands with some displays from Egypt and South Equatorial West Africa." In November 1931, Sir Cyril was engaged to conduct a survey of museum needs on the campus; his report recommending an entirely new building also called for the retention of the existing Redpath edifice as a historical monument.

Like its French counterpart Laval, the McGill campus early developed collections of outstanding importance. A museum of hygiene was established in 1893 from an endowment income, its exhibits directed, of all things, to the problems of pollution and "relating to disinfection, lighting and heating, water, buildings, soil, air, drainage, and refuse disposal, foodstuffs and clothing, vital statistics, and bacteriology and pathology in relation to public health." The medical faculty also had built up highly important collections in the areas of anatomy and pathology from 1860 but saw virtually everything destroyed by fire in 1907. Faculty members, however, were undaunted and immediately launched further collecting activities. By 1930, the McGill Medical Museum served as headquarters for the International Association of Medical Museums which had a membership of about three hundred.

The Cyril Fox report lists sixteen departmental museums on the McGill Campus, only one of which was open to the public, the David McCord Museum, named in honour of a former faculty member who bequeathed an endowment fund of approximately twenty-five thousand dollars and his personal collection of historical artifacts. The McCord, wrote Sir Cyril, has "so far as I can ascertain, no definite policy. . . . It is not clear whether the Museum is to become a purely historical or a general Canadian Museum." It had no curator and was overcrowded with exhibits in a building

112

described as quite unsuitable and "is not, and can hardly be rendered fireproof." While the objects were of equal interest to both English and French speaking visitors labels were in English only.

The same report drew attention to the haphazard method of handling collections and the most important recommendation was that a Director of Museums (and collections) should be appointed with power to bring some order out of the chaotic conditions. Such a director was eventually, appointed but with jurisdiction over only the Redpath and McCord institutions.

The Château de Ramezay at 200 Notre Dame Street East in Montreal is one of the more important museums in the province of Quebec. The Château, significant both for its architectural tradition and as the mansion of Claude de Ramezay, a French governor of the early eighteenth century, was built in 1705 and was partially restored and remodelled to house a numismatic collection in addition to artifacts relating to both French and British occupancies of the city. Its official function as a museum dates from 1895 and since that time its accessions have broadened to include Canadian historical and social material in general, along with many ethnological and French-Canadian folk items.

The one museum on the North American continent devoted entirely to the education of deaf-mutes and blind had its genesis on the top floor of the École des Sourds-Muets on the Boulevarde Saint-Laurent in Montreal. Founded in 1885, the museum devoted much of its space to natural history. The collection was an oasis in a drab institutional environment. Over many years its honorary curator, Brother Florien Crête had built up an impressive collection in areas of botany, biology, and mammalogy with a section devoted to the earth sciences in addition to having large numismatic and philatelic accessions. His museum eventually occupied an area of three thousand square feet with an extensive braille library as an annex.

In 1932 Sir Henry Miers and Mr. S. F. Markham wrote that "most of the colleges and seminaries (in Quebec) administered by religious orders have a museum, which indicates a widespread appreciation of the value of museums as aids to education. At the same time it must be admitted that the technical standard of those is not high, since the expenditure is nominal, the curatorship honorary, and few of the curators have any special qualification for the work." Brother Florien Crête is one outstanding exception, having over the years developed high qualifications for the specific needs of deaf-mutes and the blind. In addition he worked energetically with other scholastic institutions in Greater Montreal to elevate standards of conservation and display.

One such small museum, founded in 1904, can still be seen at Villa Maria, the historic mansion at 4245 Decarie Boulevard which once served as the official residence of Canada's Governors-General, and which is now a convent school for girls. On the top floor of the building, the museum functions effectively as a secondary school classroom and encourages active participation by the students. It is one of the few such institutions which contain live domestic animals for the study of biological processes. The secretary of the Museums' Association of the Province of Quebec recalls that, while association members were visiting this institution they witnessed the accouchement of a litter of white rats. The museum now serves as provincial headquarters for Le Cercle des Jeunes Naturalistes.

The Musée du Séminaire de Joliette, founded in 1890, was for many years another of the burgeoning natural history institutions. In later years, it also built up its collection of decorative arts associated with the religious life of the province. Ten years earlier in 1880, at Sherbrooke, Abbé L. Marcotte launched a natural history museum at the Seminary of St-Charles-Borromée which in 1937 occupied 5600 square feet of floor space for an ever-expanding collection embracing not only the sciences but with an area devoted to human history, along with an extensive numismatic collection.

Over a period of two centuries, artists and craftsmen, many of them sent by religious orders from France, designed and created church decoration often assisted by native craftsmen. By the end of the nineteenth century much of their work had disappeared, replaced by mass produced material of European origin. Only in the last three decades has the significance of folk art related to the church in Quebec achieved recognition. Much recovery and restoration has been carried out but here and there it is still possible to find a church which has retained the rich and honest work of the early craftsmen.

In the City of Montreal are three religious institutions which established museums in the first half of this century. The best known, founded in 1945, is associated with St. Joseph's Oratory. The museum of Notre-Dame Church concentrates on portraits, vestments, and sacred artifacts of the church hierarchy, while in the heart of Old Montreal, as an annex to the Eglise Notre-Dame-de-Bon-Secours, the Musée Marguerite Bourgeoys is dedicated to a venerated woman of the seventeenth century who dedicated her life to good works.

It is at Ste-Anne-de-Beaupré, twenty-five miles east of the city of Quebec, where the objective visitor, as distinguished from the hundreds of thousands of pilgrims, must devote time to sort out the many contradictions which have over the past half century enveloped not only the church but the entire community. Here one searches hard for the fine line of demarcation between museum, tourist attraction, and the church itself. The columns of the Basilica are covered with discarded crutches, surgical belts, wheel chairs, all symbolic of cures attributed to Saint Anne since the first miracle was recorded more than two centuries ago. Penitents crawl up the steep steps to the Stations of the Cross high on the hillside, and visit the three museums administered by the Redemptionist Fathers, one with dioramas replete with wax figures, each depicting a moment of time in which the Revered Mother of the Virgin Mary responded to the anguished plea of the mariner. The second museum is of a more general nature, devoted to religious paintings, votive symbols, and sacred relics, while in the heart of the small community, surrounded by the stores of the huckster and the temporary stalls of pedlars offering charms, souvenirs, and relics blessed and unblessed, is the giant panorama depicting the life of Christ.

One can see some of the pomp and circumstance of the religious hierarchy, the faith, humility, and dedication of the faithful – fathers, brothers and sisters – within the church, alongside crass commercialism and tourist exploitation. Perhaps Sainte-Anne-de-Beaupré and its entire community should be preserved *in toto* for sociological study.

The province of Quebec has its pockets of English-speaking inhabitants, representing approximately eleven per cent of the total population. A goodly proportion of these are concentrated in the Eastern Townships (actually in the south-western corner of the province).

The Knowlton Academy, built in 1854 was restored and adapted to house a museum and archives in 1897. It is administered by the Brome County Historical Society which more recently added "the old school house" on Tibbits Hill as a somewhat remote annex. To the south-east the Standstead Historical Society has operated a pioneer museum since 1929.

A restoration associated with the rebellion of 1837-38 opened as a museum in 1938 at Carillon on the north shore of the Ottawa River, west of Montreal. Here the former barracks of the Royal Engineers, built in 1829 to accommodate one hundred and eight officers and men, now displays among other items, articles of the seigniorial days and mementoes of Sir John Abbott.

The political scene in Quebec was not neglected, both provincial and federal authorities paying tribute in the 1930's to Canada's eighth Prime Minister, Sir Wilfrid Laurier. At Arthabaska, the provincial government administers the home Sir Wilfrid occupied from 1867 until his election to Canada's highest office. The house also serves as an art gallery. Paintings by Quebec's first impressionist, Suzor Côté, sculptures by Alfred Laliberté, and engravings by Henri

Julien are on display. The museum is appropriately enough on Avenue Laurier.

Also on Avenue Laurier, but in Saint-Lin-des-Laurentides, about twenty-five miles north of Montreal, is the diminutive cottage in which it is believed Sir Wilfrid was born. While this event has not been authenticated, the infant destined to become Prime Minister spent his early childhood here. In 1938 the building was acquired by the federal government and dedicated as a historic site on the 100th anniversary of the Prime Minister's birth. It is decorated and furnished "with authentic items such as would have been used by French Canadian villagers of good taste in that epoch."

An isolated religious edifice, La Vieille Maison des Jésuites at Sillery, built in 1702 on the foundations of an earlier Indian mission dating back to 1637, deals solely with Jesuit history of the seventeenth and eighteenth centuries. While small in size the museum serves as a significant link with the history of the role of the church and the Order in the earliest days of colonization. The museum, which is open only at limited hours, continues to be administered by the Jesuits.

Gerard Morisset, in his *La Peinture Ancienne du Canada Français* credits Joseph Legare (1795-1855), painter and one time member of the Legislative Council, with having established the first museum in Canada dedicated entirely to the fine and decorative arts in the early nineteenth century. Other areas of Upper and Lower Canada had also seen sporadic attempts to organize exhibition programs and stimulate cultural growth in the visual domain, but the first continuing gallery in Canada to emerge out of such programs was conceived in 1847 when the Montreal Society of Artists was organized. In 1860, this group merged with the Art Association of Montreal to campaign for a permanent civic art gallery. To that end a series of temporary exhibitions was initiated, awaiting the propitious moment for some benefactor to respond to their appeals. In 1879 a bequest from Benaiah Gibb and a gift of a site by the City of Montreal in Phillips Square made possible the erection of what has been described as "a building of Victorian splendor," the first Montreal Museum of Fine Arts.

Mr. Gibb, a city merchant, had also bequeathed a collection of paintings and small sculptures but with the passage of time they decreased in importance, if not in size. If they still exist, they might be resurrected when the institution celebrates its centenary. However, Mr. Gibb also proposed in his will that the Art Association should develop a library and also embody an art school, both of which have been developed over the years.

This was the era when Montreal was rivalling Boston, New York, and New Orleans as a seaport. The financial centre of Canada, it

116

was already developing its own cosmopolitan atmosphere by serving as an international market-place. In this city were concentrated the Canadian contemporaries of America's Empire Builders, although more often than not they represented absentee British and French commercial and fiscal interests. It was not surprising that the pattern of benevolence which brought into being the many major art galleries and museums in the United States would be somewhat reflected within the next half century in Montreal.

In 1892 the Montreal Museum of Fine Arts received its first major collection from John W. Tempest, along with a seventy thousand dollar bequest for the further acquisition of fine art. This benefaction seemingly spurred other collectors, among them William and Agnes Learmont, brother and sister, who willed a major collection of decorative arts along with a hundred and twenty-six paintings which included works by the Dutch genre artists and the French Barbizon School in addition to the Society's first Rembrandt drawing. With more gifts flowing in, the gallery raised funds for its present building on Sherbrooke Street in 1912, followed shortly by a change of policy and direction. Coincidently with the formal opening it was announced that the new role of the institution would be that of Museum, a fine but significant distinction.

Then came the deluge with gifts and bequests from such historical figures as Donald Smith, who had a few years earlier been elevated to the British peerage with the title of Lord Strathcona; Sir William Van Horne, recognized as a discriminating and knowledgeable collector, who loaned many important works until his death in 1915, and whose daughter bequeathed in 1941 what Dr. David Carter, the present director, has described as "the most considerable single bequest of the Museum's history." Other gifts poured in during this period (1890-1930) from many other affluent donors but it was Frederick Cleveland Morgan whose interest in the decorative arts was responsible for it becoming the first Museum of Fine Arts in Canada. Mr. Morgan was for many years president of the family-owned department store and a descendent of a family of traders.

For many years it was frequently stated that McGill University had been built on tobacco. While the tobacco fortune of Sir William C. Macdonald has played an important role in the university's development it was the gift in 1813 of ten thousand pounds, together with land "for founding of a college to bear my name" by Scottish born James McGill, businessman and philanthropist, which brought the institution into being. However, Sir William made major contributions during his life time, founding and providing a two million dollar endowment fund for Macdonald College at Ste-Anne-de-Bellevue, administered by McGill, where a botanical garden and arboretum have been established over the years.

Sir William was a bachelor and bequeathed his fortune to his secretary and long time friend, David Stewart, who continued to make major contributions to education and the cultural life of Montreal. The tobacco fortune and benefactions continue unobtrusively to help educational and cultural projects through the second and third generations of the Stewart family.

14

As Canada approached the twentieth century the museum picture was somewhat bleak in comparison to the growing interest in museums, art galleries, and other related institutions in Great Britain, Europe, and the United States. There still remained a few museums such as the left-overs from the Mechanics' Institute movement in the Atlantic provinces. In Quebec, while many of the religious institutions had amassed important collections, these were administered by clerics whose devotion was measured in terms of sacrifice and the accessions were usually housed in basement areas, corridors, or quite frequently in garrets. On rare occasions some benefactor would appear, intent on encouraging cultural growth, but the philosophy of colonialism still hung heavily over Canada.

Native artifacts picked up by the transient representatives of the Empire or of Old France were regarded as souvenirs which served as conversational pieces when shipped home. Military cartographers, many of them skilled artists who painted the Canadian scene for their own enjoyment or for military records, generally took their portfolios with them to serve as illustrations for romantic stories of exploration and conquest. The paintings by native artists were likewise bought up, usually for a song, to be hung in trophy rooms with stuffed birds, bears, and buffaloes.

Only in recent years was it discovered that there appeared to be more Krieghoff paintings in England than in Canada. Commenting on this fact, Dr. R. W. Hubbard, in his authoritative work, *The Development of Painting in Canada,* writes that "he (Krieghoff) carried on a brisk trade in Scenes of Canada which he sold to British army officers and other officials stationed at Quebec. These pictures found their way to England and, now that Krieghoff prices are so high, they appear in such quantities in the London auction rooms that one can only guess at how prolific he was."

In an earlier century officials of the Governor and Company of the Gentlemen Adventurers, later to become the Hudson's Bay Company, had seen to it that any object – animal, vegetable or mineral – with or without historic, scientific or aesthetic value was exported. The absentee landlords of "all those seas, straits, bays, rivers, creeks and sounds in whatever latitude they may be. . . together with all the lands and territories upon the countries, coasts and confines of the seas, bays, etc. . . " apparently felt no responsibility or concern to make reciprocal contributions for the development of a native culture.

In 1901, Canada had a population of slightly less than five and a half million, seventy-five percent of which were concentrated in a baker's dozen of towns and cities scattered between Quebec City and Windsor, a distance of seven hundred and fifty-five miles and in an area never more than one hundred miles from the international border.

There were no royal collections to be given, loaned or expropriated. The several Governors-General who served their four years of isolation as public duty or punishment, while each having specific interests in the field of public services, rarely followed through once the term of office had expired. Outside of Montreal and Quebec City there were few collections of native arts and crafts, Canadiana or important paintings and sculptures. Apart from a few visionaries, there was no consciousness of Canadian history or a developing and distinctive culture.

Fifty years later, Dr. Hilda Neatby of the University of Saskatchewan was to write, "An intelligent awareness of the past is generally considered to be a sign of maturity in an individual or a community; but the Canadian people, although showing unmistakable signs of political maturity, still regard their history with indifference tempered by distaste." Another writer of this same period deplored the fact that the only authentic history of Canada had to be written by Francis Parkman, resident of Boston and citizen of the United States, over-looking Garneau's 1854 history which might deserve re-examination.

In 1911, William Jacob Holland, Director of the Carnegie Institute, Pittsburg, summarizing the Canadian museum scene wrote that "In connection with the Université Laval in Quebec, the McGill University in Montreal and the University of Toronto, beginnings of a significance have been made. . . . The Provincial Museum in Victoria, British Columbia is growing in importance. A movement has begun to establish at Ottawa a museum which shall in a sense be for the Dominion a national establishment." For him, this was only "a beginning."

Historians, even those working on the periphery of the museum world, eloquently romanticize when discussing the philosophy of colonization, and tend to emphasize the political struggles between nations bent on introducing civilizing programs for the aboriginal

120

tribes, but colonialism, until recent years, was a one-way street. Whether it be the three-way struggle between the French and British, and later the American revolutionists using Canadian cod as one of the rewards, or the invasion of Czechoslovakia by the U.S.S.R., the political philosophy of the state is the all-important objective and the desires of the individual citizen, aboriginal or imported, for his right to have life, liberty, and the pursuit of happiness receive secondary consideration.

The short-lived history of Louisbourg could serve as a prototype for any program of colonization where maximun production was demanded with minimum consideration for the social welfare of the community. During the brief mutiny of December 27th, 1744, the "other ranks" sought redress of grievances which, as listed in *Louisbourg* by J. S. McLellan, comprised "half a cord of wood for each company, the return of five cords which had been kept back . . . proper rations to those soldiers who had been in expeditions to Canso and Acadia and that the recruits of 1741 should receive their clothing which had not been given them."

While the revolution freed the American people from colonialism it brought into being a new and dynamic philosophy for the exploitation of resources with a policy of wide open free enterprise which has sometimes been designated as the era of the Robber Barons. Canadians also had their period of wide open free enterprise but more often than not the absentee fiscal interests were the beneficiaries. The massive give-aways by the Indians to the British Crown followed by equally generous give-aways by the Crown in the name of economic development are one such example. It is not surprising therefore that Canada's list of public benefactors is limited. Canada emerged from full scale colonial domination too late to benefit from largesse provided by a second generation of Empire builders. In addition, for the first time in the history of man, taxation policies served to curtail the desire of an increasing number of faceless corporations to make major contributions to charities. One has only to compare the flow of gifts, for example the Corcoran, Freer, Mellon and so on to Joseph Hirshhorn to the Smithsonian and its subsidiary galleries and museums, with the almost complete lack of similar benefactions to Canada's national and provincial institutions to understand why Canadian museums remained impoverished.

An interesting parallel exists between the Congressional disputation and political gerrymandering surrounding the James Smithson legacy to the United States and the parliamentary apathy leading to the formal establishment of Canada's national museum.

Four years after Smithson's death in 1827, a Doctor Rae petitioned the Lieutenant-Governor of Upper Canada for financial assistance to conduct a geological survey which, while receiving sympathetic consideration from a minority, was denied by the House of Assembly. The subject was renewed in 1836, a committee of the House recommending that action be taken to launch a survey, but again no action was taken.

Two years later, in 1838, the bulk of Smithson's estate consisting of bullion and cases containing geological and mineral specimens arrived in the United States, but ten years had to elapse before the Smithsonian Institution was founded, and a further nineteen years before money was voted for the erection, of a National Museum in Washington, D.C.

In Canada, the first united parliament met in 1841 where a third petition, referred to earlier, and this time sponsored by the Natural History Society of Montreal and the Literary and Historical Society of Quebec, was presented resulting in a vote of one thousand, five hundred pounds being approved. The following year William Edmund Logan, Montreal born geologist whose research into the origin of coal deposits had already given him international recognition, was appointed Provincial Geologist, taking up these duties in 1843. By 1845 Logan had invested eight hundred pounds of his own money to establish on Montreal's St. Gabriel Street, a repository in which "specimens were unpacked, labelled, catalogued and repacked in numbered cases." At the same time, Logan advised the Governor-General that "the collection we have brought together is overwhelming, when I observe the small impression Murray (his assistant) and I have yet made on our seventy great boxes, most of them requiring two men to lift, I am almost in despair."

At this same time Logan wrote to Murray who was on field work in the Lake Huron region announcing that "I must get a house or set of rooms for our collection (and) we must put our economic specimens conspicuously forward; and it appears to me that the exhibition of these large masses will create a greater impression on the mind. . .(which) induces me to say that I would like you to send to Montreal, as soon as it can be done by water communication in the spring, a thundering piece of gypsum. Let it be as white as possible. . .(and) if you come across a lithographic stone, let me have a thick slab of this, 6 to 8 inches thick."

To the director of the Geological Survey of Great Britain, he wrote that "I have hired a house on speculation and am ordering proper cases to hold some of the specimens in the confident speculation that the expenditure will be sanctioned by Legislature. But perhaps I may be reckoning without my host, and may be left in the lurch after all." The rooms on St. Gabriel Street had proven too small and the house referred to became the first National Museum, financed, but only partially, out of public funds. However, in 1845 after Logan had prepared an extensive report for the legislature, a

122

sum of five thousand pounds annually for the ensuing five years was approved with a proviso that "The Geological Survey will furnish a full and scientific description of its rocks, soils and minerals. . .together with a selection of specimens to illustrate the same."

In 1851 a collection of minerals having potential economic value was sent to the Great Exhibition in London where it received top awards and citations one of which reads "of all the British colonies, Canada is that whose exhibition is the most interesting and the most complete; and one may say that it is superior, so far as the mineral kingdom is concerned, to all countries that have forwarded their products. . . ."

The initial success of the project encouraged the government to continue the policy of promoting Canada's natural resources through participation in World's Fairs and to give at least token encouragement to Logan to further his plans for a permanent geological museum.

The Canadian scene at this period in the mid-nineteenth century is of interest when discussing the impact of the Geological Survey and its neophyte museum on Canada's future economy. In his article, *The National Museum of Canada,* published in 1926 as part of the annual report of that institution, W.H. Collins, acting director, painted a descriptive picture of the Dominion as of the early 1840's.

Canada then comprised the two provinces of Upper and Lower Canada, now Ontario and Quebec. In 1843 there were about 1,100,000 people in the two provinces, less than 450,000 in the Upper, and nearly 700,000 in the Lower. These were distributed mainly in the St. Lawrence watershed and the Great Lakes as far as Lake Huron. The chief towns were Quebec, Montreal, Kingston, and Toronto. There was a small outpost settlement at Sault Ste. Marie and a still smaller and more isolated one at Prince's Harbor, now Thunder Bay. The first railway had been built in 1836 between St. Johns (St-Jean) and La Prairie in Lower Canada, a distance of sixteen miles and designed to shorten the journey to New York. Even in 1866 there were only sixty-six miles of railway.

Queen's University in Kingston had been opened in 1842 and King's College at Toronto the following year. Kingston was the seat of government until 1844 when parliament was moved to Montreal and a few years later to Toronto. In 1833 Ottawa, then Bytown, was a village connected with Kingston by the Rideau Canal. Ottawa was not to be the seat of government until 1866.

There were over 400,000 persons living in Nova Scotia, New Brunswick, and Prince Edward Island but communication between the Maritime settlements and the rest of Canada was by water. Captain Vancouver had founded a small British colony near Victoria on

Vancouver Island but, except for the small Selkirk colony at Fort Garry, there was no white settlement between Victoria and Lake Superior. Apart from these populated areas, what is now the Dominion of Canada was known only to the Hudson's Bay Company and a few adventurous explorers.

The exploitation of Canada's mineral resources had been limited to coal in Nova Scotia and on Vancouver Island. Lumber had attracted the attention of industrialists and was being exploited on both the east and west coasts. The gold rush to the Yukon was not to occur for another forty years although placer mining on the Fraser and in the Cariboo region of British Columbia had started in 1852. Lignite deposits on the Prairies would be first exploited commercially in the early years of the twentieth century. The petroleum deposits of Ontario were initially tapped around 1862 while the rush to the northern areas of eastern Canada for mineral deposits did not occur until after the turn of the century.

By mid-century, curious entrepreneurs had begun to gravitate to the neophyte museum on St. James Street in Montreal to discuss and eventually launch their own exploration and development programs.

In the United States, surveys of the natural resources of the country had been continuing for many years but frequently the persons employed to undertake such missions laid claim to the collections they amassed or, as in the case of Wilkes and Cass, the objects were placed in the custody of the Director of Patents while the bureaucrats argued over ownership and compensation. In one of his lectures, Dr. Goode quotes from a letter dated 1846 which states that The National Institute (a temporary expedient prior to the founding of the Smithsonian) "had more than one thousand boxes, barrels, trunks, etc., embracing collections of value, variety and rarity in literature, in the arts and in natural history. . . . For the preservation, reception and display of these, the Institute has neither funds nor a suitable dependency."

In Canada, Logan, making a report to parliament in 1853 proposed that consideration should be given to the erection of "an appropriate edifice especially planned as a National Museum." A select committee was appointed the following year which reported that "your committee think that they can pronounce with confidence that in no part of the world has there been a more valuable contribution to geological science for such a small outlay" (hardly more than twenty thousand pounds in all), and recommended that a greatly increased service be provided. An annual grant of $20,000 plus $8,000 for publications was passed by a large majority. (Logan, we are told, was conscious of an expanding role for the Survey and its museum with the adoption of the B.N.A. Act in

124

1867 and recommended that he be replaced by a younger man. His resignation took effect in 1869 but he continued his research and writing until his death in 1875.)

While the terms of reference for the Survey dealt specifically with geology and mineralogy, Logan like Gesner, his Canadian contemporary, had developed a wide range of interest in other branches of natural science and history thus helping to lay the foundation for the expansion of the museum into the fields of botany, biology, and associated disciplines. Logan's successor, Dr. A.R.C. Selwyn, working with a greatly increased budget and under much broader terms of reference, also received from government explicit directions for the deposit of specimens in the Geological Museum to serve as a collection "for the whole of the Dominion and which shall be open to the public at all reasonable hours." The enlarged staff made possible more extensive field exploration embracing areas and subjects of economic importance to Canada's developing role in commerce and industry, and the museum collection increased to the point where it became necessary to move again into more commodious premises, this time to a new building on St. James Street which Logan had paid for out of his personal funds at a cost of thirty thousand dollars. In his annual report of 1876 Selwyn wrote "Not long before his death, Sir William stated that he intended the whole of his library and surveying instruments, purchased at a cost of $8,532 to remain for the use of the Survey . . . besides the cost of the library and instruments he expended $8,434.38 on various items in addition to the cost of the commodious offices on St. James Street . . . and now occupied by the Survey are likewise due to his liberality." In 1881, the Canadian government paid to the estate of Sir William Logan fifteen hundred dollars for the library and three thousand dollars for the instruments.

By 1881 the Smithson controversy had been resolved. In that year the National Museum, a subsidiary of the Smithsonian Institution, was opened but prior to that the National Institute, originally organized as a quasi-governmental society "to promote science and the useful arts and to establish a national museum of history," had successfully lobbied for the establishment of The Smithsonian as an institution responsible directly to government with a Board comprising the President and other members of his Cabinet, together with representatives from Congress. Whereas the Canadian project had developed into a two-headed governmental agency, the American Smithsonian was becoming hydra-headed. An agency for receiving copyrighted works, it also encouraged, and at times, even financed research and initiated a publications program. One year after it was founded, the Institution had started work in the field of meteorology and in 1849 it became involved in telegraphic transmission. By

1878 when its second secretary Spencer F. Baird took office, it was involved in many other areas of science, had received the Corcoran collection of art, had taken over the many models from the U.S. Patent Office, and had created a repository for its various collections including cases bequeathed by Smithson. The United States Government had also received a residuary legacy from the Smithson estate in 1867 of a further twenty-six thousand pounds.

As early as 1875 the National Museum of Canada administered, what Dr. Collins calls "one of its minor activities," the preparation and distribution to educational institutions, from elementary schools to universities, of natural history collections. In that first year, a geological collection was sent to the public school at Elora, Ontario, comprising 277 specimens of rock, minerals, and fossils, each named, classified, and catalogued. By the following year, twenty-eight such collections had been distributed to all parts of the Dominion.

In 1880 the Geological Survey and National Museum were indivisible with the Montreal building housing not only scientists and administrators but the ever increasing collections which required processing, research, and storage. The building also served as information centre for schools and colleges, as well as for industry, continued to develop its public display areas and became increasingly involved in the publication of scientific papers. Before Logan's retirement, a division of biology had been created with John Macoun as its head. Macoun travelled with Drs. Stanford and Fleming on the expedition charged with siting the route for the proposed transcontinental railway and with his colleague Selwyn later studied the resource potentials of British Columbia.

It had now become obvious that both the Survey and Museum should be re-established in the capital city. The transfer to Ottawa was started in the late months of 1880 and by the following year they were lodged in the former Clarendon Hotel on Sussex Street. For the moment the premises appeared to be adequate, providing more areas for research and preparation and a much larger space for public displays. The transfer was a major moving job involving 1,729 boxes, 101 barrels, and 162 miscellaneous packages with a total weight of 282,585 pounds, but agitation for a permanent building expressly designed as a museum, which had been generated several years earlier, continued into the twentieth century. The 1899 annual report announced ". . .that no substantial progress has been made unfortunately toward the provision of a suitable building for a museum and offices of the Survey. Preliminary plans have, however, been drawn, and the necessity for such a building has been strongly supported in the House by Members of Parliament during the past session."

126

In 1892 The Smithsonian Institution received another bequest, this from Thomas Hodgins of Long Island, adding a further $216,000 to the endowment fund which by this time had grown to slightly less than one million dollars. The Freer collections of fine arts along with other lesser but equally important art gifts resulted in the formal creation of the United States National Gallery of Art in 1906. A small observatory had been built on the grounds in 1890, a zoological park opened on 266 acres of land that same year, and prizes and awards were being given to scientists both at home and abroad to encourage significant research.

One such award of $10,000 was divided between Britain's Lord Rayleigh and Sir James Dewar for "their research and investigation of atmospheric air, leading to their discovery of argon, in connection with the welfare of mankind." It was in 1891, that Samuel P. Langley, then secretary to The Smithsonian, published his paper on "Experiments in Aerodynamics" in which he proved that a heavier than air machine, if propelled by motive power, could achieve flight.

A survey of Canadian museums undertaken by the New York State Museum in 1903 pronounced Canada's National Museum collection as having "the most complete specimens illustrative of Canadian geology, zoology, botany, archeology and ethnology in the world," adding that "in paleontology alone there are sixteen thousand specimens classified and exhibited representing four thousand species." The museum also had "representative specimens of nearly all known birds and mammals of Canada (and) the most complete herbarium extant of Canadian plants."

In the early years of the twentieth century, Canada faced an era of industrial expansion and development of its natural resources. By 1900, mining activities had produced over $64,000,000, an important contribution to the national economy. Educational standards had greatly increased. The western plains had now been opened, first to the ranchers and a few years later for homesteading, and attention was being directed to the vast unexplored and largely unexploited mineral resources in Northern Ontario and Quebec. New towns and cities were mushrooming as lands adjacent to the transcontinental railway lines were thrown open. Commenting on these factors, Collins states that the need for closer specialization saw radical departures in the Geological Survey administration.

In 1901, a Department of the Interior was created by act of parliament but had little or no contact with the museum scientists. Six years later a Department of Mines was brought into being and "the original functions of the Geological Survey were divided between the Survey and a newly created Mines Branch." Museum services became the responsibility and function of both branches and in the new legislation a Museum of Geology and Natural History was specified.

While the projects within the museum had been restricted following this division of responsibility, the field work of the Survey continued to be related to economic exploitation, a situation which apparently escaped both public and politicians who over the years have viewed museum activities as some form of esoteric entertainment.

Canada, with over three and a half million square miles of known land had by 1900-01 a population density of about one person per square mile as opposed to fifteen persons per square mile in approximately the same land area in the United States. Undoubtedly Canada's small population and her gradual emergence from colonialism were contributing factors to the restricted assistance given to the National Museum. Plans for a building designed specifically to house the institution had received tacit approval but only reached the architectural drawing board in 1905 with the completed edifice formally opened in 1911.

In actual fact, Canadians had to wait until January 5, 1927, for parliament to give formal recognition to its own institution when "His Excellency the Governor-General in Council, on the recommendation of the Minister of Mines (designated) the Museum Branch of the Department of Mines 'The National Museum'. " In parenthesis, it is also recorded that the National Gallery of Canada, founded in 1880 had to wait twenty-two years before the necessary legislation was passed making it a legal entity, despite the fact that it had been receiving annual grants from the federal Treasury over the years.

Optimistically, the then director of the Museum, Dr. R.W. Brock, announced that "the museum can now expand and the work of the Survey accelerated," but the outbreak of World War I saw fiscal and staff cuts. Two years later, in 1916, a catastrophic fire completely destroyed the Parliament Buildings except for the Library and the government took over the Victoria Memorial building to provide temporary housing for Commons and Senate. "All except the exhibits and offices for anthropology, the library and certain occupants in the basement were removed to various quarters in other parts of the city and remained so scattered until May of 1920, both Survey and museum work being brought virtually to a standstill."

The dual responsibility of the museum shared by the Survey and the Mines Branch likewise affected both the efficiency and administration of the various areas while minuscule budgets limiting curatorial and technical staffs became another major factor in slowing down new and exciting policies and programs. In addition, the National Gallery had now pre-empted the building's entire east wing.

Until 1920 there had been no museum director as such, the administrative head being occupied primarily with the Survey but having a lowly curator who took charge of the day-to-day housekeeping. In this year, William McInnes was officially named Director but even then in a part-time capacity. Within four years McInnes had been replaced by Dr. Collins, who grappled with the complexities of his new office. Eventually, having been faced with increasing demands for space, he presented a plan for reorganization which, he felt, "would solve present difficulties. . .; it is," he wrote, "to share the conduct of the Museum among as many of the government departments as have a direct interest in it, under administrative control of a joint or common board of directors or trustees." Dr. Collins pointed to the fact that, at this moment of time, there were thirteen and a half halls in the building but only four of these were available for display purposes. He proposed an expansion of the institution which would provide at least three times the exhibition space currently available, but the proposal fell on barren ground.

The Miers-Markham report of 1932 speaks of "The administration of the National Museum (as being) strictly anomalous and unlike that of any other museum with which we are familiar. It is administered by the Geological Survey, which is itself a sub-department of the Department of Mines. . . .

"This extraordinary constitution of a Science Musuem comprising botany, anthropology, zoology and mineralogy, as well as geology, is no doubt largely responsible for the comparatively ineffective service rendered to the Dominion in spite of its valuable collections and expert staff." The report adds that "There is a further anomaly that the greater part of the mineral collection is housed with the Mineral Division of the Geological Survey (in a building away from the museum) where no adequate exhibition space or trained museum staff is provided."

In 1937, the report of the census of museums undertaken by the Dominion Bureau of Statistics indicated the lack of organization within the museum itself. Here it was reported that there was one officer "in charge" whose rank or responsibilities were not spelt out, plus one assistant. No record had been kept of attendance and no financial report was submitted to the census taker. Its extension services also went unreported.

The National Museum had indeed reached a low ebb, or so it was thought, just as the Depression was making its impact on the nation, resulting in further fiscal cutbacks, creating more frustrations, and cancelling those very field expeditions and research which should have been considered essential policies leading to a restoration of a badly dented economy.

15

Interest in the fine and decorative arts in Canada pre-dates the founding of the first historical museum. The Quebec Seminary established a school designed to perpetuate the traditions of French religious decor in 1668 at the instigation of François Xavier de Laval-Montmorency, at the time vicar apostolic, whose most noted student, Jacques Leblond de Latour, carved the original altar-piece for the church of Sainte-Anne de Beaupré, the one piece extant which can still be directly attributed to him but which is now in Bordeaux.

It is also recorded that in 1807 in Halifax, a Mr. M. Smith opened a school of painting at James Bowen's Academy which, appropriately enough, was next door to the Jerusalem Tavern. Also in Halifax in 1812 Ralph Stennett, described as "portrait painter and drawing master," presented a "Panarama of Optical and Graphic Spectacle" which appeared to have been of a temporary character. Something in the nature of a climax in artistic achievement in that city was attained in 1830 when an exhibition was held under the distinguished patronage of His Honour, the President of the (Provincial) Council, comprising ninety-three paintings hung in two rooms and a corridor in Dalhousie College. "Careful persons were employed" we are told, "to fetch and return the pictures without any expense to the owners; and no sticks, umbrellas or parasols were permitted to be taken into the rooms." Over the years a collection of landscapes and portraits by European minor masters and early Canadian painters were acquired to form the nucleus of a provincial collection which was eventually placed in the custody of the Nova Scotia archivist.

Russell Harper, in his *Painting in Canada,* confirms that Joseph Legare (1795-1855) was the first individual to open a public gallery in Canada. In 1817, Legare, himself an artist, collector, and politician, purchased a number of European works from the Abbé Philipe and Louis Desjardine which they had brought from Paris. Some of these were hung in his gallery along with works from his

130

own brushes, and others were given to Laval University. About two hundred works were turned over to the university by Legare's executors in 1858 to provide a foundation upon which it built its important permanent collection.

One year after Montreal had opened its permanent gallery a National Gallery for Canada was proposed by the Marquess of Lorne, then Governor-General, who, with his consort, had encouraged and fostered the creation of the Royal Canadian Academy of Arts.

The first exhibition sponsored by the Academy was held in Ottawa in 1880. Memberships or Associateships in the R.C.A. were by invitation; in return for the honour, the fortunate candidates were required to donate a Diploma Work to the Society. It was agreed that such works should be placed in the custody of the government so that a national collection could be built around them. Mrs. Maud Brown, widow of the National Gallery's first director, referred to this embryo collection as "A foundling left by its foster mother on the government's doorstep."

The problem of finding a suitable repository for the paintings was thrown into the lap of the Minister of Public Works and Mrs. Brown rationalized that "presumably because an architect was the nearest thing to an artist . . . the diploma paintings came under his care." Temporary accommodation was found in the former Clarendon Hotel on Sussex Street, then serving as the National Museum. Later the collection was moved to the old court house from which the Supreme Court Justices were about to depart for their own new quarters. With their departure a gallery area was constructed on the second floor "and a skylight was provided to improve the lighting" in 1882.

Not explained is why the peripatetic collection was on the move again in 1884, this time to the new building of the Department of Fisheries, at least a logical environment for still life works. This building, situated on Ottawa's O'Connor Street, contained a fish hatchery in the basement, an icthyological display on the ground floor, with the art gallery up one flight. Sessional papers announced that "The re-opening of the Fish Hatchery during a portion of the year may have a tendency to increase the number of visitors to the Art Gallery."

In this environment the collection languished until its next move in 1910. In the meantime, an Arts Advisory Council was officially approved by Parliament in 1907, upon the recommendation of the Hon. Sidney Fisher, Minister of Agriculture and Public Works who had responsibility for the gallery. It was fortunate for Canada that Byron Edmund Walker, later to become Sir Edmund, and his close associate Sir George Drummond were named as Council members. With these wealthy and politically important patrons of the arts

131

taking firm control, the appointment of the gallery's first director was not long delayed and the pre-empting of three floors in the east wing of the newly constructed Victoria Memorial building over the anguished protests of science museum officials, was a foregone conclusion.

Of this era in Canada's cultural growth the papers of Sir Edmund contained this comment, ". . . the government has been troubled with the log-rolling in connection with the painting of pictures for Parliamentary halls. . . .We are to stand in the gap of public criticism and try to bring good results for art out of what has not as yet been a very hopeful condition."

Despite the fact that in 1913 the terms of reference for guidance of the Advisory Council explicitly gave it responsibility for not only collecting but for the encouragement of "correct artistic taste" and public interest in the arts in general, Sir Edmund and his colleagues found themselves consistently embroiled in dialogue and dispute with artists, politicians, critics, and press as they stood in the gap and sought to change that not very hopeful condition – a condition which has sporadic outbursts even today.

One of the first controversies arose with the appointment of Eric Brown as Secretary to the Advisory Council and Curator of the yet unchristened institution. It was more of a subdued rumble than an outburst as the Academicians whose paintings this neophyte would be called upon to watch over had not been consulted. Mr. Brown's post was anomalous at best, offering a small salary, and for the moment, little or no prospects for advancement. Otherwise members of the R.C.A. might have demanded the appointment of one of their number rather than a man whose major qualifications were somewhat abstract.

Brown had spent most of his formative years in British literary and artistic circles, arriving in Canada less than two years earlier. He was not a painter and his contacts with Canadian artists had been limited, but what could one expect for a salary of $100 a month? Sir Edmund had thought he was employing a single man – actually he was – but learning that a marriage would shortly take place, His Lordship had qualms as expressed in a letter to Brown in October 1910 in which he wrote ". . .had I known about it (the forthcoming marriage), I should not have ventured to ask you to take up the duties of curator on such a small salary. . . .My only hope is that when we can show how important the work is and when the ministers and others understand your share in it, a proper salary would follow, but while I am not afraid to take the risk of disappointment in (proposing) this, for an unmarried man, I feel it is a much more serious risk for a married man. However, my dear Mr. Brown, you know the condition and if you are ready to take

132

the chance you may be sure that I will do my best in your interests."

The first task of the new curator was to design display areas on the three floors of the new museum building, followed by many lengthy discussions to formulate policies. An accessions program was of major importance as a vast number of gifts had already been showered on the institution. Other subjects included possibilities of extension services to reach across the Dominion and educational programs within the gallery itself for adults and children.

As for accessions, in 1912, the first catalogue of works owned by the nation was compiled by Mr. Brown and listed 175 oil paintings, 21 watercolours and pastels, 163 drawings, etchings and engravings, 13 architectural drawings, and 9 sculpture pieces, a total of 381. Within one year it was deemed necessary to publish a supplemental catalogue which showed well over 200 additional accessions.

The young curator and his Board were just nicely getting into harness when the outbreak of World War I. brought the curtailment of all but essential services and a cut-back in budget requirements. As already mentioned, this was followed in 1916 with the disastrous fire on Parliment Hill resulting in the national collection being placed in storage until such time as a new Centre block was built. However, within a few months cases of paintings were being regularly shipped to towns and cities from one end of Canada to the other, initiating a policy of travelling art displays – a program never before undertaken by any similar gallery throughout the world. It is worth noting that such collections were seen at the then newly created Calgary Stampede.

Agitation from the Royal Canadian Academy for representation on the Advisory Board was to continue. It was pointed out to the Advisory Council and to members of Parliament that the National Gallery owed its existence to the efforts of the R.C.A. and their initial gifts of diploma works. Therefore, it was argued, the Academy had a vested interest in the institution. Sir Edmund and his fellow trustees, all laymen, thought otherwise, Sir Edmund writing, "I can only hope that the R.C.A. will realize that the National Gallery of Canada is a state institution and that it is not in the true interest of the public that it should be, even in appearance, allied to any other body."

There is a tendency for any Academy, i.e. an association of practitioners in the arts and humanities whose purpose is, among others, to offer honours to their peers, to become conservative, or at times reactionary. An outstanding example is the French Academy. The traditional steps toward recognition call for careful scrutiny of the work of potential candidates, followed by an invitation to the nominee to display his wares. If the accepted work is approved by the academicians in conclave, an invitation is extended and an associate membership bestowed, with full membership deferred for an indefinite time. The tendency is for the academicians to perpetuate a mould which made possible their own elevation to the ranks of a distinguished hierarchy. There is no place for the immature, the unorthodox or the innovative practitioner in the world of academe. Such was the Royal Canadian Academy as Canada emerged from colonialism and World War I.

Culturally, the younger generation was shedding colonial romanticism and searching for a new national identity while an older generation clung fiercely to the accepted norm. European art dealers had found a ready market among the nouveau riche for Old Masters, many of dubious ancestry. In Quebec, the rich folk-expression of the primitives which had emerged from the seventeenth century seminary was being ruthlessly thrown out, to be replaced by imported adornment. Politically the Canadian government was making its initial bid for international recognition as an independent nation by being represented first at the peace conference and appending its signature to the Versailles Treaty, and immediately thereafter by joining the League of Nations.

The younger artists and writers, with a small minority from the older generation, were questioning traditional concepts and laying the foundations for contemporary art forms more closely related to a growing national consciousness. The development of what is now called a National Movement for the visual arts reached its climax with the initial exhibition of the Group of Seven at the Toronto Art Gallery in 1920. However, artists, particularly in the province of Quebec, had been reflecting the philosophies and techniques of the contemporary French schools as early as 1890. It was not surprising, therefore, that Sir Edmund and Eric Brown were able to convince members of the Advisory Board that the new Group was of sufficient historical importance to warrant purchases while prices were low, and also to serve as a new chapter in Canada's cultural growth. This program proved to be highly unpopular with the academicians, press, politicians, and public. The full force of criticism was directed at the National Gallery curator, culminating in attacks in the House, supported by petitions, and, at times, in the editorial columns of the eastern press.

One hundred and eighteen artists signed a round-robin which declared a boycott on the National Gallery "unless a radical reform takes place in its management." More than half that number petitioned the Governor-General in Council for dismissal of the Director but this was offset somewhat by a counter-petition signed by three hundred interested citizens expressing "confidence in the administration and its Director." Sir Edmund Walker was verbally attacked in the House of Commons for using his office for the purpose of handing out genteel graft. This furore continued well into the 1930's when the Depression resulted in another period of fiscal cutbacks and retrenchment.

In the meantime, in 1919, a customs clerk, H.O. McCurry, who had attracted the attention of the gallery was recommended for a new post of Administrator and was destined to become Director upon the death of his superior in 1939. Sir Edmund, who served on the Advisory Council until shortly before his death in 1924, was replaced by Dr. Francis Shepherd of Montreal. However, the foundation upon which the National Gallery was built by Sir Edmund and his curator protégé was well laid. Their work has made the gallery unique throughout the world for nurturing community galleries; for its entry into associated areas of art disciplines; for an accession policy which, while not neglecting the European Old Masters, gives practical support to new ideas; and for its constant resistance to political pressures.

In 1924, the gallery designed the first exhibition of Canadian artists for the Canadian pavilion at the Wembley (British Empire) Exhibition and followed this with a similar exhibition in Paris three years later. Mr. McCurry's chance meeting with a young student of art history, Kathleen Fenwick, while setting up the Wembley show, and a subsequent interview by Mr. Brown when he travelled to Paris in 1927 were responsible for still further controversy.

The fine distinction between an art gallery and art museum is normally seen in the terms of reference which state-administered institutions must follow. Generally such an institution is referred to as "a repository for the collection, storage, preservation and display of national art treasures." The art treasures listed in the first catalogue of the National Gallery indicated that, apart from the Diploma works, the rest was a mixed bag of tricks. The 1914 supplement seems to indicate that a developing policy of collecting was emerging and this becomes obvious when the future actions of the Director and his Board are analysed. The Advisory Council had little or no funds allotted for acquisitions. It was obvious, however, that two projects were pre-eminent, the first, to search for significant contemporary works by Canadian artists, a task which Mr. Brown felt, at least to his own satisfaction, he was eminently capable of handling. When his budget permitted the employment of additional professional staff he proposed, in 1921, the creation of a Print Department which immediately "gave promise of developing into one of the most important collections in America."

A Canadian Curator "with the highest attainments in this work," E.P. Rossiter, was engaged, but within two years had resigned to join the staff of the Boston Museum of Fine Arts in a similar capa-

135

city. A temporary appointment followed, the post fell vacant again in 1926. In the summer of 1927 while in Paris, Mr. Brown engaged Miss Kathleen Fenwick, a protégée of the British artist Paul Nash, and who had recently studied art history in Oxford, London, and Paris. The unpublished diary of Dr. McCurry reveals that he and Mrs. McCurry had met Miss Fenwick in 1924 while staying in the pension of Miss Pryde in Paris. A year later, he suggested in a letter to the young Englishwoman that she seek an interview. A telegram from Mr. Brown sent to Mr. McCurry from France reads "Sir Robert Borden has seen the exhibition and is greatly impressed stop who is Fenwick?" Announcement to the Canadian press that Miss Fenwick would fill the vacancy brought cries of outrage from Mr. Brown's earlier critics. The appointment of an art student, not even a practising painter, sans degree and with only a diploma was an insult to many Canadian artists and smelt strongly of Anglophile nepotism. The appointment was confirmed but the outcries against the Director, his Board and the gallery policies continued.

Unlike the Smithsonian and the majority of European state galleries, Canada's National Gallery of Art had been singularly lacking in patrons and depended almost entirely on its own slender fiscal resources for the accessions it has acquired over the years. Many of the distinguished members of the Advisory Council made contributions and succeeded in interesting art patrons who have given spasmodically to the collection but up to the mid-1930's its Old Masters, French and British schools of paintings did little or nothing to enhance the prestige of the institution which lacked the essential charisma of its Montreal contemporary.

By 1939 the National Gallery of Canada had a full time staff of sixteen with an annual attendance of 73,000; in the same year 7,115 individual items from its collection and supplementary educational areas had been circulated on loan. It also had a program of lecture tours which exposed citizens in all major cities to art authorities from Canada and abroad, thirty such lectures having been given that year. The gallery staff likewise planned and produced three national radio broadcasts and regular Sunday afternoon music recitals became a feature in the main floor gallery area. There were also available for "any art society, university or school in Canada having the necessary facilities," original works of art, reproductions, drawings and prints, all this despite drastic financial cutbacks due to the depression years.

It is worth noting that the Carnegie Corporation had in more recent years, and up to 1949, contributed $74,649 in grants, $67,419 of which was for "research, study and publication." A portion of the remaining grant was used to bring neophyte curators from the more isolated areas of Canada to the National Gallery for "familiarization programs." So far as can be ascertained, the Carnegie contributions still remain the only monies directly made available to the National Gallery by a non-governmental agency.

While the depression years bore few fruits in Ottawa or across the country, the continuing extension program was maintained and plans discussed for future development. In 1941, Dr. McCurry largely on his own initiative, introduced silkscreen processing of Canadian paintings to provide decor for armed forces canteens, messes, and other areas at home and abroad. This program emanated originally from A.Y. Jackson and Charles Comfort, and rapidly expanded to serve schools and still after to be sold commercially for the decoration of business premises. The matter of fact acceptance of this relatively new reproductive process has overshadowed its significance as the first planned project to popularize the works of contemporary Canadian artists. Thirty years later the reproductions continue as familiar decor in branch banks, schools, and other premises from St. John's to Prince Rupert.

16

Records covering the growth of Ontario museums are somewhat sparse. As a result, only general trends can be examined.

The 1932 survey discloses thirty-seven museums and related institutions in the province of which five were administered by the federal government and three by the province, while three others were under municipal control. Seven were classed as educational institutions, one was privately owned, and eighteen were shown as historical society projects. By 1937, the number had increased to sixty of which thirty-five were school and college collections, seventeen operated by historical societies, four by municipalities, one by the province and three by the federal authorities. Obviously there are discrepancies but in the five years which elapsed between the two surveys there are definite indications of steady growth. Interestingly enough, a Dominion Bureau of Statistics report of 1952 actually shows a decline but it becomes obvious as the various reports are analysed and checked that surveys conducted by mail are far from reliable. It is also well established that even the coast-to-coast surveys of 1932 and 1958 made by personal contact, and the listings submitted to the Massey Commission in 1949-50 by the Canadian Museums' Association, which disclosed sixty-four institutions, were far from complete.

The vast expanse of Canada's terrain, together with lack of communication between remote regions, undoubtedly has much to do with these discrepancies, but a more important factor was due to the terms of reference laid down for each individual survey. The 1937 D.B.S. survey was intent on locating museum collections used as educational aids whether in schools or in publicly owned institutions, whereas the 1932 survey had concentrated on institutions operated in the public interest and open to the general public. The C.M.A. report directed to the Massey Commissioners also limited its listings to non-profit institutions open to the public, whereas a still later report of the D.B.S., made in 1964, includes a number of privately operated institutions administered primarily for profit, in

138

addition to privately owned collections which lack the essential government blessing as being charitable corporations.

Contradictions are also found in the directory of the Ontario Department of Tourism and Information, published annually, which shows both private and commercial institutions including Crown Jewel and Waxwork displays, but excludes art galleries, botanical gardens, planetaria, and zoos. At the risk of being redundant it is noted that two surveys conducted over the same (1963-64) period listed one hundred and fifty, and one hundred and sixty-one Ontario institutions respectively. The c.m.a. directory of 1968 reported two hundred and fifteen institutions in the province, and one year later the Ontario directory listed two hundred and forty-one historical museums and restorations.

The Ontario museum scene following Confederation was in marked contrast to both the Atlantic provinces and Quebec. Population was almost entirely confined to the south of the province with a concentration of settled communities between Cornwall and Windsor and a few, scattered settlements following the Canadian Pacific Railway as it progressed westward. Mineral mining in the Cobalt-Sudbury area was being exploited as the nineteenth century drew to a close, but as late as 1910 the vast gold resources further north were still considered unprofitable. A few years later, with the discovery of The Glory Hole on the lease of Dome Mines with its abundance of "free gold" embedded in the ore body, the rush was on, but it was not until 1927 that Timmins was linked with North Bay by road.

Victors tend to glorify their conquests while the vanquished quietly lick their wounds. The British Crown had triumphed over the French and had even repulsed the republic to the south in the wars of 1812-14. It was natural that citizens of Upper Canada, including many United Empire Loyalists should have an intense interest and devotion for Queen Victoria and her government. It was natural also that, with the increase of literacy and the development of text book education, the need for natural history collections as teaching aids would decline. Instead, a new emphasis was developing toward the history of British colonialism and the romance of Empire building.

In 1881, virtually two thirds of the two million inhabitants of what is now Ontario lived in the more isolated rural areas and townships. Twenty years later this number had decreased by close to one hundred thousand, due to the development of more towns and cities although most of these were still isolated from the four or five major cities.

Industrial resources were rapidly developing, particularly in the south-western region, stimulated to some degree by mass immigration of German Mennonites who brought with them a knowledge of sound craftsmanship and keen business instincts, developing a compatibility with the thrifty and industrious "improved Scots." French penetration into Upper Canada tended to go northward following the fur routes, logging and a little later mineral mining, happily for the predominantly protestant population to the south.

The development of Canada's National Museum, its Art Gallery and Archives had little or no impact on the residents in outlying communities. This applied also to the founding of Ontario's Provincial Museum, the Royal Ontario Museum, and the Toronto Art Gallery. It was still the horse and buggy era, with automobile travel restricted to each immediate region, and the occasional excursion by train had all the excitement of a visit to an alien country. Highways between cities were hardly conducive for extensive touring by the Model A Ford. Settlers in the smaller communities had to rely on their own resources when considering the social aspirations of their neighbours, the philosophy of some strong-minded member frequently influencing the direction. The basic needs for food, clothing, and shelter were the first essentials, followed by education, religion, and then sports, after which the more specialized interests of individual citizens were considered. These could take any form from art to zoology.

Whereas in the Maritime provinces and Quebec the motivation for museum development was education, the thinking (call it elementary philosphy) which launched the average pioneer museum in Ontario was to pay tribute to the indomitable spirit of the original settlers with more than a dash of nostalgia added. There is ample evidence to support this premise. Surveys made in 1932 and again as late as 1957 point to the facts that the vast majority of such institutions: (a) were open only during the summer months; (b) had little or no relationship with educational authorities; (c) had collections displayed "with no definite purpose" as described by one report. A 1932 report said that historical exhibits of significance were shown cheek by jowl with much that "was sheer rubbish," while in 1958, another report stated that "only in a few instances do they (the community museums) make any constructive effort to interest teachers and school authorities in the museum as a teaching agency (whereas) other museum services are conspicuously absent in three quarters of the museums." The same report likewise infers that many such institutions "mitigate against the advancement of the museum movement in Canada" adding that local societies "are not aware that museums can play an active role in the life of the community, (the members) still living in the nineteenth century," and concluding with the devastating statement that "occasionally,

140

the evident smug satisfaction of having assembled a collection of objects, as if it were an end in itself, proved somewhat irritating."

Blame for such a condition most certainly did not rest with the well-intentioned, dedicated founders of the pioneer historical museum of Ontario. Certainly the traditions which resulted in these conditions grew out of the Ontario pattern. Public apathy might be blamed but the Canadian Historical Association founded in 1922 by academics for academics might share in the censure for their failure to recognize that history at the grass roots level was in the making while they continued to analyse a political structure which tended to denigrate cultural awareness. The Association did, however, initiate a program for the marking of historical buildings.

The report of the Massey Commission, quoting extensively from the Miers-Markham report, indicated that Canada would never acquire a museum service "worthy of her position as a leading nation until she spends as much on her museums as the leading cities of north-west Europe or the United States, and has the courage to appoint first-class curators at first-class salaries to at least 90 of her 125 museums."

In 1833 Charles Fothergill, a member of the Legislative Assembly of Upper Canada proposed that "a Lyceum of Natural History and Fine Arts" be founded in the then city of York but eighteen years elapsed before a Provincial Museum was founded. In 1903 it was reported to have "900 specimens representing Iroquois, Blackfoot, Blood, and Kwakiutl Indians of Canada – Eskimo, Navajo, Zuni, Pima, Pona." There were also life masks made by British Columbia and Washington State Indians and other collections from China, New Hebrides, Paraguay, and Africa; 300 busts of European and United States scholars and celebrities, along with 2,000 archaeological specimens, photographs, and paintings.

With Ontario firmly settled within the framework of Confederation, the amateur historians in the small communities turned their attention to memorializing native sons and daughters who had distinguished themselves during the years, played major roles in the political arena or contributed to the social development of Upper Canada in other ways.

The Elgin County Historical Society had established its museum in St. Thomas in 1895 devoting much of its space to the life of Colonel Talbot, while in the same year, at Niagara-on-the-Lake, the Historical Society established a similar institution which paid tribute to Laura Secord. Toronto's Colborne Lodge, built in 1836, had been officially opened as a museum as early as 1896 to display furniture and effects which included a large collection of paintings by John G. Howard, first architect and engineer of the city, while at

Brantford a local society created the Brant Historical Museum, named after the legendary Mohawk Chief. In the same city nine years later, a second museum, The Bell Homestead, was restored to tell the story of the invention of the telephone. In 1899, the Gage House at Stoney Creek, a few miles from Hamilton, became the prototype for future military restorations. This was thrown open to the public to re-create the story of Battlefield House, a first-aid station which functioned in the 1813 military engagement.

A museum devoted to the history of Canada's armed forces had been launched at the Royal Military College at Kingston as early as 1876, but it was not until 1925 that the Murney (Martello) Tower, built by the Royal Engineers in 1846 as part of the defence works of the region was restored and opened to the public.

The Ontario Agricultural College at Guelph had developed an important collection associated with cattle and crops at the turn of the 19th-20th century and the Perth Collegiate Institute had likewise interested itself in natural history as related to farming.

In 1900 the City of Hamilton acquired Dundurn House, former mansion of Sir Allen MacNab, Prime Minister of the United Canada (1854-1856) and opened it as a museum dedicated to His Lordship, but within a few years it had degenerated into a cabinet de curiosité, containing anything and everything including the inevitable two-headed calf. Also in Hamilton a permanent art gallery was taking shape following the organization of an Art Association in 1868.

The most isolated museum in Canada was at Fort William. It was founded in 1908 and continued in operation under the auspices of the Thunder Bay Historical Society until 1942 when it went into temporary eclipse. A miscellaneous collection comprising pioneer history, the earth sciences, and head-of-the-lake shipping was put into storage. In the same region, a small natural history museum was also in operation in Chippewa Park in 1925.

Ottawa, the capital city, saw the diminutive Bytown museum designed to pay tribute to Colonel Bye, architect of the Rideau Canal, and at Kitchener, the Mennonite culture was being preserved in the Waterloo County Historical Museum founded in 1912. Twenty years later, this second museum was still functioning on an annual budget of one hundred and fifty dollars, a sum that might be called par for the course.

The Temple Museum at Sharon in 1918 was dedicated to David Willson, a founder of a religious sect known as "The Children of Peace." The building had been originally erected in 1825.

The first museum to devote its energies to the Great Lakes Navigation was The Huron Institute Museum at Collingwood. It opened its doors in 1904, but by 1910 had added Indian relics, minerals, botanical specimens, and other assorted artifacts donated by well-meaning citizens. In the previous year, it had published a volume of Papers and Records, and received a grant of one hundred dollars a year from the Provincial government. Also in 1910, the school of mining at Queen's University, Kingston, put on display their collection of over ten thousand mineral specimens and four thousand items in the areas of geology and lithology, and on the same campus an anthropological museum and a herbarium were in operation.

In the second half of the nineteenth century the University of Toronto had various collections massed in its main building but in 1890 a fire destroyed virtually all of them. Benefitting by this tragic experience, new collections were placed in at least three buildings. A geological and mineralogical museum under the curatorship of Professor A.P. Coleman had one area; a biological collection was housed, appropriately enough, in seventy-five hundred square feet of space in the biological department; and an ethnological museum occupied the University's main building with Professor G.M. Wrong in charge. Victoria College, an affiliate, had its own collections embracing palaeontology, mineralogy, anthropology, archaeology, and "Egyptian and Indian antiquities" and it was this college which launched a building program early in the 1900's, and eventually agreed to an expansion of the program for the development of a university museum complex.

As in the case of the National Museum, and to a lesser extent the National Gallery, the story of the origin of this new edifice, later to be named The Royal Ontario Museum, is one of large personal sacrifice and dedication combined with the intense interest of a politically influential patron whose contributions both to the National Gallery and the Art Gallery of Toronto have been somewhat overshadowed.

In his book, *I Brought the Ages Home,* G.T. Currelly, first director of the Royal Ontario Museum, places its origin as a gleam in the eye of Dr. N. Burwash, president of Victoria College, as early as 1902, and speaks of the proposed institution as being initially designed for the college collection only. But with growing interest, and the 1890 disaster fresh in the minds of other faculties, the idea of a museum complex took form. It was Sir Edmund Walker who provided the essential impetus through his encouragement to Currelly for continued archaeological explorations in Europe and the Middle East and who financed out of his own purse the purchase of significant artifacts.

Sir Edmund and Dr. Currelly had known each other at school and throughout their lifetime were close friends. It was Sir Edmund, along with Sir Edmund Osler, who first approached the provincial government for funds with which to build the museum. Walker kept

143

his eye on the construction while Currelly was assembling more accessions in Europe, and interviewed, and frequently engaged staff. He also built up a mineralogy collection and spent much of his time interesting friends and colleagues in the project. Some of these such as Osler, Sir Robert Mond, Mr. and Mrs. H.D. Warren, Professor Pelham Edgar, and Dr. Sigmund Samuel, were to become active benefactors.

Even before the institution was opened, Currelly faced a continuous number of crises as he searched for and bought extensive collections at home and abroad, getting heavily in debt but continuing to be bailed out by this small coterie of dedicated people. In 1905, Currelly first broached the idea of extending the museum facilities to embrace other disciplines on the campus, Walker conspired with his colleagues to gain the consent of the Governors and Senate of the university, and the *fait accompli* was announced to the peripatetic archaeologist in December of that year while he was in Egypt, together with the good news that a purchase grant of fifteen hundred dollars had also been obtained. Currelly was to be the director of the institution, but neither salary nor expense money was forthcoming. The first wing of what was to be developed into a complex of museums under one roof was opened months before the building was completed in 1912.

From the outset the Royal Ontario Museum was designed to serve both the university and the general public. It had been strategically sited on the perimeter of the campus at the intersection of Bloor Street and Queen's Park Crescent. In 1932, the museum housed five departments, each with its own curator, in archaeology, geology, mineralogy, and zoology, and in later years it was to accommodate still more disciplines. Despite the fact that the institution has never been overly-endowed with funds and at times has occupied a very lowly place on the university appropriations program, it has consistently built up collections of international importance.

Little or no provision had been made for the accommodation of the accessions which, quite naturally, began to flood the building. Neither had thought been given to adequate accommodation for research and administrative staffs. Much of the collection of the Provincial Museum was pre-empted by the R.O.M. adding to the congestion in 1924. In 1932, wings were added to the original structure tripling the display areas but making no provision for a rapidly growing "reserve collection" or for staff requirements.

The extension program of the R.O.M. as outlined in the Dominion Bureau of Statistics report of 1937-8 was an impressive one. In cooperation with various university departments, it organized and administered field expeditions taking staff members and students to all corners of the globe. Its floor space of two hundred and sixty thousand square feet was greater than the space occupied by all the twenty Canadian museums employing professional staffs combined. It was attracting three thousand visitors weekly, averaging nine hundred and fifty-four on the three free days, and three hundred and thirty-three on days when a nominal admission fee was charged. It was not surprising that, seven years earlier, the British museum survey team had described the R.O.M. as "the largest and richest of all Canadian museums, . . .the new extensions rendering fair to make it one of the largest institutions on the North American continent."

Coincidentally with the creation of the Royal Ontario Museum, the Art Gallery of Toronto was also in a period of gestation. While Montreal was still the largest city in Canada and undoubtedly the wealthiest, Toronto was rapidly developing into a major financial hub and an important manufacturing centre. It was also attracting attention for its attainments in the field of education with its university and four affiliated colleges.

Toronto possessed a population in excess of three hundred thousand in 1910 and was rapidly being recognized as a stately residential city with large mansions surrounded by "ample lawns and abundant trees." Since the turn of the century there was also a growing interest in the arts with practising painters and prudent patrons. Public exhibitions of paintings were being held periodically by the established artists and their societies. The Ontario Society of Artists had been formed in 1872 and the Central Ontario School of Art came into being four years later. It was the Art Society's president, portrait painter G.A. Reid, who called a meeting on March 15, 1900 to discuss proposals for a permanent art gallery for the city. Byron Edmund Walker, later Sir Edmund, served as provisional chairman and three and a half months later became the first president of the somewhat nebulous Art Museum of Toronto. This museum which, for the ensuing thirteen years, was to know many homes, used the headquarters of the Ontario Society of Artists for its initial exhibitions. Eventually the trustees of the newly built public library were persuaded to design a gallery for temporary exhibitions in 1909, which was shared with the Royal Canadian Academy, the Ontario Society of Artists, and the Canadian Art Club. In November of that year an exhibition of "paintings of the English, Dutch, French and other European schools drawn from private collections in the city" attracted 12,677 visitors.

In 1903, the Museum Society had been advised that The Grange, home of Professor and Mrs. Goldwyn Smith, would be eventually bequeathed for use as an Art Gallery, but in the meantime a financial campaign had produced forty thousand dollars much of it being contributed by Founder Members who included, in addition to Sir

Edmund, the Hon. George A. Cox, J.W. Flavelle, J.W.L. Forster, Chester D. Massey, Edmund Osler, Col. Henry Pellatt, Mrs. H.D. Warren, and E.R. Wood.

Mrs. Smith died in early September 1909 and her husband nine months later. On January 1st, 1911 the property was vested in the Art Museum, and the City of Toronto developed a park area to enhance its setting. The Grange was officially opened as The Toronto Art Gallery (the original name had been changed in deference to the new Royal Ontario Museum) in June 1913, and in the ensuing two years attracted approximately four hundred thousand visitors. Three gallery areas were added to the structure in 1916 and opened to the public in March 1918. In 1924, Lord Byng, then Canada's Governor-General laid the cornerstone for the next major extension. Sir Edmund unfortunately had died in the preceding year, but the fund raising campaign had been initiated a few months earlier and the presidency turned over to R.Y. Eaton. Before his death, Sir Edmund had appointed the Hon. Vincent Massey, then Minister without Portfolio in the Mackenzie King government, to head the capital fund campaign. The sculpture court which was included in the extended gallery is dedicated to Sir Edmund.

From 1911, the year the Society obtained possession of The Grange, a collecting policy was initiated resulting in a steady growth of art works for its permanent collection. The Society also had encouraged the Canadian National Exhibition to create an art pavilion, supervised by gallery personnel and from which it received diploma works purchased by the exhibition board each year. A site adjacent to The Grange had been previously offered to the provincial government, conditionally that a building to house the Ontario School (now College) of Art would be erected. This offer was immediately accepted, along with a two hundred thousand dollar vote for the project. By 1926 the School was occupying adjacent houses.

It was at the Art Gallery of Toronto where the Group of Seven had its first highly controversial exhibition in 1920. The equally controversial Child Art Education program introduced by Dr. Arthur Lismer in the 1920's had its genesis in the same institution. With the appointment of Martin Baldwin as curator in 1932, the gallery changed direction and developed a program seeking to involve its members and the public generally. Later it was to become the first Canadian museum to introduce contemporary advertising techniques deliberately to generate controversy.

Museum proliferation was well under way after World War I. Fort Wellington, a military post in the Prescott area was pre-empted by the local historical society as a museum in 1923. At Brampton, the Perkins Bull collection, later to become the County of Peel Museum and Art Gallery, was thrown open to the public and today is listed as the first county art gallery in the province. In 1925, a museum was launched in the public library at Peterborough, and at Barrie, the Women's Institute organized the Simcoe County Museum in 1928. At the National Experimental Farm in Ottawa, an agricultural collection was started in 1930, and in the same year the National Research Council initiated an aeronautical museum, later to be taken over by other government agencies.

At Cayuga, south of Hamilton, the Haldimand Historical Society created its pioneer museum in 1934, the same year that the Norfolk Museum of Art and Antiquities opened its doors at Simcoe, a town in the same general region, later to be named the Eva Brook Donly Museum with a collection of over three hundred paintings of local scenes and portraits from the brushes of W. Edgar Cantelon, in addition to other historical memorabilia. Mohawk Chief Joseph Brant came in for more posthumous recognition in 1937 at Burlington where a replica of Brant's last home was constructed, an indication that ethnology was penetrating the consciousness of historians. At Norwich, also in south-western Ontario, a museum to perpetuate the pioneering efforts of the Mennonite culture was opened in the following year as was coincidentally the Lundy's Lane Museum at Niagara Falls, an institution occupying all of four hundred square feet of floor space on the site of a battlefield of 1812.

The recently organized Ontario Historical Society was actively encouraging museum development throughout the province and subsequently established a Museums' Section which held its own workshops in association with the annual meetings of the parent body. This signpost indicative of a new interest in museum growth could be viewed as a turning point in the history of the Canadian museum movement, insofar as the provincial society and its satellite served as a political lobby arising out of the frustrations engendered at its annual seminars. As one disillusioned delegate remarked, "We go to talk over problems but when we leave we still have them to take back with us." It required more than two decades for the lobby to become effective.

Increasingly, the society and its museums' section were involving the professionals working in the major institutions of the province but the seeds being sown had to await a more propitious moment for germination.

Radical departures from the norm in Ontario's museum policies and techniques were being discussed in the final years of the depression. In the field of the visual arts the impetus was stimulated both by the National Gallery and the Toronto Art Gallery whose programs were reaching out to the more isolated communities.

The City of London had received a bequest to be used for the

147

building of a library-art gallery complex which was formally opened in 1940. A travelling exhibition program was immediately designed to serve libraries and art societies in the smaller communities of south-western Ontario. It also established links with permanent galleries appearing in neighbouring cities.

In 1943, the City of Windsor acquired a mansion in Willistead Park and opened its own library-gallery complex which today ranks along with London and Hamilton as one of Canada's major galleries.

The University of Western Ontario at London opened its McIntosh Art Gallery in 1942, while Hart House on the University of Toronto campus became the second campus gallery in 1948, but as late as 1951 there were still only eight galleries in Ontario in the fields of fine and decorative arts. The Western Ontario circuit was regularly supplying twelve communities with travelling shows and a small art circuit had been organized in Northern Ontario to serve the more isolated communities between Sault Ste. Marie and North Bay.

Public response to the five Historic Parks developed under federal auspices in the Atlantic Provinces and Quebec was making its impact on Ontario historians in the 1930's, although recognition of such restorations as museums had to wait for a number of years. Initial emphasis was on military installation relating to the 1812 unpleasantness and the pioneer village did not make its appearance until 1954.

In 1934 the Women's Canadian Historical Society (Toronto) obtained possession of what remained of Fort York in the west end of the city with the intention of preserving it for its historical significance. Within a few years the site became the centre of controversy when proposed freeway construction threatened its demolition. The site and buildings were eventually rescued by the relatively young Toronto Historical Board and were later to become one of a chain of restorations now being administered by that civic body. The Fort comprises eight original buildings constructed during the war of 1812. Its displays depict the beginnings of the Province of Upper Canada along with the early history of the Canadian militia.

Shortly before World War II, the federal Department of Northern Affairs and Natural Resources started a series of restorations in Ontario. The first such project, Fort Malden at Amherstburg at the extreme south-western tip of the province, was a fortress constructed in the final years of the eighteenth century following the evacuation of Detroit. It was officially opened as a National Historic Park and Museum in 1941. Old Fort Henry at Kingston is another massive fortification which had served as the major military stronghold of Upper Canada and which came in for restoration by the province at about this period. It continues to function as a significant tourist
148

attraction in the summer months with a daily display of nineteenth century ceremonial drill complete with fife and drum band.

Such restorations reached almost epidemic proportions with Fort Wellington at Prescott also coming under the aegis of the federal agency. This military compound, originally built to maintain the lines of communication between Montreal and Kingston during the 1812 hostilities, had also seen service in the Mackenzie rebellion of 1838 and was garrisoned by an artillery battery at the time of the Red River troubles of 1860. It later saw more service in the Fenian raids of 1866 and housed a reserve garrison at the time of the 1885 North-west skirmishes. The restoration was completed and opened to the public in 1940.

In the same year, the Niagara Parks Commission, intent on building up tourism in their particular bailiwick, opened the Old Fort Erie Museum to the public, another testament to the 1812 confrontation with Canada's neighbour to the south, and almost simultaneously reconstructed Fort George at Niagara-on-the-Lake. This fort, built in 1796 by John Graves Simcoe, has fourteen buildings and served as the major British military establishment on this particular frontier during the War of 1812. Navy Hall, adjacent to Fort George was a third project of the Commission, a building which served as winter quarters for the Provincial Marine in the late eighteenth century and which became headquarters for Simcoe during his term of office as Lieutenant-Governor.

Although the depression was drawing to a close, museum developments remained almost at a standstill reflecting the still shrinking economy. However, for the moment the pattern was well established. The few major institutions in the larger cities struggled to keep alive on miniscule budgets. The National Museums had been subjected to drastic cut-backs in the name of political expediency, with the local historical societies continuing to hold their regular meetings where they discussed their impossible dreams and vied with each other to boast of accessions stored in the basements — awaiting the moment when a fairy godmother would appear.

The major institutions still lacked a central association to serve as an effective lobby, and what staff they had was generally recruited from the ranks of enthusiastic amateurs whose main attribute was dedication to a hopeless cause. Of the half million dollars expended by not more than one hundred institutions in Ontario, the federal government is estimated to have provided not more than two hundred thousand dollars with the province and its Crown corporations, notably the Niagara Commission and provincially administered universities, spending an equal amount. The remaining twenty per cent came from municipalities, voluntary organizations, and endowments. Fortunately, the forties saw an increase in both general interest and financial support.

17

Well over one million square miles of wilderness stretched between the more settled central region of Canada and the Rocky Mountains when Charles II extended the "beneficient despotism" of the Hudson's Bay Company for "trade and administration of justice" to include all the lands and waters "in whatever latitude they shall be, that lies within the entrance of the straits commonly called Hudson's Bay"; later to become Rupert's Land. The French likewise had eyes on what was believed to be rich and profitable regions for the fur traders and the North-West Company of Montreal raised itself in opposition from time to time.

While trading posts were soon established, these were only temporary expedients until Pierre Gaultier de Varennes, Sieur de La Vérendrye erected forts at Lake of the Woods in 1732, Fort Maurepas on Lake Winnipeg in 1733-34, and Fort Rouge at the confluence of the Assiniboine and Red Rivers where present-day Winnipeg stands, before pushing westward to the Rockies.

In 1870, when the Province of Manitoba was founded and entered Confederation, its known population was less than 19,000 but by 1901 it had grown to a quarter of a million and the land and inland water areas had been increased from 13,000 to 73,000 square miles. In the intervening thirty years, wholesale immigration policies had brought 15,000 Mennonites and about 20,000 Icelandics, and a few years later were to come Germans, Ukrainians and other Slavs to establish ethnic communities.

The French voyageurs had remained, many to cohabit with members of the Indian tribes and create their settlements to the south and west of Winnipeg as place names of the region testify. Out of this ethnic mixture came the Métis or half-breeds and Louis Riel.

Fort Rouge, shortly to be named Fort Garry, continued as the western outpost of the Hudson's Bay Company. A map circa 1910 showed six major towns or cities in addition to twelve smaller settlements and nine Hudson's Bay Trading posts.

Historians have to wait for what might be called the objective truths to emerge and so with museums. It is not surprising to discover that, while a Provincial Archives was proclaimed in 1885, its sole function was to preserve and collect public documents. It was only in 1946 that its services were officially extended to assist the Manitoba Historical Society with research and publication services.

In natural history and the earth sciences, at least one collection, "a few interesting local fossils", was on display at the Winnipeg rooms of the Historical and Scientific Society of Manitoba in 1900. A museum with a paid curator at the Agricultural College was reported in 1932 but fails to appear in subsequent directories. In 1922 the Hudson's Bay Company opened its historical exhibit on one of the upper floors of its department store in downtown Winnipeg and which can be considered as the first human history museum west of the Great Lakes. Its collections were then described as "relics of the fur trade and pioneer life with some Indian and Eskimo material, ships' models, furs, a diorama and model forts." This museum managed to cover the entire gamut of the history of Rupert's Land drawing accessions from its vast network of trading posts and factors spotted between Labrador and the Rockies.

Until 1937 the Hudson's Bay collection was divided between its Winnipeg and Vancouver stores, but in that year the artifacts were brought together in Winnipeg for recataloguing and a more ordered and specially designed display area was opened in its store there. While custodians had been employed it was not until 1938 that a professional curator was added to the staff. His duties eventually included those of librarian, researcher, and editor of the official house organ, later to become *The Beaver,* first publication in Canada dedicated to historical documentation. These developments encouraged the local historical society to work for the restoration of Ross House in the heart of Winnipeg and led to the use of the long abandoned Lower Fort Garry to serve as depository and later display area for surplus relics which Hudson's Bay factors had salvaged.

In 1905 the Zoological Garden in Assiniboine Park had a precarious beginning but as the city became financially involved it developed rapidly and by 1918 the University of Manitoba had established faculty museums of zoology and geology. During the ensuing two decades, eight scholastic institutions in Winnipeg had acquired natural history collections and were listed as having bona fide museums.

Brandon, one hundred miles to the west, had its B.J. Hales collection of natural history, comprising "fauna of the province, geological specimens and Indian relics" occupying twelve hundred square feet in the Normal School. While this collection temporarily dropped out of sight in subsequent surveys, it now is established in its own right on the campus of Brandon University.

The art scene had its own connotations. In 1876 an art society was founded in Winnipeg following the establishment of a society in Brandon. The Winnipeg group was the forererunner of the local art gallery, finding quarters in the Exposition Building of the Industrial Bureau in 1912 with the Lieutenant-Governor, in the presence of a distinguished company, officiating at the opening. In the official history of the art gallery it is recorded that the initial exhibition, loaned by the National Gallery of Canada, consisted of two hundred and thirty paintings from the Royal Canadian Academy collection and that "three of its most respected members, Homer Watson, Maurice Cullen and F.C. Challoner, had come from the east (which) certainly underlined the importance the organizers and the art world gave to the event."

Other exhibitions shown at this time suggest a lively and catholic interest as collections included one from the British Colonial Association, Dutch Masters, original drawings from English publishing houses, and a comprehensive exhibition of Scottish art presumably arranged by its first gallery director, A.J. Musgrove, who had recently arrived from Scotland to serve in the dual capacity of curator and principal of the newly organized art school. Two artists who later had associations with The Group of Seven, Francis H. Johnson and Lemoyne L. FitzGerald, had earlier filled curatorial roles.

Among the younger artists associated with the gallery who later achieved national and international fame were Walter J. Phillips, watercolourist and printmaker, Frank Brigden, known mainly for his watercolours, and Dr. Charles Comfort who eventually joined the faculty of the University of Toronto from which he resigned to become Director of the National Gallery of Canada and who had his first one-man show in Winnipeg in 1910.

For its first ten years the gallery was administered by the Board of Trade but in 1923 the Art Gallery and Art School were formally incorporated as an independent entity. However, two years later an annual grant from the city was discontinued and the gallery was forced to close. Exhibitions were continued regularly in local department stores or in the corridors of the Art School and in 1933 the gallery was revitalized when it was offered space in the new Civic Auditorium complex, a building which deserves to be preserved as a prime example of architectural ineptitude and of civic relief works planning. The gallery originally occupied "one half of the corridor on the third floor," a corridor which served as upper floor foyer and emergency fire exit from the adjacent auditorium. Gallery officials were strictly forbidden to hold any activities in the

152

gallery area at times when the auditorium was in use.

A bequest of twenty-nine paintings to the gallery association influenced the city to make more space available and three years later a second bequest of ninety paintings from the estate of the late James Cleghorn resulted in a second area being set aside in the same building for gallery display. Included also in the Civic Auditorium were two widely separated areas to accommodate a recently organized natural and human history museum administered by a community association "and for thirty-three years, in spite of unrealistic budgets, limited facilities and an almost inaccessible location (a parallel corridor to that of the gallery, serving also as fire exit and foyer and subjected to the same restrictions), the association managed to maintain a small but scientifically sound museum." While the major emphasis was in the field of natural history, another area, on the main floor corridor, was later made available for ethnic and pioneer historical exhibits.

The first federal relationship with museums in Manitoba occurred in 1933 with the opening of a nature centre and museum in Riding Mountain National Park, near Wasagaming, and at that time accessible only over a dirt road north of Minnedosa. Now it is only one hour's drive on black top from the Trans-Canada Highway at Brandon.

Saskatchewan and Alberta were admitted into Confederation on September 1, 1905, at which time the joint population was somewhat less than half a million, including the aboriginal tribes. These two new provinces each occupied approximately a quarter of a million square miles of what had been part of the North-West Territories and Rupert's Land. Fifteen years later Saskatchewan had tripled its population, Alberta lagging behind with still less than 600,000. The influx of population coincided with the throwing open of lands for homesteading, but the Alberta foothills country was still reserved for the ranching fiefdoms which had been in existence since 1802.

Early explorers had penetrated across the prairies in the second half of the seventeenth century but major colonization did not get under way until after the survey of Palliser and others. Toward the end of the nineteenth century, Russian and Ukrainian immigrants began moving into this region, intent on establishing their own self-contained, and at times insular settlements such as the Doukhobors, eight thousand of whom were given lands in the Prince Albert area of Saskatchewan in 1899. The Slav immigrants, encouraged by railway interests, tended to settle in colonies in the more northerly regions. This was also the country for the remittance men, younger sons of a highly prolific British aristrocracy, with migrants also coming from the Dakotas, Iowa, and the grain-growing states to the immediate south.

As late as 1910 there were only two cities in Saskatchewan. Regina, founded in 1907 as the provincial capital, had then a population of just under ten thousand, and Moose Jaw, forty miles to the west had about six thousand inhabitants. Saskatoon, later to become the second largest city, was a town of three thousand. Prince Albert, which at one time had hoped to be the provincial capital, was the fourth largest incorporated municipality.

The Hudson's Bay Company, now long merged with the North-West Company, built and mounted its forts at strategic points to protect its traders and trade from what was viewed as unfair and immoral competition by the whiskey runners from the south.

The process of colonization did not permit anything but the bare essentials for survival – food, clothing, shelter – all of which made necessary wagon trails leading to crude roads and on to the nearest settlement. It was essentially a man's world but soon came the church, followed closely by the school house serving also as community centre.

As in the Maritime provinces and Quebec a century or so earlier, the study of the natural resources of the immediate region was tied in with this need for survival. Once the Indian tribes had been pacified, subjugated, and segregated, the victors collected their souvenirs as the initial step toward a naive story of the civilizing processes.

There were individual collectors of artifacts but there was virtually no museum growth in Saskatchewan until after World War I. A Provincial Archives had been created in Regina in 1913 but its function was primarily to preserve and catalogue official government documents. However, only one year after the province had entered Confederation, a natural history collection had been assembled and officially named as a provincial institution. By 1932, the collection occupied six thousand square feet of space in the legislative building and had a staff of three.

The University of Saskatchewan in Saskatoon had collections of art, biology, geology, and human history, including archaeology prior to 1910, and shortly after hostilities overseas were at an end, the student body of the Nutana Collegiate in Saskatoon established an art collection in a permanent gallery area as a memorial to its World War I casualties.

At Bulyea, forty miles north of Regina, a museum was launched in 1921. Its direct descendent reopened in expanded quarters in 1967 to celebrate Canada's Centennial, this in a community which has yet to qualify as being an incorporated municipality and with a population of less than one thousand.

In Prince Albert, the most northerly community of any size, a

154

local Historical Society opened a museum which was reported to have collections of pioneer artifacts in addition to Indian and Eskimo relics but was confined to a floor space of six hundred square feet. Ten years later the collection had been taken out of circulation and by 1966 its whereabouts was unknown. In the same city one of the most outstanding yet smallest displays of wild life in Canada was created by a former superintendent of the Prince Albert National Park. In 1934 within the park at Waskesiu a Nature Centre was established by the park authorities.

The political history of Prince Albert is unique insofar as it was a focal point in the struggle of the Métis under Louis Riel. It was also viewed at one time as a logical city to serve as capital of the new province, and it is the only constituency in Canada to have elected three Prime Ministers: Laurier, Mackenzie King, and Diefenbaker.

The first community museum in Canada to devote its entire display area to palaeontology was at Eastend, a small and isolated community in the Cypress Hills region of Saskatchewan where the explorations of an amateur palaeontologist, H.S. Jones, uncovered significant fossil deposits in the early 1900's. A museum was organized to house his finds in 1921 and later these were placed in corridor areas of a new consolidated school. At Shaunavon in the same region, the local Canadian Club opened the Grand Coteau Museum in 1922 with emphasis on natural history and the earth sciences, while at Maple Creek, gateway to Cypress Hills, a pioneer museum was founded in 1930. All three institutions are still functioning.

The North-West Mounted Police force was established in 1893 made up of a five hundred man unit, many of whom were British expatriates, for policing the North-West Territories and with headquarters in Regina. The force was granted the use of the prefix "Royal" in 1904, and in 1920 when it had absorbed the already established Dominion Police, headquarters were transferred to Ottawa but the training school remained. A museum, which until recently placed more emphasis on crime and criminals than on the traditions of a police force unique throughout the world, was opened at the training centre in 1934. Now with a professional curator and a greatly enlarged area the new administration had relegated the sometime grisly exhibits of man-hunts and murders to the storeroom in favour of material relating to less spectacular but more significant achievements of the Red Coats.

Fort Battleford, another link with the R.C.M.P., relates to the social and historical impact of the Riel Rebellion, an impact which was all but lost following the abandonment of the fort in 1903. The fort was subjected to wholesale theft and vandalism before "outraged citizens" attempted restoration with the aid of provincial funds. Agitation for federal assistance resulted in the National Historic Sites Service moving in. Restoration in depth was undertaken and the fort reopened this time as a museum *in situ* on July 1, 1951, while at Batoche, scene of the Riel uprising of 1884-85, the federal department restored a segment of the 'zareba' in which grave markers of Métis killed in the battle of Batoche are preserved, together with the church and rectory of St. Antoine de Padoue, built in 1884.

In the first thirty years of Saskatchewan's life, sixteen museums were opened including the campus collections at the University of Saskatchewan, the art display at Nutana College, a school museum at Meunster, and community museums at Bulyea, Swift Current, and Yorkton.

Alberta was a late-starter in the museum field, for its free-booting early inhabitants (exlcuding the aborigines) were too busy creating a colourful historical background to concern themselves with cultural growth.

The federal government planned a Natural History exhibit for the new Rocky Mountain National Park as early as 1893. Two years later a small collection of minerals, plants, birds, and mammals was installed in a wooden building "of bungalow style." The collection was moved in 1899 to a combined museum and administration office building. An entry in the 1910 Museum Directory published by the Buffalo (New York) Society of Natural Sciences states that space used for exhibitions measured three thousand one hundred and twenty-eight square feet with only four hundred and ninety-one square feet for offices and workrooms. The museum even had a curator, a Mr. N.B. Sanson, and was "supported by grants from the Dominion Government which vary in amount." A small research library developed and by 1908 annual attendance was climbing to around ten thousand. The museum, augmented somewhat but now almost neglected, occupies a wooden structure on Banff's main street.

The new University of Alberta in Edmonton had built up a respectable geological collection by 1914. Other collections associated with the sciences could also be found on the campus. The two normal (teacher training) schools at Camrose and Calgary both boasted displays which were open to the general public in the late 1920's.

The Edmonton Art Society in 1924 was given space for a permanent display area in rooms beyond the cashiers' cages in the civic block, moving in the mid 1940's to an equally illogical but more practical area in the municipal baby clinic.

In Calgary a museum, financed by minuscule funds from the city

156

exchequer, got under way in 1911 receiving seven mentions in the Miers-Markham report of 1932 for being one of the few institutions in Canada seeking to involve schools and pointing also to the fact that one area had been set aside for art gallery purposes "in which to display exhibitions of paintings by local artists." It was one of five museums in Canada which was municipally financed but the survey team deplored the absence of a qualified curator.

This museum was typical of its period, being located in a decrepit downtown office-warehouse building adjacent to skid row and one block removed from the tacitly accepted brothel district. An exposed half-section of a beehive occupied the better part of the small window facing the street with bees actively doing their thing but the interior was dingy, illuminated by unshaded light bulbs. Its main floor was devoted to dinosaur bones, fossils, Indian artifacts, antiquities, and curiosities, along with a well ordered and extensive display of entomological specimens. Stuffed animals and birds were on show in the basement. The art gallery space was, in 1928-29, housing several paintings and sculpture pieces which formed the nucleus of a civic art collection with the local Art Society bringing small collections from the National Gallery and other agencies from time to time. The museum was listed in the 1937 report of the Dominion Bureau of Statistics, but its activities had been discontinued two years earlier by the city "as an economy measure" and the contents dispersed with no record kept as to their disposition.

Dr. O.H. Patrick, colliery owner and entrepreneur, conceived the idea of a zoological garden in 1927, persuading city council to turn over the island of Saint George in the eastern sector of the city to him. The doctor devoted time, energy and money into building up the collections of mammals reptiles, and birds but found the city fathers singularly disinterested in helping to finance the project. A small coterie of interested citizens joined Dr. Patrick, and in 1932 the dedicated and enthusiastic founder turned his attention to the creation of a palaeontological park on the same grounds, importing carloads of fossil remains, including petrified wood and dinosaur bones from the Alberta Badland country to the south-east of the province, and building at his own expense two fossil houses in which to display the smaller pieces. With the active assistance of Charles Sternberg, then palaeontologist at the National Museum of Canada, cement dinosaur replicas, ranging from the giant brontesaurus to the diminutive pterodactylus, and eventually totalling fifty specimens, were displayed in a simulated environment.

A small privately owned museum in Galt Gardens, Lethbridge attracted visitors in the 1920's, and remained active for approximately twenty years before the retirement of the owner. At St. Albert, north of Edmonton, the Father Lacombe Museum and Shrine was opened in 1928 in the restored home (c.1861) of the reverend father, and tells of the missionary work of the Oblate Fathers.

As in other parts of Canada the Depression and war years served as effective deterrents to further museum developemnt. The provincial government, however, did set up in the cupola of its legislative building an archives of sorts. Privately owned collections are known to have been available had public interest been awakened but major projects which had been discussed in the brief period of affluence of the 1920's were shelved and forgotten.

Alberta, and to a lesser degree Saskatchewan, began to feel the full effects of the Depression in the spring of 1930. At the same time the first grain combines made their appearance. However, along with the combines came drought and insect defoliation, effectively wiping out what had been a prosperous agrarian economy. This situation, which prevailed until the advent of World War II, was a traumatic experience for Albertans and one which not only developed sociological overtones, some of which are still obvious, but also saw wholesale migrations. Many farmers left their devastated wastelands to travel by Bennett Buggy to the mountains or north to resettle in what today is known as the Peace River block.

British Columbia has a lengthy and colourful history and an equally rich cultural heritage. While the west coast Indian tribes developed a highly sophisticated folk art through totemic symbolism, the Spanish explorers who landed on Vancouver Island in 1774 brought with them the techniques upon which modern agriculture is founded. Captain Cook's survey of the entire coast line of British Columbia closely followed by a second survey conducted by Captain Vancouver are historic landmarks and it was a few years later that, rather than fight over the spoils, the North-West Company merged with the Hudson's Bay Company to rule this territory of 366,000 square miles. By 1901 the population had reached 190,000, thirteen per cent of which were Chinese whose contribution to the development of Canada's west coast economy is only now being given a somewhat grudging recognition.

In 1849 Vancouver Island was proclaimed a British Colony and following the first gold rush of 1858 the mainland territory was added, with the colony entering Confederation in 1871 as the sixth region to be admitted. Unlike its sister provinces in the West, British Columbia was a pioneer in museum development. The Provincial Museum was founded in Victoria in 1887 and its Public Archives opened eleven years later. In 1897 the Provincial Department of Mines had an extensive display of mineralogy. In Vancouver's Stanley Park, a zoological garden was created in 1886 later to be expanded into one of the major zoos in the Dominion. The origin of the Provincial Museum at Victoria follows a well-known pattern of one man's dedication.

Jack Fannin, born at Kempville, Ontario in 1837 had shown early interest in natural history. He was attracted west in 1862 after hearing the stories of major gold discoveries in the Cariboo but faced disillusionment. However, he turned his prospecting experience to good use when he was appointed head of the Provincial Department of Surveys. Throughout his travels, Fannin collected specimens and accumulated twelve cases of birds and mammals which he turned over to the province as the nucleus for a proposed museum. Fannin was appointed its first curator on the 25th of October 1886, his personal collection filling a fifteen by twenty foot room in one of the government buildings.

One year later, in his first annual report, the curator announced that "slightly over five hundred names have been recorded" of interested visitors. Thirteen years later, the collections had outgrown their initial home and were transferred to more commodious quarters in the Supreme Court building. In 1897, they were again moved, this time to the east wing of the newly constructed legislative building where a wing had been expressly designed for museum purposes. John Fannin retired due to ill health on February 13th, 1904, dying a few months later.

By 1921 the institution had once again been expanded with additional space in the basement of the existing premises being utilised. By 1928 reserve collections had found temporary (if thirty years can be considered temporary) storage space in the attic. The museum was launched primarily for natural history with concentration on birds, mammals, and marine life of the west coastal regions. With the appointment of more professional staff the earth sciences and the cultural heritage of the west coast Indian tribes became of major concern and by 1932 a rich ethnological collection had been ammassed.

The Archives of British Columbia, which had been established by the Act of the Legislature in 1898 and which occupied an adjacent area in the legislative building, quite early fulfilled a dual role as custodian of pioneer history, collecting not only manuscripts, books, maps, prints, and photographs, but also pioneer relics, and important works of fine art, thus complementing the program of the adjacent museum.

Victoria and its neighbouring municipalities which make up the metropolitan area have become a mecca for the entrepreneur interested in the tourist dollar resulting in a proliferation of attractions, frequently called museums which are frankly commercial in character. Out of this group at least one may be considered as worthy of mention.

159

Buchart Gardens, internationally famous for its botanical displays, is one attraction whose present owners are quite happy to have it viewed for tourists rather than even a distant relative of the museums. Located at Brentwood, about fifteen miles east of Victoria, it has a fascinating history. Its founder, Mrs. Robert P. Buchart, a pioneer anti-pollutionist, despite the fact that her husband was despoiling the environment through quarrying operations, sought to offset the spreading blight with a landscaping program in the quarries being excavated in the interests of Portland Cement. Eventually the beautified landscape was thrown open to the general public as a hospitable gesture and immediately became a major attraction to out-of-town visitors. Toward 1904, Mr. and Mrs. Buchart offered the entire botanical estate to citizens of the region as a gift with the proviso that it be maintained and the policy of public admission continued. The citizens in their collective wisdom and speaking through their municipal voice rejected the civic gesture. Had the municipalities involved taken up the offer, the two dollar admission fee now charged and paid by hundreds of thousands of visitors each year would be providing considerable tax relief. In 1951, the *Garden Journal,* official publication of the New York Botanical Garden, pronounced Buchart Gardens as "the outstanding showplace of the Pacific Northwest."

For the most part, other museum developments, both on Vancouver Island and in the lower Mainland, had to wait until the late 1920's. One exception was the Vancouver City Museum which was in the planning stage in 1892 but failed to open its doors until 1903. This institution after a spectacular launching began to languish as civic grants were curtailed and disagreements arose between members of a quasi-civic board of trustees drawn from city council and the local Historical Society. The museum which was first located at Dunn Hall on Granville Street later moved to the old Carnegie Library on Main Street. At the official opening of its second location visitors were exposed to "pictures and curios" including "skulls, bones, teeth and sea beasts, dried and in skeleton form with birds being added shortly thereafter." The collection eventually included "over one million sea shells and one million and sixty thousand other items."

In the period just prior to the stock market crash of 1929, the Native Sons and Daughters of British Columbia, an organization concerned with the preservation of the province's history, began work on restoration of Fort Langley (a former Hudson's Bay post); the Nanaimo Bastion; the Old Hastings Mill Store on Vancouver's Alma Road; and the Craigflower Schoolhouse on Admiral's Road in the Esquimalt-View Royal district near Victoria. These four restorations represent the first conscious step to develop historical museums at the community level.

Despite this sudden surge of museum growth in the province the 1932 survey listed only nine institutions including those previously mentioned and the Ethnological Museum on the campus of the University of British Columbia. The ninth institution was described as "the charming art gallery built in 1932 (on West Georgia Street), well designed and housing an interesting collection of fine art due to the generosity of Mr. H.A. Stone and other citizens." This Vancouver gallery was one of nineteen in Canada which employed professional staff.

Six years later, the Dominion Bureau of Statistics added five more institutions to their listings; the isolated Museum of Northern British Columbia at Prince Rupert, overlooked in the 1932 survey, a Geological Museum on the University of British Columbia campus, the now celebrated Vancouver Public Archives, as well as two school museums, one at Duncan on Vancouver Island, the other at Vernon in the heart of the Okanagan.

The Lipsett Collection of historical paintings by John Innes was opened in 1941 in the British Columbia Building on Vancouver's P.N.E. Grounds. In Victoria, as annexes to the Provincial Archives, the restored Helmcken House was opened in 1942 to memorialize one of Victoria's pioneer medical men. The same year Thunderbird Park was created, an open-air display of Community House, Totem Poles and other artifacts of the Kwakiutl tribe, and which saw the initiation of the first museum activities program in Canada.

18

From the first years of the nineteenth century to the mid-twentieth century, museum development in Canada had been sporadic. In the Bulletin of the New York State Museum (1903) a listing of only twenty-one museums in Canada was published. Of these, six were in the Maritime provinces, one in Quebec City and three in Montreal, nine in Ontario and one each in Manitoba and British Columbia. The Acadia College Museum at Wolfville, Nova Scotia, was described as "the most instructive and attractive in Nova Scotia." The Provincial Museum in Halifax had, in addition to extensive collections in the various sciences, "specimens relating to the various industries; a numismatic collection; some local historic specimens; and a few oil portraits of merit."

F.J.H. Merrill, compiler of the directory, also recorded that fifteen institutions were associated with scholastic establishments. Four of these were on the University of Toronto campus and two on the campus of Queen's, with the Universities of New Brunswick, Acadia, Dalhousie, McGill, and Laval each having one museum. Three museums were administered by provincial authorities, at Halifax, Toronto and Victoria, and the National Geological Survey was a federal responsibility. The Newfoundland museum was also included as an adopted child through its geological survey of the colonial administration. Only the museums of the Montreal Natural History Society and the Hamilton Scientific Association were admisistered by community organizations. As the Directory dealt only with natural history the overall picture of Canadian museum growth is incomplete insofar as there were museums housing fine and decorative arts and the beginnings of institutions featuring military and pioneer history.

A 1910 survey reported on forty-one institutions, disclosing an increase of two in Ontario, ten in Quebec, two in New Brunswick, four in Nova Scotia, one in British Columbia, and the first museum on the Prairies in the Rocky Mountain National Park at Banff.

Both of these reports were far from complete; instance the fact of the Pictou Academy collection which still existed in 1932. In addition the Des Brisay collection at Bridgewater, Nova Scotia, by this time almost a half century old, went unreported. In the adjacent province the Owens Art Gallery at Sackville had been functioning for at least two decades. In Quebec the omissions were even more numerous, as well before the end of the century museums had existed in seminaries at Joliette, Ste-Anne-de-la Pocatière, Sherbrooke, Sillery, St. Hyacinthe and Trois Rivieres. In Montreal the Musée de l'Institution des Sourds-muets had been in operation since 1885, while in Ontario there were museums in Hamilton, Niagara-on-the-Lake, and Stoney Creek.

The museum picture twenty-two years later was eloquently described in the Miers-Markham report which had been financed by the Carnegie Corporation. In the interim, Canada had been involved in World War I, a war which had threatened to split Confederation wide open but which had also brought unexpected prosperity as wartime industries were founded. There had followed industrial strife, for example the Winnipeg general strike of 1919. There had also been an influx of wheat growing farmers and a takeover of much of the ranching lands in the Alberta foothills country. In addition, the development of mineral and coal resources in the Maritimes, Northern Ontario and Quebec, and the industrialization of central Canada, all had made possible a population explosion.

The Miers-Markham report arrived at an inopportune moment following the disastrous stock market crash of 1929 which was making its impact felt on the Canadian economy and social mores. The first combines had been successfully demonstrated in the wheatlands and this factor, coupled with depression, drought and pest defoliation brought to an end the "harvester excursions." Mineral production had more than doubled in the thirty years from 1901. Manufacturing had increased five-fold but a fiscal system which had developed wide speculation had conspired to plunge Canada into seven years of depression. The paper millionaires of 1927, who might eventually have become patrons and benefactors, had, some literally and others figuratively, wiped themselves out. Although Messrs. Miers and Markham made no mention of this situation, one could hardly expect their report to be any more than pessimistic. Their survey listed one hundred and twenty-five institutions; twenty-three of these were west of the Great Lakes, sixteen in the Maritimes (excluding Newfoundland), thirty-seven in Ontario and forty-nine in Quebec. Included were, "the national and provincial museums, also such of those belonging to societies as are accessible to the public (with) the teaching museums being included so far as they are accessible not only to students, but also to the general public."

Commenting on museum conditions across the Dominion, the sur-

163

vey team found in British Columbia and the three Prairie Provinces that "comparatively little has been done by the provincial and municipal governments to provide a museum service. . .and, in the matter of art, the three (Prairie) provinces are even worse provided. The only public gallery is at Edmonton (which) has received some support from the city and is granted the use of two rooms in the city block."

In the Maritime provinces the only bright spots were "the new museum at Saint John, New Brunswick, the Archives of Halifax and the Provincial Museum in the same city." The latter "although congested and disordered, contains much material and might be made into a good museum." The Saint John Museum, it was pointed out, "contains a children's department, which is at present unique among Canadian museums."

Ontario, the report continued, had in addition to the National Museum and Gallery and the Public Archives in Ottawa; a Provincial Museum in Toronto used largely by teachers and scholars; campus museums at the Universities of Ottawa and Toronto; and "The Royal Ontario Museum, which is now the largest and richest of all Canadian museums. . . and so administered and displayed that its collection cannot fail to be of educational value to all visitors."

It was also discovered that the existence of the Ontario Historical Society had stimulated museum growth in the more remote areas through the previous decade. The report added that "seven of these society collections are housed in odd rooms of Public Libraries, generally in the basement, but five others have their own separate buildings. However, all these society museums are comparatively small and. . .should not be over-emphasized." In no case did any of them employ a paid curator; "all are honorary and do the work of amateurs rather than experts, generally with the help of a caretaker." The average annual expenditure did not greatly exceed one hundred dollars.

The exceptions, however, were noted. The Howard House, now listed as Colborne Lodge in Toronto, was receiving financial support from the city, and the Waterloo Historical Society's museum (no longer listed) had an annual grant from the municipality of one hundred and fifty dollars with the Society providing cases and curator, the Public Library Board donating utility costs, together with accommodation, the local Department of Education handling printing costs, and "with small grants also from the adjacent cities of Galt and Kitchener."

Reviewing their tour through Quebec, the two British museologists, Miers-Markham, mention that "most of the colleges and seminaries administered by religious orders have a museum which indi-

164

cates a wide-spread appreciation of their value (but) at the same time, it must be admitted that the technical standard is not high, since the expenditure is nominal, the curatorship is honorary, and few of the curators have any special qualifications for the work." Apart from these study collections, forty-nine institutions were listed as bona fide and open to the public. Twenty-two of these were administered by religious orders; of the remaining twenty-seven, ten were on the McGill University campus (and presumably open to visitors) but "presenting little to attract the general public." The survey added that "there are, however, already vigorous indications of far-reaching improvements which may extend also to interesting collections of the Chateau de Ramezay and those of the Art Association of Montreal."

This book-length report, which signally failed to attract the attention of politicians, public or press, or even museum personnel, decried the lack of support given to museums and galleries from coast to coast but offered many constructive suggestions and hopefully saw a greater growing interest which might blossom forth as Canada developed into a more or less independent nation.

Commenting on facilities in the larger cities, the report gave a somewhat dim view of existing conditions remarking that "in Montreal, Toronto, Winnipeg, Vancouver, Hamilton and Ottawa, all great and growing centres with populations exceeding 125,000, and in Calgary also, with a population of 85,000, there are public museums of considerable size, but with the exception of Toronto and Ottawa, none really worthy of their province and country." In London and Windsor, the report continues, "adequate museums are entirely lacking. Each of these towns has more than trebled in population in the last thirty years; the next thirty years will probably see each with its population doubled again, and it would seem that the time is now ripe for bold and consistent planning to meet the future. As yet in neither Montreal nor Winnipeg nor Hamilton nor London is there any visible sign that the civic authorities are even aware of the importance of museums, and the combined effort of the four does not equal, either in energy or finance, that of some of the smaller towns of Great Britain or the U.S.A.

"In Winnipeg, since the control of natural resources has been handed over to the province, materials have been collected for a comprehensive exhibit illustrating the natural resources, if and when a museum can ever be established. . . .In Vancouver the public museum is poorly housed and overcrowded but the new art gallery is most appropriate to its purpose." Of Ottawa "the political heart of a vigorous and prosperous nation," they found "a city scarcely equalled on the American continent for the beauty of its surroundings or the dignity of its public buildings, containing within it the

National Museum of Canada, the fine collections of the National Gallery and the Dominion Archives. Of these, the National Museum is, in our opinion, handicapped by its peculiar administration. The present accommodation is sadly inadequate for the immediate and most urgent requirements. . .and the National Gallery too is somewhat cramped."

Summarizing this depressing picture, the visiting authorities recognized that "Canada has not been very long in the collectors' field, that her educational museums are embryonic, and that her museum endowments are negligible. If these points are borne in mind, one is bound to feel the utmost admiration for what has been accomplished against almost insuperable odds by a few enthusiastic individuals," adding that "less is spent on the whole group of one hundred and twenty-five institutions than is spent upon one of the great museums of Great Britain, Germany or the United States. . . By contrast the museum expenditure of Chicago's Field Museum (a heavily endowed institution) is more than twice as much as all the museums and art galleries of Canada put together."

The American Museum of Natural History in New York had, in the mid nineteen-thirties, an endowment income of $577,000 annually, revenue from local taxes amounting to $300,000 and an additional sum of like amount from subscriptions and voluntary donations. It would take another quarter of a century before conditions in Canada would materially improve.

This report had one important aftermath. The Educational Branch of the Dominion Bureau of Statistics was made aware of the development of a relatively new cultural force and conducted its own first museum census five years later. To a large degree this report complemented the conclusions of the earlier survey, and might have created considerable concern had its publication not been delayed until the final year of the Depression and just a few months prior to the declaration of World War II.

This new survey, officially listed as "Educational Bulletin No. 4 1938," concentrated largely on museum services, financing, and staffing. It also revealed that the total estimated budgets of all museums, art galleries, historic parks, and archives in Canada "is considerably less than one million dollars annually." Seven institutions were administered by federal authorities; six of the nine provinces administered or helped to finance a total of twelve institutions; and two corporations, Bell Telephone of Montreal and Hudson's Bay Company of Winnipeg, had opened Company museums with a total staff of two.

An editorial comment pointed to the fact that "on a per capita basis the expenditure on museums is eight or nine cents, compared with about twenty-eight cents for public libraries," and added a further comment by comparing the low per capita cost against $3.77 per capita (in 1937) and not including amusement tax, spent on motion pictures, which the anonymous writer called "another variety of visual education and entertainment."

The possible training of museum staffs was investigated. It was learnt that a bilingual course in museum techniques had been given at McGill University in 1933, but the general feeling among museum personnel was that "wages paid across the country were not sufficiently remunerative to make possible to spend any part of income on such a visionary project."

The years of the Depression and six years of war had a profound effect on Canadians, perhaps more so than in older and more settled countries. Throughout this period there was a radical change in the political climate. Reluctantly government had to face issues for which there were no precedents. Social and welfare legislation was hastily passed; relief works introduced; moratoriums and other measures designed as temporary expedients were adopted. Politically through these fifteen years Canada was evolving out of colonialism to become a member of the Commonwealth of Nations, and still later to achieve recognition as a young but energetic international power. Canada had a seat at the San Francisco conference where the United Nations was born, but prior to that the Dominion government had made its own declaration of war, delaying this action in order to assert its own token independence in external affairs.

In 1941, the government initiated a policy for the appointment of High Commissioners and Ambassadors and in 1952 it established its own permanent delegation at NATO headquarters. In that same year Canada demanded, and got the right to nominate a native born Governor-General with a commitment that such nomination would be acceptable to the British Crown.

IV

Canadian Renaissance
And The New Look

*A National Consciousness,
Cultural Maturity,
Centennial Celebrations,
and the Centennial
Aftermath*

19

The salutary lessons learned throughout the Depression combined with the political responsibilities and rapid expansion of industrial plants during the war years, brought the nation out of its period of adolescence into mature nationhood, but still with slender apron strings attached to Westminster. It was also at this time that a new economic colonization was taking shape, as much needed capital was poured into the country from the United States while British capital was being discreetly withdrawn.

Canada's assertion of sovereignty was reflected in the development of a new historical consciousness and a richer cultural pattern. The Canadian Broadcasting Corporation had been founded as early as 1932 and the National Film Board seven years later, both corporations providing a modicum of encouragement to creative and interpretive artists.

While museums and art gallery developments were virtually at a standstill the ferment continued. Canadian authors were struggling for exposure and a national Authors' Association was born. In the first year of the 1930's a Dominion Drama Festival was launched, playwriting competitions were announced in Ottawa and Edmonton, while from coast to coast community art, literary, ballet, and music groups came into being.

A proposal to organize a national Museums' Association initiated by Dr. H. O. McCurry, Director of the National Gallery, was discussed in 1939 but the outbreak of war saw the plans shelved, to be revived eight years later by Dr. McCurry in association with Dr. F. H. Alcock of the National Museum and Gérard Morisset of the Musée du Québec at a one day meeting held in Quebec City. Fourteen museums had direct representation with five others from more distant regions sending proxies in lieu of attendance. The Director of the British Columbia Provincial Museum sent apologies and advised his colleagues that his absence was due to the fact that he had been unable to get an expense account authorized for such an extended trip.

170

The Canadian Arts Council was founded in 1945 following a series of preliminary meetings which had started in 1941. That year Dr. Lawren Harris, founder member of the Group of Seven, made a nation wide lecture tour on behalf of the recently organized and short lived Federation of Canadian Artists, advocating the building of cultural centres in Canadian cities as a post-war project. Dr. Harris visualized complexes to house both visual and performing arts along with museums and other related activities. A citizens' committee in Calgary took up the challenge but had to content itself with a pilot experiment.

There were other signs of cultural consciousness in Canada as citizens sought to readjust following the austerities of Depression and combat, much in the manner of a long delayed infant bursting from the womb to demand, in a language not even known to itself, both attention and sustenance. Members of the performing arts were, quite naturally, the most persistent and vocal, producing shows quite frequently which were more often than not immature and of dubious artistic quality.

Writers there were, seeking to interpret the Canadian scene but finding that their manuscripts were rejected because there was no such thing as a paying Canadian audience. Painters and sculptors were still searching for patrons who had faith in new forms of expression. A.Y. Jackson wrote, "We never put prices on our paintings because, what's the use, no one buys them anyway."

"The Group" had made their slight dent in the international cultural scene at Wembley. The Hart House Quartet, a foursome which included Boris Hambourg, member of a distinguished musical family, and which had Vincent Massey as its patron, had also made the occasional appearance abroad in the 1920's in addition to subsidized visits to some of the isolated regions of Canada, even as far north as Timmins, Ontario in 1926, but the tendency on the part of press and public was to denigrate Canadian creativity in the arts.

Nine Canadian composers entered competitions in the fine arts class at the 1948 Summer Olympics, the same Olympics where Barbara Ann Scott skated off with the gold medal. Miss Scott received red banner headlines in the nation's press and a ticker-tape parade through downtown Ottawa climaxed with a gift of a gold-plated Buick for bringing fame and renown to Canada. Her fellow Ontarian, Professor John Weinsweig, a member of the Royal Conservatory of Music faculty, won the highest (silver medal) award in his particular class for his Divertimento No. 1 for solo flute and string orchestra; this singular and unique triumph merited all of two paragraphs over the Canadian Press.

The Canadian Arts Council which had instigated the entries records that "only a few of the compositions had ever been played by

Canadian orchestras and none had been published." When questioned recently about the reception of his achievement, Professor Weinsweig confessed that he had been overlooked as a guest star in the parade and had failed even to receive a pair of silver-plated civic cufflinks; however "my work subsequently was published – in England, [and] has since become my most widely performed work and a repertoire piece in Canada."

Fritz Brantner, Montreal painter, got honorable mention at the same Olympics with an oil dedicated to Canada's national sport entitled "Breakaway." Mr. Brantner's success also went unheralded. The Arts Division of the International Olympics, incidentally, was terminated in 1952.

In the field of history, the comment that the only definitive history of Canada had been written by the American, Francis Parkman, could now be replaced by a statement of Dr. Hilda Neatby who in 1950 wrote "The professional [Canadian] historian, operating almost exclusively within university walls. . .has produced a sound and creditable, if not distinguished volume of work, but he has produced it too exclusively for an academic public. He has not reached or touched the Canadian people." The author, a distinguished historian in her own right, added a footnote to the effect that "it must be remembered, of course, that much of this work is done outside Canada. Two leading workers in Canadian history today are Canadians, professors in American universities writing and publishing in the United States."

The ferment resulted in other forms of expression. In 1949, Prime Minister the Rt. Hon. Louis Stephen Saint Laurent appointed a Royal Commission on National Development in the Arts, Letters, and Sciences which two years later produced its 517 page report, itself a masterpiece of prose. Another volume, titled *Royal Commission Studies,* had been published a few months earlier which contained essays by distinguished and knowledgeable Canadians dealing with the contemporary scene in the arts and humanities.

In the Report, the chapter dealing with museums quoted extensively from the Miers-Markham report of 1932. The Commissioners emphasized that the comments had been written two decades earlier but added their own devastating footnote which said in part that "We assume that it was thought that Canadians, if informed of this regrettable situation, would take immediate measures to correct it. No such measures were taken. We believe that during our own admittedly superficial survey of a matter, which, important as it is, lies only on the periphery of our Terms of Reference, there appeared the first evidence of general public concern for museums since the publication of the [Miers-Markham] report. Those who compare the record of our own impressions with the findings of the [1932] report will see that the present shows little if any sign of improvement. The annual per capita expenditure in terms of real value has probably decreased. Canada's relative importance in the world has decidedly increased. If our distinguished visitors of twenty years ago could then reproach us for being blind to our responsibilities as a 'leading nation,' it is perhaps as well that they are not required to pass judgment on us today."

This Commission, now popularly known as The Massey Commission, saw "a more cheering picture" when reviewing the progress and development of art galleries which had, over the years, enjoyed close co-operation with the National Gallery.

Co-operative effort in two regions, western Ontario and western Canada, had made possible the circulation of exhibitions, not only to established galleries but to small art societies in rural areas. Such services were performed "by voluntary effort and in the 'spare time' of [some one] Gallery Director." The extension program of the Art Gallery of Toronto, out of which grew the Art Institute of Ontario, also deserved passing mention.

Even with these encouraging notes, the Commission commented that "It is, however, scarcely necessary to mention that there is no gallery in Canada to compare with the wealthy and established institutions to be found in the United States and abroad. All galleries in Canada regard themselves as poor; but with their limited resources they try to carry on all usual functions of such institutions and to make the most of what they have."

One year later the Dominion Bureau of Statistics published its own highly objective second report on Museums and Art Galleries, almost wholly a statistical record, covering the administration, activities, and finances of one hundred and eighty-five institutions. A brief editorial, written as an Introduction, commented on the fact that "Canada's best known museums have passed the stage where relics are collected, named and put on shelves in a random manner. Exhibits are now formed into representative groups or built around unit themes." Certain recurrent reservations were voiced in the report. Many collections were in storage and away from public view due to lack of suitable display areas and the necessary funds to care properly for them. One cynical but anonymous curator was quoted as saying, "Those responsible for the establishment of this museum forgot to provide funds to maintain it, so the exhibits and building are deteriorating fast."

One encouraging sign contained in the report dealt with the growth of public interest. Whereas in 1938 the same federal agency had reported that, at the rate of museum attendance, it would require ten years for each of the ten and a half million citizens to pay just one visit to any one of the institutions, the 1952 report dis-

173

closed a recorded attendance of 2,754,805 in only eighty-seven of the one hundred and eighty-five institutions polled. Canada's population in the fourteen years had increased to just over fourteen million citizens.

Some further highly revealing statistics were also made public for the first time. Federal involvement in museums due to the developing program of the National Parks Service of the then Department of Resources and Development had increased to twenty (a department which has since changed its nomenclature but not its skin and is now the Historic Sites Service of the Department of Indian Affairs and Northern Development). Provincial governments were financing in whole or in part twenty-one institutions, and municipal sponsorship from coast to coast had actually reached eighteen. There were now 475 full time and 248 part time employees. Gross expenditures of only sixty-two of the total listed had reached a record of $1,895,000 with the federal government contributing 29.6 per cent, the provinces 25.2 per cent, municipal governments 26.5 per cent and endowments having climbed to all of 2.4 per cent, or approximately $45,480. What might be called an anticlimactic note suggested that the remaining one hundred and twenty-three institutions which had failed to supply the essential fiscal statistics were perilously existing on little more than $100,000, or an average of $812 per institution.

Twelve years later, in 1964, 214 museums and related institutions reported total income of $9,500,000. Federal and provincial authorities jointly contributed fifty per cent with local governments paying out slightly less than $1,000,000, but endowments had increased to only $77,371 for administrative purposes. However, $4,500,000 had been contributed by benefactors for capital development projects.

In 1952, Montreal was the only city in Canada with a population of one million. Toronto had passed the half million mark, and the thirty-eight other cities had populations of from 50,000 to 300,000. While air travel was developing into an accepted form of transportation, the jet age was still a few years away.

In the museum field, as opposed to art galleries which were being served by seven exhibition circuits, there was only one regional association. Co-operation between the major museums and the small community institutions was virtually non-existent although it was viewed as highly desirable. Too many small museums were operating in complete isolation.

Of the 185 institutions listed in 1952 only fifty-two were housed in their own buildings and of that number not more than twenty were in buildings expressly designed for museum or gallery functions.

During the ensuing eight years museum growth gained momentum

174

and along with it philosophies, policies, and programs were to undergo radical change. Historical and science museums were emerging from their vacuum which had seen an insularity with concentration on research and preservation at the expense of display and involvement of the general public.

In 1958, Dr. Guthe stated that the community museum "does not take an active part in community life (and even shows) smug satisfaction of having assembled a collection of objects, as if it were an end in itself." The same man and wife team had some critical comments concerning "the wide-spread failure to recognize the museum as a community service agency. . . accentuated by contrast with the varied services offered by most art galleries, [and frequently] a defeatist attitude toward the need for improving the exhibits." The Guthes recognized the fact that an organized system of communication between museums was still lacking. The recurring theme of the museum as a social institution with a responsibility to Canadian society was emphasized as a companion to the library, which sought to interpret "the treasures of life in an attractive, logical and stimulating manner."

The step by step progression in museum growth from 1960 to 1970 is not hard to assess. By 1960, according to a directory published late that year by the American Association of Museums, the number of Canadian museums had risen to 272. Four years later a second directory published under the same auspices showed a further increase to 348. In 1963 the Bureau of Statistics had launched its independent census, which was completed in June 1964 but not published until February 1966. It corroborated this surprising growth, the listings disclosing 385 institutions.

Centennial year celebrations were approaching. Governments were urging comunities to develop original and exciting programs and projects to mark the event. The federal authority had announced grants of one dollar per capita to municipalities on condition that the junior governments would make matching contributions, and that these monies be used for the creation of capital projects to serve as monuments of the 100th anniversary of Confederation.

A mushrooming interest was generated by the appointment of a Commission expressly designed to develop national participation in the Centennial Festival and it was not surprising to discover a sudden and intense interest in Canada's history and its accomplishments in areas of social intercourse. Almost overnight appeared a sense of cultural maturity and a feeling of national destiny. Local historical societies, natural history groups, and scientific bodies vied with community art clubs to produce imaginative, and at times impossible, schemes to memorialize this one moment in history. Competi-

175

tion was keen as sports, recreation, and other interests visualized alternate projects with some municipal authorities seeing the grants in terms of civic improvements which included new city halls, tourist information bureaus, and occasionally comfort stations.

Out of the 2,018 incorporated cities, towns and villages in Canada 140 elected to build, restore, or reconstruct community institutions associated with the visual arts, history or science. The federal government also had offered two and a half million dollars to nine of the ten provinces for similar projects in the capital cities. (Prince Edward Island had already opened its Confederation Centre aided by federal funds in 1964.) Four of the provinces elected to build museum complexes and a fifth, Newfoundland, decided on a cultural centre in which to house theatre and art gallery.

The impetus to develop museums which got under way in the last years of World War II had created its own momentum and by June 1968, when the Canadian Museums' Association published its Directory of Museums and Related Institutions, 715 entries were listed. For the statistically minded, this growth represented one new such institution each four days over the three year period since the 1964 census. If this is viewed as abnormal, a statistical report of museum growth in the United States, published in 1965 by the American Association of Museums, disclosed that "one-third of the nation's [U.S.] museums have been established since 1950, one every 3.3 days."

The capital costs of all the projects undertaken in Canada during what can be called the one thousand days devoted to centennial preparations have not been totaled up, but a conservative estimate would be that not less than one hundred million dollars were spent. Another interesting sign points to a broadening of interest in other areas of history, science, and the humanities; a contemporary review of Canadian museum development indicated that, whereas in 1964 museums were grouped under only nine categories or disciplines, the 1968 directory gave seventy-two major categories extending from aeronautics to zoology.

While the approach to Canada's centennial year undoubtedly was a major contributor, many other influences have to be considered. Canada as a mecca for tourists certainly had played a role in encouraging museum growth. While tourist agencies over the years had stressed scenery, fishing, hunting, and other outdoor attractions, the jet age was offering counter attractions abroad in the form of festivals, museums, and art galleries, making necessary a new and more sophisticated pitch for the tourist dollar in Canada. Also there was a growing consciousness of the need to preserve examples of distinctive Canadian architecture, the pioneer homes and settlements, early military fortifications, and even ships.

176

In the three years (1964-1967) art galleries and cultural centres had doubled from 71 to 148. With advances made in the various sciences – natural, social, and applied – a rapid increase in museums specializing in specific disciplines also occurred. Whereas in 1964 there were only five institutions with areas devoted exclusively to children this number was quadrupled.

In 1932, the Miers-Markham report had expressed amazement that, despite the fact that Canada was primarily an agricultural nation, there was no museum dedicated to this subject (the survey team had by-passed Guelph). Now twelve such museums were in operation.

The all important factor in relation to the growth of museums was their more general acceptance, not only as tourist attractions but also for their educational value as these institutions came increasingly to be used as annexes to the classroom.

Much was made of the fact that Expo '67 attracted fifty million visitors during its six months of operation. In 1966 a poll was taken of one hundred and sixty-seven institutions or only one third of museums operating in Canada, which showed an attendance of 12,984,250. A 1970 survey conducted by Statistics Canada and which admittedly had drawn replies on this subject from somewhat less than seven hundred institutions disclosed attendance in that year had now reached fifty million, give or take a few thousands, and there is still more evidence that attendance continues to climb. The National Historic Sites Service announced that visitors to thirty-seven of its historic parks and buildings had increased in 1971 by 14 per cent.

Museum development was also keeping pace with attendance. An unofficial survey in early 1972 indicated that listings of bona fide institutions were reaching the eleven hundred mark and that further expansion involving the expenditure of $185,000,000 could be expected during the present decade.

20

Although Newfoundland pioneered in museum development in the early nineteenth century a serious setback to further growth occurred during the Depression years when the small provincial museum was closed as an economy measure and the contents dispersed.

Newfoundland joined Confederation in 1949 and only then did Newfoundlanders start to emerge from a stagnant society into an era which at least had promise of a richer economic and cultural future. The Hon. Joseph R. Smallwood, last of the Fathers of Confederation, who was deposed in November 1971, not only had a keen awareness of history, but also over the years concerned himself with the preservation of the Island's historic resources which had been accumulating since the eleventh century. Undoubtedly both early and later developments in the museum field can largely be attributed to this remarkable figure.

Newfoundland's history is dominated by its association with the conquest of the Atlantic. There is evidence, at the northerly tip of the island at L'Anse aux Meadows on the Strait of Belle Isle, that Viking ships landed in the eleventh century to establish the first known settlement of explorers on the east coast of North America three hundred years before Cabot sailed past the spot. Excavations have uncovered significant artifacts which have aroused interest not only in Canadian archaeological circles but also in Scandinavia. In the past six years additional excavations have been carried out and temporary buildings erected to protect the digs. Despite its isolation some 5,000 visitors came to the site in 1971. Access to this small outport is by chartered boat, the familiar bush plane, or by an unpaved road 312 miles north of the Trans-Canada highway and 764 miles from St. John's. A chance archaeological discovery at Port aux Choix, approximately 180 miles north of Corner Brook on the Gulf of St. Lawrence and on the dirt highway leading to L'Anse aux Meadows, is currently under investigation. Tentative indications point to a culture which existed during the period 3000-4000 B.C.

John Cabot landed at Bonavista in 1497 and was followed by

English, Scottish, Basque, and Spanish sailors attracted by the vast quantities of cod. The Cabot Tower, built in 1897 on the peak of Signal Hill overlooking St. John's harbor, commemorates the 400th anniversary of the explorer's landing, doing double duty insofar as it was in that tower that Guglielmo Marconi received the first trans-Atlantic message in 1901. Signal Hill, itself designated a national historic park, has its own museum, officially opened as a Visitor Interpretation Centre in the summer of 1968, and commemorates the last formal battle between the English and French for domination of the Atlantic coast and the extensive fishing reserves. In 1971 the Hill and its two museums attracted 562,780 visitors.

The *Great Eastern*, the ship used to lay the Atlantic cable, was based at Harbour Grace and here it was that the cable from England was surfaced. Also from the same area Alcock and Brown took off on their spectacular and historic flight to Ireland. A museum which had been in the planning stage here for many years was opened in 1972.

The Gander airport likewise has its historic connotations before the jet age made possible direct flights over the north pole. It was also the scene of a major aviation disaster in 1967 when a Czechoslovakian plane crashed. As a monument to the tragedy the Czech government turned over their Expo '67 pavilion for erection at Gander, but in face of a continuing austerity program, this project likewise has been postponed. On the airport mezzanine the thousands of air passengers who land or stop over see "The Conquest of the Atlantic" aviation display which was formally opened in 1967, expanded in 1969, and further enlarged in 1970. A temporary exhibition area for prints and paintings drawn from Memorial University sources was also opened in 1967. A remodelling program by the Department of Transport has resulted in a permanent display area which is described as "a fairly respectable gallery" and which was opened in the fall of 1971. A smaller Czech pavilion which had served as annex to the main structure at Expo '67 now serves as an Arts and Culture Centre in Grand Falls.

At Corner Brook another civic centre containing swimming pool, fine art display, activities areas, and a small museum was opened in 1968 as a delayed centennial capital grant's project.

What was a badly overcrowded provincial museum in the Gosling Building on Duckworth Street in downtown St. John's, has now more commodious accommodation with the removal of the regional library to the university campus. Individual display areas are related to the history and the economy of the island, together with relics of the now extinct Beothuk Indians, in addition to Viking artifacts. The reactivated museum was formally opened after Confederation, about 1952, while the Newfoundland Archives, also in St. John's, occupies the historic Colonial Building on Military Road having been moved from its original quarters on the university campus in 1960.

This province will wait until March 31, 2049 before celebrating the centenary of its entry into Confederation. On July 1, 1967, while the rest of Canada was in a festive mood, the people of Newfoundland continued the tradition of Memorial Day to honour the members of their Regiment who were completely wiped out fifty years earlier at Flanders. To commemorate this event and tell the story of the military and naval roles of the island, the Naval and Military Museum on the eleventh floor of Confederation Tower was opened in 1963; and at Quidi-Vidi, outport on the northern edge of St. John's, a restored military battery was opened in 1967. Nearby is a small derelict church which has officially been proclaimed a historic building. A lighthouse at Cape Spear, on the south-eastern tip of the harbor of St. John's, also has been marked as a national historic site but restoration has been postponed.

As previously indicated, the province of Newfoundland elected to construct an arts and cultural centre on the campus of Memorial University as its centennial project. The edifice embraces art gallery, library, theatre, and restaurant and is designed for involvement of both the university and the general public. The theatre was officially launched in May 1967 with a Dominion Drama Festival. Six months later, the art gallery had an equally auspicious opening with a major exhibition of Henry Moore sculpture.

In 1970, Memorial University, through its now-thriving art gallery, established exhibition areas in thirteen schools extending from Bonavista on the north-east coast to Springdale on Notre Dame Bay, three hundred miles west on Highway 1. For this program, the university has made available a continuing flow of works of art drawn from its permanent collection which as of mid 1971 totalled approximately five hundred paintings, prints, and sculptures. A second program has now been launched in another region and will be followed by others until the entire province is covered.

In the St. John's dockside slum area, the old Newport wine maturing cellar made up of two lengthy tunnels with vaulted roof was rescued by the recently established Natural Resources Division of the government, restoration getting under way in 1970. While the cellar is a unique historical attraction in its own right, the university authorities have been viewing it as a logical site for a downtown gallery with an arts and crafts workshop in the adjacent warehouse on the same site. They view the projects as "a tremendous challenge and gamble."

Meanwhile the Director of Historic Resources reports more archaeological digs at Saglek Bay in Labrador where skeletel remains indicating human habitation over a span of four thousand years have been discovered. The historic Bonavista Lighthouse is undergoing restoration. At St. Thomas more restoration of historic buildings are under way, and on the Isle of Bois-Ferryland a gun position associated with the British occupation of 1815 has been partially restored. Modernization of displays at the Newfoundland Museum was completed in 1973 giving this institution a contemporary look within its nineteenth century architectural framework.

Except for the National Historic Sites restorations and three small privately owned museums at Hibb's Cove, Bona Vista Bay, and Trinity, all museums and related projects are financed and administered directly by the province or through Memorial University.

In December 1970 restoration started on the Castle Hill National Historic Park to serve as a make-work project for 400 local people who were jobless following the closing of a United States armed forces base at nearby Argentia. A uniquely designed interpretation centre adds to the attractiveness of this point of land which had dominated the rich fishing banks in the seventeenth century and which, in 1713, the English gained by diplomacy after all efforts to capture by force had failed. The long abandoned French defences are in process of restoration and while work progresses the park is open to the public.

The Provincial Historic Resources Authority continues its archaeological explorations at L'Anse aux Meadows and Port aux Choix, while the National Historic Sites Service in association with the National Museum of Man has entered into an international agreement with the Scandinavian governments for the establishment of an international research team relating to the saga of the Vikings.

Remains of a prefabricated Moravian mission building erected in 1781 were recently discovered at the virtually inaccessible outpost of Hopedale, Labrador, approximately 250 miles due east from the Goose Bay airport. There are no road connections and tentative plans for a reconstruction are still low on the list of priorities.

In 1972 two more museums had their official openings even while awaiting completion of their exhibition areas, one at Grand Bank near the southern tip of Fortune Bay and only 30 miles from the French island of Great Miquelon; the other at Heart's Content on the east coast of Trinity Bay and less than 100 miles from St. John's. In the heart of St. John's, the St. Thomas Rectory dating from 1820 was proclaimed a historic site in 1973, and is open to the public.

21

In the years immediately after World War II, not only did museum growth increase but interesting departures from the norm developed. In Prince Edward Island, a province with a population actually decreasing by three thousand in fifty years and almost as isolated as Newfoundland, an arts and crafts centre was merged with the Robert Harris Gallery in 1947 when funds were raised through provincial and municipal subsidies for the engagement of a professional director. The centre was to be patterned after a Toronto project which had flourished under the inspired leadership of Dr. Arthur Lismer in the 1920's. An Act to incorporate the Prince Edward Island Art Guild was passed by the provincial Legislature and was given Royal Assent on March 23, 1949.

Occupying two large rooms in the Market Building in the civic square, the Centre was designed to serve all segments of the community but the emphasis more and more stressed children's creative activities. The new director, who had studied under Dr. Lismer (Miss Frances E. Johnston), took up her duties in 1949 and for the next six years developed a program which "included a changing scene of art exhibitions monthly, through the co-operation of the recently formed Maritime Art Association, lectures, classes for adults, workshops for teachers, film showings, recorded concerts, classes for children, a Saturday morning Open House for youngsters, a weekly radio program known as The Radio Art Class in addition to hobby activities for residents of the provincial home for the aged." In a recent letter to an art gallery colleague, Miss Johnston, in a postcript wrote, "If we hadn't run out of money and I had stayed on the island, I would have worked toward the establishment of a museum pertaining to the Island history and ecology, because I saw that a centre devoted exclusively to the arts had limited usefulness to the farmers and fishermen who make up most of the population of the province." Miss Johnston added, "Although the art centre closed in 1955, the Guild did not vote itself out of existence until after the Confederation Centre was opened. Their remaining funds were used to buy furniture for the children's room in the [Confederation Centre] art gallery."

The nine years which elapsed between the curtailment of activities at the Guild workshops and the opening of the new Federal-Provincial Centre in Charlottetown were far from sterile. With the approach of Canada's centennial year, the role which the island province had played in preliminary discussions leading to Confederation assumed greater significance in the minds of local historians. Possibly also the eyes of politicians and members of Chambers of Commerce were turned toward the development of tourism as an antidote to the declining fisheries, ship building, and agricultural industries, particularly as a causeway from the mainland to the island had been promised and seemingly was nearing reality. This project, however, was indefinitely postponed in 1969.

The colony of Prince Edward Island had waited until 1873 to become the seventh of the colonies to enter Confederation but Province House, which had been built in 1864, was the scene in that same year of preliminary discussions leading directly to the historic 1867 decision to create a Dominion of Canada. And was it not Robert Harris, Welsh-born but almost native son, foundation member and early president of the Royal Canadian Academy who, in 1883, had been given a commission to paint the mural for Ottawa's Parliament Buildings depicting the Fathers in session?

Continuing agitation for a permanent cultural centre was quietly kept up by members of the Guild and other civic-minded individuals. Out of the discussions came the suggestion for a permanent memorial to the Fathers of Confederation to be built in Charlottetown. Unlike many another such dream, it developed as a grandiose edifice far beyond the capability of the Island government to maintain, let alone provide the necessary capital funds for its construction. Eventually the problem was resolved by persuading first the federal government and then the nine remaining provinces to participate in a memorial which would symbolize the bonds of unity from coast to coast at a cost of over five million dollars. This memorial, formally opened by Queen Elizabeth II on August 2, 1964, embraces a theatre, regional library, art gallery, and historical museum, social areas, sculpture court, restaurant, and rooms designed for other cultural activities.

Following the Centre's opening with its fanfare, pomp, and circumstance, local citizens and governments, both provincial and municipal, took a second look at this monolithic and, to the average man in the street, alien structure figuratively dropped into their midst overnight and which was already taking the form of a massive and somewhat austere off-white elephant. Local cynics and some opposition M.L.A.'s were beginning to mutter that here was another project dedicated to political short-sighted if not blind folly. After all, the argument went, this was the winter of 1964, when Charlottetown's population numbered less than twenty thousand and the net personal income of the one hundred and eight thousand Island residents was the lowest in the country.

As other communities were to realize a few years later, it was one thing to raise capital, one-shot funds for centennial projects; to keep them operating for day to day events was another kettle of fish. It was obvious to the harrassed taxpayer that the newly opened Centre could not survive on revenues from its summer festival program. The much publicized visit of Her Majesty had undoubtedly resulted in a flood of tourists, but could this flood be augmented or even maintained at the 1964 level? And there was a limit to what the somewhat slow and at times temperamental ferries, and an even more temperamental railway, could transport.

Consultants who visited Charlottetown that winter to investigate alleged technical deficiencies in the building and to report on potential programs found what was primarily a caretaker staff already quietly and effectively working on projects designed to involve the community and residents of the other Island regions – a film society, a quick renewal of the arts and crafts programs, amateur theatre, and music groups, social events, lectures, and the occasional booking of professional entertainment from classical to rock from the mainland. Schools in outlying rural and urban districts were being urged to bring their classes for tours and lectures – all this while the regional committee responsible for the day to day housekeeping was frantically seeking ways and means for continued financing.

Several months had to elapse before a formula was reached making possible continuing federal grants supported by funds from the provincial treasury and with grants for various projects from The Canada Council. All this was required to augment monies raised by the summer festival and other activities including rentals and catering profits.

In 1969, Confederation Centre attracted 180,000 visitors excluding patrons to the theatre; the art gallery area reported a summer attendance of 66,235. Increased tourist traffic together with year-round activities for the Island residents continue to mushroom according to a statement made by one senior official to the effect that "the various components in Confederation Centre" had attracted just over one million visitors in 1971, with an added comment that "naturally for the 1973 Centennial we are expecting even better figures."

In 1970 a Director of Extension Services was appointed, resulting in a steady increase of community activity throughout the island

184

relating primarily to revival of crafts and art classes, a program which by 1972 had reached the Indian reserve of Lennox Island. The appointment of Confederation Centre as an Associate of the National Museums of Canada in late 1972 has made possible still further developments in extension services to coincide with the 1973 centennial celebrations. In addition, the gallery staff assembled the first comprehensive show of paintings by Robert Harris ("The Making of a Portrait Painter").

While Charlottetown's Centre has assumed its rightful place in Canada's political history, there is still one fact which should not be forgotten. From 1816, the year of the founding of the first museum in Canada, to the opening of Confederation Centre, not more than twenty museums or art galleries were occupying buildings expressly designed for their highly specialized functions. For fifteen years, during the final phase of the Depression and until the end of World War II, there was little or no building under way. From 1950 to 1964 there was a mild flurry during which time seven or eight small institutions moved into new quarters. Four of these were in Saskatchewan, but it was Charlottetown that created an impact on the body politic across Canada and undoubtedly served as a stimulus to both provincial and municipal governments. It served also as a pilot experiment in providing facilities and competent technical administration to men and women living in one of the more isolated and economically depressed regions of the country. Over the years, they had been starved for cultural expression and almost overnight they took part in what can only be called a sociological revolution.

In 1963, The Garden of the Gulf Museum at Montague was opened with its exhibits related to the pioneer life of early settlers. One year later, at Miscouche, the Musée Acadien, founded by the Sisters of the Congregation of Notre Dame, moved into a log cabin to tell the story of the French settlers. Also in 1964 the Green Gables farmhouse at Cavendish, in which Lucy Maud Montgomery had spent most of her girlhood and which is now immortalized in her famous book, was restored by the National Historic Sites Service and turned over to the province to administer. The rambling and charming house, at the entrance to a public golf course and presently serving as a non-alcoholic nineteenth hole and tourist attraction, contains many memorabilia of the island's most famous author. Another cottage at New London was recently turned over to the province for museum purposes having been the birthplace of Miss Montgomery but from which she was carried away three weeks later never to come back, at least to take up residence. A blue trunk is exhibited along with other furnishings which may or may not have been there at the time of her birth.

One of the more interesting community museums on the Island, a

185

restoration of a typical Prince Edward Island home of the early nineteenth century, was opened in 1967 at Alberton in the North Cape area, while at Bonshaw, a suburb of the capital city, an automobile museum displays antique cars and pioneer farm machinery. In Charlottetown, the Provincial Archives has moved into new quarters in the library area of the Centre.

At times it is difficult to differentiate between the bona fide museum and what is known as the Tourist Attraction; national and regional museums' associations are still grappling with this problem. Prince Edward Island is one such region having a profusion of the latter; for instance, the Old Homestead at Strathgartney, a restored two and a half storey home of one of the original settlers. The restoration is authentic but the owner frankly admits a primary interest in commercial promotion and profits.

There is an octagonal all-glass building in Cabot Park near Malpeque; its windows were brought from the Cabot building in Charlottetown and it can be described only as a historical showcase for pioneer artifacts. The re-creation of a sixteenth century Mic Mac Indian Village at Rocky Point also attracts many people who can purchase authentic Indian crafts as souvenirs. The Woodleigh Replicas near Burlington, a collection of miniature castles and other world-famous buildings of varying dimensions but authentically reproduced, defies classification. It can be classed only as a tourist attraction despite the fact that the owners consistently refuse to open their grounds on Sundays. Given another half century it may eventually be recognized as a museum dedicated to one family's hobby and idiosyncrasies. The one contribution to natural history is to be found in the Prince Edward Island Wildlife Park at Rustico, an eighty-seven acre wildlife refuge where guided tours are featured for teachers, school groups, and in the summer months for Island visitors. An active research program also continues.

Quite naturally the impact of the Charlottetown Centre is reflected in greater historical awareness, and as in other provinces a centennial cannot be celebrated without a proliferation of museums. Anticipating this event eight new museums have been opened. Two community owned projects are the O'Leary Museum which has already enlarged its display space, and an Acadian Village at Mount Carmel.

The recently organized provincial Historical Resources Administration was given the responsibility of spending a $900,000 birthday gift from the federal government, two thirds of which will have produced The Scales Mill restoration in Freetown, an early electrical development; The Green Park Shipbuilding Memorial, another restoration; the purchase and renovation of "Beaconsfield," a fine example of Victorian architecture which will serve as the Admini-

186

stration headquarters; a reconstruction of a group of fishing shacks, dories, and drying racks at Basin Head "to recreate the mood and even the smells of an industry now more mechanized"; and at Orwell Corner a rural cross-roads settlement to reflect the social centre of an early farming community.

Encouragement has also been given to community projects at Tignish, Dundas, and Lennox Island, the latter being a tribute to the Mic Mac culture, while the Federal Historic Sites Service has erected its own interpretation centre at the site of the Fort Amherst National Historic Park.

22

Nova Scotia, with its population of approximately three quarters of a million in an area of little more than twenty-one thousand square miles, has an intimacy making possible a close relationship between government and people. It is a province with three major ethnic groups and cultures embedded in its history and a series of economic reverses in more recent years has made it one of the depressed areas of Canada. It also has developed a colour problem, arising out of its acceptance of Negroes fleeing more than a century ago from the United States and of more recent arrivals from the West Indies. This has led inevitably to a segregated area in its capital city and adjacent communities. The three dominant cultures, Acadians, United Empire Loyalists, and "improved Scots," live amicably within their own regional concentrations.

Halifax and its neighbouring city Dartmouth had their moment of deep tragedy in 1917 when the explosion of the munitions' ship *The Black Tom* devastated the two cities, leaving thousands of their citizens dead, scarred or homeless.

Essentially the province is dependent on fishing, shipping, and coal; the two latter have suffered heavy declines in the past half century. These major industries play an important role in its museums. Curiously enough, despite an early interest in the various arts, the province had only two permanent collections of paintings both of which were housed until recently in the Provincial Archives where they were treated essentially for historical content rather than for aesthetic appeal.

In 1952, Nova Scotia had sixteen museums or historical restorations. Four of these were administered by the federal government, three by the province, two by educational institutions and one as a town project; the remaining six were under the jurisdiction of community societies. By 1964, the number had increased to twenty-three, with the National Historic Sites Services adding three more to their list of restorations and the province taking over three historic houses in the interim. In the three ensuing years, 1965 to 1968, museum growth had more than doubled, with fifty-three listings in the Canadian Museums' Association Directory, ten of which were Centennial Capital Grants projects. Of the museums added to the provincial list, six can be viewed as historic restorations and, as their titles indicate, these represent both diversified disciplines and cultures. They are the O'Dell Inn and Tavern at Annapolis Royal; La Vieille Maison at Meteghan, Digby County; The Ross Farm Agricultural Museum at New Ross, Lunenburg County; Sherbrooke Village in Guysborough County; and the Prescott House at Starr's Point, King's County. The last three are directly under the jurisdiction of the Provincial Museum; Sherbrooke Village and the Prescott House are joint federal-provincial restoration projects and were opened in 1972. The two remaining pioneer museums are the Archelaus Smith Museum at Centreville on Cape Sable Island and the Cobequid-Yorkshire Museum at Oxford in Cumberland County. Also in 1972, the Canadian Department of National Defence announced that at the S.S. *Stadacona* naval training base, the Admiral's House was to be converted into a museum; a classroom annex it is to be open to the general public.

The change of emphasis from the natural sciences to human history in Nova Scotia was a slow-evolving process. Thomas Haliburton, first provincial archivist, had recognized the need for historical documentation but it is necessary to turn to the policies initiated by Harry Piers, first Curator of the Provincial Museum, to find the source for this subtle transformation. J. Lynton Martin, third curator of this same museum, in his article "Museums in Nova Scotia" discusses the rise and decline of the Mechanics' Institute museums by pointing to the fact that in their heydey, "the sciences were young, scientists were few, books were comparatively scarce and expensive, and the museum collection provided the only readily available means for the identification of the hosts of strange rocks, minerals, plants and animals," adding that". . . by the end of the Second World War all [collections] except those in the Provincial Museums had been destroyed or had become inactive. . . due to the increasing availability of good scientific literature." Mr. Piers, he points out, had seen the need for the museums to change direction and create new philosophies and "with little or no encouragement, he spent his lifetime collecting artifacts, documents and pictures related to our historical heritage."

The historical collection and paintings of Judge Mather DesBrisay were dispersed following his death in the last decade of the century, the Provincial Museum taking the Mic Mac Indian artifacts with pioneer artifacts being privately purchased by a Mr. E. D. Davison for presentation to the municipality of Bridgewater.

Nova Scotians, however, had to wait until after World War II to see a revival of interest in pioneer museums which, Mr. Martin argues, was probably due to the "increasing alarm about the accelerated drain of things of historical value." From 1947 to 1964, new museums made their appearance at the rate of one every two years. However, in 1960 a Museum Act was passed by the Legislature which provided for a Board of Governors under the chairmanship of the Deputy Minister of Education, with the Museum director serving as a board member. The Board was given power to "operate such museums, branches or other institutions. . . administer grants to museums, organizations or individuals for the promoting of the purposes of this Act. . . ."

In practice the province, through the director of provincial museums, makes grants of ten dollars a day to community institutions with seasonal operation of from two to four months with a maximum sum of $1,200.00 annually. For year-round operation the grant is increased to twenty dollars a day, or $7,200.00 annually, but such grants are available only if it is felt that such public expenditures are warranted after scrutiny by museum staff members. Practical encouragement is given to community societies to improve their standards of operation through visits by technicians who provide study papers and essential equipment with which studies can be turned to effective use. The size of the grant is dependent on the use to which the local society puts this added knowledge. Staff members also are available to design displays, advise on the authenticity of accessions and generally give aid and succour when called upon. Workshop sessions are held at irregular intervals, and in 1971 grants to community societies had reached $74,000, a $30,000, increase over 1967.

Although the Board had been administering the Simeon Perkins House at Liverpool, the Uniake House at Mount Uniake, and the former home of Thomas Chandler Haliburton at Windsor for a number of years, a new dimension was added to the provincial takeover of community institutions in 1967 when the Balmoral Grist Mill near Tatamagouche was officially adopted. The project had been initiated by a regional historical society two years earlier. Today the mill operates during the summer months with one of the few millers left in the region in charge.

At Barrington, a decrepit and neglected woollen mill was rehabilitated in 1968 by the province and is seen in operation twice daily during the tourist season to illustrate "unique methods of wool production and its use among Nova Scotia fishermen." A New England church on the highway at Barrington, erected by Cape Cod émigrés in 1765 and believed to be the oldest non-conformist church in Canada, has also been restored. Tombstones in the adjacent graveyard date back to 1766.

The province also rescued the Marine Museum in Halifax which had a period of decline due to lack of community and municipal support, taking it under its wing as an annex to the Historical Museum at the Citadel.

The Lawrence House at Maitland, linked closely with Nova Scotia's ship-building industry, has been restored and was opened to the public in 1970. The Ross-Thomson House at Shelburne, which had been in sorry straits, was taken over by the province in this same year.

Presumably expressing the philosophy of his Board, Mr. Martin points to certain factors in museum growth which should be applicable to the remaining nine provinces, when he writes that "too many local museums of the same type can fragment the museum picture so badly that no one institution can provide a worthwhile experience to the visitor. There is, after all, a limit to the amount of valuable historical material in Nova Scotia," adding "It is hoped that future development will be measured largely in terms of improved quality and performance."

During the time the museum program of the province was being diversified, the government-administered Museum of Science, still on the Institute of Technology campus, was being slowly strangled. Its quarters were required for an expanded school of architecture and by 1966 the museum was occupying only fifty per cent of its original area; it was only a matter of time before it would be called upon to relinquish the remaining space. It had already seen the disappearance of its small planetarium, the first in Canada, which had been a popular attraction. Incidentally this institution was one of the early pioneers in radio and television programs in the various areas of science with Mr. Pier's successor, Donald K. Crowdis as moderator.

Plans for a new museum were launched in 1966, and the completed contemporary edifice including administrative and educational areas was opened four years later, but the Human History and Marine displays still remained on Citadel Hill.

Communications museums, until recently seen only in Montreal, are today extending from coast to coast. The Maritimes Telephone and Telegraph Company opened its exhibit on the second floor of the company's new Halifax headquarters in 1967. Other museums in the province specializing in technology and industry include the New Glasgow Museum, with its large collection of glassware, much of it of local origin, pioneer furnishings and agricultural equipment. At Stellarton, two miles away, a Miners' Museum with simulated mine workings tells the story of the internationally famed Pictou dragermen or mine rescue workers. In this same general area, en route to the Prince Edward Island ferry, the Mic Mac Museum embraces an ethnological park displaying burial mounds, pioneer relics and stone implements.

The *Theresa E. Connor,* last of the Lunenburg salt tankers, is today moored at a Lunenburg quay and "portrays the gallant era of the Nova Scotia schoonermen, re-created through relics, photographs, graphics and color slides." A section of the ship is devoted to the story of the schooner *Bluenose*, the legendary Queen of the Atlantic.

Along the south shore of the province other small museums crop up at unexpected intervals and places. The DesBrisay Museum previously mentioned is now in its own Centennial building in the twenty-five acre municipal park at Bridgewater, while further west the De La Tour Musée et Bibliothèque D'Entremont has preserved the history of the D'Entremont family and the Acadians. This small museum-archives complex is at Middle West Pubnico (not West, nor Lower West, nor East, Middle or Lower East nor Pubnico itself, not even Pubnico Beach). At Yarmouth, ferry port for Bar Harbor, the county museum deals with marine history of the region, with an extensive collection of shells. Across the highway the Firemen's Museum, the only one in Canada solely devoted to fire-fighting, is a historical project of the local fire department.

The Churchill House at Hantsport, built in 1860 near the mouth of the river Avon, is another restoration which has marine associations. The original owner pioneered in the building of wooden ships in the mid-nineteenth century, and the ground floor areas of the house are now devoted to the story of early ship building.

Throughout the mainland pioneer historical museums can be found at Aylsford, Old St. Edward's Church at Clemensport (c.1784), Parkdale, Parrsboro, St. Peter's, South Rawden, Sunrise Trail Museum at Tatamagouche, Walton and Wolfville; the last-mentioned is located in a restored home which contains domestic artifacts in large number. A geological park and natural history museum is located at Rose Bay, and there is a wildlife park administered by the province at Shubencadie.

A Centennial museum-gallery-library project was conceived for the city of Dartmouth, the culmination of an involved project which resulted in a relatively new city hall being replaced by a brand new Centennial civic centre with the abandoned municipal building being remodelled for historical and cultural purposes. The new tenants put the building to excellent use, providing regional library services on the main floor with historical museum and art gallery one flight up. The museum displays have areas devoted to maritime history including whaling and commercial fishing, domestic fashion and taste, with the gallery area being used for locally organized and travelling exhibitions.

Another civic complex at Amherst, a few miles south of the New Brunswick border, was opened in 1967 with offices of the municipal administration being adjacent to a small museum dedicated to four locally born Fathers of Confederation.

In 1603 the government of France proclaimed that all lands lying between latitudes forty and forty-six in the new world should be called Acadie. Two years later Pierre du Gua, Sieur de Monts, and his friend de Poutrincourt established the settlement of Port Royal in the Annapolis Valley along with Samuel de Champlain. At Annapolis Royal, to the west, another Acadian settlement was established in later years, which was eventually taken over by the English and developed into a military stronghold. It was here that the Duke of Kent designed buildings, earthworks, and defensive emplacements. The two historic areas are now serving as museums *in situ,* Port Royal Habitation having been restored and reconstructed with reproductions of the furnishings of the early seventeenth century and the Annapolis Royal building displaying artifacts relating to the Acadian settlement and the struggle between the English and French during the eighteenth century. Both parks are administered by National Historic Sites Services as is the Grand Pré National Park, seventy miles to the east of the same highway. The location of another Acadian settlement of the period 1675-1755, this park has more romantic implications being the locale for Longfellow's immortal "Evangeline." It contains the replica of the original Acadian church, attractive gardens, a statue of Evangeline and a museum.

The same federal agency has partially restored and is administering the Citadel National Historic Park, a stone fort and moat built in 1828; the York Redoubt National Historic Site, base of a late eighteenth century Martello Tower; along with remains of gun emplacements which served as part of the Halifax Citadel Defence Complex. In 1972, it announced that it had assumed responsibility for restoration of many waterfront buildings in the same city.

Two of the bakers' dozen of exciting and unique architectural concepts embodying small museums are on Cape Breton Island, reached by driving over its half mile umbilical causeway. At Baddeck, the Alexander Graham Bell Museum erected in 1956 by the National Historic Sites Service, is a glass and metal structure in the form of a tetrahedron, the geometric design used by Bell in his aeronautical experiments. The building houses exhibits relating to many of the scientific achievements of this noted Canadian in the fields of communications and to his work on hydrofoil crafts.

193

One of the most successful monuments to Confederation is undoubtedly the Miners' Museum at Glace Bay, a centennial capital project which miraculously achieved a distinction of being architecturally well designed and technically functional. The building is a stylized abstraction of typical colliery surface buildings with a memorial tower in the form of head-frame. Although relatively small, the interior areas are economically designed with space devoted not only to mining history but including displays dealing with the economic uses of coal, a geological section, and similar associated subjects. Constructed on a bluff overlooking the Atlantic, the museum has its own operating coal mine, forty feet below surface and reached by a slope where visitors are shown mining techniques in action. Equally important is the fact that while it attracts many thousands of visitors in the summer months, the building with its small auditorium serves through the winter as an arts and crafts centre.

At nearby Sydney, the St. Patrick's Church Museum, a stone structure built in 1828, was restored by Xavier College students in 1966 and opened as a centennial project the following year.

Twenty-three miles to the south of Sydney is the sparsely populated and frequently fog-enshrouded Fortress of Louisbourg. Developed as a massive French military and civil encampment in 1713 it became almost overnight a vital military commercial and governmental centre. More a fortified community than fortress, its seventy acres were surrounded by a wall two miles long and at times eighty feet thick. Yet despite its defences, an untrained New England force captured it by 1745. It was returned to the French four years later only to be re-taken by the British under General Amherst and Admiral Boscawen. In 1760 the British systematically razed the fortifications leaving the town to sink into obscurity.

Reconstruction of this all but forgotten historical landmark was launched by the federal government primarily as a make-work project for displaced Cape Breton coal miners, although a museum had existed on the site since 1928. With a revival of coal production in the mid-1960s many of the miners left Louisbourg, but the reconstruction project continues to employ scores of men and women, many of whom have developed into skilled weavers, metal workers, stone cutters, and timber hewers. The National Historic Sites Service which administers the restoration has one of the best-equipped artifact laboratories in Canada and employs a large staff of historians and archaeologists in its research section.

At its zenith the Fortress had a combined military and civilian population of over five thousand. One third of the town and fortification will be restored and already an interpretive staff, attired in costumes designed and made within the Louisbourg complex, are reviving the many trades and crafts that were part of the everyday life of the community.

The Citadel, including the once well protected King's Bastion and Barracks, was opened in 1969. The Barracks measuring 365 feet in length has fourteen furnished rooms with several display rooms in which the history of the building is told in addition to a behind the scenes story of the reconstruction techniques. An adjacent and truly magnificent chapel is nearing completion. In addition, although incomplete, the Governor's Stables with livestock, carriage house, guard and ice houses are open to visitors. Fifteen other buildings have been started with others still in the planning stage. As the Fortress of Louisbourg continues to grow it will undoubtedly be recognized as one of the outstanding restorations on the North American continent. Further park developments will continue until the end of this decade.

Although the project has not yet been widely publicized it attracted over 100,000 visitors in the two summer months of 1972.

The Gaelic College Giant MacAskill Highland Pioneer Museum, with surely the longest name for any museum in Canada, is on the Cabot Trail, about twenty miles east of Baddeck, and is dedicated to the Gaelic tongue, arts, crafts and other facts of Scottish colonization. The patron saint, Angus MacAskill, supposedly stood eight feet tall and was a man who performed legendary feats.

On the north shore trail, at Cheticamp and almost at the gate of the Cape Breton Highland Park, the Musée Acadien dedicated to the French culture of the region occupies the rear of a two room arts and crafts centre. While diminutive, this museum has a fascinating and honest collection of domestic objects, including glassware, looms, and spinning wheels.

Where the Trail turns inland to become Highway 33, another small museum is a converted two-room school house called the Margaree Salmon Museum, the only such institution in Canada specializing in the sport of salmon fishing. It is located at Margaree Northeast, one of the five Margarees – East, Forks, Southwest, Northeast, and Upper. Here the life cycle of the salmon is outlined with other displays relating to fishing techniques, including poaching.

South and east on the Cabot Trail toward Little Narrows a byroad turns south again to Iona and the Nova Scotia Highland Village Museum, a small complex of pioneer buildings dedicated to as the name implies, the Scottish traditions. Further along the main highway beyond West Bay, the small community of St. Peters has its Nicolas Denys Museum with memorabilia of the museum's namesake and a small collection of Robert Harris paintings. A final call to Madam Island, east of Chedubucto Bay, to view the Lenoir Forge restoration site of an industry which prospered in the second half of the nineteenth century and in its hey-day produced ships' chandlery and anchors, completes what can be described as one of the most picturesque and entertaining tours in what is virtually unspoilt country.

Despite the interest in fine art which was evident in the early nineteenth century, the Province of Nova Scotia lacked an art gallery other than two temporary expedients until 1967. In 1953 Dalhousie University had created an improvised display area; a second collection belonging to a non-existent Nova Scotia Museum of Fine Art occupied space in the Provincial Archives where it was displayed more for historical connotations than for aesthetics. A number of art works drawn from these accessions provided decor at Government House.

With the 1964 announcement of federal funds for Centennial capital projects, the local Centennial committee discussed plans for an art-gallery cultural centre complex. However, this project was rejected. The Nova Scotia Museum took over an additional building in the Citadel Park in 1967 to serve as an art gallery, after which came the deluge. Galleries opened at Saint Mary's and Mount Saint Vincent universities the same year. Both these institutions have since opened galleries expressly designed to meet National Gallery standards.

An expansion of the venerable Nova Scotia College of Art in 1968 led to a new annex dedicated to Anna Leonowens, Nova Scotia born woman now immortalized in *Anna and the King of Siam* and who, we are told, helped to found the college and had "a probing creative spirit directed toward service."

In November 1971, Dalhousie University opened a new arts complex embracing music, drama, and the visual arts. The new gallery area was, at the same time, designed to meet basic requirements for the display of major works. In the past three years Acadia University has created gallery space in its art department. Even the excellent Military Museum within the Citadel walls is now in the art scene with its displays of paintings by Canadian war artists of World Wars I and II drawn from Canada's national collection.

The appointment of the Nova Scotia Museum as one of the National Museum "associates" in the fall of 1972 is already being reflected in further developments throughout the province. A new exhibition centre serving as display annex and distribution base was built as an annex to the Thomas McCullough House at Pictou, and similar centres were established at Sherbrooke Village, the Yarmouth Fire Fighters Museum, and at Bridgewater.

196

23

Unlike its provincial neighbour to the south, New Brunswick basks in a more rarefied atmosphere, despite being a depressed economic region. The casual visitor receives the impression that the province's bicultural and bilingual problems, if not entirely resolved, have developed an accommodation resulting in a truce which has tenuous overtones. The Acadian descendents for the most part occupy coastal and northern regions as place names indicate, with the United Empire Loyalists and New Englanders well entrenched in towns and cities along the Saint John River and the south-westerly shore.

It is a province of twenty-seven thousand, nine hundred and eighty-five square miles, one third of which, lying north of the 46th parallel, is virtual wilderness. Its population in 1901 was a little more than three hundred thousand and consistently increased by about ten thousand a year until 1961 when the rate declined somewhat. The total population as of January 1968 was six hundred and twenty-three thousand.

Over the years, many of the community museums in this province came under the benevolent wing of the county councils, with regional historical societies initiating and administering the institutions. With the abolition of the county system in 1967 these institutions faced an interim adjustment. However, without too much delay, a new provincial policy was formulated making provision for continuing grants.

Five of the thirty-three museums listed in 1968 are devoted to miltary history, the two major projects being the Fort Beausejour Park Museum at Aulac, still administered by the National Historic Sites Service and dedicated to both the French and British occupancies; and the Military Compound in the heart of Fredericton, currently under restoration with the help of the federal authority and which is linked wholly with the British. In 1932, a regional museum was installed in one of the Compound buildings to display the artifacts of the York-Sunbury Historical Society, but major restoration of other areas was delayed until the mid-1960's. On September 25, 1971, restoration of two of the three remaining buildings had been completed, with the Guard House being formally opened on that day. The third building, the Men's Barracks, is due for restoration in the near future. At Saint John, the Martello Tower was partially restored in 1963 with the aid of the federal government, as was the Saint Andrew's Blockhouse in 1967. Both are now administered by local authorities.

With all this emphasis on military achievements it is worth noting that the Campobello International Park, jointly administered by a United States-Canadian Commission, is more meaningful as a symbol of international amity than similar parks in Manitoba and British Columbia. This is probably due to the fact that the Franklin Delano Roosevelt summer home serves as Interpretative Centre and Museum. The home and park were given to the Commission by the Armand Hammer Foundation.

A few years before his death, Lord Beaverbrook, formerly Max Aitken, created his historical niche in his own inimitable manner by purchasing The Old Manse at Newcastle, converting it into a library "to house books and other pertinent materials," and presenting it to the municipality. In Fredericton, he founded the Beaverbrook Fine Art Gallery as a repository for his extensive collection of paintings, as well as a five hundred seat theatre, The Playhouse, both of which are endowed and administered by a foundation. The gallery now circulates segments from its collections to rural areas throughout the province.

Also in the capital city, the Provincial Archives received formal official status in 1967 and was housed in the Bonar Law-Bennett Building on the university campus. In addition, three restorations in the immediate area are open to visitors: the original university building built in 1791; the astronomical observatory (c. 1851); and The Burdon Schoolhouse dating back to the 1850's.

Visitors to the legislative buildings can also see a collection of portraits, including many examples of the British schools of the eighteenth and nineteenth centuries, some painted by Sir Joshua Reynolds. In this same building a first edition portfolio of the Audubon *Birds of North America* is on display.

The most extensive and best documented record of the Acadian occupancy of New Brunswick is at the new cultural and historical complex on the campus of the University of Moncton where a wealth of artifacts and archives cover domestic, agricultural, and industrial developments of the French settlers dating from the Treaty of Utrecht. The open display technique provides an exciting environment for the visitors. The adjoining art gallery serves as an-

198

nex to the school of art and provides areas for contemporary works, lecture programs, films, and classes to reach out to the large French minority in the city and district.

Also at Moncton is the Free Meeting House, used intermittently from 1821 to 1961 as a place of worship for all denominations. This building which over the years had accommodated twelve faiths involving Protestants, Catholics and Jews, was restored in 1966. More recently a civic museum was opened on Mountain Road. Unfortunately, the bilingual image of the city remains tenuous.

The New Brunswick Museum at Saint John has in the past few years undergone extensive face-lifting with its display areas attuned to contemporary philosophies. As the oldest continuing museum in Canada it has long outgrown its space and a planning committee has been delegated to devise a long range program for implementation within the next few years. At the present time, the museum houses departments of natural history and earth sciences; pioneer Canadian and miltary history; a department of fine and decorative arts; an extensive archives. Each department has its own curator and staff. The children's museum still provides exciting and stimulating displays.

Perpetuation of the United Empire Loyalist tradition in Saint John is exemplified in the restored Loyalist House (c. 1810-17) at 120 Union Street and opened as a museum in 1960. In the downtown area, on King Street, a century-old general store was restored and restocked with authentic merchandise or facsimiles thereof under the signboard of the Barbour Food Manufacturer and Distributor to celebrate this company's own centennial in 1967. This fascinating general store continues to attract thousands of visitors annually and is now administered by the city.

In 1932, the province had eleven museums which in the ensuing twelve years had increased to sixteen. In 1968, of the thirty-three listings in the *Canadian Museums' Association Directory*, seven were created under the Centennial Capital Grants program.

In Caraquet, a predominently French-speaking settlement, as the name implies, the Musée Acadien was built with centennial funds on a promontary overlooking Chaleur Bay, complementing an adjacent ichthyological (federal) display providing a varied menu including arts and crafts in the French tradition along with natural science under the microscope.

Some years prior to 1890 a miscellaneous collection of paintings was displayed in Saint John. These were later transferred to the Mount Allison College at Sackville where the first art gallery in the province was built in 1893. Cataloguing and classification of this collection had to wait until 1965 at which time the gallery area was radically remodelled to provide a more contemporary climate for a proliferation of other art works that had accumulated over the years. Rarely does lightning strike twice in the same place but not so bequests. In the spring of 1971, an announcement was made that the Mount Allison University had received two bequests to provide half a million dollars for art gallery renovation from two estates. The unexpected funds have made possible what curator Christopher Young describes as "more of a re-building job than just a renovation." The existing standing walls remain but with an entirely new interior structure, with three eighteen-foot storeys replacing the existing two floors.

The Miramichi Museum at Chatham continues to function but lacks its once exciting educational program. At Hopewell Cape, twenty-five miles south of Moncton, the Albert County Museum occupies the former county jail which does double duty as a historic restoration and pioneer museum. The lower floor is maintained as an austere and somewhat forbidding warning to the evil-doer, with the upper floor devoted to more amenable subjects relating to the more law-abiding pioneers. One of these, the Rt. Hon. Richard Bedford Bennett, is remembered with a bronze bust placed there by his good friend the late Lord Beaverbrook, to remind visitors that Canada's fifteenth Prime Minister had spent much of his childhood in Hopewell Cape.

Travelling north along the Saint John River, the Royal Canadian Dragoons Museum at Oromocto is located at the Canadian Forces Base and further upstream at Hartland a civic historical collection is on display in the town hall.

Dalhousie, in the Chaleur Bay region, has a new historical museum-library complex, only partially opened in centennial year, which, in addition to its existing collections of domestic and industrial artifacts, is hopefully seeking to encourage exploration for the rich fossil deposits in the nearby bay area. The Keiller House at Dorchester is a restored residence c. 1813 designed to have period rooms of three generations of the Keiller family; and at Gagetown the Tilly residence, dating from 1786, has the decor and furnishings of the first generation as well as later occupancies. Both are owned by the province but administered by local historical societies.

One of the more ambitious centennial projects is on the Island of Grand Manan at Grand Harbour where the comprehensive Moses Memorial Collection of Natural History has, at long last, found a more appropriate environment than the one occupied since 1862. Closely associated with the island schools, the museum serves as a year-round nature centre in addition to housing historical articles and documents relating to the pioneer life of Grand Manan. While in this area the visitor can time his arrival and departure by ferry to make a stop-over at Campobello Island, mentioned earlier, and a visit to the Campobello Library at Welshpool to see exhibits relating to the first of the Welsh settlers, and in particular memorabilia of the Owens family, one-time owners of the island.

The Kings County Museum at Hampton with its displays connected to county history is another centennial project and forms part of the city hall complex. At Upper Woodstock the original court house and county office built in 1883 was restored by the regional historical society assisted by grants from the province. The building not only served as the seat of justice but had functioned as a regular stopping place for coaches and was also used as a community centre where political rallies, concerts, and levees were held.

The Sunbury Shores Arts and Nature Centre at Saint Andrew's has been endowed by its founder, Mrs. Frank F. Eidlitz, to serve the community. During the summer months it attracts the tourist with lectures, exhibitions, and other activities related to the two disciplines indicated in its name.

Sooner or later Saint Andrew's is destined to have its own historical museum. The local historians have been collecting artifacts over the years while optimistically anticipating an announcement that the last surviving beneficiary of a bequest probated thirty or more years ago will have died, the will having stipulated that the two storey Georgian house, its contents and the bulk of the Kerr estate would be used for such a museum but only after all other benefactions had been provided for. Anticipating this windfall – the last surviving beneficiary now ninety-five years old – the Charlotte County Historical Society has opened a temporary museum on Water Street.

A little known museum-aquarium, jointly operated in the municipality by the Canadian Fisheries Research Board and the Huntsman Marine Laboratory also in Saint Andrew's was enlarged in 1972 as a work incentive project. The new building has 3,600 square feet of floor space and "a more adequate outdoor pool for the harbour seals," in addition to a small theatre for lectures and film shows. A unique innovation is "a large-scale model of Passamaquoddy Bay, featuring the topography of the ocean floor and the ebb and flow of the high tides for which the Bay of Fundy is famous."

A $125,000,000 hydro project on the Saint John River north of Fredericton brought with it political repercussions as farmers envisioned their homes and acreage being inundated. The reclamation project, directly affecting two hundred and forty families, called for the eventual flooding of some thirteen thousand acres of low-lying lands to provide a head-pond for operation of hydro turbines downstream. While the land-owners had rarely enjoyed great wealth, they had felt security of tenure which had always provided them with a pleasant, if uneventful life. New Brunswick people, particularly the descendents of the United Empire Loyalists, are acutely conscious of their history and with the proposed flooding many buildings with historical connotations would be demolished or buried in the avalanche of water. It was to be an Aswan Dam in miniature with hydro development as an initial step toward the rehabilitation of this depressed province. The provincial officials prophesied that, while a few hundreds would suffer inconvenience and possibly some social upset, the benefits achieved would outweigh temporary dislocation. Out of the controversy and following entensive surveys came the answer which at least partially resolved the problem – the salvaging of buildings, furnishings, implements, and other objects of historical significance and the creation of a typical riverside settlement designed not only to preserve for posterity some of the pioneer history but also to build up the tourist industry. The added cost of approximately four and a half million dollars represented a very small percentage of the overall development, particularly as other federal monies from the Federal Economic Development and Agricultural and Rural Development funds became available.

The historical community of King's Landing near Prince William, twenty miles upstream from Fredericton, was opened in 1970 as the first phase of this reclamation attracting seven thousand visitors in the two months. Estimated attendance in 1971 was given as in the neighbourhood of fifty thousand. Eventually the colony will occupy three hundred acres with one fourth being developed into a typical rural settlement of the 1870's, the remaining land transformed into a pioneer agricultural project raising crops and animals common to that period of time. The completed settlement will include eight residences with the essential outbuildings, church, school, store, and community hall, most of which were salvaged as the dam was under construction. The Loyalist farm, opened in 1971, serves as the second phase of the restoration and by 1974, when the entire area will be in operation, it will also have the last of the covered bridges of the area, barns, grist and other mills, and its own somewhat personal dam complete with hand-propelled ferry. Crafts of the nineteenth century will be among the featured attractions.

Complementing King's Landing, work commenced in 1972 on the reconstruction of an Acadian Village at Bertram, six miles inland from Caraquet in the Chaleur Bay region. When completed in 1975 it undoubtedly will serve as a major tourist attraction as it is planned to revive interest in Acadian crafts. As with its United Empire Loyalists' counterpart, planning and operation is the responsibility of the province's Historical Resources Administration.

In recent years the City of Saint John has built a replica of the Fort Howe Block House which served as part of a British garrison toward 1777, and has restored Pleasant Villa School (1875). At New Denmark near Edmundston, a recently opened museum is dedicated to the early Danish settlers. The Restigouche Art Gallery at Campbellton has a small permanent collection but relies heavily on travelling shows; while at Edmundston the St. Louis College art gallery is open to the public.

A Historical Resources Administration, founded in the late 1960's, provides grants in aid to community institutions until such time as a long-range policy has been resolved which undoubtedly will embrace major extension services in association with the National Museums' Board. In the meantime, training programs for museum personnel at all levels have been launched in association with the Canadian Museums' Association and the office of the Historical Resources Administration is now providing counselling and giving technical direction to the community institutions.

24

Two major developments in the museum-art gallery disciplines in the province of Quebec have still to make their impact on the museologist, enthusiasts, and the general public. The most important and by far the most spectacular project is the somewhat less than quiet transformation of Expo '67 into what undoubtedly is one of the larger museum complexes on the continent, "Man and His World." Within six months of the official closing of Expo '67, three permanent museums emerged with many other pavilions housing temporary displays.

Mayor Jean Drapeau, whose creation of Expo brought to him and to the city he governs international acclaim, takes umbrage when the word "museum" is applied to any of the pavilions, but might still be agreeable to settle for some other word to denote centres of educational entertainment. The fact that two professional museum workers were employed to search for appropriate collections is indicative of the direction His Worship had in mind for his brain child even at the moment when he and his colleagues were battling for the essential authority and finances to develop a continuous international exposition. Provincial legislation was delayed until February 1968, but by mid-May "Man and His World" was in business.

The most popular exhibition that year was an antique auto show, a private collection displayed in the former British Pavilion. The Longueuil electrical display which had been evicted from its home in 1959 but which had gone on the road as a peripatetic exhibition was accorded space in another pavilion, and was invited back for an encore performance in 1971 where, in what had been the Maine Pavilion, it attracted over one hundred thousand visitors.

The Ontario Pavilion housed "The Face of Winter," a display related to primitive and pioneer forms of transportation with firearms appropriately having their day in the Steel Pavilion. A railway museum was another popular feature and the philatelists also found space for their special interests. Younger fry viewed over five hundred works of art from children thoughout the world – this exhibition having the intriguing title of "From Youth with Love." The Montreal Museum of Fine Arts, in co-operation with a major commercial gallery, created period rooms with a French flavour, in quite naturally the former French Pavilion.

An attraction, which in 1969 received international acclaim, was the ethnological collection from the University of British Columbia's Department of Anthropology. So successful was this particular exhibition that it was held over for the 1970 season. Also in 1970, the Hungarian government loaned painting masterpieces from the world famous Budapest Museum.

The temporary displays are major contributing factors to the continuing popularity of "Man and His World," but other and more permanent projects have been introduced. The most important of these is the conversion of the International Pavilion of 1967 into the Musée d'Art Contemporain to serve as a major branch of the Musée du Québec administered by the provincial government. The pavilion had been designed as a permanent installation and had served as an experimental station for engineers, scientists, and technicians involved in the problems of environmental control for such institutions. The Musée now displays its permanent collection of contemporary paintings and sculptures purchased by the provincial authorities, and is also busy with a continuing program of travelling exhibitions the year round.

The geodesic sky bubble designed by Buckminster Fuller which served as the United States Pavilion was transformed into the Biosphere, an aviary and botanical garden, but in 1971 it temporarily returned to the United States for its "Festival of American Folklife." The former ALCAN Aquarium and Dolphin Pool was donated to the City of Montreal, and is now being administered by a separate civic agency.

Seventeen years prior to Expo, a historic fort on Saint Helen's Island, scene of the 1967 play area known as La Ronde, had been turned over to the Société Militaire et Maritime de Montréal for restoration. In 1964 the Fort was formally opened as The Military and Maritime Museum of Montreal with an added attraction featuring drill demonstrations throughout the summer months. This museum filled an important role in the year of Expo and continues its program on the Island operating outside the administrative orbit of "Man and His World."

These developments should not surprise, other than for the numerous pavilions salvaged for continued display. References have been made to International Expositions in earlier chapters, and the list can readily be expanded. In Europe the Paris Exposition of 1855 saw the takeover of the Palais d'Industrie, to be replaced in 1900 by the Palais des Beaux Arts. It is only necessary to name other expositions to bring to mind permanent museums and galleries which were brought into being; Vienna (1873) and Melbourne (1888), followed by Brussels, Antwerp, Dublin, and Madrid, but the concept of Mayor Drapeau of Montreal is, for the moment at least, the most imaginative to date.

Unfortunately, in 1973 "Man and His World" began to shrink in size. Despite its continuing popularity it had run up a $46,000,000 deficit, but with the prospects of the 1976 summer Olympics pavilion shrinkage was inevitable, with approximately fifty per cent of the buildings being removed or dismantled. The eastern portion of Isle Notre Dame has vanished to make way for the Olympic rowing track and adjacent spectator facilities. However, the dwarfed "Man" managed to attract major displays from Japan, the U.S.S.R., Bulgaria, Czechoslovakia, France, and Switzerland.

The second major development in the province was another product of Canada's centennial celebrations despite the fact that the political climate in Quebec developed a coolness which reached to deep frost during the visit of the late Charles de Gaulle.

Quebec is the largest of the ten provinces with just under thirty-four thousand square miles, or about twenty per cent of the total land area of Canada if the Northwest Territories are excluded. One fifth of this terrain contains ninety per cent of the organized communities, the vast majority of which are south of the 50th parallel. Of the more than two thousand cities, towns, villages, and hamlets only about three hundred and fifty have populations exceeding one thousand, and it is safe to say that of the six million residents (actually 5,780,849 at the 1966 census) one third reside in cities of fifty thousand or over. Montreal alone has two and a half million, with the remaining two thirds living in a closed society which, well into the twentieth century, revolved around the Church. This condition is not peculiar to Quebec alone as a similar environment may be found in the northern reaches of other provinces. Added to this, however, and peculiar only to Quebec was the philosophy of a feudalistic political society of the late Premier Duplessis.

The Quebec habitant had an isolated life out of which developed the many crafts for which the province is deservedly famous. A natural step was the growth of community movements leading to the creation of arts and crafts centres, fostered and encouraged by the church. It is understandable that the Centennial Capital Grants program in Quebec devised by a provincial commission placed emphasis on regional rather than local projects, and viewed the cultural and recreational needs in terms of providing essential services at the county level.

Reviewing the overall comprehensive program as portrayed in an official book published early in 1965, it was apparent that the centennial projects had been designed to fill basic functions in fields of recreation and culture by creating facilities in areas which never before had been able to enjoy leisure activities other than in the church hall or some all but abandoned building. In 1966, a provincial election turned out the party in power and the incoming administration took a second look at the proposals. While the scheme was not scrapped, construction was delayed with some projects being abandoned and others amended.

In spite of delays, by early 1968 the Province of Quebec ·had twenty-eight new cultural complexes containing art galleries or exhibition areas and with the occasional museum or library serving as units. Three such projects were dedicated to the younger generation and significantly christened "La Cité des Jeunes." A few years prior to Canada's centennial a Fédération des Centres Culturels had been organized and undoubtedly the philosophy of its dedicated founders was in large part responsible for the initial concept.

In June 1968, the Provincial Minister of Cultural Affairs announced that his department would "restrain and even refuse funds to some of the new centres" which, he claimed, had already become a problem to his administration. The solution to this political situation would be to divide the vast territory of the province into ten cultural regions in which a series of "maisons de la culture" would be established.

The defeat of the Union Nationale government and the return to power of the Liberal Party saw a new program implemented "for the stimulation of cultural awareness in all regions through active participation and the linking together of cultural agencies through Bureaux d'Aménagement Culturel." Development of this program would be completed within the ensuing three to five years. By December 1972, six regional centres had been established to serve about fifty communities which had resulted in "nearly four hundred cultural programs in the field of films, concerts, literature, art exhibits and lectures" being presented in more than sixty centres. Over seventy Maisons de la Culture are now affiliated with the provincial federation, with seven associates in Ontario and two in New Brunswick. Despite this surge only a few cultural complexes have been built due to the shaky fiscal condition of the province but local arts councils are encouraged to develop temporary expedients to keep the momentum alive.

A proposal made to the government to provide subsidies for local purposes was submitted by the Fédération to the appropriate Minister in 1969 and has been approved in principle. In the interim the province provides funds for the Fédération to maintain a central secretariat and staff, and also pays salaries and expenses of the regional directors, a cultural investment of about one and a half million, dollars annually.

The Federation has now close liaison with the Ontario Council of the Arts and recently purchased a collection of works by Ontario artists for circulation through Quebec. A few of its exhibitions are on loan from the National Gallery of Canada but generally comprise reproductions rather than originals.

One art centre, as distinguished from art gallery, in a predominently English speaking community and endowed by a charitable foundation, is the Stewart Hall Cultural Centre at Pointe Claire. This remodelled mansion stands in three acres of landscaped parkland and is an excellent example of architectural adaptation. It houses library, small auditorium and music room, in addition to work areas for ceramists, painters, weavers, and camera fiends, and has an exciting art gallery on the upper floor. Along with the endowment, the late Mr. and Mrs. Walter Stewart deeded the mansion and grounds to the city.

It is possible to visualize the extent of the arts council program as one studies regional maps of the province. North from Ottawa and serving the mineral mining region of Noranda are four such complexes: at Maniwaki, one hundred miles north of Ottawa; Rouyn a further two hundred miles north; and on the perimeter of the paved highway still further north, at Amos and La Sarre.

In the Chicoutimi-Lac St-Jean region, also in the northern reaches of the province, a cultural complex at Mistassini includes a Musée de l'Homme; while at Jonquière the facilities are geared largely to the performing arts but also provide art gallery space. At Chicoutimi, the major city of the region, there are plans for a centre including museum, library, art gallery, and music conservatory. Older institutions around the lake embrace an excellent zoological garden at Saint-Felicien, the Musée Louis Hémon-Marie Chapdelaine at Peribonka, and a civic art gallery in the city hall complex at Arvida. And M. Villeneuve's Musée de l'Artiste in North Chicoutimi must not be overlooked.

One of the more delightful and highly functional centres opened in October 1967 at Shawinigan, a city which has expanded with the development of the Alco aluminum plants in the area. Not quite so isolated as the previously mentioned centres, this cultural complex is designed to appeal to a much larger rural population having a five hundred seat theatre, art gallery, activities' workshops for photographers, painters, and craftsmen, and an olympic-sized swimming pool on the lower level.

Along the north shore of the St. Lawrence River, an art gallery and crafts council is alive at Baie-St-Paul, a community immortalized by The Group of Seven and other nationally known painters. Still further east at Baie Comeau, approximately three hundred miles from Quebec City, the centennial project took the form of a historical museum and regional library.

Another one hundred and fifty miles on Highway 15 is Sept-Iles, a thriving distributing and shipping point with a population of twenty thousand. A dual purpose centennial project saw the restoration of a Hudson's Bay Post to serve as a tourist attraction in the brief summer months but designed to encourage winter-time activities in the fields of the visual and performing arts and crafts.

On the south shore of the St. Lawrence, east of Quebec City, similar centennial projects were erected at Rivière-du-Loup and at Amqui, forty miles south-east of Mont Joli, which in addition to its art gallery has a botanical garden and conservatory. A cultural centre has also been promised at Gaspé. The Gaspé Peninsula is not well endowed with either museums or art centres. A centennial project at New Carlisle is dedicated to sports and recreation, while at Bonaventure, what was to have been a cultural centre ended as a city hall. This small community on the Bay of Chaleur has its own interesting museum housed in a former jail with historical implications and displays of pioneer artifacts, as well as a good collection of fossils.

In the more populated areas of the province to the north and west of Montreal, centennial centres opened in 1967 are more numerous. A Cité des Jeunes was established at Vaudreuil, with other centres serving adults and children at Lachute, Saint-Jacques-de-Montcalm, and Dorval. In the Eastern Townships, south of the metropolis, centres are strategically placed at Saint-Prosper, Châteauguay, Cowansville, and Farnham. Postponed centennial projects which opened in 1968 are located at Asbestos, Bécancour, Black Lake, Hauterive, Lac-Etchemin, La Tuque, Tracy, and Trois-Pistoles.

The three cultural centres directed almost exclusively to youth are undoubtedly the most intriguing developments to emerge out of Confederation celebrations. The most ambitious one is at Rivière-du-Loup, originally launched a few years prior to 1967. The almost self-contained "cité" occupies four or more civic blocks with sports facilities including indoor and outdoor swimming pools. A theatre, exhibition areas, studio, and workshop accommodation for arts and crafts, including photograph and cinematography, were formally opened on July 1st, 1967. Adjacent to the complex are high-rise dormitories for the rural children attending regional high schools in the city.

25

The excitement of Expo, together with the developing cultural awareness as shown in the growth of Quebec's cultural centre movement, overshadows the depressing plight of the province's historical and scholastic museums in the mid-1960's. Whereas in the remaining nine provinces a developing historical consciousness was translated into positive action, no more than ten historical museums came into being in Quebec in the second half of the 1960's, and these gains were partially offset by the disappearance of some of the early institutions. At Longueuil in 1959, the Musée Historique de l'Electricité LaBadie collection was in storage, while the college museum in the same city was closed ten years later.

Many of the scholastic museums were curtailing their activities or closing down. Included in this lengthening list were the Musée des Sourds-Muets of Montreal, the Abbé Marcotte's collection at the Sherbrooke Seminary, at La Pocatière and Nicolet, and the prestigious Redpath on the McGill campus. The Musée Historique de Vaudreuil, a community project housed in a historic building, was in precarious shape in 1967, and the Musée Sagueneen at Chicoutimi had suspended operations.

It is not difficult to pinpoint causes for what proved to be a tempory situation. Undoubtedly many of the scholastic collections had outlived their usefulness in face of more authorative text books and the advent of television. As for the community institutions, the unassailable fact of museum life from coast to coast revolves around the problem of providing continuing funds for administrative purposes.

Quebec's Ministère des Affaires Culturelles not only has jurisdiction over museums but has "sections" within the areas of music, letters, theatre, and the visual arts. The Provincial Archives is under its control as are libraries, historic monuments, archaeology, astronomy, and allied disciplines. The Ministry had concentrated almost wholly on the Musée du Quebéc for interpretation of the Province's history and only in 1970 did it place responsibility for liaison with

210

the community institutions in the hands of the Director of the Musée du Quebéc following representations by the provincial museums' association. The following year such non-profit museums were given exemption from property taxes.

In 1972, under a new dynamic Cultural Affairs Minister, Madame Claire Kirkland Casgrain, an overall review of the problems both faced by cultural organizations and museums was undertaken. At the same time the National Assembly enacted Bill 2 for the establishment of a Cultural Property Commission to advise the Minister of Cultural Affairs concerning the protection, preservation, and acquisition of any property, archaeological site, works of art of "aesthetic, legendary or scenic interest" and generally to control the destruction or loss of significant objects of man and nature. The Commission is headed by G.E. LaPalme, who in 1961 was the first to serve as a Minister of Cultural Affairs on the North American continent.

The Province of Quebec Museums' Association, founded in 1958, and which celebrated its one hundredth meeting in February 1973, has consistently worked toward higher standards and more fiscal support for the museums and art galleries within the provincial jurisdiction.

The art scene in Quebec, and particularly in Montreal, was not too bright at the end of the sixth decade of this century, despite the proliferation of galleries attached to scholastic institutions at the higher level and the growth of Cultural Centres. The Montreal Museum of Fine Arts, having one of the richest collections in Canada, faced financial problems for several years and was unable to raise the requisite funds to expand its 1912 structure other than through temporary expedients and superficial remodelling of existing areas. By 1970 the institution had built up an administrative deficit close to $1,000,000 and the Board had to stand by helplessly as important works of art, many of which had been on indefinite loan, were withdrawn by their owners and sold by auction in New York and London.

For this institution a ray of light made its appearance in 1972 with the drafting of provincial legislation to ensure its financial security. As an earnest of its intentions the province voted $150,000, an increase of $90,000 over the previous year. The Arts Council of Greater Montreal added a further $100,000, and The Canada Council likewise responded to the appeal with a special projects' grant of $50,000. The financial report for the year showed a small surplus for the first time in a decade.

With the passage of a provincial Bill in the spring of 1973 the museum is now assured of more adequate financing while retaining its identity as a community association, the province having minority representation on its Board. While for many years the museum had been viewed as having a program essentially designed for the English-speaking minority, it has consistently acquired a solid and significant collection of French-Canadian decorative arts and has encouraged Quebec painters to exhibit. In the mid-1960's its administration became fully bilingual.

The closer relationship between the province and the Montreal museum is indicative of a much brighter future as seen in the announcement in January 1973 that seventy-nine works of art from France would be shown at the museum. Lending institutions included The Louvre and the Bibliothèque Nationale, with exhibits dating from the Romanesque and Gothic to the end of the Middle Ages. A musical program including troubadour and minstrel songs, Gregorian chant, and other compositions from the eleventh to the fifteenth centuries added another dimension to the exhibit.

The David Ross McCord Museum has been more fortunate insofar as in 1957 Mr. and Mrs. Walter M. Stewart provided funds which eventually totalled $750,000 for the redesigning of the former McGill Students' Union house at 690 Sherbrooke Street West in which to continue the policies of the museum's founder whose avocation had been the preservation of Canada's history. The McCord collections include paintings by Canadian artists such as Kreighoff, Hamel, Ozias Leduc, and more than two hundred commissioned works from the brush of W. H. Bunnett, a one-time British officer. These paintings are now viewed as "an architectural record of streets and buildings in Montreal, Quebec and Trois-Rivières." The Notman Archives comprise about 350,000 glass negatives and prints of historic significance dating from as early as 1856, with other departments related to Canadian ethnology which had been collected in 1878 by George Mercer Dawson and pre-empted from its former sister (The Redpath) museum. The McCord also has extensive collections of costumes and toys. This rejuvenated museum which re-opened in early 1971 has been transformed into an institution which is the epitome of good taste and erudite display. Unfortunately, at the present time, it continues to occupy a lowly place on the McGill University budget.

The Redpath Museum which had officially closed its doors in 1970 became one year later a research centre dedicated to geology, palaeontology, zoology, anthropology, and the marine sciences. Almost coincidentally the university received as a gift and with some endowment funds a twenty-three hundred acre wilderness area southeast of Montreal in Rouville, now named the Mont St-Hilaire Nature Centre, and under the direction of Miss Alice Johannsen, the former director of The Redpath and McCord. The gift, from the estate of Brigadier Gault, includes a large summer home now serving as research centre and library. Approximately fifty per cent of the acreage is reserved for ecological research, with the remaining wilderness used for nature walks open to the general public. Dormitories have been erected for students and scholars and provision made for small conferences related to the overall policy.

As of December 31,1972 there were thirty-one museums in Greater Montreal, with a further six or seven within a fifteen mile radius beyond current boundaries representing approximately twenty-three per cent of the provincial total. In the field of the fine and decorative arts Sir George Williams University, the Université de Montréal, and the Université du Québec (Montreal) all have galleries. A museum of primitive art is on the Collège Sainte-Marie campus, and a collection of traditional French design can be seen at the Institute of Applied Arts.

Two smaller galleries, one at La Maison des Arts la Sauvegarde which emphasises the plastic arts, and a community art gallery known as the Centre d'Art du Montroyal, are administered by community societies.

The Sadie Bronfman Centre of the Young Men's/Young Women's Hebrew Association, built in 1967 and endowed by the Bronfman interests, is making its own contribution to the visual and performing arts. The Bank of Montreal has its replica of the original banking office in its present elaborate headquarters on St. James Street. Displays include a Canadian numismatic collection. In the same neighbourhood The Dow Planetarium was opened as a public relations' feature by the brewing company. As another centenary contribution the Aluminum Corporation of Canada opened its Musée Alcan in Place Ville Marie where documents, photographs, and historic mementoes of the company are on display, as well as the story of the contemporary uses of this useful metal. La Maison de Calvat, within the perimeter of Old Montreal, serves as a museum dedicated to French-Canadian decorative arts and is administered by Ogilvie's Department Store.

One major surprise was the announcement on February 21, 1972 that the Château de Ramezay, one of Montreal's foremost sight-seeing attractions, was on that day in the process of being restored to the condition it enjoyed in the early 1700's, with the approval of the Quebec Historical Monuments Commission and paid for under the winter works program of the federal government. This project was first proposed forty years ago by the Montreal Antiquarian and Numismatic Society, the oldest historical society in Canada, which has administered the museum since its inception. Cost of the complete restoration is expected to be no more than $300,000. By the end of 1972, five rooms had been virtually completed with work continuing toward a projected re-opening in 1974.

Plans of the original structure are non-existent and structural changes were made from time to time. The decision concerning the ultimate refurnishing of the Château will be influenced by the results of research currently under way. The Château served as the official residence of Claude de Ramezay, first French Governor from 1705 to 1765, and was later taken over by the British until well into the nineteenth century with a temporary occupancy by the United States between times and later to become the seat of the first Canadian government.

Most of the vast collection which literally filled almost every square foot of available space prior to the restoration is in storage. Curator John D. King had his eyes on an adjacent city owned tunnel from St. Paul Street to the Champs de Mars as an ideal display area but this was vetoed when Mayor Drapeau stated that he used the tunnel daily to reach his office. An alternate suggestion may result in the take-over of a neighbouring building to serve as museum annex and preparation area for its proposed travelling displays.

One of the oldest museums administered by a public corporation in Canada was the Telephone Historical Collection which opened in the Montreal offices of Bell Telephone in 1930 with a staff of three. By 1964, the historical and archival department had a staff of thirty-seven plus a major display area. Its climax was reached in 1967 with a Communications Pavilion at Expo but within two years the permanent exhibit on Beaver Hall Hill had been closed down although the company continues to add to its vast collection of obsolete equipment from the initial telephone used by Alexander Graham Bell to satellite communications. Throughout the years, Bell Canada has made consultants and artifacts available to museums directly or indirectly involved in communications and applied science in Canada, the United States, and abroad while its archives are consistently used by historians and scholars. Plans are being studied for a proposed major development of the Bell Homestead at Brantford, Ontario.

Within the Montreal area, the religious museums continue to serve a predominantly French Catholic population as islands in one of North America's most cosmopolitan cities. Many of the churches are themselves historic edifices and architecturally unique. A new addition to this general classification and designated "museum" only in 1966, is La Maison Saint-Gabriel at Pointe-Saint-Charles, an early land concession ceded in 1662 to Marguerite Bourgeoys, foundress of the Congrégation de Notre Dame. Six years later a convent was opened to function as a centre for the community projects of this order of nuns; this convent remains substantially in its original state today.

214

The story of this historic building starts with Cardinal Richelieu who in the final years of Louis XIII organized the Company of New France. One of the company's commitments was to recruit three hundred colonists each year during the lifetime of the fifteen-year charter in return for a monopoly of trade in the St. Lawrence valley, but thirty years later "there were not more than two thousand French in the whole country." As a result, the company's charter was revoked by Louis XIV in 1663, and New France then became "a royal province."

The sisters of the Saint Gabriel Convent were given the responsibility to meet, shelter, and arrange for the betrothal of contingents of Les Filles du Roi. A meticulous record of all the symbolic "Daughters of the King" succoured by the religious Order remains as archival material. Many of the Daughters, if not all, received royal dowries of from fifty to two hundred Louis. One entry in Sister Marie-Louise Beaudoin's book *Les Premières et Les Filles du Roi à Ville-Marie* lists Catherine de Lavaux as having been betrothed to Gilbert Barbier, "charpentier," on November 14, 1652, one of whose daughters, Adrienne, was espoused at Ville-Marie on January 10, 1667 to Étienne Truteau, direct ancestor of Canada's twentieth Prime Minister, Pierre Elliott Trudeau.

To the north, the Joliette Seminary which had been compelled to close its museum to visitors in 1966 is scheduled to open a new building in 1974 at a cost of $300,000 in which to display its European paintings and an important collection of religious decorative arts and sculptures, with a small area dedicated to contemporary French-Canadian painters. South of the city at St-Constant, the Canadian Railway Museum continues to expand, having acquired well over one hundred Canadian and European locomotives and other rolling stock, in addition to urban street cars and buses. Founded only in 1965, this museum is destined to be one of the major institutions in North America which specializes in this somewhat bulky form of artifact. At Lachine, west of Montreal, the Musée Saint-Anne and Manoir Lachine, one time home of Robert Cavalier, first mayor of Montreal, are open to the public.

In more recent years, the Historical Societies of the Eastern Townships have sponsored many new institutions, some occupying buildings of historical significance. In 1961 the Compton County Historical Museum was opened at Eaton Corners, while the Stanstead County Historical Society has its regional history museum in Stanstead, and the Barn Museum, dedicated to pioneer agricultural techniques, is located on the estate of Lady Banting at Rock Island. The Cornell Mill Museum Society took over the local grist mill in 1964 and partially restored it for the display of pioneer artifacts, and for a historical library and archives. At Knowlton, the Brome County Society restored the Knowlton Academy building in 1967 in which to house its archives, and in addition took over the Tibbetts Hill (1844) School House. The newest museum in this region is at Sutton, conceived in 1967 but opened only recently for public inspection. While it contains many pioneer artifacts, the emphasis is on the early history of communications. The founder, Mr. Edmund Eberdt, is a retired communications engineer, who in addition to donating his collection to the local museum society has built up an extensive archives.

In the realm of the fine arts the University of Sherbrooke opened its campus gallery in 1963, while at Cowansville a Centre d'Art was also a centennial gesture making its quiet contribution to bi-culturalism.

The smallest museum in Canada undoubtedly is at Rock Forest, about five miles south-west of Sherbrooke, where the Cercle des Jeunes Naturalistes des Pics-Dorés meet on summer evenings to study the stars, then bed down until the first crack of dawn to engage in bird-watching and nature walks. The size of the museum prohibits the display of anything much larger than impaled insects.

As has been emphasized earlier wildlife refuges and nature centres are included in museum disciplines. In 1973 The Canadian Wildlife Service completed two major centres in the Province of Quebec: a $350,000 project at Cap Tourmente on the north shore of the St. Lawrence, east of Sainte-Anne-de-Beaupré, and a somewhat larger wildlife centre, costing $400,000, at Percé on the Gaspé Peninsula.

216

26

A writer in 1910 describes the City of Quebec as being "divided into upper and lower town – access to the former being obtained by steep and winding streets, by several flights of narrow steps, or by an elevator. Much of the lower town recalls the older portion of such French provincial cities as Rouen or St. Malo. The streets, with one or two exceptions, are narrow and irregular. . . . In the upper town, where the streets are wider and well paved, are the better class of dwelling-houses and public buildings, most of the churches, the public walks and gardens and many of the retail shops."

Lower town continues much as it was half a century ago with some deterioration intermixed with haphazard restoration but retaining its picturesque and historical atmosphere. The upper town has fared better, with organized rehabilitation being evident. If one ignores urban sprawl on the perimeter of the two areas, Quebec City remains one of the few communities on the North American continent which can be viewed as a museum *in situ*. In the mid-1950's, local government and interested citizens successfully resisted attempts by commercial interests to introduce neon lighting, false fronts and other symbols of modernization in the upper town, including its main thoroughfares Grande Allée and Rue Saint-Louis.

Situated in the Parc des Champs de Bataille is the Musée du Québec. Here one finds a vast concentration of significant artifacts and archival documents. Despite the fact that the Musée du Québec is the oldest and largest repository in Canada dedicated solely to the preservation and interpretation of the French culture, its activities have been only sparsely reported. Reasons for this apparent neglect are many, the obvious one being, until recently, the lack of bilingual communication.

In the report of the Massey Commission, while the Quebec Provincial Archives got passing mention, the museum was completely ignored. But it is also obvious that the then Provincial Minister, under whose jurisdiction the museum functioned, likewise chose to ignore the Commission, neglecting to submit a brief or make representations to the Commissioners.

The directors and staff over the years have quietly worked to build significant collections, do research and, within the terms of reference, interpret the French fact to museum visitors. In 1937, the museum was attracting about seventy thousand visitors annually; thirty years later, when attendance was restricted due to a major remodelling program, attendance was reported at three hundred thousand.

While this book is not too much concerned with political ideologies, it has to be recognized that the end of the Duplessis regime resulted in the revitalization of museum policies in the province. In 1964, an annex was formally opened at the rear of the existing structure with the Director of the National Gallery of Canada participating as a token gesture of amity. For the first time in the museum's lengthy history, a program designed to encourage contemporary arts and crafts of French Canada was launched, together with a flow of exhibitions from abroad.

In 1966-67, the gallery areas were modernized and a contemporary display philosophy introduced. The miscellaneous collections in the areas of the natural sciences which formed a large part of the display in 1952 had disappeared. Activity programs now include constantly changing exhibitions, lectures, films, and concerts aided by a restored seventeenth century baroque organ which was installed in 1967. Both museum and archives, the latter now occupying the ground floor as a distinct entity, are sadly lacking in space in which to function.

The Province of Quebec through its Fish and Game Department administers the Aquarium du Québec at its biological centre. At the city limits of Orsainville the Jardin Zoologique is one of the outstanding zoos in Canada.

Place Royale, a complex of historic buildings surrounding the church of Notre-Dame des Victoires in lower town, has been restored at an estimated cost of $2,700,000 of federal money in grants and loans stemming from the "Canada-Quebec Agreement for Special Areas." The project embraces fifteen buildings with a further fifty-five destined for restoration at a future date. $800,000 was also allotted under the same agreement for the rehabilitation of the Quebec Seminary. Both projects were completed in 1973. Coinciding with this make-work project the City of Quebec proposed that "a corporation be created to restore and administer all of old Quebec within the city walls as a long-range undertaking." It came as no surprise, however, when the Federal Department of Indian Affairs and Northern Development announced in October 1972 that "a consensus on the general concept for the development of old

Quebec has been reached between various federal and provincial agencies and that a six point program would get under way forthwith. . . for the rehabilitation of Artillery Park and the immediate environs [to] suit contemporary requirements without losing its historical significance," with the Hotel-Dieu Hospital as one of the major focal points. Restored buildings would be used for low-cost housing and offices of the Federal government in addition to interpretation and reception centres along with an underground parking lot to accommodate one thousand cars. In making the announcement the Hon. Jean Chrétien intimated that the overall restoration would equal that of Fort Louisbourg and Lower Fort Garry. It would also provide much needed temporary and permanent employment and add to the city's tourist potential.

In the spring of 1973 work started on the restoration of Dauphine Barracks. Completion date of the entire project will be 1981 or 1982 and the estimated cost is sixteen million dollars. Other projects include a mooring basin at the Cartier-Brébeuf National Historic Park in which a replica of Cartier's flagship *La Grande Hermine* will be on display; reconstruction of the first Fort Levis, on the Lauzon Heights; and, further afield, the creation of two more National Parks at Florien in the Gaspé region, and La Mauricie in central Quebec.

Visitors to the provincial capital can find a wealth of historic sites, buildings and museums, one of which is Les Voûtes Jean-Talon, the first brewery in Canada and just a stone's throw away from the Hôtel de Ville. The low-ceilinged vaults, originally built by the intendant Jean Talon in 1668, contain artifacts of the seventeenth century, including furniture and a gun display. After visitors have explored the cavernous dungeon they are regaled with a bottle of contemporary ale at the expense of the present owners, a practice which may not be considered ethical by some members of the museum profession, but one which undoubtedly helps to build up attendance.

The museum of Le Monastère des Augustines Hospitalières depicts the story of the hospital's origin in 1639; the displays go far beyond the religious intent to become at once a study of nursing and medical techniques of the period. The Centre Marie de L'Incarnation at the convent of the Ursuline Order is also a historic edifice built in 1644 and serves as a sociological document of that period with nursing history playing a secondary role, while La Vielle Maison des Jésuites at Sillery built in 1702 on the foundations of the original Jesuit habitation (1637) illustrates the early work of that Order in New France.

Within the walls of Quebec's Citadel, a historic monument under the jurisdiction of the federal government, the Musée du Royal 22e

Régiment is dedicated to the history of one of Canada's most famous regiments, the Van Doos.

In the heart of the upper town, the Quebec Chamber of Commerce occupies La Maison Mailleu at 17 Rue St-Louis. This building serves as an example of the typical French architecture of the mid-eighteenth century and is restored to show to advantage the techniques of construction.

Laval University collections are not generally available to the public but with the opening of the Lemieux Art Pavilion in 1972 a town-gown relationship is being stimulated through the activities of the Loisirs Socio-Culturels. Exhibitions are generally related to the contemporary scene. The Musée du Séminaire de Quebec, which is affiliated with Laval, still occupies the building at 6 Rue de l'Universite in the heart of old Quebec. Here may be seen traditional paintings of Canadian and European origins, displays of gold and silversmithing, antique furnishings, numismatics, philately, and "curiosities."

The first settlement deliberately designed for functional efficiency, and which today could still serve as a prototype for study by the town planning engineer, is Le Trait Carré de Charlesbourg. Now a suburb of Quebec City, Charlesbourg was designated a "Historical Zone" only in 1965 and placed under the jurisdiction of the Quebec Historical Monuments Commission. It is now protected "against any form of transformation which might change its historical or architectural character."

Originally designed and established by Jean Talon in 1666, the settlement is now described as a "charmante localité de la banlieue de Québec." Founded by Talon at the request of Louis XIV, it had forty homes built for colonists who were despatched from France in groups. The project called for the establishment of a series of communities adjacent to the young Quebec colony, the land being part of the Seigneurie Notre-Dame-des-Anges owned by the Jesuit Order. Each community had the church as the hub with lands ceded to the settlers fanning out in the manner of wheel spokes. The homes formed the first line of defence against attack and made possible the ordered retreat to the church where a massed force could be organized to repel Indian or other invaders.

Directly south of St-Jean, on the Richelieu River, at Île-aux-Noix, Fort Lennox was taken over by the federal Historic Sites agency for restoration in 1940. The compound, forming part of the defence against possible invasion from the south, was occupied by the British from 1820 to 1829. Another important military restoration in the same general area is the Fort Chambly National Park, also on the Richelieu River. This fort was built by Captain de

Chambly in 1655, rebuilt in 1711, and later occupied by the British. Unfortunately the historic village founded by Jacques de Chambly, a restoration which was the scene of a major fire in the mid-1960's and represented a community designed for more peaceful pursuits, is now permanently closed.

At Coteau-de-Lac, where Lake St. Louis joins Lake St. Francis, a fortress comprising fifteen buildings is being restored and is open to visitors. Included in the same massive program essentially designed to provide work is an allotment of $280,000 for continued underwater archaeological research in the Baie des Chaleurs and the erection of an interpretation centre at Restigouche.

The federal government came umder severe criticism for having announced its intention of constructing a new International Airport at Ste-Scholastique, north-west of Montreal. This decision caught politicians by surprise but, accepting the inevitable, the Quebec Ministère des Affaires Culturelles concerned itself in seeking ways to preserve many of the historic buildings due to be razed. Since late 1971 two proposals have been under investigation by the provincial authorities and discussions opened with their federal colleagues which will no doubt result in a major restoration project based on (a) the pattern of Ontario's Upper Canada Village, or (b) a complex of complexes with three groups of buildings each surrounding one historic focal point in three separate locations.

One of the major archaeological projects currently being undertaken by the province in assocation with Laval University is the research, exploration, and eventual partial restoration or reconstruction of the Village des Forges de St-Maurice, a few miles from Trois-Rivières, where the foundations of what is believed to be the first foundry in Canada have been uncovered. As work continues, the Commission of Historical Monuments is creating a park site where artifacts will be on display. In Trois-Rivières itself, at 1260 Rue Royale, is one of the few museums in the province dedicated almost solely to archaeology. Also a small but interesting art centre is located in a converted house at 1580 Rue Des Chenaux, which, in addition to having a continuing program of exhibitions, is involved in other areas of the visual and performing arts.

The economic rehabilitation of Quebec as a mecca for tourists interested in becoming acquainted with a rich culture, as portrayed through its history, its crafts, and its arts, goes hand-in-hand with a conscious effort on the part of the Cultural Ministry to involve all regions of the province and all classes of society in a cultural renaissance which will also serve to create better understanding between the two founding peoples.

221

27

What Dr. Loris Russell, one-time director of the National Museum calls "the resurgence" of that institution dates from 1947 when Canada was host to the Annual Meeting of the Geological Society of America. "For this event," Dr. Russell writes, "various renovations of the building and modernization of the exhibits were authorized, and from time to time the development of the museum has been continuous" pointing to the fact that four main display areas for permanent collections were created with the large rotunda being devoted to temporary exhibitions. Eventually the museum engaged a staff of designers, artists and technicians "to develop colourful dioramas which by 1961 were attracting almost half a million visitors," the writer predicting that by 1967 it could be visualized that at least a million persons a year would be "enjoying the benefits of the Nation's premier museum and one of the world's centres of culture," somewhat of a non sequitur.

In other federal areas the Department of Northern Affairs and Natural Resources had firmly established its Historic Sites Service and a policy which had both public and political acceptance of historic park development, including costly restorations of military fortifications.

In 1942, the Canadian War Museum was founded and established on Sussex Street in the Capital with eight thousand square feet of floor space and a staff of five. Initially the museum was administered as an annex to the adjacent Public Archives.

However, the museum revolution of 1947 had still to face a number of setbacks. In 1949, the National Museum was transferred to the National Parks Service of the Department of Resources and Development with the official status of "a section of a branch" of that department. Its budget for that year was a minuscule one hundred and seventy-seven thousand five hundred dollars, but its policies and programs had been extended "to illustrate Canada's rocks, minerals, ores, fossils (both vertebrate and invertebrate), soils, topography, scenery, birds, mammals, reptiles, amphibians, fish,

222

forests, waterpowers," with the people and their culture seemingly added as an afterthought. Its full time staff of scientists involved in these disparate areas of science and history "equalled the number of scientists employed in the Insect and Spider Division of the American Museum of Natural History, New York." Actually there were ten professional staff members employed who devoted virtually all of their time to research "although aiding and co-operating in exhibition and educational activities" in the public areas.

In 1951, the Massey Commission published its report in which it recommended, among many other things, that the existing Victoria Museum building be entirely converted to museum purposes, with "adequate funds for these purposes and for general educational services." It was also proposed that the Museum be given a Board of Trustees of its own to direct its policies, and that greater emphasis be placed on educational services including loans, travelling exhibits, and lecturers with special attention given to information services and advice to small museums throughout the country which would include a simple and practicable scheme for the training of museum curators.

So far as the Massey Commission members were concerned, these recommendations would serve as a stop-gap before further recommendations could be put into effect. Long range projects, it was suggested, should include the establishment of (a) a Canadian Historical Museum "in its own adequate and appropriate building," (b) a Canadian Museum of Science "to illustrate in general the contributions of Canada to scientific research, to applied science and medicine, to invention and technical development, particularly in physics, chemistry, engineering, and other appropriate fields"; (c) a National Botanical Garden under the Department of Agriculture and to "assist in the establishment or support of other botanical gardens in certain of the various climatic regions of Canada"; (d) for the federal government to organize "a zoological garden, under the Parks Branch of the Department of Resources and Development"; and (e) "the establishment of a National Aquarium or National Aquaria, under the Department of Fisheries, in suitable regions in Canada."

By 1964 a Dominion Arboretum and Botanical Garden had been given formal recognition.

In 1967 the National Library and Public Archives moved into its new and greatly enlarged promises which included large display areas, and its former premises were used to expand the Canadian War Museum which became a division of the recently created National Museum of Man. Also in the same year, a National Museum of Science and Technology was opened with great fanfare in a leased building originally designed as a wholesale bakery, but which, curiously enough, provided a near ideal environment for the several disciplines which included mountain locomotives and other rolling stock, antique road transportation, aircraft, electronics, communications, and exhibits of contemporary science and technology.

Plans for a new museum complex which had been designed to accommodate the existing institution had been completed by the architects in 1964 "except for a few minor changes," but the project was first delayed and then totally scrapped in 1966. This resulted in the resignation of the director and a number of senior staff members when high hopes were seemingly dashed. In rapid succession, the new appointee to the directorship also resigned, ostensibly due to general frustration, despite the fact that on December 2, 1967 an Act was unanimously passed creating a Crown Corporation responsible to the Secretary of State whose major function was to administer the National Museums of Canada including the National Gallery. However, on April 10 of the following year, a third director, Dr. A. W. F. Banfield, resigned after twelve years of service. In a press interview, Dr. Banfield declared that there was no indication that frustrations would be decreased under the new administration; that the budget of the Canada Council in the current year equalled the total budgets of the National Museums (excluding the National Gallery) over half a century of operation; that his (Natural Sciences) museum was "literally hanging on the ropes" due to budget curtailments and lack of staff and facilities; and any possibility of an improvement in conditions had all but disappeared with the abandonment of plans for a new building.

Viewing the situation objectively, the scrapping of architectural plans in 1966 for the thirty million dollar building as an economy measure "to ease pressure on the construction industry," as stated by Prime Minister Lester B. Pearson, was justified for an entirely different reason. In 1961, when the proposed new building came under discussion, the planners had failed to take into account a burgeoning interest in museums or changing philosophies and techniques. By the time the plans were completed they were approaching obsolescence and would have resulted in many expensive modifications as work progressed. The *coup de grâce* was inflicted as costs for the new National Centre for the Performing Arts continued to mount from its original nine million dollars eventually to reach an astronomical forty-six million dollars.

A new survey in depth was immediately launched projecting into the mid-twenty-first century. In 1967, one proposal was hinted at by the Hon. Judy LaMarsh in a parliamentary debate when she said "we have been looking into possibilities and perhaps having in centre town [Ottawa] a display area with other buildings which are less expensive per square foot outside the core of the city for research

224

and laboratory work." In the same speech, Miss LaMarsh also expressed disappointment that, due to curtailment of funds, also brought about because of the mammoth escalating costs for the National Centre of the Performing Arts, a proposal to create a national zoological garden had been deferred.

On April 22, 1969, the Hon. Gerard Pelletier, Miss LaMarsh's successor to the office of Secretary of State, intimated another radical proposal when he stated that he favoured "making the Federal presence known throughout Canada in a way other than by post offices and national revenue buildings." In the interim, the decrepit Victoria Memorial Museum, which reportedly has been sinking by a few millimeters each year, was closed in 1970 to permit a complete remodelling of its interior. This was to make possible fourteen contemporary display areas as opposed to the previous six, equally divided between the Museum of Man and the Museum of Natural Sciences and providing a total display of seventy thousand square feet. In May of the same year, the National Museum Board announced that it had created a Design and Display Division appointing "Canada's leading expert in exhibition design" as its chief.

As the Museum building was being modernized, task forces were doing research and planning contemporary display areas to add new dimensions to museum philosophies and techniques. One such project is the orientation hall leading to the Museum of Man called "The Immense Journey" – a series of visual and aural statements relating to man's evolution through pre-history to contemporary society, as a precursor to exhibits in the fields of archaeology, anthropology, ethnology, folklore, and pioneer history. The Museum of Natural History embraces displays relating to palaeontology, geology, mineralogy, botany, birds, reptiles, and mammals. The overall concept includes areas for temporary exhibitions, with a social area and adjacent restaurant to add to the attractiveness of the two museums. A proposed Children's Museum has been delayed due to lack of an appropriate budget.

The grant for this major modernization which propels the two national institutions into the 21st century was $3,500,000, but this failed to include Public Works costs for basic construction. While some areas were thrown open to the public in late 1973, the museum complex will not return to full operation until 1974. In the interim the museum staff was kept fully occupied with a variety of public service activities including the circulation of twenty-nine exhibitions in addition to six new displays in the Canadian War Museum, and four multicultural exhibits travelling to Eskimo and West Coast Indian communities.

In the final three months of 1972 fifty-seven technical papers were published while throughout the year one hundred and fifty research projects were under way. The War Museum received and catalogued ten thousand individual items; the History Division acquired the remarkable Schwartz collection of French-Canadian furniture; the Archaeological Survey Division launched a new "rescue program"; and the Ethnological Division embarked on what is called "a salvage project."

The lifetime of this revitalized institution is expected to be one full decade. When it is considered that the Canadian Pavilion at Expo '67 and its successor at Japan's Expo '70, each with a life expectancy of six months, cost twenty and fifteen million dollars respectively, the costs are low, particularly as it is anticipated that these two museums will attract from two to three million visitors annually. For the present, the National Museum of Science and Technology continues to expand its exhibition program and increase its somewhat bulky collection of artifacts.

Major changes are also planned for the National War Museum still serving as a somewhat detached annex to the Museum of Man in its own quarters on Sussex Street. The proposed takeover of the adjacent National Mint building in 1974 will provide additional space for display, storage, and workshop uses. The National War collection of paintings which had led a peripatetic life since the end of World War I has now a permanent display area in the War Museum building. This collection numbering 5,400 individual works of art lends items to satellite military museums in other cities.

The War Museum has continuing daytime and evening lecture series for adults and children, and has a firm liaison with the Regimental Museums in Armed Forces camps across the country. These small institutions numbering thirty-five, which over the years have been administered and financed by Regimental Committees, were recently given quasi-official recognition by the Department of National Defence together with annual grants for their operations.

28

The first Canadian art circuits were organized and well under way in Western Ontario and the four Western provinces toward the end of World War II. A Maritime Art Association adopted a similar program shortly thereafter, followed by the organization of a circuit in Northern Ontario, thus blanketing most of the country with co-operative agencies whose primary function was to tour art exhibitions to smaller, more isolated communities.

Despite inadequate finances and staff shortages, the National Gallery responded to the demands by these circuits. The Massey Commission Report refers to the fact that "exhibitions of Canadian paintings have increased in number from thirty-one in 1928-29 to two hundred in 1947-48" despite the fact that there were "two major limiting factors, apart from cost. One is the absence in other Canadian cities of fireproof buildings in which to hang pictures, and the other is the want of experienced staff in local galleries to take care of unpacking, display and repacking." The Report added that there were only six local art galleries in the country completely satisfactory in these respects.

A brief presented to the Commissioners by the National Gallery Director and his Advisory Board eloquently outlined the limitations of the gallery staff to implement new programs and even questioned whether it could carry on its existing services unless immediate needs were met. The brief asked that "the present anomalous position in relation to the Department of Public Works [to whom the Gallery reported] be clarified, "that the National Gallery be established as a distinct branch of government under its own Board of Trustees and a competent authority be created for "advising the Government on such art matters as are properly a matter of public interest." This latter suggestion was designed undoubtedly to curb uninformed criticisms which continued to find their way into the pages of Hansard.

Another pressing need was for a new building, for the existing space lacked proper facilities, was overcrowded, "and the temporary partitions together with the highly inflammable materials used in the basement workshops [by staff members of the Geological Survey] form a serious fire hazard." A new gallery should have adequate display areas, the Commission was told, a reference and library section, air conditioning plant, photographic studio, and a laboratory for inspection and repair of works of art to serve not only the gallery itself but all public galleries across Canada. A greatly increased staff was also suggested. All the proposals were endorsed by the Royal Commission.

About the time of the Massey Commission hearings, two new staff members were appointed to the Gallery. Dr. Robert Hubbard, a young art historian, was named Curator of Canadian Art, and Donald Buchanan, joining the staff initially to develop special projects, within a brief period became Director of the Industrial Design Section which was establishing its own small Design Centre on a site where the present National Gallery now stands. Working with the Department of Reconstruction, National Research Council, and the National Film Board, Mr. Buchanan created a major exhibition with revolutionary overtones, stressing contemporary Canadian design, which had its premiere showing at the annual convention of the Canadian Manufacturer's Association in 1958 before being sent across the country for display in every large city. Out of this project the National Gallery established an agency under Mr. Buchanan to investigate problems of industrial design and to serve as information bureau. So far as is known, the dovetailing of fine art into industrial design by a National Art Museum had never previously been undertaken in any other country.

A small portion of a Carnegie Corporation grant was used to launch *Canadian Art*. A quarterly edited for several years by Mr. Buchanan, it served as the prototype of succeeding art publications in Canada out of which grew *Arts/Canada,* a bilingual magazine now published by an independent non-profit agency with Canada Council subsidies.

The Royal (Massey) Commission on National Development in the Arts, Letters and Sciences received its Commission of Appointment from the Governor General in Council on April 8, 1949. Two years later, in May 1951, its completed report was presented to His Excellency for reference to the government of the day. A total of one hundred and forty-seven recommendations were included in the report of five hundred and seventeen pages, sixty-eight of which referred specifically to the various areas and disciplines associated with Canadian museums. Possibly with tongue in cheek, the Commissioners announced that "If all our recommendations were accepted, the total figure might in isolation appear substantial, but in

228

comparison with the costs of other activities of Government, it would be modest, almost insignificant."

Just over six years elapsed before the federal government brought into being The Canada Council following providential windfalls of one hundred million dollars and lobbying by the Canadian Arts Council. However, in the interim some of the less spectacular and certainly less expensive recommendations were implemented.

In 1951, the National Gallery was placed under the management of a Board of Trustees, replacing the former Advisory Council but retaining a majority of the former advisors. The new Board was called upon to report, not to Public Works but to the Minister of Immigration and Citizenship, certainly a forward step. A substantially increased budget was approved by the House and, during the ensuing months, an ambitious international architectural competition was announced for a new gallery. Eventually a winning design was selected, but possibly the ghost of Public Works hovered over the Trustees as this project was shelved. In the interim, the new administration had made contact with the House of Lichtenstein establishing a rich source for purchases of important Old Master paintings.

Dr. H. O. McCurry, second Director of the National Gallery, retired in 1955 after thirty-six years service. An accolade written by A. Y. Jackson in his autobiography says, "What funds there were [for gallery acquisitions] were administered cautiously and wisely by McCurry, and during his regime important paintings were acquired: Daumier's *Third Class Carriage*, *Pieta* by Massys, Rembrandt's *Bethsheba at Her Toilet*. Paintings by Gaugin, Cezanne, Van Gogh and Degas. . . . Whether McCurry had more discretion or the Academy Royal Canadian had become more liberal, there were no disagreements. When he retired there was a general feeling of regret in Canadian art circles."

The new dynamic director, Alan Jarvis, at once became the storm centre of controversy. Many of the plans he inherited and which had remained just as gleams in the eye of his predecessor, were brought to fruition overnight. A greatly increased budget was demanded and obtained. Mr. Jarvis had refused to accept the appointment as a civil servant and at the same time requested that he have the status, if not the title, of Deputy Minister making possible direct representation to his Minister. Appointments were announced almost weekly to head new departments and services. A Director of Extension Services was engaged with liaison officers for west and east given roving assignments.

The first meeting of art educators and directors with senior National Gallery staff members and representatives from the Trustees was held at the University of British Columbia in 1956 to discuss co-ordinated programs and long range projects. The new crop of Canadian abstractionists were having their day at court. Jury shows, open to any and all Canadians in the varied fields of the visual arts, were announced only to produce critical comment from the die-hard traditionalists who saw their works rejected out of hand. Major acquisitions were being purchased in addition to works by the younger generation of native artists.

Another major accomplishment of the director was the appointment of Dr. Nathan Stolow to take over the conservator's workshop in the gallery basement, and who, in the next five years, was to gain an international reputation for his significant contributions to the sciences associated with environmental control and art restoration. A new morale was rapidly developed as Trustees and Director established a rapport not only with the responsible Minister but also with other members of the Cabinet. One set-back was the cancellation of plans for a new gallery, but a compromise was arranged whereby a new building, eventually to house the Department of Immigration and Citizenship, would be constructed forthwith and adapted to serve as still another temporary expedient. While all this was in progress, a change of government brought a minister hostile to all contemporary art forms and who preferred the traditional civil service attitude to the swinging and somewhat independent Director, resulting in at first private disagreements eventually developing into public recriminations. Paradoxically, it was another proposed Old Master purchase from the Lichtenstein collection which brought issues to a head and precipitated the resignation of Mr. Jarvis in 1959.

Prolonged negotiations had been under way with Count Lichtenstein for many months prior to the defeat of the previous regime and verbal assurances had been given that funds well over two million dollars would be available for the purchase of three important paintings. The deal was consummated, or so the Director assumed, but the new Minister, supported by the Minister of Finance, now actively hostile to the Director and all his works, declared the contract null and void, leaving the embattled Mr. Jarvis with no option but to resign. The resignation brought about an incipient crisis within the gallery but, while rumours of other resignations of staff and trustees were in the air, no positive action was taken and the controversy faded away as the name of a new appointee was announced.

The appointment in 1960 of Dr. Charles Comfort to succeed Alan Jarvis came as a surprise to the majority of interested bystanders. Had the then responsible Minister followed her personal instincts an academician representative of the turn of the century vintage might have been given the post. In retrospect, it is possible to say that Dr. Comfort was a logical choice – a director who could
230

be a stabilizing force and one who could hold office only for five or six years before reaching the mandatory retirement age. The new Director had been closely associated with The Group of Seven and was a founding member both of the Canadian Group of Painters and the Canadian Society of Painters in Water Colors. He had even served as President of the Royal Canadian Academy; had written a special study on Canadian Painting for the Massey Commission; served as a senior combat War Artist in England, Italy and Northwest Europe; served also on the advisory and purchase committees of the Art Gallery of Toronto; and was, at the time of his appointment, Associate Professor of Art and Architecture at the University of Toronto. In this last capacity, a number of young directors and curators in major galleries across Canada had been his students. Dr. Comfort had also built up a national reputation as a muralist. It was not generally known, however, that about the time of his appointment he was experimenting with hard-line abstractions.

The last few months of the Jarvis regime had been taken up with the preparations for the opening of the new six storey Lorne Gallery in downtown Ottawa. One of the first duties of the new director, and one which possibly was the most difficult of his short tenure of office, was to mastermind the formal opening of the building. So far as the Minister was concerned, Dr. Comfort's predecessor was *persona non grata,* yet his contributions in planning the new gallery could not be overlooked. In the end, quiet diplomacy prevailed.

The new gallery quite naturally demanded a major reorganization of an exhibition program and a further development of staff, particularly as tentative plans for centennial celebrations and more major exhibitions were even then being discussed. Staff and services had to be expanded to meet the various challenges, a major one being to persuade the government that the purchase program of Old Masters should be continued or even accelerated. At the same time, there should be no slowing down of accessions by contemporary Canadians.

During Dr. Comfort's term of office, the gallery displayed a succession of exhibitions, some initiated by his predecessor, the like of which had never been seen in Canada. These included the Tukankhamen Treasures; Heritage de France; the Van Gogh retrospective; the Controversial Century, 1850-1950; Victorian Artists in England; and Eighteenth Century Paintings from The Louvre. In 1964 the National Conservation Research Laboratory was established as a major branch of the gallery. Dr. Comfort was also responsible for the founding of the Canadian Art Museum Directors' Organization which now serves as a link between the major galleries throughout Canada and the national institution.

In 1963 the government in power was replaced by the administration of the Rt. Hon. Lester B. Pearson. One of the early decisions of the new government was to pave the way for more Massey Commission proposals by transferring responsibilities for both National Gallery and the Museum Complex to the new Department of the Secretary of State. There was almost immediate loosening of purse strings, making possible, for the first time in the gallery's history, a realistic approach to greater expansion of its policies and programs.

Jean Sutherland Boggs, the fifth Director, assumed office in 1966, a time when most of the senior staff members were engaged in organizing more shows of international importance, both at the gallery and in Expo pavilions. By 1967 a Deputy Director was engaged and Dr. Hubbard was elevated to the post of Chief Curator. There were now seven curatorial divisions made up of Canadian, European and Contemporary Art, Research, Prints and Drawings, the Canadian War collections, and Photography. Extension services were reorganized as were the areas of education. The films on art programs developed in co-operation with the National Film Board and the Canadian Film Institute likewise have grown into another major service. Early in 1968 the extensive reference library and some of the offices were moved into an adjacent building to make possible the creation of more exhibition areas as a further temporary expedient.

In an article published in *The Canadian Collector* of November 1969, Miss Boggs indicated that repercussions still occurred at times. One recent accession had apparently "aroused more ire than any other object in the National Gallery's collection since I arrived in June 1966." However, undaunted, she added, "History suggests that a work as provocative as this in the period in which it was produced is apt to have a meaning which may endure." In the same article, the writer pointed to the fact that, unlike many of the Canadian galleries and national art museums abroad, monetary and other gifts were virtually non-existent.

In the fall of 1968, Dr. Boggs faced criticism when, in an effort to hold down costs, she persuaded her Board to charge admission fees of one dollar for the Jacob Jordaens exhibition, the largest ever to be mounted by the gallery and comprising three hundred and fourteen works drawn from eighteen countries. Over the years a tradition had been developed that, as taxpayers' money was involved, admissions should be free. An immediate resistance to this precedent was felt with letters pouring into the papers, particularly the media in the nation's capital. Editorial writers and columnists joined the hue and cry accusing the Director with wilful extravagance and waste of public funds. The inconsistency is that The National Centre for the Performing Arts, heavily underwritten by the taxpayers, provides cultural entertainment of high calibre at box office prices.

Recently Dr. Boggs created another curatorial department dedicated to mediaeval decorative arts, and initial purchases were made in 1971. Acquisition of avant garde works continues unabated.

The National Museums Act of December 1967 decreed that a Trust Account be opened "to which shall be credited all monies received by the Corporation by gift, bequest or otherwise." Article 17 of the same Act gives the Corporation powers to acquire by gift, bequest or otherwise any real or personal property. The National Revenue Act makes provision for a one hundred per cent tax deduction, subject to certain conditions, of such gifts received by the federal authority in the name of The Crown. In 1968 the regulations were changed to permit gifts to the provinces to receive similar tax benefits.

In 1970 Miss Margaret Hess of Calgary donated $25,000 to the Museums' Board to establish "a fund for important studies and research projects." At the time, Dr. William E. Taylor, Jr., Director of the National Museum of Man, announced that "This is a new and dramatic event. . . and a distinct source of encouragement for those involved in the work of our National Museums."

Comparative figures over the past two decades reflect the growing consciousness in Canadians of cultural matters. In the fiscal year 1951-52, the National Museums complex in which the National Gallery is included occupied less than 90,000 square feet and staff for the three units stood at 64. Gross attendance was reported by the Dominion Bureau of Statistics at 413,230. For the fiscal year 1971-72, six museum units were occupying 398,000 square feet, staff had increased to 428, and attendance had reached 1,124,902. As for revenues, the expenditures of the museums complex in 1951-52, including funds for acquisitions, was less than half a million dollars ($438,270 to be exact). The approved budget ten years later had mounted to an impressive $8,209,517.

In the overall renaissance of the National Museums, many innovations were debated from 1964 to 1972 at seminars and consultations within months after federal cultural responsibilities were placed in the hands of the Secretary of State. The first such meeting at Ste-Adèle, Quebec, saw the Hon. Maurice Lamontagne and a corps of senior officials closeted with representatives drawn from diverse cultural groups and museum societies for five days. It was here that the Canadian Museums' Association was promised grants of $30,000 a year for three years to establish its National Secretariat in Ottawa and conduct a national survey of museum resources.

Under Senator Lamontagne's successor, the Hon. Judy LaMarsh, the National Museums' Board, a Crown corporation, was created, and in 1971, when the Hon. Gerard Pelletier took over the office, further consulations were held with the new Minister outlining his own radical plans to make it possible for the National Museums to go to the people. In the first days of March 1972, Mr. Pelletier placed his proposals before the Cabinet and was given the essential approval to implement this program, which within the coming decade will reach out to the most isolated communities in the country.

In summary the new policy will make available to all regions of Canada displays and services drawn from the national and regional collections; will recognize up to forty major institutions in the ten provinces and the Northwest Territories as "associated" museums which will receive both capital and operating grants "to ensure full and safe utilization of items loaned to them"; will establish "National Exhibition Centres" manned by cultural development officers to provide services to smaller art galleries, museums and communities; will set up liaison agencies with other federal and provincial agencies designed to provide cultural programs through the various media; will launch an inventory of artistic, historical, and scientific collections in Canada; and will provide legislation to curtail wholesale exportation of objects considered "part of our national heritage."

The administrative machinery to get the wheels turning was promptly set into motion with the National Museums' Board and The Canada Council being immediately involved. A consultative committee representing all regions of Canada was linked with the National Museums' Board in May 1972 to assist in establishing terms of reference, surveying immediate needs, and nominating museums and art galleries to serve as "associates" to the national institutions. As of March 31, 1973, the initial grant of $8.1 millions had been allocated to finance projects and get administrative machinery under way.

Among projects submitted for consideration were: the creation of suburban display areas; museumobile projects designed to travel into more isolated regions, including the Northwest Territories and the Yukon; building of "Exhibition Centres" to serve as distributing agencies, and provide stimulation in areas hitherto neglected.

Additional projects relate to more active involvement of the public sectors in what is described as "Popularization" along with multcultural projects, the training of museum personnel, and encouragement to small community institutions to spread their wings. An increase of the original grant to $13,000,000 for 1973-74 makes possible the acceptance of more "Associate" institutions as the second phase of this plan with $18,000,000 ear-marked for 1974-75.

234

In the overall program, multi-culturalism is one of the keynotes encouraging displays representing all ethnic folk ways, both native and adopted, and is planned to strengthen the ties of nationhood. The impact of this project, unique throughout the world, has already been felt through massively increased attendance levels and individual involvement while the theme of "Decentralization and Democratization" has subordinated the federal presence to that of the cultural aspirations of men and women at the grass roots.

Yet the federal presence persists but in an entirely new light. All National Museum components are also designated as "Associates" and must assume responsibilities for initiating their separate programs, as in the case of the National Museum of Man which in November 1972 staged an exhibition of West Coast Indian decorative arts in the National Centre for the Performing Arts, later making the collection available for travel to other regions. The same museum in January 1973 had the first of ten museomobiles (patterned after The Ace caravans that have been touring Alberta for the past four or five years) taking the story of the Eskimo into the Atlantic provinces as far as the outports of Newfoundland.

A senior member of the National Museums' Board when interviewed declared that such travelling displays were not intended to be shown in the more populous communities but were designed to reach boys, girls, men, and women in the remotest settlements of Canada. During the summer months they will be placed in the more isolated recreational areas for the entertainment – and education – of tourists.

The exhibition centres currently being built in many of the smaller towns likewise will be used to bring from the Ottawa repositories significant stories in three-dimensional form of Canada's heritage. Miraculously, these innovations were happening within one year after the program was announced in Calgary on March 20,1972.

If the National Gallery is to expand its extension services efficiently and at the same time make provision for a continuing flow of gifts, bequests, and purchases, its first priority must be a new and expressly designed building which will serve not merely as a showcase but will indeed be a National Museum of Art, a fine but important distinction. The federal government has long felt the need for such a repository but bureaucratic wheels turn slowly. In the fall of 1972 the Canadian Press carried a despatch to the effect that a new building had been authorized at a cost of $40,000,000, a report which was only partially correct. Approval in principle undoubtedly has been written into Cabinet minutes but the estimate has yet to be placed before the Treasury Board.

If Canada's twentieth century culture is to have any meaning for future generations, much of the story will be told through its artistic heritage. Already Canada's art collections occupy twenty-six warehouse buildings in and around the capital city – works of art which were bought for a song (and the occasional prayer) and which today can be valued in millions of dollars. Paul Duval, Canadian art critic and historian, recently cited one such example, a painting by an Italian renaissance artist that had cost the nation $25,000 in 1937 and today could readily be sold for $1,400,000. Whether the work is judged for its cultural values or as a continuing national financial asset, it serves no purpose being hermetically sealed in a fireproof vault for a posterity one thousand years hence.

One of the initial steps taken by the National Museums' Board under the new program was to divorce the National Conservation Laboratory from the national museums and establish it in its own right as The National Conservation Institute. A 30,000 square foot central headquarters is located in Ottawa with regional laboratories to serve British Columbia, the Prairie provinces, Ontario, Quebec, and the Atlantic provinces. Conservation services will be available to art galleries and museums operated in the public interest with restoration services made possible to the private sectors of the country at cost.

As the new policies are implemented, a greater flow of art works will be pulled out of storage and sent on the road, some even reaching "the most isolated communities." Initially, in 1973, and in cooperation with the Vancouver, Edmonton, and Dalhousie Art Galleries, ten exhibitions travelled to thirty-eight galleries. The collections included an Augustus John Retrospective; photographs by Charles Gagnon; and "Comic Art Traditions in Canada."

Two more national Museums will open in Ottawa in 1974-75. A National Museum of Numismatics administered by the Bank of Canada will occupy the entire main floor of the existing bank building on Wellington Street and serve as centre-piece to a considerably enlarged repository for Canada's bullion. The numismatic collection deals primarily with Canadian monetary forms from Indian wampum and Hudson's Bay vouchers to contemporary coinage and notes. Since 1966 the Bank has been unobtrusively building up an impressive and significant collection that, of necessity, has been kept in close security.

The Canadian Postal Department likewise has been in the field of historical collecting over the years, and in May 1974 will formally open the National Postal Museum on the ground floor of the Alex Campbell Building. Already plans are in the making for specially designed space in the new headquarters of the Postal Department. Although exhibits will be somewhat restricted the Department has acquired many large three dimensional artifacts, including one of the once-familiar mail coaches, for subsequent display.

236

29

The National Historic Sites Service, as a federal agency, emerged out of the National Parks administration, following its Minister into the Department of Resources and Development in 1950, and eight years later making another departmental switch into Northern Affairs and National Resources. It is now seemingly well established under the aegis of the Department of Indian Affairs and Northern Development.

In October 1971, a comprehensive policy was drafted by the National Historic Sites and Monuments Board; the thirty page document proposed criteria for the designation of sites of national historical significance and also outlined a long range development policy. A task force was appointed to establish thematic and regional priorities in addition to producing a master plan for the next decade. Provision has also been made for closer co-operation with governments at the lower levels and for the creation of buffer zones to preserve and enhance the surrounding terrain.

In addition to administrating its historic parks, the Service consistently provides money and technical aid to municipalities to preserve or restore buildings of national significance such as Ermatinger House at Sault-Ste-Marie and the Emily Carr birthplace in Victoria, B. C. The Board also concerns itself with field work and research covering archaeology on land and under water.

In 1969 a national survey of important architectural and historical buildings was launched and within two years a list of close to one hundred thousand had been compiled. A second phase got under way in 1972 to select those premises deemed to be worthy of more detailed study. It goes without saying that the erection of plaques, cairns, and other monuments continues unabated. The capital budget for this relatively unobtrusive program for 1970-1971 was $7,000,000, plus a continuing grant for the Fortress of Louisbourg project. This funding did not include restoration programs financed through the Local Initiative and Depressed Regional Economic Expansion programs, and make-work projects undertaken by other federal departments.

The 1972 capital development program of this Service involved forty-two individual projects, many of which are new and extending into all provinces, the Northwest Territories, and the Yukon.

The activities of the Board and its services spread far beyond the more publicized historical showplaces. For instance, in February 1972 it was announced that eight canals with important historic links and previously administered solely by the Canals' Division of the Ministry of Transport, had been placed under the wing of the Historic Parks branch "which will work closely with the provinces to develop the recreational potential of these waterways and to protect their park, wildlife habitat and historical values." The eight canals are The Rideau, Trent-Severn, Murray, Carillon, Ste. Anne, St. Ours and Chambly, both on the Richelieu River, and St. Peters Canal in Cape Breton.

Two major developments within the Department were outlined by the Hon. Jean Chrêtien, then Minister of Indian Affairs and Northern Development, in a speech delivered in Vancouver, September 12, 1972, when he announced what he described as "two initiatives which will complement the work of the Conservation Program of my Department." The first was a survey to be known as the Canadian Engineering Achievement Record to be conducted by volunteer members of the Engineering Institute of Canada to "identify engineering and technological achievements which have contributed to the historic, economic, cultural, technical, scientific or military development of Canada." The second initiative was the formation of a national trust to be known as Heritage Canada, an independent, nonprofit corporation which would make possible "the protection of buildings of architectural and historical value for workable contemporary use, and as well, to keep natural areas and scenic landscapes unspoiled for future generations."

Heritage Canada has been provided with "the authority to acquire through purchase, donation, bequest, exchange or lease lands, buildings, structures and artifacts... and to enter into cost-sharing arrangements for the preservation and protection. . . of such accessions." It received a $12,000,000 federal endowment to get under way, but, said the Minister, "it is expected that it will generate its own funds from private sources, membership fees, revenues from the sale or rental of renovated buildings and from other investments."

A United States organization, "Partnership in the Arts," issued a bulletin in 1971 disclosing that federal contributions to the arts in that country had reached a per capita funding of seven and a half cents; the organization urging a massive increase of thirteen times its current appropriations "for the National Endowment." The writers pointed to the fact that contributions to the arts by the Aus-

238

trian government had reached $2.00 per capita; the New York State largesse being just half that amount; while Canada's contribution to the same cultural cause at the federal level had reached an eyebrow-lifting $1.40 per capita. It is unfortunate no detailed break-down was given, but it is obvious that the millions of Canada Council monies played a major role in this documentation.

An analysis of Canada Council grants for 1971-72 discloses that out of $32,000,000 awarded for grants and subsidies, the academics in the disciplines of the humanities and social sciences received the lion's share amounting to over $19,500,000; the performing arts received a little more than $9,000,000, most of which was shared among seventy-three professional companies. This left approximately $3,300,000 for the visual arts. Out of this sum twenty-four galleries benefitted to the extent of $638,838; the balance was used for grants in aid to individuals and societies working in the creative fields. However, five years earlier, twenty galleries had received only $271,960 out of a $4,400,000 appropriation.

The Council, however, had been building up its own fine art collection since 1960, having invested $90,000 over a ten year period. The collection was sent on tour in 1970 culminating in a full-scale exhibition at the National Gallery; it was then sold to the Department of External Affairs in that year "at current valuations" for $160,000. The art works now serve as decor in the Department's new Sussex Street home and in embassies throughout the world. The $70,000 profit is being used to build up a second collection.

In 1972 The Canada Council launched its "Art Bank" with a $5 million budget to be expended over five years for the purchase of more art works by established Canadian artists for a self-liquidating rental project in association with most if not all federal Ministries and Crown Corporations. Its avowed intention is to establish new aesthetic standards in federal public buildings across the nation.

The need for continued advances in the humanities and social sciences is beyond dispute but The Canada Council has some reservations as stated in its 1971-72 annual report. "While the Council has reason to be proud of many achievements of scholars, we are less sure that we can point to this entire field of scholarship with confidence that we are lending our support in the most productive way" – adding that "we must examine the full spectrum. . . to discover whether we have been too disjointed in our efforts and whether gaps remain in which the Council might usefully take the initiative."

According to André Fortier, appointed Director in the summer of 1972 to replace Peter Dwyer who had retired due to ill health, the entire spectrum in the arts would also be reviewed due to the National Museums' Board having initiated a program of financial aid to art galleries and museums. Mr. Fortier expressed a personal opinion that major revisions in policy could be anticipated and new long-range programs implemented.

One such program was announced in February 1973, tentatively called "Explorations," designed to reach into Canada's grass roots and to aid aspiring artists or groups in the areas of "folk art and popular culture." For this project a one million dollar budget was created, and for the first time in the short history of The Canada Council regional advisory committees were established to review applications.

Injections of federal funds from departments not generally associated with culture are not to be discounted. Temporary expedients to help bolster sagging employment and stimulate economic growth are now taking on permanency. Major grants under the Department of Regional Development, known as DREE, have been made available for historic restoration in most provinces. British Columbia, one of the more affluent provinces, received approximately one million dollars in LIP grants for forty-three museum projects and provided temporary employment for four hundred and forty men and women in 1972-73.

Other federal funds designed for make-work projects include Opportunities for Youth, and at the other end of the spectrum the New Horizons' Fund made available for senior citizens. One such example of the latter program is a fifteen thousand dollar grant to a group of Saanich, British Columbia, pioneers who have been rounding up antique farm machinery for restoration and display as historical artifacts.

30

The surfeit of military restorations along that portion of the four thousand miles of undefended border within Ontario was replaced in the post-war years with programs calling for the salvaging and preservation of buildings and communities having more peaceful connotations. Air travel, indoor plumbing, electrical gadgetry, and radio were now being taken for granted, at least in the more populated urban areas. Emphasis on the struggle for survival had shifted from primitive improvisations to the products of mass production. Pioneer homes were being torn down in the name of progress, and with them the other remnants of primitive tradition were vanishing – the swaddling clothes of a young civilization.

However, a few echoes of border disagreements remained. During the American Civil War, Canada had served as a refuge for fleeing slaves and two way-stations on "the underground railway" within a few miles of Detroit were among the early restorations of the 1940's. At Dresden the home of the Reverend Josiah Henson, the legendary principal figure of the Harriet Beecher Stowe novel, was christened "Uncle Tom's Cabin" when it was opened as a historic ethnic restoration in 1946. In the same decade at Chatham, twenty miles away, the First Baptist Church, site of John Brown's anti-slavery convention of 1858, was restored to display relics of the event.

The Mennonites, who at the time of their migration from Germany in 1786 had settled in the Kitchener-Waterloo area, were among the first to gather objects relating to their search for religious freedom. In 1953 a pioneer village was developed at Doon as a symbol of the Mennonite way of life. Among the early buildings were the Peter McArthur House, Freeport Church and a roller flour mill, along with Conestoga wagons in which members of the sect had transported their possessions. Other buildings have been added in recent years, and in the summer months folk festivals, pioneer days, and religious celebrations are held to perpetuate the Mennonite traditions while craft workshops continue to preserve their pioneer industries.

Dr. Wilfrid Jury at the University of Western Ontario in London, began a collection of Indian Pioneer artifacts on the campus as early as 1935, developing a museum twelve years later. In 1957 Dr. Jury planned and brought into being the Fanshawe Pioneer Village north of London, a typical crossroads community of the pre-railway era where, in the manner of Doon, displays of pioneer skills are featured during the summer months.

A few years later this indefatigable Doctor turned his attention to the Huron Indian culture at Midland, where he supervised the building of a replica of an ethnic village compound. Throughout the summer months, visitors are exposed to continuous demonstrations of the daily primitive life of the Hurons, including not only sights and sounds, but also pungent odours as they existed three hundred years ago. His major achievement, however, is Ste. Marie Among The Hurons in the same city of Midland, an authentic reconstruction of Ontario's first European community where lived six of North America's martyr saints from 1639 until their assassination ten years later. This replica is undoubtedly one of the all-important of its kind on the continent. In 1971 a new and large orientation centre, which includes two auditoriums and an interpretative museum comprising an additional 20,000 square feet, was opened and Dr. Jury is still working on plans for an Indian agricultural colony of the seventeenth century. Within a stone's throw is the Fort Ste. Marie Jesuit Church and Residence with its own museum and Martyrs' Shrine, while in the small city itself, the local historical society administers the Huronia Museum, founded in 1947, and since 1967 located in a new centennial museum building.

Adjacent to all this is the recently developed Wye Marsh Wildlife Centre, a federal undertaking directed toward conservation of regional birds and mammals. Midland has a year-round population of slightly more than ten thousand.

In 1957 at Madoc, one hundred and thirty miles west of Ottawa on Highway 7, a group of historic buildings of the period of 1800 was assembled,. including farm house, school and a water powered sawmill. Within ten years, thirteen more pioneer villages developed in Ontario partially as a result of a provincial-wide conservation program designed to deal with problems of ecology. The most famous, at Crysler's Farm Battlefield Park, a few miles east of Morrisburg, was originally conceived as a small cross-roads settlement. Now not only a re-creation of forty buildings of the late eighteenth – early nineteenth centuries, it also serves as a permanent monument to the development of the St. Lawrence Seaway. Today, Upper Canada Village is ":a living village museum portraying the evolution of life in the province from 1795 to 1860." The restored buildings moved from areas in the region now flooded, include

242

churches, mills, stores, farm buildings, homes and taverns, the latter strictly limited to non-alcoholic drinks, for the moment at least. One of its major contributions to the museums' field is its concentration of pioneer activities in virtually all areas, a living museum in truth.

Coincidentally, the City of Toronto opened Black Creek Village in 1960. Approximately five miles north of the city centre near Highway 400, it has undoubtedly been overshadowed by the fame of the Upper Canada project. However, it is equally important not only as a tourist attraction but also as an authentic re-creation of a settlement of the 1860's. Unlike most pioneer villages, Black Creek Village has a year-round program, initiated in 1966, concentrating on organized school visits during the winter months. In mid-1970 the Metropolitan Conservation Authority advertised for charitable contributions toward further restoration and to provide extended facilities at the "Albion Hill Conservation School" where more than 25,000 pupils, student teachers, and conservationists had taken natural science courses in the preceding five years.

While many individual buildings in the province have been restored or taken over for museum purposes as temporary expedients, authentic restorations have been relatively few, but authenticity emerged gradually from examples established by the National Historic Sites Services. Its initial project in Ontario was Laurier House in the nation's capital, originally occupied by Canada's eighth Prime Minister and later by the Rt. Hon. William Lyon Mackenzie King during his term of office.

Ordered restoration programs became prevalent in the early 1950s, reaching a peak during centennial year, although only two of the twenty-four Ontario centennial capital museum projects, the Allan MacPherson House at Napanee, and Dundurn Castle at Hamilton, were professionally completed by 1967. Dundurn, undoubtedly, is the epitome of all such restorations from its ostentatious Victorian decor in the family area to the dark, dank servants quarters below stairs. The success of Dundurn Castle as a tourist attraction and prestige symbol for the city has resulted in the acquisition and restoration of the McQuestion House, built in 1840 and occupied by descendants of the family until 1966. This latest addition to a growing number of museums was opened to the public in the summer of 1971.

While about one third of the historic buildings listed in Ontario are dedicated to the original owners, the collecting programs in many have strayed far away from the initial intent. One of the more intelligent approaches to this situation in which compromises were effected without prejudicing restoration is the Jordan Historical Museum of the Twenty, a name derived from the culture of the Twenty Mile Creek region of the Niagara Peninsula and developed by a local wine company. This museum complex is a prototype in miniature of the pioneer village, and includes the Fry and adjacent homes and schoolhouse, in addition to the original vintage house dating from 1815. The exhibits, unlike those in the general run of pioneer museums, are changed annually, many of the artifacts being borrowed from descendants of the pioneer families in the immediate region, and the entire project is financed by the winery.

Pioneer grist mills have proven to be popular restorations in the southern region of the province. One of the more exciting is at Almonte where the Mill of Kintail serves also as a memorial to surgeon-sculptor R. Tait McKenzie, who not only used the mill as home and office, but created a large studio where he could practise his avocation and which now houses many of his works.

The era of the 1950's saw eighteen rehabilitation programs largely dedicated to regional history. Some of the more attractive ones include the Eldon House at London, former home of the city's first treasurer, and administered by the Public Library Board; the McFarland House at Niagara-on-the-Lake, a Provincial Parks' Commission project; the old Post Office and Thomas House at Oakville; the Dr. Charles Duncombe Home in St. Thomas; the 1836 residence of Mrs. Susan Sibbald in Sutton, and the Françoise Baby House (c. 1811) in Windsor.

Prime Minister Mackenzie King, in the manner of Laurier in Quebec, is memorialized at the Woodside National Historic Park near Kitchener which is administered, quite naturally, by the federal Historic Sites Service. Here the boyhood home of Mr. King has been completely restored to depict "the family life and atmosphere of the King home as it could have been in the 1880's."

Pioneer village fever spread northward as centennial year approached. Blind River got its Timber Village established in time for an official opening on July 1, 1967. On St. Joseph Island near Richard's Lodge to the south of Sault Ste-Marie the ruins of the fort were partially restored and church, school, and barn added to round out a story relating to the origin and development of a small island settlement. At Port Arthur, now Thunder Bay, an authentic replica of a logging camp, including bunkhouse, cookhouse, stable, and blacksmith shop, with the appropriate outbuildings, was set up in the adjacent bush country.

The most isolated historic restoration in the province opened in 1968 on the island of Moose Factory at the northern terminus of the Ontario Northland Railway, on the shores of James Bay, and over six hundred miles north of Toronto. Here is the first English settlement in what is now Ontario, a Hudson's Bay Trading Post, still in operation, which was established in 1673. The museum park on the site of the early Factor's post has forge, powder magazine, and orientation building dealing with the development of the area by the Hudson's Bay Company and other trading companies. It is open to the public during July and August, and in its second summer of operation attracted approximately six thousand visitors. The five hundred mile train ride from North Bay to Moosenee is reported to be an illuminating and historical experience in itself.

A continuing and increasing record of historic churches deserves mention. The Historical Branch of the Ontario Department of Records and Archives lists twenty such buildings, including one Roman Catholic, one Quaker Meeting House, two Anglican, four Methodist, two Baptist, one Congregationalist. Six show no religious affiliation but their names strongly suggest that they could be Anglican. Two Indian (non-denominational) missions are also included, one such mission, Her Majesty's Chapel of the Mohawks at Brantford, having been built in 1785.

The approach of Canada's centennial produced a spate of miniature pioneer villages. The Pickering Museum at Brougham, east of Toronto, was opened in 1961 and expanded six years later to include a number of log buildings of the mid-nineteenth century. Each September the local historical society sponsors a "History in Action" festival. At Trent River near Havelock a complex of eight pioneer buildings have been salvaged and rehabilitated, while at Milton, the Halton Museum, a county project, has as its focal point the restored Alexander homestead. At Lang in Peterborough County, Century Village, a centennial project, as its name suggests, has thirteen buildings to form a pioneer settlement of 1867; across the Indian River the Lang Mill Museum was also put into working order in 1967. Rockton in the Brantford region has its Westfield Pioneer Village.

Museums in the 1950's were broadening their interests. The traditional pioneer institutions, which, while emphasizing human history usually degenerated into all-purpose repositories for natural history, antiquities, and curiosities, were twenty in number. Four community museums were devoted to mining, logging, milling, and miscellaneous manufactures, four interpretation centres were founded in provincial wild-life parks, and a children's zoo made its appearance in London. The first of a series of military museums on encampments, established during World War I, was opened at Camp Borden. A planetarium was built at McMaster University in Hamilton, and the Botanical Garden in the same city underwent major development. The first ethnic museum dedicated to the immigrant culture of the Ukrainians opened at Oakville in 1952 and the Stephen Leacock summer home at Orillia was restored to serve as shrine for Canada's most distinguished humourist.

Agitation for assistance to the small museums of Ontario had been initiated by the Ontario Historical Society in the early 1950's but without too much success. Spasmodic grants of not more than two hundred dollars were occasionally offered, "mainly for publications," but the very isolation of the majority of community institutions militated against them. Of the ninety-one museums and art galleries visited by Dr. and Mrs. Guthe in 1957, twenty-six were shown as being partially or wholly financed by the provincial government. These included nature centres, the tourist attractions on the Niagara Peninsula, art galleries in major cities, the provincial archives and museum; only nine of the forty-eight small museums benefitted. The Society continued to develop its series of annual workshops directed toward the honorary curators of the local institutions. The program was augmented by technical papers but administrative standards remained low.

In 1961, a provincial Act was passed making possible a grants' program, and amendments in 1963 broadened the terms of reference. Under the Act grants were made available to "any municipal corporation, conservation authority or the council of a [Indian] band which owns and maintains a museum open for at least three hundred and sixty hours and at least sixty days in that year, in the sum of six hundred dollars annually. . . and thirty-three and one third percent of the annual salary of each curator or assistant curator, but not exceeding four hundred dollars each museum," with an additional proviso making such grants available for museums in the planning stages.

The natural outcome of this legislation was to encourage town, city or county councils to accept legal responsibility for administration of the local institutions, leaving operations in the hands of the historical society. More important, however, the government now employs a corps of advisers who travel extensively to give technical assistance, in co-operation with the Canadian Museums' Association museum training seminars. In 1972, the Department of Public Records and Archives made over one hundred grants for a total of approximately $100.000.

Undoubtedly the new legislation was partially responsible for the phenomenal increase in Ontario museums from 1960 onward, but the growing interest in the forthcoming centennial celebrations was also an important factor. In the first half of the decade one new community museum in the province was opened every thirty days, but in the ensuing twenty-four months (1966-68) fifty-three new institutions appeared on the Ontario scene of which only twenty-three received funds from the federal-provincial capital grants program. With an additional thirteen historic parks opened in these same two years, an impressive one hundred and fifteen museums dedicated to history and the natural sciences came into being.

Ottawa had a substantial increase in museums by centennial year to augment the existing national institutions. The National Film Board opened its Photo Centre Picture Gallery for the display of works drawn from its Still Photo Division, and also officially announced the establishment of an Archives available to interested members of the public. A little known museum dedicated to the history of scouting forms part of the National Headquarters of the Canadian Scout movement located on Baseline Road, and the Governor-General's Footguards maintains a museum collection of historic artifacts dating from 1872 at its Armouries on Cartier Square. At Uplands Airport and on the Rockcliffe R.C.A.F. airport, aircraft which cannot be accommodated at the already enlarged National Museum of Science and Technology are kept on display.

A short-lived Wheelhouse Museum concentrated on under-water archaeology of the Ottawa River opened in 1966 but, lacking suitable accommodation, was required to close the following year. Its dedicated members continue their field operations and have charted over one hundred and sixty wrecks ranging from schooners to sidewheelers. In 1970 their collection was turned over to the National Museum of Science and Technology.

National headquarters of the Canadian Amateur Ski Association, with over four hundred affiliated clubs, is in Ottawa. In 1965 efforts were made to launch a Ski Museum but only in mid-1971 did this project get off the ground in a diminutive vacant store building at 238A Sparks Street, moving into a rehabilitated building at 457A Sussex Street in December 1972. In spite of its cramped quarters an ambitious program has been mapped out which will include the establishment of an archives section, along with active canvassing for historic artifacts relating to winter transportation and sport. Already memorabilia dealing with Dr. A. E. Possild's researches into the migration of reindeer from the Bering Straight to the Northwest Territories and the National Geographic Society's 1935 Yukon expedition led by Bradford Washburn are on display, along with mementos of Canada's recent triumphs in international competitions. Plans are under way to develop a series of travelling displays for use of member clubs.

Ontario's major cities are now generally involved in financing and, on occasion, administering museums, art galleries, and other related institutions, the City of Toronto being a pioneer in this field. Casa Loma, the Sir Henry Pellat architectural monstrosity, could almost be dismissed save that in recent years the museum of the Queen's Own Rifles has occupied one area in this architectural maze.

The Toronto Historical Board maintains headquarters in its Marine Museum of Upper Canada, once the officers' quarters of

"Stanley Barracks" and now within the grounds of Exhibition Park. Early water exploration of Central Canada is depicted, along with the development of shipping on the Great Lakes. The Ned Hanlon tug and ice-breaker, recently restored, is in the adjacent dry-dock and the H.M.C.S. Haida, former R.C.N. destroyer, rides at anchor on the lakefront. Only a few hundred yards distant Old Fort York, a military post founded in 1793, is now administered by the same Board. Each summer there is a re-enactment of the Fort York Guard on parade. Scadding Cabin, oldest remaining building in Toronto, and preserved as a log cabin pioneer residence of the late eighteenth century, is located nearby.

The last home of William Lyon Mackenzie, Toronto's first mayor, leader of the Rebellion of Upper Canada, and journalist, is another Historical Board responsibility. The print shop, still fully operational, turns out replicas of the once seditious pronouncements which led to his imprisonment. In marked contrast is the picturesque Colborne Lodge with a nearby studio displaying the many watercolours by John Howard.

In the past few years the Historical Board has worked on the restoration of two further historical buildings. The original house of David Gibson, active supporter of Mackenzie in the 1837 Rebellion, was set afire by the Loyalist troops, and on his return from self-imposed exile in 1849 he rebuilt the Georgian-style brick residence currently standing. And to complete the story, Montgomery's Tavern, a two-storey stone building erected in 1832, serving as stopping place and court house in which Gibson briefly held prisoners on December 7, 1837, was restored and opened in the summer of 1972.

An overall picture of Ontario's art scene, including Toronto's contribution, deserves its own chapter, but in other related projects Metropolitan Toronto is presently involved in developing a zoological park with emphasis placed on the preservation and conservation of nature and the role men play in ecology. The beauty of the zoo site will be sustained and enhanced with nature trails.

Situated in the Rouge River region, twenty miles east of the city, a seven hundred acre conservation area has been transformed into a park with man-made natural settings to simulate the flora of the six continents which, in the words of the designer, will "give man's eternal fascination full scope while transforming the animal from a moronic environment," or as another of the architects phrased it, "Things must look right to the animal before they look right to the people."

Work on the site started in 1970 following lengthy planning between Metro agencies, a new Zoological Society, and the Regional Conservation Authority. Phase One of the project is costing

$20,000,000 plus an additional $1,500,000 for acquisition of animals. There is parking for six thousand cars and forty buses close to a terminus for a mini-train service. Pavilions and restaurants located at strategic points make possible year-round operation. The environment provides total immersion for visitors, who with the completion of a new six-lane highway are now able to reach the zoo in less than half an hour from downtown Toronto. The Dr. Jackson (Roman Meal) mansion on the property serves as research centre and can be used for small conferences. Animals, birds, reptiles and, hopefully at a later date, marine life, from the six continents will be nurtured and displayed.

Formal opening of what will be the most contemporary zoo on the North American continent will be in the summer of 1974. Already being discussed is the development of a massive botanical garden on adjacent lands, to be dedicated to the legendary City Parks Administrator Tommy Thomson, on which, says Dr. Gunter Voss, general director of the zoo project, "we would hope to grow most if not all the vegetation, including food, for our animals and birds while we would like to include an aquarium also." Cost of this annex would be another $20,000,000.

Although Metro Toronto continues to expand its museum program, the provincial government established its Ontario Heritage Foundation in 1967 for the purpose of acquiring, preserving, and restoring properties of historical and architectural interest and to accept donations of properties (real or personal) of aesthetic, recreational, or scenic interest for "the use, enjoyment and benefit of the people of Ontario." The Foundation works closely with the National Historic Sites Service and other federal agencies. It also advertises that "all donations are deductible for Federal and Provincial income tax purposes *to the full extent of the donor's income*" which now makes possible gifts of art works to the province. These in turn are loaned to its galleries and museums for safe custody and display.

The concentration of population in the province continues to hug the St. Lawrence and Lake Ontario with a subsidiary growth in Northern Ontario. The museums in these two disparate regions illustrate two distinct cultures and economies. Driving from the Quebec frontier to Windsor on Highway 2, the smaller historical museums tend to become repetitious, illustrating the triumphs and tribulations of the original settlers of the late eighteenth and early nineteenth centuries, the God-fearing (usually Protestant) hard-working founders who now provide a modicum of reflected glory to the community, with here and there a restored grist mill or military fortification.

The towns and cities in the northland are comparatively young, having first been opened for settlement in the 1880's following discovery of the vast nickel resources in the Sudbury area, and silver in the Cobalt region, and in 1909 the opening of gold mines still further north in the Porcupine area. Just after World War II the already discovered deposits of pitchblende saw another "rush" to the north as uranium, almost overnight, became essential to the growing nuclear developments.

Surprisingly the pulp and paper industry gets only casual recognition in Northern Ontario museums. One such museum was projected in 1967 at Abitibi but proved to be abortive. Timber Village at Blind River emphasizes the history of lumbering and also houses a small aquarium stocked each spring by the National Wild Life Services. The only museum dedicated to uranium and the nuclear age is at the town of Elliot Lake, midway between Sudbury and Sault Ste-Marie.

In Centennial year, the Sudbury Chamber of Commerce obtained local financial support to restore and remodel one of the older small mansions of the district, The Bell Rock House. This was then presented to the fledgling Laurentian University for use as a cultural centre accessible to both local citizens and the university community. The house contains a small museum and art gallery as well as an activities area and is dedicated to bilingualism and biculturalism – a unique pilot project.

A few miles to the south of this area is Manitoulin Island, approximately eighty miles long and thirty miles wide at its eastern end, and which now sustains five community museums devoted to the natural and human history of this sparsely populated outpost. In 1967, one of the institutions, the Manitoulin Historical Marine Museum, was devoted almost solely to underwater archaeology but closed its doors two years later. Also in the Georgian Bay region and to the west a spate of community museums appeared during the 1960s with seven opening in 1967. A natural history museum was built in Algonquin Park by the Department of Lands and Forests. At Golden Lake, on the perimeter of the park, a museum dedicated to the Indians of the region, and administered by the Council on the reserve, was established in 1963. Other museums opened in this same general area are at Colbalt, Kirkland Lake, Porcupine, and Bruce Mines in the Northern Ontario mineral mining region, with others at Fort Frances, Atikokan, Kenora, and Sault Ste-Marie. The Fort William (now Thunder Bay) museum which had been out of operation for a number of years was also revived.

The Simcoe County Museum, five miles north of Barrie, celebrated centennial year with a major expansion. A new gallery wing of three thousand square feet built in mid-1970 now accommodates its ever-increasing flow of artifacts dating from 2,000 B.C. The small community of Sarnia has both a railroad museum and a library-art gallery complex.

Retracing footsteps somewhat one finds well established museums at Tobermory and Penetanguishene which has both a pioneer museum and the Naval and Military Establishment reconstruction. A similar situation prevails at Wasaga Beach with Schoonertown, a museum built on a naval base site which operated in the early years of the nineteenth century. On Nancy Island, in the same region, the relatively young Museum of the Upper Lakes exhibits relics of the good warship *Nancy,* destroyed by the Americans in the 1812-14 unpleasantness. The naval tradition is also maintained by the Segwin Steamboat Museum at Gravenhurst, while at nearby Huntsville the Muskoka Museum Society administers a complex of six pioneer buildings.

Museum growth continues unabated in Canada's most populous province. In December 1971, the Provincial Museums' Adviser, Mr. V. N. Styrmo, announced that six more institutions had opened in the previous six months: the Wiser's Canadiana Museum which had moved to Corbyville from Montreal; an Indian Village named SKA-NA-DUT in the Longwoods Conservation Area; a pioneer museum at Strathroy; the Valens Log Cabin Museum north of Dundas operated by the Hamilton Regional Conservation Authority; the Whitchurch-Stouffeville Museum at Bogartown, east of Newmarket; and The Apothecary, a restoration of an early chemists's store at Niagara-on-the Lake, the first museum to come under the direct jurisdiction of the Ontario Heritage Foundation but operated and maintained by the Ontario College of Pharmacy. Mr. Styrmo later reported that at Thunder Bay construction of a replica of the original Fort William had been approved. For over a century this fort had served as headquarters of the North-west Company, which in 1816 merged with the Hudson's Bay Company. It is anticipated that the historical complex of fifty buildings from the Great Hall capable of seating two hundred people, to prison and dog kennel, will be completed by 1974. Much in the manner of Fort Louisbourg, plans are afoot to train native artisans in many of the old skills and trades.

In the same report a footnote was added to the effect that "the City of Kingston is working on 'The Pump-house Museum' for its tercentennial in 1975 being on the original 1839 site. . . the objective being to restore the ancient machinery to illustrate the age of steam." Two Martello towers have already been opened to the public, and it is anticipated that the Port Clark Lighthouse at Kincardine on Lake Huron will shortly be restored.

The centennial celebrations commemorating the founding of the Mounties in 1873 overshadow the invention of the telephone by

Alexander Graham Bell that same year. The federal government in association with the Province of Ontario and the city of Brantford may mark this lesser-publicized occasion by opening a National Museum of Telecommunications in a downtown park area at Brantford without disturbing the Bell Homestead, already designated a National Historic building, a few miles away.

Agreement has been reached with Bell Canada to furnish most if not all the artifacts, and to make available its historical staff for research. Capital costs are expected to be about twelve million dollars.

In October 1969 a joint statement was issued by the federal Minister of Indian Affairs and Northern Development and the Chairman of the (Provincial) Niagara Parks Commission to the effect that "three properties of national historic significance in the Niagara area will be transferred from provincial to federal responsibility." The properties in question are Fort George, Navy Hall, and part of the Queenston Heights area, including Brock's Monument at Niagara-on-the-Lake. A long term program for the extensive development of these sites is currently under way, with new and more sophisticated displays being installed at the Rainbow Bridge Interpretation Centre and stabilization work also projected at Fort George. Another development of historic sites at Niagara-on-the-Lake was also launched in 1970 by the federal authority starting with the transfer of lands from the Department of National Defence and the re-location of the provincially owned golf course to make possible the development of Fort Mississauga and Butler's Barracks as historic interpretation centres. The latter building will be used to tell the story of the United Empire Loyalists and also to serve as a museum depicting the history of regional architecture.

The Niagara Parks Commission continues to be involved in these projects which include the leasing of lands to the Shaw Festival and Toronto Symphony Association "to help create a suitable environment for interpreting the history of this most important and attractive area."

31

From the 1940's well into the 1960's the older established art galleries were making their quiet contributions to the cultural maturity of the province. The late Arthur Lismer of Group of Seven fame, who had initiated creative arts classes at the Art Gallery of Toronto, saw other galleries developing similar programs. It remained, however, for the London Public Library and Art Gallery under Dr. Clare Bice, himself an author and illustrator of children's books, to launch an all-embracing program in creative activities for children that had many unique features and which became the subject for a documentary produced by the National Film Board in the late 1940's.

Entering the 1950's the Toronto Art Gallery initiated its Wednesday evening "five ring circus" with varied activities, including music recitals, lectures, panel discussions, films, and tours, attracting large crowds who wandered at will from one excitement to the next. This institution also initiated the first Madison Avenue type publicity program in Canada, one of the hightlights being its "One Million Dollars' Worth of Rembrandts."

The Royal Ontario Museum was also changing its format to attract more school classes as well as the general public, and in 1951 opened its Sigmund Samuel Museum annex to display its collections of decorative arts and a large number of Paul Kane paintings.

Entering the sixth decade of the century, Ontario had eleven art galleries in operation, all of which were suffering from lack of fiscal support. By 1963 this number had increased to sixteen. In other cultural areas the Toronto Symphony, National Ballet, and the Canadian Opera Company were making valiant attempts to develop a public consciousness in their respective fields. In the world of theatre, Stratford was now well established, but two or three professional companies in Toronto were leading precarious existences.

On December 31,1963, The Province of Ontario Council for the Arts was created by the government of Premier John Robarts with an initial grant of $1,000,000 along with a knowledgeable and inspired citizens' committee to administer the fund. Terms of reference of the Council gave the directors considerable latitude. Initially the Council devoted its energies to keeping existing institutions alive while searching for a long-range policy.

In the three succeeding years, a number of pilot projects were launched with what appeared to be gay abandon to some of its critics, but which served only as preliminaries to what was christened "The J. Keiller Mackay Five Year Plan" with the added slogan that "Instead of handing out raincoats and rubbers, we'd like to change the weather." A three point program included plans for Coordinated Regional Arts Services, and a Centre for Arts Research in Education. With the release of the 1969-70 annual report these services were in operation and the government grant had been increased to $1,650,000, making possible a continuation of subsidies to about eighty-five organizations. In 1970, two grass-roots pilot projects were under way, one embracing the Niagara Peninsula and south-western Ontario, the other with headquarters in Thunder Bay serving the greater portion of Northern Ontario to the west.

The Arts in Education program had reached out to seven educational regions, and a fourth project, the creation of a Franco-Ontarian Affairs branch, had been launched with the appointment of a liaison officer. The seventh annual report released early in 1972 disclosed that the provincial grant had taken another jump to $1,750,000. Twenty-four art galleries out of a total of thirty-three received $170,000 in grants from this fund. The eight campus galleries at the various universities receive their subsidies indirectly through university funds, while the major funding of both the Art Gallery of Ontario and the Royal Ontario Museum is in direct grants from the Provincial Department of University Affairs.

Canada's centennial celebrations brought many significant developments to Ontario's art scene. At the municipal level, a memorial gallery, originally planned ten years earlier, was finally opened in a building expressly designed for the purpose at Owen Sound, birthplace of Tom Thomson, one of Canada's most revered artists. A Homer Watson Memorial Gallery at Doon, in the Kitchener-Waterloo area, also had its official launching. The Rothman Corporation built a contemporary art gallery at Stratford to serve as permanent headquarters for much of its international art collection which, in addition to serving as an important part of the Stratford Festival, functions as a year-round community attraction. From here a continuing program of travelling exhibitions is organized which today are eagerly sought after by practically all major galleries throughout Canada, not only because the company defrays all costs but also because the individual works are of such fine quality. The Rodin sculpture show of 1970-71 is one such example.

It was in Centennial Year that the London Public Library moved into its new building which provided for greatly increased space in its art gallery annex. At Niagara Falls, in the same year, the Parks Commission remodelled the former home of Sir Harry Oakes, one time mineral mining pioneer, as a museum of the decorative arts with accompanying arts and crafts studios and workshops. The Peterborough Centennial Museum was also provided with an art gallery area to display its small collections of paintings and sculpture. Reflecting the literary scene, the Guelph home of the late Canadian poet, Colonel John McCrae, built in 1872, was restored and formally opened in early 1968 to honour the author of "In Flanders' Fields."

The centennial celebrations also produced a new generation of public benefactors. From the advent of World War I until late in the 1960's gifts and bequests for cultural organizations had been at a low ebb. There were patrons who gave support to various areas of the performing arts, Lady Eaton being one of the more persistent; or who, through purchases, provided encouragement to the younger painters, but gifts to museums and art galleries were few and far between.

One of the lesser publicized, but more important, benefactions was the gift of Mr. and Mrs. Robert McMichael, who designed, built, and stocked what is now known as the McMichael Conservation Collection of Art, a one-storey gallery recently expanded, which, in 1967, was turned over to the Province of Ontario as an outright gift. Surrounded by six hundred acres of conservation forest the building has all the intimacy of a private residence including an indoor swimming pool which does dual service as a humidifying agent. The galleries are filled with paintings and sculptures, with emphasis on The Group of Seven, and on those who had come under the influence of The Group, such as Emily Carr, Tom Thomson, David Milne. In addition there are works by the founding members of the Canadian Group of Painters. The McMichaels, who serve as honorary curators, continue to occupy their private living quarters. A small piece of hallowed land adjacent to the gallery contains the remains of three of the illustrious Seven, while, also on the property is the restored Tom Thomson shack recently salvaged from a land developer's scrap heap.

Somewhat delayed as a Centennial project but similar in intent to that of the McMichael project is the Robert McLaughlin Gallery in Oshawa. Initially dedicated in 1968 the gallery reflects the philosophy of the short lived Painters Eleven, a more recent group than the Seven and which has had a major influence on contemporary Canadian painting. Painters Eleven had its genesis in the studio of Miss Alexandrea Luke who later married Ewart McLaughlin of Oshawa.

In its six years of active life, the group had for its mentor J. W. G. (Jock) Macdonald and the other members were Oscar Cahan, Hortense Gordon, Walter Yarwood, Harold Town, Jack Bush, Tom Hodgson, Kazuo Nakamura and William Ronald, all of Toronto, with Ray Mead of Montreal being the eleventh member. The gallery's permanent collection has for its nucleus one of the major works of each of the Eleven but as accession funds are made available more such works are purchased. The McLaughlin estate contributed $100,000 as an accessions endowment fund when the gallery opened and has added similar amounts in 1971 and 1972.

One undertaking that can be viewed as a valuable annex to the art gallery development of the province and which already had provided incentives to a number of small library boards to expand their cultural programs was the Art Institute of Ontario, a voluntary society launched in 1952 by Dr. Martin Baldwin, at that time Director of the Art Gallery of Toronto, as a co-operative art circuit. In 1964 the Institute received its first grant from the new Provincial Arts Council. By 1966-67, the Institute was circulating sixty exhibitions to over one hundred community societies, such as libraries, schools, women's institutes, and local sketch clubs. In a three-year period the Institute's full time director, who also served as lecturer, addressed one hundred and sixty groups. The several art shows had one hundred and seventy-five individual bookings, and were viewed by approximately two million individuals. In 1966, the Institute administered a provincial government scheme for the purchase of one hundred and seventy-five works of art from Ontario and Quebec artists, which were exhibited at the Toronto gallery and later shown in Montreal and Quebec City as a gesture of bicultural harmony. They were then sent on a two-year tour reaching the smallest provincial communities equipped to handle such a display. The ultimate disposal of the collection saw the paintings distributed to join the permanent collections of Ontario's established art galleries.

In 1967 it was obvious that the Art Institute needed a further fiscal injection. Talks with the provincial authorities resulted in the decision that the Art Gallery of Toronto should serve as the official gallery of Ontario. Undertaking province-wide responsibilities, including the take-over of the Art Institute by 1970, the gallery continued to be administered by an independent and largely elected board. One of the top priorities in this new departure was a major capital expansion program for the gallery itself. With its increased budget, the Institute had called for more active participation from the major galleries of the province, and by the time it was finally phased out to become part of the now designated Art Gallery of Ontario, eleven art galleries and two exhibition societies had become actively involved in the program, thus providing liaison with

256

every region within the four hundred and twelve thousand square miles of the province and serving a population of approximately seven million.

Although the gallery was renamed the Art Gallery of Ontario, the administrative structure is relatively unchanged with the province having only minority representation on the Board. In 1971, the institution received $610,000 from the provincial Treasury, augmented by $15,000 from Metropolitan Toronto, with a further $50,000 from the city as rent for use of Grange Park as a municipal green spot in the downtown section. Also in 1971 the gallery received $500,000, which came indirectly from the Samuel Zacks estate, for a building fund to augment an earlier government vote of $12,500,000 for a major expansion of the existing premises to be spent prior to 1980.

In 1970, Henry Moore, internationally-famed sculptor, announced that the major portion of his sculptures, prints, and drawings would come to Toronto in recognition of the gesture made to him when the city commissioned one of his highly controversial works for the square in front of the new city hall. In the next year, along with the financial developments mentioned above, the gallery became heir to the Charles Band collection of works by the Group of Seven, Tom Thomson, Emily Carr, and David Milne, viewed as one of the most important accessions in this field.

In the same year Premier Robarts announced that Mr. and Mrs. Samuel Zacks had turned over their entire collection, numbering over one thousand individual works of art, to the province. The benefactors expressed the hope that the collection would be made available "on indefinite loan" to the Art Gallery of Ontario and the Royal Ontario Museum. Another press release emanating from the Premier's office was the announcement that Mrs. Jack Barwick of Ottawa, sister of the late Douglas Duncan, millionaire art patron and collector, was giving the province more than twenty-seven hundred paintings by Canadian artists for distribution to The National Gallery and the art galleries of Ontario, with a further proposal that nine hundred should be placed in art galleries in the remaining nine provinces.

To accommodate the new accessions and find space for the ever increasing extension services and activities' programs, the Art Gallery of Ontario Board embarked on a symbolic ground-breaking ceremony in September 1971, and at the same time launched a drive for $5,000,000 to augment its capital funds. Architectural planning had started in 1966, but the overnight metamorphosis of the institution and the successions of benefactions resulted in extensive modifications to the original proposals.

The first phase which will add 156,000 square feet should be completed in the summer of 1974, making possible a reopening of the institution with display space approximately five and a half times larger than the original galleries. The cost of phase one is approximately $18,000,000. An immediate start on phase two will be made and if all goes well completion date could be December 1975, but if inflationary trends continue the opening may have to be delayed.

Enveloped within the existing complex is The Grange, restored "as a gentlemen's house of 1835-40" and officially reopened on April 19, 1973. Originally built in 1817, many of the unique features of this building have been reconstructed making possible a dual role as a historical document and reception area. The Grange is the centre for the activities of the Women's Committee. When the entire expansion is completed the gallery will have a staff of 150 with an annual operating budget of $1,500,000.

Major developments in Ontario's art milieu are not confined to Toronto. The cultural pattern of neighbouring Hamilton is represented in the somewhat unspectacular but well-planned program of its art gallery, which moved into a new building in 1953 when it received a group of Canadian and European paintings from the estate of Mr. and Mrs. Newton D. Galbraith. Since that time, a steady stream of gifts has enabled the gallery to build up its collections of paintings, prints, drawings, and sculpture with emphasis on Canadian works, but also including significant and well-planned collections of American and British artists. In 1970, the gallery acquired four seventeenth century Dutch paintings which, says T.R. MacDonald, the gallery director, "is a new field for us." In August 1971 plans for a new $3,300,000 gallery got under way on a site provided by the city with a projected completion date of 1973-74.

The London Art Gallery had been expanded on two occasions since opening its doors in the Memorial Library in 1940 when the city had a population of 70,000. By 1972 a census disclosed a growth to 220,000 and discussions were under way to create a Metro government which would embrace half a million residents.

Branch display areas had earlier been opened in the suburban libraries, and in 1964, community societies interested in the arts petitioned for a new gallery as a centennial project. It was not until January 1972 that a steering committee was appointed to "study in-depth proposals and existing facilities relevant to a new gallery" and to make recommendations to the city. Five months later a report was submitted to the local authorities recommending that "a new gallery be built in the core area," approximately 45,000 square feet in size with provision for future expansion; the report also advised that the proposed institution be granted administrative autonomy. London city council approved in principle authorizing an *ad hoc*

258

committee to get things moving. Cost for building and furnishings excluding land was estimated at somewhat less than $2,000,000. However, the concept upon which the decision was reached suggests that when the gallery is formally opened, possibly in 1975, the City of London will have "not a neo-classical temple to an invisible tribunal of beauty, truth and goodness, nor should it in any self-conscious and therefore pseudo way ape the European art styles of an era when Canada was a magnificent wilderness populated by a proud people whose present condition is in part the result of a perverse and misdirected worship of those styles. . . . The exterior should be a warm invitation to enter without removing shoes, or bowing heads, or lowering voices. . . . it should be able to house the cultural heritage of our region much of which is still stored away in attics and barns, without in the process imposing upon that heritage a meaning entirely alien to it." "One of the chief functions of a new gallery" the committee continued, "is to eradicate by its inviting presence those elitist notions about it that exist in the popular mind."

The City of Windsor in the south-western corner of Ontario has also taken an unconventional approach to the expansion of its Willistead gallery which for many years was administered by the Public Library Board, but for an entirely different reason. The new building on Riverside Drive West certainly is no "neo-classical temple," its architectural exterior suggesting a plebian way of life free from any "élitist notions." The all important factor is that it has space – 55,000 square feet, as compared with one tenth that amount in the venerable library/gallery complex in Willistead Park.

There has been some face-lifting to make this edifice more acceptable as the home of the muses, rather than its former image as brewery warehouse dedicated to more prosaic recreation. In fact, gallery director Kenneth Saltmarch declares that this could be "well among the most exciting projects in Canada," and all at a cost of $1,400,000.

In its thirty years of existence the Willistead has acquired approximately 800 art works conservatively valued at half a million dollars with assurances of many new gifts now that it has found a permanent home. Not content with exhibiting its own collection and the many travelling exhibitions now available, it has set aside 3,000 square feet for a display area for a continuing flow of artifacts drawn from the Royal Ontario Museum.

On July 1st, 1968, the Royal Ontario Museum divorced itself from its founding alma mater, the University of Toronto, to become essentially a provincial institution, administered by an independent corporation but receiving grants directly from the provincial treasury. The museum, over the previous fifteen to twenty years, had been facing decreasing operational and accessions revenues from benefactors and increasing demands from both the university and the general public. University grants to the museum had failed to keep pace with rising costs.

Facing an intolerable situation, the new director, Peter Swann, publicly declared early in the year that now was the time for the federal government to institute a takeover, declare the Royal Ontario Museum a national museum, and kick through with an initial $1,000,000. Mr. Swann's diatribe brought him under attack from various sides, the existing National Museum directors in Ottawa pointing to the fact that they too had been treated as the poor relation of government, and if any further grants were to be dispensed through the Secretary of State or any other department, they had priority.

Some provincial officials, recognizing that Ontario's centennial capital commitment was already costing taxpayers several millions of dollars in excess of the original estimate, saw no reason at this time to aid the Royal Ontario Museum, which after all, was comfortably housed, moderately well staffed and seemingly able to find benefactors to finance field operations in exotic corners of the earth. Mr. Swann's agitation resulted in what can be viewed as an initial step toward the major expansion of the one museum in Canada which had, over the years, developed a score of curatorial departments, had its Sigmund Samuel Canadiana Museum as an important annex, and was just getting ready to open the McLaughlin Planetarium within its complex of buildings. Also, it was the one museum in Canada that had established solid international status.

The Royal Ontario Museum had faced problems and at times internal conflict throughout its somewhat brief history. It had grown in reputation and erudition under a succession of brilliant directors. Dr. Gerard Brett who followed Currelly introduced new disciplines and display techniques. His successor, the internationally known Dr. Theodore Heinrich, was a *bon vivant* but also a discriminating authority in the decorative arts. Dr. William Swinton, British palaeontologist, the fourth director, also made radical and at times controversial changes in philosophy and policy. The museum had also attracted equally brilliant, but less publicized, curatorial and research staff members.

Mr. Swann came to the Royal Ontario Museum in late 1967 from the Ashmolean and shortly thereafter confessed to a colleague that "I have two years to do an almost impossible reorganization. If I fail, I'll get out but even if I succeed only partially I may still be out – booted out possibly." In June 1971, Mr. Swann was indeed facing possible enforced retirement although the new public image of the museum was reflected in substantially increased attendance.

260

Included in his lesser publicized innovations were the founding of a postgraduate degree course in museum curatorship in association with the University of Toronto; a drastic reorganization of the internal administrative structure; making his curatorial and research staff available to all Ontario universities; the publication of a scholarly Quarterly directed to the lay public; and a radical development of the museum's program for children.

The revitalization of the Royal Ontario Museum had actually started several years prior to the appointment of Mr. Swann, with the introduction of contemporary displays in its geological and mineralogical galleries, but shortage of finances and a beclouded administrative policy brought the work to a virtual standstill. The persistent needling of the provincial administration and the university hierarchy had the desired effect, the province increased its grant by five hundred and fifty thousand dollars; Mr. Swann announced that this increase was both "too little and too late."

Today the Royal Ontario Museum has taken its displays on to the street, while the entire interior environment also adds to the air of excitement. "We had to bring the museum out into the street to get rid of the sort of minimum security prison impression everybody had of this place," the controversial director told one reporter. "For years, the museum just sat there and everyone thought of it as a sort of mausoleum. They failed to understand that it could be a dynamic place." By late July 1971 the much publicized differences between the director and his Board appeared to have been resolved but in July, 1972 the irascible Mr. Swann was summarily dismissed "due to irreconcilable differences," resulting in a barrage of letters to the newspapers and questions in the Legislature.

However, at the Royal Ontario Museum the mushrooming of programs continues unabated by sheer momentum. An oversized museomobile which had been sent on the road in 1970 had been replaced by two smaller peripatetic models; the 60th anniversary shows and celebrations continued, culminating with a major display of its internationally famed oriental artifacts and complemented by an impressive collection of Japanese decorative arts from the Art Gallery of Greater Victoria. An expanded educational and extension program was also launched during the year, including the creation of a teen-age research and laboratory club.

In the fall of 1972, *Rotunda*, the Royal Ontario Museum Quarterly, announced that the Dr. M. Hans Froberg Collection, the "finest private mineral collection in Canada," had found a permanent home in the museum through the generosity of the International Nickel Company. This comprises some 3,000 specimens including many unique display pieces, large suites of gold and silver and priceless reference material ranking behind only the Dorfman Collection. The donor company also sent a cheque for $150,000 for construction of a gallery in which to house their gift.

The annual grant for administrative purposes which had been $1,200,000 in 1966 had grown by an additional $3,000,000 by 1972. By that same year, attendance had reached an impressive 1.4 millions and this figure cannot help but increase as the museum has now extended its hours until 9:00 p.m. six days a week. A major expansion program, which undoubtedly will run to $50,000,000, is virtually assured; a provincial capital grant of $12,500,000 has already been voted, and a further $250,000 have come from the Zachs' Foundation. An architectural firm has already been commissioned to conduct a feasibility study.

Dining facilities are now augmented by a members' lounge complete with cocktail bar. But over and above these innovations valuable field expeditions by staff members representing many diverse disciplines continue throughout the world, financed by endowments and special research funds. A new Board with some of the old members re-appointed has been brought together to serve, with Dr. W.H. Tovell, acting director, as an interim administrative body until survey reports by consultants have been studied and new terms of reference spelt out. A search for a successor to Mr. Swann got under way in January 1973.

In mid-1972, the Royal Ontario Museum was named an Associate Museum under the Decentralization and Democratization program implemented by the National Museums Board. As a result, it became possible to create four satellite display areas as annexes to major museums and galleries in other regions of the province, providing for a continuous flow of exhibitions drawn from its various departments.

The foregoing vicissitudes and triumphs of the Royal Ontario Museum, however, pale beside Ontario's centennial grants project which officially opened in September 1969, over two years behind schedule.

32

In 1963 a young Toronto architect, Raymond Moriyama, was given a free hand to produce "a building of international significance" for a Centennial Centre of Science and Technology. The designs and technical specifications were well advanced before consideration was given to the appointment of its first director, one who had built up a national reputation as historian and administrator, and his associate director with a similar reputation but who had specialized in the areas of natural sciences and children's programs. The architect had produced a contemporary complex of buildings demanding contemporary philosophy and techniques in the fields of applied science and technology. It is easy to imagine how bewildered was the Minister of the Crown under whose jurisdiction the Centre was placed and his entire staff when they later examined the plans. Whatever policy did emerge from the Department seemed to be at odds with the policies being evolved by the director and his staff of approximately one hundred. Compounding the problems which became obvious while construction was still under way, was the fact that a business administrator had been recruited from industry, and the entire project was placed under the jurisdiction of the Department of Tourism and Information.

The original estimate for the new centre had been set at fourteen million dollars but prices escalated with architectural modifications adding to costs. Extensive trips were made by the higher echelon of staff to view similar centres throughout the world, but progress appeared to slow down. Critics of the project publicly questioned the snail-like progress and suggested that, somewhere in the administrative structure, disagreements were widening. Early in 1967, the director resigned taking with him fifteen other staff executives including his associate director and the director in charge of interpretation.

William O'Dea, Chairman of the ICOM, the International Committee for Museums of Science and Technology, and one-time Keeper of the Aeronautics and Sailing Ships Division at London's

Science Museum, took the directorship and pronounced the situation "a mess." This resulted in threats of legal action if a retraction was not forthcoming – an apology was published a few weeks later, but in January 1969 Mr. O'Dea tendered his resignation and shortly thereafter left the Science Centre to return to England.

Mr. O'Dea's successor, Douglas Omand, a forty-nine year old biologist, emphatically declared that the institution was not a museum. The policy, he emphasized, would be "to take science out of the laboratory and put it where casual browsers could observe and experience some of its challenge for themselves." Earlier Mr. O'Dea had announced similar objectives stressing "audience participation at the maximum levels." He had also stated that history would not be neglected in its entirety but possibly "up to twenty-five percent of the total." His successor rejected a proposal to install examples of early agricultural machinery but did agree to a re-creation of the laboratory where Banting and Best discovered insulin. A little later were installed a 1907 steam locomotive in its appropriate environment as well as a pioneer printing plant.

The only individual who remained untouched through all the various controversies was the young Toronto architect who was quoted by *Time* in its Canadian edition of June 27, 1969 as saying "if it looks as though it will make a beautiful ruin some day then I feel it is good architecture." *Time* editors added that "the Centre very nearly achieved that distinction at several stages of construction." Along the way, the Centre was plagued by so many staff changes, policy disputes and other delays that Ontario's Tourism and Information Minister, James Auld, admitted to days "when I would have shed few tears if this whole concrete complex had slipped into some large crevice in the Don Valley."

The exterior appearance and setting of the Centre has inspired imaginative writing. Thus Rosemary Speirs, reporting to *The Vancouver Sun* on September 2, 1969, speaks of the complex "squatting like an immense modern version of some ancient Mayan temple. Its three buildings, including a strange triangular office edifice, spread over two knolls and a leafy ravine on the edge of seven miles of rolling. . . parkland." In more prosaic language the Centre is a split-level cluster of three units on twenty acres of land in the geographic heart of the Metro region with a total floor space of 485,000 square feet. The interior has nine major exhibit areas in the fields of space and earth exploration, Canadian life, communication, the story of the molecule, genetics and allied subjects, engineering, transportation, and a science arcade with a total of approximately five hundred exhibits, a large percentage of which can be activated by the curious visitor.

Writing of the Centre for *Museum,* a UNESCO quarterly, shortly before his resignation, Mr. O'Dea outlined some of the more imaginative developments that were then taking place. He stated that "the car parking arrangements have been devised so that over fifty bus-loads of children may be accommodated, representing up to three thousand children at times in any one day," adding that "at a later stage it is intended to build dormitories."

Mr. Omand, director-general of the Centre, insists that exhibits will never remain static but will continuously be up-dated or replaced. Plans are already under way to add an area dealing specifically with human ecology. In October 1972 and throughout the winter months, amateur astronomers were able to view the planets, moon, nebulae, and galaxies in the evening hours. As a Christmas gift to old and young alike, there were outdoor and indoor activities relating to what was intriguingly called "Gliding and Sliding on Ice and Snow," with a natural ice loop 400 feet long as a major attraction, along with exhibits, films, slides, and lectures on "The Science of Gliding, Puck Power, Historic Winter Equipment," and allied subjects. The Centre is serving as host to the first World's Crafts Exhibition held under the auspices of the World's Crafts Council from June to September 1974. A distinguished jury drawn from many nations met in New York in March 1973 to make selections. More than one thousand delegates from seventy countries will be exposed to the exhibition as they attend the sixth biennial meeting.

In the meantime, the anticipated one and a half million visitors to the Centre each year can relax in the dining room and cocktail lounge or on benches scattered throughout the buildings and grounds before continuing their press-button education while the youngsters discover, in the Science Adventureland, a new world where fantasy and reality are bridged.

The Centre has experienced some backlash from adult visitors whose silent contemplation of man and his works is at times disturbed by exuberant children. A partial answer to this problem has been to extend visiting hours into the evening with children admitted only if accompanied by their parents.

On April 1, 1972 the Hon. George A. Kerr, Minister of the Department of Colleges and Universities, announced that a new Ministry had been established to integrate branches and agencies related directly or indirectly to culture, history, education, health, community, and social services. Prior to this innovation no less than six government departments had assumed jurisdiction over varying elements in the field of museums and related institutions. At the same time task forces were put to work to review past programs and introduce proposals for more co-ordinated operation and administration, with projections going well into the 1980s.

Also keeping pace with contemporary growth in the museum field, the Museums Branch of the Ontario Historical Association issued its own declaration of independence and became the Ontario Museums' Association. Initial steps have been undertaken to conduct ten training seminars in co-operation with the Canadian Museums' Association and to create eleven "area museum committees to make possible more frequent communication in an effort to face the fact of our geography as a vast province with regions almost completely isolated from the urban centres."

33

Winnipeg, Canada's fourth largest metropolitan area, is fourteen hundred miles by rail from Toronto, a comfortable three days' drive by automobile, twenty-eight hours by train, or two and a half hours by jet aircraft. Until the Trans-Canada highway was completed in the mid-1960's, the city was relatively isolated, tourists by road having to make detours through the United States. The advent of air travel had helped to break down the isolation somewhat, but the massive wilderness area of the Pre-Cambrian Shield to the east with its pockets of muskeg, although serving as a geologist's paradise, had been viewed as a roadbuilders' nightmare.

This isolation had quite naturally affected relationships between the east and mid-west. Vancouver, third largest metropolitan area in Canada, is still another fourteen hundred miles westward. The territory between Toronto and Vancouver was generally dismissed as "a cultural desert," yet within its isolation Winnipeg had fostered the Royal Winnipeg Ballet, oldest professional company in Canada; one of Canada's outstanding symphony orchestras; an important art gallery dating back to 1912; and the Manitoba Theatre Centre, the second oldest continuing company after Stratford. It had also produced a number of notable painters.

Fifty per cent of Manitoba's population reside within metropolitan Winnipeg. The ethnic diversity may have been somewhat responsible for its developing cultural maturity. The presence of The Hudson's Bay Company and its regard for historical documentation, if somewhat biased to support a reputation for ruling as a "benign despotism" in a more colourful era, has been somewhat responsible for a belated historical consciousness expressed in the restoration of Lower Fort Garry. This complex of stone buildings at Selkirk originally built by The Hudson's Bay Company served in more recent years as a country club for Winnipeg's elite until it was turned over to the federal government in 1966 and became another link in the chain of federal Historic Parks.

Here much of the historical collection which had occupied space in the Winnipeg "Bay" is again on display supported by a more objective story line, including other facets of the fur trade and early colonization of the west. The complex includes the main residence, store, jail, fur loft, and a two storey museum containing until recently elegant, expensive and exciting displays in diorama form with Indian masks on the second floor seeming to reflect surprise at finding themselves surrounded by so much opulence. One area deals with the Métis Rebellion of 1869-70 and the role played by Louis Riel. Further restorations will include the early jail-house, riverside landing, distillery, brewery, saw and grist mills, and the fort's original agricultural area to make it "one of the finest historic sites on the continent."

Upper Fort Garry, twenty miles to the south-west, also built to guard the river traffic, is recalled only by the gateway still standing in the heart of Winnipeg's business district. Visitors driving from the Lower Fort can stop off at West Kildonan to inspect the Seven Oaks House, a historic building restored to a residence of the 1850's, and former home of pioneer merchant John Inkster, before proceeding to Saint Boniface to see another authentic restoration completed in 1966 by the National Historic Sites Service. Here stood the Saint Boniface Basilica, unfortunately gutted by fire in 1968, but still standing is the Convent and Chapel of the Grey Nuns erected in 1846, serving as a pioneer museum related to the French occupancy of the region with the chapel itself being its own museum *in situ*.

The new Museum of Man and Nature in Winnipeg, opened on July 15, 1970 as a provincial centennial gesture, is the first museum in Canada to concern itself almost entirely with the ecological relationship between man and his environment. A single storey display area provides thirty-seven thousand square feet for the public, which for the moment, accommodates exhibits relating to the arctic, subarctic, northern forest, southern woodland and grassland zones. There is also what can best be described as an earth history gallery, in addition to a large area devoted to "the evolving urban centre."

While the civic complex includes a lavish all-purpose auditorium, the museum proper, which had 400,000 visitors in 1971, embraces a planetarium which attracted 170,000 adults and children. A six story structure accommodates administrative and curatorial personnel together with conservation and research areas. As explained in an initial brochure, the philosophy of this mult-million dollar institution, part of a massive urban rehabilitation plan, is "to look at the cultures of the earliest known human beings and their descendants and their basic relationship to this landscape. The second approach is concerned with the adaptation of the historic immigrant population, emphasizing the influence of environment on immigrant cultures and vice versa through exhibits integrating natural and human history."

Accepted as an Associate by the National Museums Board in mid-1972, the Manitoba institution wasted no time in implementing a program involving ethnology and multi-culturalism. While these disciplines have found their respective niches in the realm of academe, the museum has now translated both into an exciting visual experience.

In July 1972, a travelling display which speaks in terms of the original settlers took to the road, or more literally to the railroad, for a thousand mile educational journey to Churchill stopping at every settlement en route, including all Indian reservations and encampments. Museum officials had salvaged a C. N. R. day coach from the scrap heap. After a major rehabilitation job, it was loaded with exhibits going back to pre-historic times in which the story of the migration of the forefathers of Indians and Eskimos was presented as well as the roles played by their descendants in the social structure of Canada. The exhibit is bilingual with an accompanying brochure printed in English and the syllabics of the Cree. The car has been christened "The Rolling Stock Museum" which in the idiom of the Cree is "The Travelling Long-ago News." Two more rail coaches have already been pre-empted for similar uses and a total of five is envisaged in operation over the next five years.

A second project calls for the creation of a branch display at the Polo Park Shopping Centre at a cost of $1,500,000, while adjacent to the existing downtown complex an annex housing the replica of the S.S. Nonsuch, an early trading boat of the Hudsons' Bay Company, is on view.

In October 1972 the Manitoba Museum of Man and Nature made the first gesture to Canada's Jewish community with a major exhibition, jointly organized by the museum staff and the Jewish Historical Society. Entitled "Journey into our Heritage – the Saga of a People from the Ghettos to Freedom and Adventure," the exhibition was initially subsidized by the provincial government. Following its closing in the spring of 1973, it is destined to tour other museums.

The Manitoba Museum Association originally founded the earlier museum in the Winnipeg auditorium. The association, throughout the years from its inception, had a staff of two and its annual grants came from the City of Winnipeg and the School Board. A provincial historical society had also come into being but, receiving only token support from the government, frustration developed. The same occurred with the local museum societies proliferating in other regions and the situation came to the surface at a Historical Resources Conference held on the university campus in 1965 at which the plight of museums was discussed. Resolutions calling upon the government to take some positive action had to wait until the completion of the new provincial museum complex when a comprehensive program for extension services was designed to serve "established and embryonic museums whenever they are requested by bona fide interested groups in the province." Today co-ordination of display and educational services with the curricula of school districts and divisions throughout the province is being encouraged, while additional extension services include illustrated lectures, film strips, television and radio programs, and "where they can be effective, travelling exhibits."

In 1970, the provincial Legislature passed *The Museums and Miscellaneous Grants Act* establishing a consolidated fund to assist municipalities, Indian Bands and incorporated non-profit organizations administering museums, but limiting individual grants to two thousand dollars in any one year. A further clause makes possible similar grants to "organizations, or associations [involved in] any cultural, historical or archaeological project or undertaking." At the same time, a Department of Cultural Affairs was created to administer the new legislation. Regulations under the Act make provision for incentives to museums and galleries based on the visual quality of exhibits, quality, and condition of collections, the knowledge and efficiency of staffs and educational activities; a ministerial review of rejected applications has also been established.

In September 1971, the Association of Manitoba Museums was founded to promote the advancement of museums services throughout the province; fortunately it has established a harmonious liaison with the director and staff of the provincial institution. A further hopeful sign was the appointment by the provincial government of a Director of Historic Sites, part of whose duties involves the monitoring of grants to the community museums.

The Winnipeg Zoo in its earlier years housed its exhibits in traditional cages but since 1946 has developed contemporary display techniques to place the animals in a simulated natural environment. The Zoo today ranks as one of the major institutions of its kind in Canada. It is closely associated with a botanical garden and conservatory, all located in Assiniboine Park.

In 1965, the University of Manitoba opened Gallery III on its Fort Garry campus, replacing a temporary art display area in the university library. The new gallery devotes most of its display space to contemporary Canadian paintings and sculptures, organizes a steady flow of didactic shows, and is rapidly acquiring an impressive permanent collection with emphasis on faculty and senior student

270

works. Also on the campus are museums of natural history, geology, and zoology, the latter having recently undergone a drastic redesigning.

Also within the perimeter of Greater Winnipeg are several community and municipal museums. At Transcona the public library has an annex devoted to pioneer artifacts and the Ross House continues to be an attraction. In this log cabin post office built in 1855, relics of the early Red River settlement are exhibited, with one display providing particular attractions for philatelists. Ukrainian folk arts and crafts quite logically assume a significance in this region and recognition has been given them in the small museum at 1175 Main Street by the Ukrainian Women's Committee.

In 1969, historical museums in the southern regions of the province included a reconstructed Mennonite village at Steinbach depicting a settlement of the 1870's, with farmstead, church, schoolhouse, log cabin, grist and saw mills, cheese factory, and blacksmith shop. At Emerson, a border point, the Gateway Stopping Place Museum was opened in 1958 with exhibits displayed in the former jail house (1879) at one time an enforced rest home for many fugitives from justice. The first Customs' House in the west, built in 1870, is also on the site. In the same general region, the Carmen Pioneer Museum was founded in 1954, and at Portage-la-Prairie a log cabin museum was opened in 1967. Other community institutions north and south of the Portage-Brandon section of the Trans-Canada were operating at Minnedosa, Dauphin, Killarney, and Boissevain.

As the Saskatchewan border is approached the town of Elkhorn pridefully offers its Manitoba Automobile Museum which also includes antique agricultural implements. An Agricultural Museum at Austin, sixty-two miles west of Winnipeg, has been operating for many years with the financial assistance of provincial and federal agencies, and in recent years its operation has been substantially expanded.

The city of Brandon is the second largest community in the province and the only other municipality to have an art gallery, unfortunately still occupying a remodelled building which until 1959 had served as a Home for the Aged. The Brandon Allied Arts Centre has involved itself in creative programs for adults and children and the B. J. Hales natural history collection, mentioned earlier, now occupies greatly increased space on the campus of the young University of Brandon. The Canadian Forces base at Shilo, west of Brandon, has an excellent museum dedicated to the regimental history of the Canadian Artillery and is open to the public.

Central Manitoba is largely lake country, one paved highway threading itself northward between the west shore of Lake Winnipegosis and the Saskatchewan border. Over three hundred and fifty miles from Winnipeg is The Pas, a mining community developed in the second decade of the century, with its Little Northern Museum dedicated largely to mineral exploitation of the region. From The Pas, approximately six hundred and fifty miles by air or seven hundred and fifty miles by rail, the port of Churchill has a museum, founded in 1944 by Brother Jacques Volant, O. M. which continues to display and interpret the folk ways of the Eskimo, and includes a collection of sculptures which has achieved international recognition. Fort Prince of Wales at Churchill, the first stone fortress west of Quebec City, which took forty years to build and two days to be reduced to rubble save for thirty or forty feet of its outer walls, can be reached in the brief summer by boat or canoe, or by dogteam in the remaining nine to ten months. The fort, now a National Historic Park, has undergone some restoration but other than its outer wall only traces of the various habitations remain.

The site for this Hudson's Bay post was explored in 1686, two years before King Charles II granted a charter to Prince Rupert and seventeen other "gentlemen adventurers seeking to trade into Hudson's Bay." A temporary fort was built a few miles upstream on the Churchill River in 1717 but construction of the stone fort at Eskimo Point, a rocky promontory, got under way in 1731. In 1769, The Royal Society established an astronomical station at the fort to make observations of the planet Venus. Three years later Jean-François de Galaup, Comte de Pérouse, led a fleet of three ships intent on attacking the fort as part of the Franco-British feud. The fort was well armed with guns – forty-nine of them – but lacked the four hundred and twenty gunners trained to man them. De Galaup spent the ensuing two days destroying the wooden buildings and stone structures before sailing off with a complement of prisoners. Despite its isolation, the fort attracted over two thousand visitors in the summer months of 1971, but further restoration of this interesting historical document will have to wait until a more propitious moment. In the meantime, research continues by the National Historic Sites Service.

This same federal agency announced in 1969 that the Manitoba government had turned over for restoration the family home of Louis Riel in St. Vital, now within the perimeter of Greater Winnipeg. The building is currently being converted into a museum to pay tribute through graphics and artifacts to this historic figure, long viewed as traitor by some but who in recent years has been acclaimed by many as martyr and hero.

In 1952 the Province of Manitoba could boast of four museums and one art gallery; in the following twelve years eleven more institutions had opened their doors. As of December 31, 1968, the province had twenty-nine museums and related institutions, of which six received finances from the Centennial Capital Grants fund in 1967. Further impetus has been given to museum development, however, with the province's own centennial celebrations of 1970. Capital grants from both federal and provincial exchequers became available for local committees seeking to memorialize a local event with some permanent monument and the historically minded seized upon the opportunity to advocate their own pet projects.

By the end of the celebrations, twenty new musuems had been launched, one in Winnipeg called The Aquatic Hall of Fame and Museum; two devoted to the Ukrainian culture at Gilbert Plains and Gardenton; a museum at Hadashville concentrating on forestry, and a threshermen's museum at Winkler. The remaining fifteen were classified as institutions dealing with pioneer history.

Other museums, most of which emerged out of these same festivities, are at Carmen; La Rivière; Pilot Mound; St. Andrews where the former rectory (1853) contains miscellaneous items from at home and abroad; and The Red River House, former residence of Captain William Kennedy, fur trader and arctic explorer – all in the south central region. In the south-west, Bowsman, Dauphin, Eddystone, Grandview, Hargrave, Souris and Virden are now listed. As of April 1973, the Provincial Museum's Advisor listed sixty-nine museums in operation and a further twenty-one in the planning stage, including one dedicated to the Icelandic settlers.

Contributing not only to the development of cultural consciousness in the fine arts, the Winnipeg Art Gallery's new building, formally opened by Princess Margaret and Lord Snowden in September 1971, makes a major contribution to contemporary architectural design. The triangular site provides 120,000 square feet of space, and architect Gustavo de Roza has put to effective use every inch. An activities area shares the basement with storage and workshop facilities, an auditorium is located on the main floor vertex area, and administration offices occupy the balance of the second or mezzanine floor. The entire third floor, with 25,000 square feet, is divided into nine gallery areas, with an additional 15,000 square feet of open display for sculpture on the top floor adjacent to a cafeteria and lounge. Space is also provided on the main floor for a commodious lobby with a small concourse of specialty shops. The opening was far from formal. The horde of visiting dignitaries from Canada, the United States and Europe were met by striking picketers and viewed a structure far from complete, the event being transformed into a hilarious celebration dedicated to the Moment of Truth.

Having assembled an important collection of paintings, graphics and sculptures the gallery had long outgrown its previous quarters.

Its late Gothic and early Renaissance panels from Germany and the Low Countries are outstanding and it has continued to acquire European Old Masters, French Impressionist and Post-Impressionist works. In addition, it has consistently developed a Canadian collection dating from 1830 and has the "richest and finest collection of paintings by the late Lemoine FitzGerald," who in 1932 became the last member of the Group of Seven. Within the past decade the gallery has also benefitted extensively from the estate of the late Douglas Duncan, and other benefactors including Lord and Lady Gort, John A. Macaulay, former president, and Montreal architect Peter Dobush, who presented the institution with one hundred and twenty-five paintings by Canadian artists.

A Curatorial Department of Primitive Art has been created, the first of its kind in Canada. Recent accessions to its Eskimo sculptures and prints include gifts from the Bessie Bulman estate, and the Twomey collection of four thousand items, making it the most extensive and distinguished Eskimo collection in the world.

In its extension program, the gallery has conducted the usual Saturday classes for children and in co-operation with the Junior League established a policy of circulating exhibitions for schools within the metropolitan area, in addition to sponsoring and administering a similar service for the more isolated communities of the province. In 1972 more funds became available for an expansion of the art gallery program. Much of the $300,000 grant from the National Museums Board, as a token of its status as one of ten Associate institutions that year, is being used in the planning and organization of major exhibitions to travel from coast to coast. The delayed opening of the new gallery took place on January 19, 1972 and by July 19th of the same year had welcomed 155,000 visitors.

34

While Confederation Centre at Charlottetown serves as a cornerstone upon which Canada's contemporary museums have been built, the Province of Saskatchewan saw four museum buildings of architectural interest erected in the decade and a half after 1950, three in Regina and one in Saskatoon, a record unsurpassed in Canada up to that time. The Provincial Museum of Natural History at Regina, which was installed in its new building in 1950, gets credit for being the first museum in Canada to install a complete gallery of thematic displays using diorama techniques. In 1955 the Norman Mackenzie Gallery was opened on the Regina College campus and in 1962 a downtown art gallery formed part of the new public library. Two years later the Fred Mendel Gallery and Conservatory was opened in Saskatoon.

In Regina, Norman Mackenzie, a prosperous lawyer, acquired extensive collections of Old Master paintings and drawings, miscellaneous objets d'art, and antiquities and had also cultivated a taste for western Canadian paintings before his death in the early 1930's. The entire collection was bequeathed to Regina College, along with downtown real estate from which a fund would be created for both capital development and administration. In the meantime, the paintings were hung in the manner of the late eighteenth century, floor to ceiling, frame to frame, in a dimly illuminated octagonal hall, awaiting the propitious moment when real estate values would increase. Prints, sculpture pieces, and cases of miscellaneous objects were stored in basement rooms.

Not until 1951, when the Norman Mackenzie Art Gallery was opened on the campus, was any attention paid to having the works authenticated or restored where necessary. The superficial examination of the paintings, to say the least, was disappointing, although here and there some valuable works were discovered, particularly among the Old Master drawings which a few years earlier had been considered of little value.

The gallery, an interesting architectural achievement in design, sadly lacked technical areas. Through its endowment fund it has developed a progressive accessioning policy, and was one of the first campus institutions to encourage community participation. Undoubtedly its presence was responsible for young artists from other regions of the west joining its art school faculty and the development of a school of painters which has received national and international recognition.

It would hardly seem possible that a city of the size of Regina with a population of just over one hundred thousand could support two art galleries, yet the Regina Public Library pioneered in this field in 1948, allotting two rooms in its Andrew Carnegie building for small travelling exhibitions and local shows. In 1962 a new library building was opened with an art gallery annex and full-time curator in charge. Art rental along with lectures and film shows have since been included in an all-embracing program, complementing what can be viewed as a more sophisticated program of the campus. The Mackenzie Gallery concentrates on major, and at times highly controversial exhibitions, while the downtown gallery offers smaller travelling shows and works by regional artists.

Museums, particularly the community institutions, have always held a tenuous place in Canadian society. They are often orphans left on the doorsteps of civic authorities by their progenitors after they have discovered only a lukewarm response and an absence of welfare checks with which to keep the infant alive and thriving. The situation has changed, not as rapidly as it should, but the full significance of the community museum is making its impact felt on the body politic. Saskatchewan is heading in this general direction.

In the cultural field, serving the community art societies and galleries, the Saskatchewan Arts Board was created in 1948 with the express purpose of increasing both quality and quantity in the disparate fields of the arts and crafts. The ultimate aims, as outlined in its brochures, are: "to assess through research and study the developing needs of art, artist and audience in each field of visual and performing arts; to formulate plans to fill these needs in the best possible way; to determine whether the plans fill the needs adequately so the budget and effort expended on the arts in the province will achieve maximum results." The Arts Board has been kept free from politics and can be credited with the development of a climate which has responded to experimentation and improved standards of performance, in both the visual and performing arts. Until recently historical museums were operating in a grey area, but in 1972 a new government took the first positive steps to involve the small community institutions in an all-embracing program under a newly appointed museums advisor.

The Provincial Natural Science Museum has made its staff avail-

276

able for technical advice, and has, on occasion, provided some financial assistance for projects considered of regional importance, the Eastend palaeontology display being one such example. Staff members also have accomplished significant work in the fields of ethnology, anthropology, archaeology, and the earth sciences. The Department of Fisheries opened a Fish Culture Station at Fort Qu'Appelle in 1958, and since that time has expanded many activities, including organized tours, lectures, library and research facilities, and a film service.

As a Centennial project the Hewett Home on the Souris Trail at Cannington was restored, and as another Centennial gesture to honour one of the province's most colourful sons, the boyhood home of the Right Hon. John George Diefenbaker, eighteenth Prime Minister of Canada, was restored and transferred to the Wascona Centre in the capital city.

Over the years the government has concerned itself with the preservation and retention of historic furnishings and decor in its legislative buildings. The Saskatchewan Government Telephones, a Crown Corporation, as its name implies, opened its Telerama in its downtown administration building in 1965, a display which tells the chronological story of telephonic communication from the original Bell experiments into the era of the satellites.

The province has been directly involved with the Western Development Museum, originally opened in 1949, which has built up impressive collections of all pioneer forms of transportation, agricultural equipment, domestic tools and appliances, virtually all having been restored and put into working condition. The museum was formally brought into being in 1948 when the provincial Legislature approved a special act, named a Board of Directors, and provided for an annual grant from the provincial treasury. Originally established in North Battleford, the new Board acquired abandoned airplane hangers in that city, in Yorkton, and in Saskatoon. In 1963 a new building was erected at North Battleford, and four years later, as a centennial gesture, a small pioneer village was created to portray village life of the early twentieth century.

Plans for a permanent museum building in Saskatoon were initiated in 1964 but not until May 1971 was the sod turned for a single level structure of 120,000 square feet at a cost of $1,100,000. After its formal opening in mid-June 1972, construction on a new multicultural museum costing $107,000 got under way at Yorkton with initial floor space of 10,000 square feet and provision for two additional wings of the same size. This museum had its opening in September of the same year.

The new Saskatoon museum, logically sited near the agricultural fair grounds, has a typical small town main street as the focal attraction which serves as a covered mall with railway station at one end, and a hotel of the late nineteenth century at the other. Five large display areas each measuring 100 by 130 feet are used for permanent exhibits of antique farm equipment, horse-drawn and energy powered vehicles, with a sixth area for specially organized or travelling exhibits.

Not content with these achievements, the Western Development Museum Board entered into negotiations with the City of Moose Jaw for a take-over of the former fairgrounds for the establishment of an Aviation Museum dedicated largely to the days of the bush pilot. At the same time, it helped to persuade the provincial government to purchase a reconstructed pioneer village for $500,000. This village had been built and used by a Canadian film company as location for a movie titled *Alien Thunder* based on the story of The Riel Rebellion, and starring Donald Sutherland as the legendary Indian Almighty Voice. All research for the instant village had been undertaken by museum personnel who also recruited the supporting cast from the Duck Lake community and loaned virtually all the artifacts used in the production. The Alien Thunder village and adjacent lands are now officially designated as a Provincial Historical Park with the Saskatchewan Museum of Natural History named as custodian until such time as a permanent policy can be implemented.

The three museum complexes at Saskatoon, North Battleford, and Yorkton operate with a total paid staff of thirty-eight. However, it has from its inception involved citizens in many ways, encouraging, instructing, and supervising large rosters of volunteers in restoration and learning to operate equipment from ox-drawn carts to seat of the pants aviation, all of which is brought into action at the drop of a stetson. The three came under the jurisdiction of the Department of Culture in January 1973, thus indicating a reorganization of government policies. The museum has also joined the growing list of National Museum Associates thereby accepting responsibilities for the expansion of its educational services, which include major improvements to the North Battleford Pioneer Village. A further four hundred thousand dollar expansion is envisaged for the Yorkton complex.

Saskatoon with a current population of one hundred and fifteen thousand, is almost equal in size to Regina, and like its sister city has two exciting art galleries. One gallery at Marquis Hall on the university campus has a small but important collection of nineteenth century Western Canadian works along with contemporary paintings and sculptures. The campus also has its varied collections in the areas of anthropology and archaeology and a herbarium. In 1967

278

the Saskatoon Council of Women, in co-operation with the university authorities and other interested societies, restored an early (1887) stone schoolhouse, which throughout the pioneer days had served also as community centre and church.

In 1945, a civic art gallery was opened in the downtown area, occupying space on the second floor of a warehouse building. A few years later, the gallery was transferred to the basement of the King George Hotel where it languished due to lack of finances. In 1965, Fred Mendel, for many years a consistent and knowledgeable art collector, who had arrived from Czechoslovakia some thirty years earlier and re-established his international packing plant in Saskatoon, presented the city with a representative cross-section of his accessions, together with a cheque with which to build a contemporary gallery and conservatory as a memorial to the province's sixtieth anniversary.

The completed building, containing two gallery areas, with workshops for the arts and crafts, is an outstanding piece of architectural design. The transition, however, from the modestly financed basement gallery to the new cultural centre was not accomplished without severe labour pains. The existing community association was loath to lose control, yet found itself unable to raise the essential administrative finances. The civic administration, unaccustomed to making any major contributions to such erudite enterprises, was called upon eventually to face the facts of a cultural renaissance. That first step has since developed into a well-rounded program embracing along with the Mendel Gallery a twenty-two hundred seat auditorium, serving also as convention centre and adding to the architectural beauty of a city which has been acutely conscious of its urban scenic setting for many years. The city now assumes major responsibility for financing its cultural activities.

Saskatoon, as in other northern communities arching out from Winnipeg, attracted many ethnic groups during the days of colonization, with the Ukrainian community becoming a dominant ethnic factor. Two museums devoted to the decorative arts and crafts of the Ukraine are to be seen in the city. The Museum of Ukrainian Culture at 202 Avenue M South, organized and administered by the Eparchy of Saskatoon, has an excellent display of exhibits dating from the eighteenth century. It was opened in 1967 as a Centenary project. The Arts and Crafts Museum of the Ukrainian Women's Association occupies an extensive area in the Mohyla Institute adjacent to the university campus. This Association has established branch museums in Toronto, Winnipeg, Edmonton, and Vancouver. The museum also has an active research department and is heavily involved with inter-museum loans and circulating exhibitions.

Duck Lake is seventy-five miles east of Battleford, and a little more than a shot-gun blast from Batoche, the small community made famous during the Riel Rebellion. In 1960, Fred Anderson, local historian whose knowledge of the Rebellion is highly respected, launched the local historical museum and saw its major expansion in 1967. This included the restoration of the former North-West Mounted Police jail, where the Indian outlaw "Almighty Voice" had been incarcerated. A schoolhouse of the same era was also restored and now houses a rich and impressive collection of relics of the Rebellion, in addition to artifacts related to the Hudson's Bay post.

In what can be described as the north central region of the province, Denare Beach, near the mining community of Flin Flon, is at the end of a circuitous and somewhat nondescript highway, approximately three hundred miles from Prince Albert. A small museum was opened in the isolated community in 1954 with exhibits concentrating on Indian culture, mining, and geology of the immediate region. At the westerly boundary on a fully paved highway leading to Edmonton the museum of the Barr Colony was opened as a Centennial Project in 1967. The Barr Colony was a short-lived community which has been both praised and damned by historians, viewed as an altruistic experiment in communal agriculture by one element, and as a well planned con game by more cynical students of the subject. Unfortunately, the museum ran into problems at its founding, but is now concentrating on the story of the "Reverend Mr. Barr" and his followers. Its collection also includes the Imhoff religious paintings, mostly copies of European works, and a wild-life exhibit with an abundance of nature's freaks displayed in its own semi-detached area.

One of the better and older museums of the province devoted almost exclusively to the natural history of the region is the Thoreson Memorial Museum at Swift Current. If justice were done, the museum would be in a building considerably larger and better adapted to its multiple functions. The institution owns, among other things, the George Warren collection of native birds; has well designed displays of associated subjects; recently initiated a policy providing temporary loan exhibitions; and encourages an exciting hobby group for children who send their own small exhibits to schools within the immediate region.

Canada's centennial celebrations saw somewhat more museum projects developed in this province than are to be found in her sister provinces to east and west. In 1952 only eight institutions were listed in the federal directory; at the end of 1964 when the province celebrated its fiftieth anniversary, the total had increased to twenty-seven. By the time Canada's 1967 celebrations were over, nineteen new institutions had been launched and others were being expanded as capital funds became available, and by May 1973, sixty-three were in operation.

Discussions on new museums developed in all regions, including as far north as Flin Flon, but there were a number of shattered dreams. At Nipawin, where a local citizen had proffered a fairly substantial sum for an art gallery, legal complications concerning a proposed site shelved the project indefinitely. Prince Albert, which had once enjoyed a historical museum, viewed architectural plans, but a three-dimensional mock-up submitted by the local Historical Society was rejected in favour of a recreational building in centennial year. Canora also discussed the restoration of an early Greek Orthodox church which had been officially named for a 1967 opening. Residents of the Spy Hill-Esterhazy district, dreaming of a revitalized community when potash mining got under way, had to be content with sharing a twenty by twenty foot space with the Regional Library and the Canadian Legion while members of the museum society continued to store specialized collections in their respective homes.

It was in the area further to the south that plans materialized, as at Kindersley and Rosetown, west of Saskatoon; here the municipalities are administering regional library-museum complexes; at Craik, Raymore and Foam Lake in the less travelled central area; at Veregin, where not surprisingly the Doukhoubor Prayer House was restored as a tourist attraction and is now also used for "public gatherings and religious festivals"; and still further south at Fort Qu-Appelle, a community that had attracted artists and craftsmen in recent years, a former Hudson's Bay Trading Post was restored and now serves as a historical museum. The City of Moose Jaw built one of the best designed art gallery-museum complexes in the west as an annex to the existing library. It is situated on the perimeter of Crescent Park and rounds out an overall recreational program and beauty spot.

To the east, a centennial museum was opened at Rocanville devoted largely to pioneer agricultural techniques. At Weyburn, the Soo Line Historical Museum had got a little off the tracks in its enthusiasm to embrace all manner of gifts, but developed a new direction when it took over and transformed the former transformer station. Fifty-five miles to the south on highway 39, the Estevan Lion's Club restored a former North-West Mounted Police Barracks with the aid of the Capital Grants Fund, and now operates a museum displaying natural history collections and pioneer artifacts.

In 1966 the Saskatchewan Museums' Association was organized after receiving encouragement from the provincial administration. Since then, the association has initiated annual workshops, prepared briefs for submission to the provincial authorities, and generally is paving the way for more community and governmental involvement in addition to linking itself with the national museums' association.

For close to fifty years Notre Dame College, located in the small prairie community of Wilcox, twenty miles south-west of Regina, has continued to grow through hard work and prayer, according to its founder, eighty year old Monsignor Athol Murray. Occasionally the college made the headlines for its ability to turn out superb hockey players and, during the Depression, for its unique program of manual services in return for education. The college, throughout the years has continued the policy of student participation in day-to-day housekeeping, and the philosophy of Monsignor Murray, who is still at the helm, anticipated much of the contemporary "free school" techniques of today.

What was not generally known is that throughout the years Father Murray was collecting incunabula, rare manuscripts and books which today rank as one of the best ten collections in Canada. Recently the college gained more publicity when it was revealed that in its temporary archives it had the original papers of Confederation formulated in Quebec in 1864 bearing the signatures of John A. Macdonald and George E. Cartier. Also included in its ten thousand items are manuscripts of the twelfth and thirteenth centuries, many works of the fifteenth and sixteenth centuries, "Most of the first edition of Erasmus and one or two of Thomas More, a fifty-three page treatise by St. Thomas Aquinas, the Nurnburg Chronicle by Schedel, the life of Martin of Tours written in ink on sheepskin and an *Encyclopedia of All Knowledge* published in 1517."

A one million dollar capital fund drive was launched in Toronto early in 1971. When about one third of the money had been collected, Father Murray indicated that his recipe for hard work and prayer will make possible a library-archives building with appropriate display areas within the present decade.

A further tribute to the Rt. Hon. John G. Diefenbaker was made in 1971 at the small town of Wakaw, forty miles south of Prince Albert, where his former law office was restored, while about seventy miles to the south, at Humboldt, a historic park was dedicated to commemorate the "telegraph site of 1885."

As in other provinces the National Historic Sites Service continues to work in the general areas of restoration, taking over Fort Walsh from the Royal Canadian Mounted Police in 1971. This Fort, originally founded to combat the whiskey trading traffic, had in more recent years been used as an equine training centre, finally serving as quarters for the internationally famous R.C.M.P. Musical Ride. The Fort and adjacent lands which were the scene of the Cypress Hills Massacre are currently undergoing restoration and were opened to the public as a National Historic Park in 1972 although completion date will not be until 1975. At Batoche the federal agency has acquired more land to make possible the reconstruction of the battlefield of the North-west Rebellion of 1885, while at Fort Battleford new modernized displays are being installed to replace the somewhat sketchy exhibits of artifacts. The Royal Canadian Mounted Police also took positive steps to celebrate its one-hundreth anniversary by formally opening a new $300,000 museum on the campus of their barracks in Regina on July 4, 1973. Although the Mounties have over the years developed a reticence concerning publicity, the new museum will remain open three hundred and sixty-five days a year and for the accommodation of tourists during the summer months will welcome visitors from 8:00 a.m. to 9:00 p.m.

One of the major contributions to prairie agricultural history made possible through National Historic Sites was the opening of the William H. Motherwell farmstead at Abernathy, seventy-five miles east of Regina. The stone Italian Revival style residence was built and occupied by Mr. Motherwell in 1882 and for the ensuing sixty years the owner devoted his major energies to improving the lot of his fellow agriculturists. As one of the first graduates of the Ontario College of Agriculture he came west with a well founded knowledge of scientific techniques, and conducted experiments in both grain and livestock raising. At the same time he agitated for improvement of grading and shipping. Mr. Motherwell was elected first president of the Territorial Grain Growers' Association, became first Agricultural Minister in the provincial Legislature, and after fourteen years' service was invited into the Mackenzie King Cabinet with the same portfolio, a position he held until 1930.

35

As Alberta approaches the twenty-first century it is still mainly cattle and grain country, but since the 1940's, gas and oil in addition to large deposits of lignite and bituminous coal have enriched its economic structure. To the north are large forest reserves still virtually untapped. From its easterly boundary at one thousand feet, the land rises progressively into foothill country and then, more abruptly into the several gateways of the Rockies and the National Park areas which have become meccas for tourists, hunters, anglers, and, in more recent years, skiers.

Until recently the province had developed a reputation for political unorthodoxy, while its economic development has resulted in many disparate cultures and traditions now reflected in its changing social structures. It was a region that, well into the twentieth century, had its wide-open proclivities, but almost overnight it changed its spots to become saturated with fundamentalist evangelical zeal and puritanical philosophy.

Quite naturally Alberta's museums today are seeking to interpret the legendary stories of the past century. The small community institutions, many of them still literally saturated with artifacts and other memorabilia relating to the fur trade, tribal warfare, whiskey runners, horse and cattle rustling, round-ups, homesteading, early mineral exploration and exploitation, the dirty thirties and the more recent oil and gas developments, are now receiving more professional guidance with which to tell the stories effectively. The perpetuation of at least some of these traditions is left to The Calgary Stampede – part county fair with all the razzmatazz which characterizes such western expositions – with its rodeo keeping alive the history of early ranching days and the nomadic life of the Plains Indians. Some of Calgary's excitement is reflected in virtually all regions of the province where little rodeos are held, along with other events relating to pioneer days.

In Edmonton, a somewhat synthetic reconstruction of Klondyke Days as a parallel to the Calgary whoop-de-do is celebrated annually although it might well be more properly staged at Cache Creek, British Columbia, or in the Yukon. Despite this fall from historical rectitude, Alberta's capital city has in recent years developed an exciting museums program. The city government currently administers its Storyland Valley Zoo, opened in 1959, and, as the name implies, dedicated to the younger population; the John Walter Historical Site opened in the same year in two restored buildings which had once belonged to this man, one of the city's earliest businessmen (around 1880); the Queen Elizabeth Planetarium in Coronation Park opened in 1960; and also in 1960 the city archivist developed a historical display in the civic centre complex. Under reconstruction, and now open to the public, is a pioneer village on the historic site of Fort Edmonton near Whitemud Creek. The primary object of the restoration is "to tell the story of the city from the beginning of geological time to the present and into the future"–truly a monumental task. In addition to audio-visual techniques and three-dimensional models, boats, ferries, streetcars, and small factories are being restored, while a coal mine which operated on the site in 1905 is being made safe for public inspection. The development, although sponsored and administered by the city, depends largely on private donations with the provincial government financing some of the operations. The planned completion date is set at 1987.

Following trends in other major centres, the Alberta Government Telephones designed its own communications display area in a new and contemporary headquarters building which logically deals with the development of telephone services in the west.

A revitalized art gallery at the University of Alberta, located on the south side of the Saskatchewan River, has a continuing program of temporary exhibitions. In addition, collections relating to scientific disciplines continue to exist on the campus. However, the only such museum open to the public is devoted to geology, palaeontology and mineralogy in the basement of the Biological Sciences Building.

The Provincial Museum and Archives, founded in 1905, had collected, if not too well preserved, a number of miscellaneous artifacts, stuffed birds and animals, documents and historical booklets, including two complete collections from the estates of Ernest Brown (historical photographs) and Judge Grey (pioneer artifacts), which were placed in storage or displayed intermittently in the Cupola and adjacent corridors of the Legislative Building. This institution had its metamorphosis in October 1967 when the Provincial Museum and Archives of Alberta was formally opened, a project partially financed through the federal centennial gift of two and a half million dollars, augmented by a further four million from the Provincial Treasury. The building occupies approximately half of a thirteen and a half acre park. The former Government House, which occupies the rest of the park, is now being used as a reception area for the entertainment of visiting dignitaries.

Architecturally, the building is not as spectacular as the Ontario centennial project, nor as monumental as that of the new British Columbia centre at Victoria, but, more than anything it interprets the Bauhaus philosophy that form follows function. As in Charlottetown, the architects were called upon to blend the contemporary structure with the early twentieth century architecture of Government House. The building occupies two hundred and fifty thousand square feet and has four display wings for its human and natural history collections. In addition there is an archival area which has its own independent displays.

From the two or three unqualified civil servants who administered the archival museum as late as 1964, the staff now numbers seventy-five full time and sixty-five part time employees, all highly trained for their respective functions. Attendance was just under three hundred and seventy-eight thousand in 1972.

The museum is primarily designed to interpret the pioneer and natural history of the province but its program of temporary exhibitions has included "A Salute to the Northwest Territories"; a show drawn from the Smithsonian Institution entitled "Silent Cities – Mexico and Mayas"; "Easter Island"; "The Preservation of Abu Simbal"; "The Color of Man"; and "Pionèer Life of Early Alberta Settlers." The archives gallery also has changing exhibitions relating to the documented history of the province.

The Edmonton Art Gallery was still functioning in the civic baby clinic building in the late 1940's when the society received a bequest of an older three storey residence in the downtown area of the city. Forthwith it was remodelled to provide a ground floor gallery, the second floor being utilized for a child art program. In 1952, the gallery had a staff of two and a budget of approximately fifteen thousand dollars. Twelve years later the staff had increased to seven and its budget was now forty-one thousand dollars, with attendance in the neighbourhood of twenty-five thousand. Both its children's and adult classes had overflowed out of the restricted gallery area and were threatening to take over a nearby elementary school during off-hours. The City of Edmonton was contributing in cash and services approximately nine thousand dollars, with the province giving an annual grant of two thousand dollars.

In 1964 gallery officials were surprised to learn that it was to receive a bequest of six hundred thousand dollars for capital expansion. A proviso in the will of the benefactor, however, stipulated that if such expansion was unduly delayed the monies would go

286

elsewhere. By 1967, as the deadline approached, the society had raised one hundred and fifty thousand dollars through the sale of its existing premises, had a promise of a two hundred thousand dollar grant from the province, and had raised through public subscriptions a further three hundred thousand dollars. The government grant, however, was conditional that the sum be matched dollar for dollar over and above monies already pledged. The estimated capital cost of the proposed gallery was a million and a half dollars. The city would provide the site and give title to it, city fathers being aware that once the edifice was open, their annual grant for administration would have to be substantially increased. The Junior League, as Junior Leagues elsewhere, had long been actively supporting gallery programs and had voted fifty thousand dollars as "a Centennial Project" to set up and operate (but not to build) a Children's Gallery over the ensuing three years.

On May 1st of that year tenders were called for a new building with a total floor space of fifty-two thousand, six hundred and eighty-seven square feet, and in April 1969 the new art gallery was formally opened, with an administrative budget of two hundred and ten thousand dollars, this being increased by a further nineteen thousand dollars in 1971. Full time staff has been increased to ten with five part-time security guards and twenty-one part-time teachers. Attendance for the first full year of operation had built up to two hundred thousand. The gallery was given Associate status by the National Museums' Board in 1972 and immediately devised plans for the development of exhibition satellites in suburban areas.

The Glenbow-Alberta Museum occupies the former Provincial Court House building in downtown Calgary and was until recently a one-man show, reflecting the personal taste and wide-spread interests of its founder, Eric L. Harvie, Q.C., It was Dr. Harvie who, when the Provincial Government planned to tear down the sixty year old building, helped to persuade authorities to preserve it as a historical example of government architecture and to serve as a repository for his collections.

While adhering to the original philosophy of its founder "to preserve in permanent form the history of Western Canada and to maintain a record of its living history," the collections have included from time to time numismatics, Chinese ivories, European antique porcelain, and even replicas of the Crown Jewels, displayed logically enough in an old vault which in earlier days had protected legal documents of the government.

One area records the history of weapons from the neolithic era to the small arms of today, along with chain mail and armour. In-depth displays deal with the history of the Royal Canadian Mounted Police; early transportation; The Riel Rebellion; fur trade; Indian and Eskimo cultures with complementing exhibits devoted to the aboriginal tribes of other continents; followed by the story of pioneer life on the prairies.

If anywhere in the museum there is any mention made of the founder of this oversized *cabinet de curiosités* it would be difficult to find, not because government and the administration now operating the museum and its subsidiaries are not grateful, but out of respect for Dr. Harvie's "intense passion for anonymity," as one writer has phrased it.

In 1967 Dr. Harvie, in the name of his entire family, turned over his Glenbow collection to the provincial government with the proviso that an independent corporation be established "as a memorial to Centennial year." The corporation, known as The Glenbow-Alberta Institute, would administer in the interests of the people of Alberta buildings and other properties, including the Glenbow collection shown in a 1966 balance sheet as having "an insured value of $4,950,000."

A provincial Act spelled out the terms of the benefaction which included a cheque for $5,000,000 to be matched dollar for dollar by the province, and to serve as a perpetual endowment fund, with the province also called on to contribute $100,000 annually to the Institute, along with an additional $35,000 for administration of the Calgary museum.

A summary of collections shown in the Act ranges through archaeology, archival material, earth sciences, ethnography, fine art, a library of 20,000 volumes, and military, natural, and pioneer history. The art collection alone totalled "over 14,000 items by upwards of 1,000 artists."

Historically Dr. Harvie's philosophy is parallel to that of Sir Hans Sloane who spent his entire lifetime collecting. In 1753 Sir Hans left to the British government his entire collection of 70,000 individual objects, in addition to 50,000 books on the condition that the sum of 30,000 pounds be paid to his estate for the collection, and that "a repository for the better reception and more convenient use of the said collections" should be created and thrown open to the general public. In like manner Dr. Harvie is never content to restrict himself to a single object or discipline as visitors who have seen his more recent (Riveredge) collection can testify. And while the Riveredge Foundation continues collecting, a fleet of mobile museums visits the smallest of rural communities during the school year, and adds lustre to the western parks system in the summer months. T.J. Honeyman, Scottish author and art critic writing in the *Scottish Field,* summarized his impressions of the many Harvie projects as "something more comprehensive in both cultural and historical fields than anything I had seen."

288

The Harvie (and associated) charities have extended into other disciplines and wider fields. A program of archaeological exploration continues to produce significant artifacts relating to the history of the west. Financial assistance has been made available to the Royal Ontario Museum for its digs in Egypt. Dr. Harvie served first as a member and later as chairman of the Charlottetown Confederation Centre Foundation and was also one of the charter members of The Canada Council.

The oil boom of 1948 produced more millionaires per capita in Calgary than in any other city in Canada. With one or two exceptions they diverted their excess wealth to what is known as "the improvement of the breed," football and similar pursuits. One recent exception was a matching gift by the late Sam Nickle, president of an independent oil company, of one million dollars to provide an art and archaeology museum on the campus of the University of Calgary. This museum will contain an extensive numismatic collection donated by his son, Carl.

The Glenbow-Alberta Institute presently has its improvised art gallery in the former small parts warehouse of the Ford Motor Company. While the exterior appearance is somewhat uninviting, a spacious uncluttered interior has been intelligently transformed into a pleasing display area capable of housing major exhibitions.

A downtown rehabilitation project to be completed in 1975 will have as its focal point a convention centre and hotel but included in the overall plans will be an eight storey Glenbow-Alberta complex which will bring together the various collections under one roof. This museum expansion is being financed by the provincial government and is expected to cost $8,000,000. The 80,000 square feet of space provides for both historical and fine art galleries, archives and reference library facilities in addition to a 375 seat lecture hall and other educational facilities.

In late 1972 the Glenbow Institute was accepted as a National Museums "associate." As a result, one or more areas will be earmarked for temporary exhibitions drawn from the nation's capital.

In 1912 a Provincial Institute of Technology was founded in Calgary. Provision was made for a department of commercial art but not until 1926 was a full time instructor appointed for a daytime class of five or six. Despite this lowly beginning, the school attracted teachers of outstanding ability who concerned themselves with fostering the philosophy of sound painting. Although the school never received much recognition it has produced over the years a substantial group of practitioners with national reputations in the diverse areas of the arts and crafts.

The school was given college status in the 1960's while remaining within the technology structure and in 1973 moved into its own multi-million dollar building to accommodate approximately five hundred students. The college campus now occupies 156,000 square feet 5,000 of which have been set aside for two art galleries that are open to the public. Other small areas have been allotted to local societies involved in the visual arts at the professional level. A mall seventy feet high by forty feet wide and extending through the mid-section of the building serves as a sculpture court.

A pilot project initiated by a small group of cultural opium eaters in the spring of 1946, while having made a significant impact on the visual and performing arts elsewhere, signally failed to achieve its goals in its own bailiwick. Born out of desperation due to lack of civic interest and equal lack of funds, the Calgary Allied Arts Council was organized that year, and as a temporary expedient rented The Coste House, a twenty-room mansion which had been doomed for wrecking as a civic white elephant. A philosophy was evolved to embrace a centre designed to encourage participation of both artists and lay public. The ninety-hour a week "open-house" principle was alarming to more orthodox institutions, not only in Canada but in the United States, although here and there more liberal programs were being introduced by art galleries to build up a declining attendance.

The Calgary Allied Arts Council had accepted the fact that if cultural progress was to be made it would have to adopt radical departures from the norm in a city geared to the culture of the wide open spaces. In addition to spectator involvement the organization initiated children's programs, something which local educational authorities had banished as a luxury item in the depression years. It also sought to assist the struggling cultural societies while keeping in mind political pressure for greater recognition of all cultural affairs.

For ten years the Calgary Arts Council administered, and subsidized so far as its limited exchequer would permit, the Western Canada Art Circuit, a co-operative agency for the circulation of art collections. Initially it served six public galleries and four or five burgeoning art societies. When the Circuit was temporarily suspended in 1970 its membership included ten campus galleries, eleven permanent community institutions, and six exhibiting societies.

From 1956 to 1960, the Calgary organization was encouraged through Canada Council grants to publicize and counsel similar projects in other regions of Canada, one such being the production of a brochure in French and English for nation wide distribution.

Unable to get the essential fiscal support for construction of a permanent centre the Arts Council, in 1958, settled for a heavy road machinery sales and service building large enough to accommodate a five hundred seat theatre, galleries for adults and children, together with studio and workshop facilities where it continued its ninety hour, seven days a week program. Capital assets of approximately half a million dollars were built up only to see the Centre closed down on December 31, 1969 when a deficit of approximately three hundred thousand dollars had been incurred.

Three months later, the Riveredge Foundation had taken over the property and contents after providing funds for the payment of debts. At the same time, temporary accommodation was also provided for the young professional theatre group and the child arts activities were continued. Simultaneously, workmen moved in to refurbish and redecorate the interior as a first step to revitalize the institution. If this hope fails, the building could continue to be used to display segments of the ever-expanding Riveredge collection of antiquities, curiosities, natural history, and ethnology.

The Calgary Zoo, after overcoming civic inertia, presently claims to be the largest of its kind in Canada with over four hundred specimens, many unfortuantely still behind bars. A step by step modernization program has been launched to provide a more simulated environment for the captive exhibits at an ultimate cost of around ten million dollars and to be completed by 1980.

Certainly this Zoo is the only one on the continent that can boast of another collection of inanimate but authentic replicas of prehistoric reptiles dominated by a thirty-two foot high Brontosaurus, and with new replicas added from time to time as palaeontologists discover hitherto unknown species. Added to the attractions in this somewhat restricted St. George's Island is a Children's Zoo and a delightful Aviary-Conservatory dedicated to exotic plants and birds which serves as a year-round attraction.

A few blocks distant from the Zoo, the Calgary Brewery created a Fish Hatchery in 1938 dedicated to raising trout with which to stock Alberta lakes and rivers. Such was its popularity that the brewery owners, the Cross family, opened the first inland aquarium and a museum dedicated to the pioneer ranchers of the foothills. In 1972 the new brewery owners closed the aquarium. While the livestock was being transported to the Provincial Aquarium in Quebec City public outcry created second thoughts and the brewery agreed to match province and city for a new aquarium on the site of an equally new provincial fish hatchery located near the Zoo. The vacated space on the brewery complex now houses a new and unique exhibit telling the story of the horse on the North American continent.

Calgary's 1967 centennial project is one of the few outstanding architectural developments to emerge from the Centennial Capital Grants project. Originally designed as a Planetarium and Space-Science Museum, capital cutbacks and restricted administrative financing resulted in a greatly reduced program. Much of the building, apart from the celestial theatre, is being used for other community cultural activities, mainly in the performing arts which normally should have found their way into the ill-fated Arts Centre. An aeronautical display has been developed using adjacent parklands for the larger artifacts. Continuing this rationalization relating to transportation, the local Model Railway Club has enthusiastically pre-empted a display area for its miniature rolling stock.

Heritage Park, launched in 1964 by one of the Harvie Foundations, is sited in an ideal environment, adjacent to the extensive parklands surrounding the Glenbow reservoir, and only a short drive from the Calgary downtown core. Committed to the interpretation of the foothills pioneer culture prior to 1904, the reconstructed village continues to add more buildings, and in the manner of similar projects has costumed guides and artisans practising the crafts of its own era. A one mile track makes possible the addition of historic rail cars in motion, a nineteenth century opera house is consistently used for the professional production of tabloid westerns and other stage plays, and a halfsized lake sternwheeler circles the Glenmore Dam.

36

Banff, internationally known mountain resort town, has in recent years built up a reputation for its School of Fine Arts. Originally planned for summer activities, it now has expanded into a year-round educational institution. Facilities for the performing arts include a 1,000 seat proscenium theatre, a 250 seat concert hall with full stage, and an all purpose experimental playhouse in addition to facilities for teaching in the fields of drama, opera, ballet, and music.

Well-equipped studios and workshops for the visual artist and the many craft workers are more than adequate, while its chalets and dormitories add to the exhilarating environment on the slopes of Tunnel Mountain. Although the school has built up an extensive collection of fine arts, the quality is uneven and no provision as yet has been made for a permanent gallery. The works presently hang in halls, corridors, and the theatre lobby.

Attached to the campus, now known as The Banff Centre, is a School of Business Administration which in the spring of 1973 linked itself with the museum-art gallery movement by initiating a year-round series of courses from three day refresher sessions to six week advanced studies into administration, public relation, financing, and other essential areas of public service management.

In the Banff townsite on Bear Street, the Whyte Foundation opened its own cultural centre in 1968 which includes an archives-library complex in addition to the Peter Whyte Gallery, a memorial to one of the lesser known but important painters of the Rocky Mountain region. The building has made a significant contribution to the architecture of the National Park and is an aesthetic show-piece in its own right.

Community services at the centre provide citizens and tourists with a wide selection of reading material including reading room facilities, a continuing change of exhibitions drawn from its own collection of approximately 400 works, and evening activities in the form of film shows, recitals and lectures. Scholars, historians, and writers have access to manuscripts, publications, photographs, and early maps relating to the environment and culture of the Canadian Rockies. In 1971 the foundation was entrusted with the extensive archives of the International Alpine Club.

The parkland area on which the present building stands provides ample room for a major expansion of its existing premises and provisional plans have been designed for a further contemporary building. Another site has been reserved for a small group of early log residences including the Whyte and Brewster log homes. The foundation has provided an endowment to ensure that adequate funds are available for the proposed developments, administration, and projects with regional Indian bands.

Banff also has its Norman Luxton Museum administered by the Glenbow-Alberta Institute and founded by the colourful Indian trader who was also one of the two-man crew of the Tillicum. This ketch essayed a round-the-world voyage which ended in near disaster. The museum built of logs in the manner of a traditional western fort has two display areas relating to the ethnic culture of the plains and mountain Indians as well as the birds and mammals of the Rocky Mountains.

A National Park Museum founded by the federal government at the turn of the century is somewhat neglected but continues as a year-round attraction for visitors.

Lethbridge is another Alberta city with its own cultural personality. While the much publicized Mormon Temple is in Cardston, members of the sect have established themselves throughout the Lethbridge area. The enforced settlement of west coast Japanese, who during World War II were sent into the interior from British Columbia, is another important sociological factor, as are the homesteaders from the Dakotas and Montana.

The social climate of Lethbridge until a few years ago was puritanical. Major recreational activities revolved around the outdoor sports of fishing and hunting. Its vast civic centre area in the heart of the city, a gift from the local brewery, was designed to promote both winter and summer sports with little concentration on the arts and crafts groups who were provided with two or three small rooms. The Pemmican (senior citizens') Club held its regular meetings in the civic centre as did members of the local Historical Society.

The city had its Sketch Club, Handicraft Guild, The Playgoers, a competent and dedicated amateur group that always rated high in drama festivals, and a Musical Club. In 1962 Lethbridge citizens were not surprised to learn that Dean B. Yates, a prominent resident who had been interested in many community activities throughout his lifetime, had bequeathed $250,000 for the erection of a cultural complex to house most if not all of these societies. By

294

the time the will had been probated escalating construction costs had obviously ruled out such a visionary concept. An architect and cultural consultant were called in to work with a civic committee, and as an initial step two early schoolhouses on the perimeter of the civic centre were taken over for remodelling to accommodate the senior citizens, crafts groups, and the historical society. More ambitious plans for a five hundred seat auditorium and art gallery were placed before the taxpayers and two plebiscites were enthusiastically defeated. However, by some feat of legerdemain Mayor and Council found essential legal loopholes along with federal write-off loans and grants to enable the terms of the bequest to be fulfilled at a cost of $546,000. Formal opening of the new centre took place in May 1966.

While the controversy was raging, the civic Centennial Committee was advocating creation of The Nikka Yuko Japanese Garden in Henderson Park as a graceful tribute to the growing Japanese community. Monies available from the three governments were far from adequate but additional funds were raised by public subscription. The project, designed by architects brought from Japan, while being viewed somewhat sceptically by many citizens, was completed and opened in 1966, and since that time has been administered by a civic committee on which the Japanese community is well represented. Manned by younger members of the Japanese families, the garden has attracted approximately 100,000 visitors annually to view the grounds, its tea ceremony pavilion, bell tower, pond and island, and the Azumaya (shelter).

A temporary museum opened in 1964 in the former Bowman School. Within two years, it had proven inadequate and the second floor of the former Sir Alexander Galt Hospital was taken over. A local service club has reconstructed the legendary Fort Whoop-Up on its original site along the river flat, a battlefield parkland where the last war between Indian bands was fought. The first phase was opened in 1972, and the second phase, including a typical Indian encampment of the mid-nineteenth century and a pioneer settlement, is due to open in 1980.

One hundred and ten miles east of Lethbridge we come to Medicine Hat, Alberta's fourth largest city. Here one finds the community administered historical museum which deserves study as a prototype for other such institutions in the more isolated communities of Canada. For seventeen years the museum had occupied 500 square feet of floor space in a dilapidated downtown building and operated on an annual budget of approximately $500. Attendance in 1952 had been given as 2,100, and it is doubtful if it ever exceeded that number. For its centennial project, the Medicine Hat community elected to build a new museum on the outskirts of the city, adjacent to the Trans-Canada Highway. It is of simple design yet highly effective as a sound architectural concept. With the assistance of professionals drawn from the Provincial Museum in Edmonton its displays are interesting and authentic. It now has a professional curator and is annually attracting several thousands of visitors. In fact, so popular has the museum become that floor space was doubled. The community has its small art gallery in the lower floor of the regional library.

The Alberta Badlands have played a significant role in palaeontology and an equally significant, but less publicized, part in the exploratory areas of the petroleum industry. The dinosaur graveyard exposures in the cut-banks on the Red Deer River flats, from Rumsey in the north going south-east to the Saskatchewan border and beyond, have produced many skeletons and other fossils which today serve as important contributions in the museums of North America.

Despite the fact that the first evidence of dinosaur remains was discovered near Drumheller in 1884, the significance of the area was appreciated only by scientists until the 1930's when agitation was launched to have the Drumheller Valley declared a Provincial Park and the fossil deposits controlled. In 1955 the provincial government proclaimed an area in the Patricia-Brooks district, about seventy-five miles down stream from Drumheller, as a protected park which now has skeletal exposures *in situ,* together with an interpretation centre. The Drumheller and District Museum Society was organized two years later, and immediately sought cooperation from local citizens for the development of a "Dinosaur Trail" extending north to the Munson ferry and over gravelled trails to Rosedale ferry, fifteen miles to the south of the city. In this region, exposures not only of dinosaur bones but other fossils, including fresh and salt water mollusks, petrified wood, trilobytes, and early plant life are constantly being uncovered by erosion.

The Drumheller Museum (not to be confused with the Homestead Antique Museum in North Drumheller which is devoted to pioneer domestic, agricultural and mining history) opened its doors in 1960 placing emphasis on the now well marked and documented trail, and occupied an area fifteen feet square. A promise of a skeletal reconstruction of an Edmontosaurus, a member of the duckbill family, by the National Museum of Canada called for a radical expansion of the museum. The reptilian remains measuring thirty feet from stem to stern, standing eight feet high and with a three and a half foot skull occupy the place of honour in the substantially enlarged new building. The Drumheller Museum is one of the few community museums devoted to the earth sciences on the North American continent which has concerned itself with faithful specialization and interpretation. Its one publication, a sixty-eight page dissertation made possible through profuse advertising, includes scholarly essays translated into the language of the casual visitor or for school use.

Historical museums in Alberta tend to grow in clusters. The community institutions adjacent to the 49th parallel such as Coutts, a border point, Pincher Creek, and Fort MacLeod place emphasis on the whiskey traders and the early days of the Mounties. An exception is in Cardston where the 1887 home of Mormon pioneer C. O. Card has been restored and serves as a museum of the Latter Day Saints' migration from Utah. North on Highway 2, the local historians look westward into the foothill country to recall early ranching days, and the stories are revealed at Claresholm, Stavely and High River. Eastward to the Saskatchewan boundary, at Rosebud, Hanna, Castor, Consort, Czar and other communities, the story is told of the homesteading and sod breaking of the 1900's, with initial prosperity and harvester trains followed by drought and depression of the thirties, in a land known as "next year country."

Further north the topography changes with museums reflecting other interests. At Rimbey The Pas-Ka-Poo Historical Park contains a log schoolhouse, pioneer Anglican Church, and the first town office. A nursing museum, one of the few in Canada, occupies space at the Alberta Hospital in Ponoka, and still further north The Reynolds' Museum is a sprawling acreage of antique agricultural machinery, automobiles, the occasional airplane, and household furnishings, guns, and other weapons, in addition to Indian and Eskimo artifacts.

In an easterly direction, the Camrose museum received a citation in 1968 for its Centennial museum project, while directly north the town of Tofield established its schoolhouse museum with a wild life exhibit. The neighbouring town of Viking, not to be outdone, took over an old store building and added a replica of an early gas well (1913) as an added attraction. Forty-five miles further to the southeast at Wainwright, site of the federal Buffalo Reservation, an abandoned telephone building became the Battle River Historical Museum.

There are enclaves and open lands of ethnic settlements through the province, Hutterites and Mennonites, Danes, Poles, and of course the descendants of the French Voyageur, but their stories are to be found chiefly in major city museums.

The Indians and Metis have as yet to build their first museum but this situation is expected to be changed shortly on the Stoney Reserve at Morley. The Ukrainians on the other hand established settlements shortly after steel was laid by The Grand Trunk Railway. They have preserved or restored a historic village, including a sod house, church and schoolhouse at Willingdon. The Basilian Fathers have a religious museum with an extensive collection at Mundare, while at Sandro, gateway to Elk Island Park, a few pioneer houses have served as show place for Ukrainian costumes and other folk art for many years. In 1972 a federal Local Initiatives Grant of $177,000 made possible the expansion of this project into a full-fledged Ukrainian village where folk crafts and festivals are encouraged.

The Alberta Game Farm at Ardrossen, fifteen miles east of Edmonton, is an experimental station devoted to the breeding of animals drawn from all areas of the world. The "wildlife park" occupies fifteen hundred acres, and in the words of its owners, is devoted to "the propagation and preservation of rare species through scientific captive breeding and primarily devoted to hoofed mammals ranging from Muskoxen to giraffes, along with fifteen hundred birds representing eighty species." A few miles to the east in the Elk Island Park is another wildlife refuge containing buffalo, elk and deer, administered by the National Wildlife Service.

A small museum at Fort Saskatchewan occupies a pioneer home of the community, and further north of Edmonton reaching almost to Athabaska are five more museums. A former Hudson's Bay Fort is now the Fort Victoria Museum at Smoky Lake. Three pioneer buildings, including an early log school, community hall, and municipal office, were restored as the centennial project of Westlock fifty miles north of Edmonton. At Barrhead on the highway leading to Thunder Lake is the one museum in an expressly designed building in this rather remote region. Five miles south of Athabaska the Kinnoull Historical Society as a centennial operation restored a pioneer home at Colinton in which to display the arts, crafts, clothing, and furnishings of the early settlers.

The Peace River country lying between the 55th and 56th parallels is isolated from the rest of Alberta and is reached via Highway 2 starting at Valleyview, the first settlement in the Peace Block. It is in this area that many of the dispirited and at times almost penniless victims of the Depression years migrated to begin a new life. The Peace River district has prospered and with the opening of the Alaska Highway (1513 miles from Dawson Creek to Fairbanks) the region is destined to continue growing. The seven communities listed in 1966 having populations over one thousand had a sixty per cent increase over the years.

A 1910 map shows Dunvegan and the Peace River Landing as the only organized settlements with two Hudson's Bay trading posts further to the north on the Peace River. Sir Alexander Mackenzie, first man to reach the Pacific coast, did so by traversing the Peace River 1792-93, but apart from fur trading the entire region was neglected and virtually unpopulated until early in the twentieth century. Of the four museums in the region, the Mission Saint Charles at Dunvegan was opened only in 1957 with the restoration of the Catholic Church and Rectory today administered by the province. A small museum existed at High Prairie in 1959 and in 1967 it moved into the centennial building.

Both Grande Prairie, by far the largest community with a population now over 12,000, and Peace River, one hundred and twenty-five miles to the north, whose population has climbed to 5,000, had museum buildings as their centennial projects. The latter emphasises the travels of Mackenzie, and the Grand Prairie institution has areas devoted to pioneer and natural history, including the Bernard Hamm collection of birds and mammals and the Robert Cochrane display of rocks and fossils.

A new and young breed of politician has taken command of provincial governments from coast to coast in the past few years, bringing with them a sophistication that recognizes the need for cultural growth and awareness. One of these is The Hon. Horst Schmidt, Alberta's Minister of Culture, Youth and Recreation, who said in an interview recently that "Alberta is to have the most progressive cultural program in Canada," while announcing the establishment of an "Arts Foundation" for the purchase of art works to serve as decor for public buildings throughout the province. Within three months, a purchasing committee was at work accumulating paintings and sculpture pieces, while also acquiring a number of gifts with an estimated value in excess of twenty thousand dollars from public-spirited citizens including some artists.

The Minister also called public hearings to discuss multi-cultural development which, he says, ranks high on his list of priorities. In addition, he has appointed a task force to study the frustrations and needs of the small museums and has devised a master plan for historical restorations. Art galleries operating at the professional level will receive annual grants equal to ten per cent of their annual budget as a matter of rote, all of which, Mr. Schmidt says "will lead us to a new social climate."

In 1932 the Dominion Bureau of Statistics listed eight museums in the province. The Father Lacombe Museum and Shrine was the only one located outside the urban areas. Twenty-two years later thirty-nine institutions were reported, and by 1968 the number had reached sixty-six. As of mid-1973, ninety-two museums were in active operation, and the provincial museums' advisor reported that there were thirteen more in various stages of development.

Until the present decade, Alberta had been the one province in Canada lacking a National Historic Park. Proposals had been made for the deeding of lands and mineral rights on the former homestead site of the Cochrane Ranch founded in 1802, but provincial authorities rejected the offer although the project would have included a historical story of early agriculture. The federal service was still awaiting a decision from a new political administration in 1973, but in the interim has been developing a small historic park at Rocky Mountain House willed to The Crown some years ago, where stone chimneys and a plethora of small artifacts indicate the site of early trading posts. A temporary interpretation centre was opened in 1972 and adjacent lands acquired to serve as a buffer zone. The same federal agency is reconstructing a buffalo jump west of Fort MacLeod which likewise will be given the federal blessing as a Historic Park upon completion.

37

Centennials are developing into a Canadian tradition, providing incentives for local societies to agitate for museums with which to honour the event. British Columbia has officially celebrated five such centennials in the past quarter of a century and it is a matter of interest to study not only the growth but a more sophisticated development of museums in relation to these festivities.

In 1849 Vancouver Island was proclaimed a Crown Colony which, one hundred years later, gave Island residents a brief moment of glory but had little or no effect on museum origins. In 1858 the mainland territory, up till then the more or less exclusive fiefdom of the Hudson's Bay Company, also acquired the status of Crown Colony and was christened British Columbia. The anniversary of the christening rather than the Colony's birth was sufficient excuse for provincial authorities to proclaim a 1958 celebration accompanied by cash grants to the communities for appropriate symbols, and which found the Native Sons and Daughters providing leadership in museum development. No less than twenty-four such institutions were added to augment the twelve or thirteen already existing. For the next eight years there was sporadic growth with another surge as still another historic event called for the appropriate commemoration.

In 1866 Vancouver Island and the mainland were absorbed into one political entity and once again, despite the proximity to Canada's centennial, the British Columbia populace was urged to commemorate this historic coupling, thus adding another nine or ten museums to the fifty-six then officially recognized. By the time the nation-wide Confederation party ended on December 31, 1967 there was a total of ninety-eight museums, art galleries and other related institutions. Twelve of the existing ones had used funds for expansion or other forms of capital development.

Barely six months had elapsed when another proclamation advised all loyal British Columbians to make ready for another centennial – this time to celebrate the province's admission into Canadian Confederation on July 20, 1871. Organized communities were advised that sixty cents per capita would be forthcoming for appropriate and approved capital projects, with a subsequent announcement that the federal government was sending a gift of ten million dollars as a birthday present to its sixth offspring.

Museum developments which directly or indirectly came into existence around the 1958 celebrations reached into some of the more isolated outposts coinciding with the expansion of the Native Sons and Daughters whose major officer took the title of 'factor'. The local society was also tabbed as 'post,' indicating quite clearly their objectives.

The legendary mining town of Barkerville was considered ripe for rehabilitation at this time despite the fact that to reach it one had to drive over a tortuous logging road for sixty miles. At the height of the Cariboo gold rush of 1850, Barkerville had a population generally estimated at 10,000. Also emerging from this movement were museums at Ashcroft and Cache Creek, while at Clinton the historic 47-Mile House on the Cariboo Trail became the South Cariboo Historical Museum. The citizens of Dawson Creek launched their museum in the late 1950's, and in the same period at Alert Bay a library-museum complex was opened.

Campbell River, one hundred and sixty miles north of Victoria, established what is believed to be the first wholly ethnic museum in the province. This institution, in the basement of the municipal hall, initiated projects to encourage local high school students to investigate the rich culture of the West Coast aborigines.

Isolated, but now becoming more accessible as highways are developed was the S.S. *Moyie,* beached at Kaslo on the Kootenay Lake which in 1958 was pronounced a historic vessel for future restoration. At Nelson the beginnings of a museum got under way in which emphasis was placed on geology and mining with token recognition to the Doukhobor environment. Seventy miles to the southwest the citizens of Rossland, at that time virtually a deadend community, sought to keep alive the romance of the gold mining days. The S.S. *Sicamous,* beached at Penticton, was restored for the 1958 centennial, the lower deck (boiler room) more or less adapted for museum display with the upper deck (saloon) converted into a dine and dance restaurant. At Kelowna a two storey log cabin was erected to provide a more permanent home for a historical display first collected in 1932.

In recognition of the Crown Colony celebration, or it may have been coincidence, the provincial government created Nature Centres at Miracle Beach on Vancouver Island, and Manning Park on the Hope-Princeton Highway, and in 1962 established a third centre at Shuswap Lake.

302

On the lower mainland a small art gallery was opened at Burnaby, one which has built up a national reputation for its annual shows devoted to Canadian contemporary graphics. Historical museums also were launched at Cloverdale, Haney, and Chilliwack.

In 1931 the Native Sons moved into the abandoned Hudson's Bay Post at Fort Langley, later building their own museum on an adjacent site in which to display their increasing collection of pioneer artifacts in 1958. In the interim, the National Historic Sites Service had undertaken a major restoration at the Fort proclaiming it a National Historic Park, as the nation's contribution to that year's centennial festivities. There were other developments in more populated areas; for example, Vancouver built an attractive Maritime Museum as its centennial gesture even though it lacked an adequate collection; but by reviewing the overall pattern of museum growth in British Columbia it is readily seen that the momentum, which was little more than a wash on the beach in 1949, became a tidal wave in the ensuing twenty-two years.

By 1965 Dawson Creek had its new museum-gallery building with one area set aside for industrial technology, and about two years later the Campbell River museum moved into a delightful architectural complex sharing space with the regional library and tourist bureau while continuing to emphasize the culture of the Island Indian tribes. The S.S. *Moyie* at Kaslo was completely rehabilitated and transformed into a floating museum by the time of the 1966 centennial, while at Rossland, now reached by a hardtop highway which still is an adventure in itself, the museum was expanded and now has effective contemporary displays including a mine entry made safe for visitors. In 1968 the society created another annex dedicated to its most illustrious citizen, Nancy Green, Canada's contribution to Olympic ski champions.

Such has been the success of the three Nature Centres administered by the provincial Department of Recreation and Conservation that a fourth one was opened in Mount Robson Park, high in the Canadian Rockies, with a temporary tent-frame structure serving as lecture hall and exhibition area. In 1970 this latest addition recorded six thousand visitors; In the same year, the original three built up a record attendance of 140,000.

The somewhat desultory start at Barkerville was accentuated as the 1966-67 celebrations loomed on the horizon and both restoration and administration were taken over by the province. By the time the 1971 festivities approached a new hardtop highway had been completed and many more buildings restored, exciting activities for visitor participation were introduced, and large picnic and camping grounds developed. As a result, attendance rose to well over 175,000. Restoration of what is described as The Chinese Settlement is now under way.

The popularity of Barkerville encouraged the provincial authorities to develop a second and more accessible historical park at Fort Steele, six miles north-east of Cranbrook, a region with many historical connotations. A full quota of adventurers and explorers had passed through this region including David Thompson, Sir George Simpson, and Captain Palliser, and it also had been the scene of a rich placer mining discovery that historians claim paid off to the tune of $25,000,000. The townsite, now nearing completion, represents a pioneer community of the last decade of the nineteenth century. A replica of the Waso Hotel serves as museum and interpretation centre. It has its theatre where nineteenth century vaudeville is staged during the summer months. A replica of the North-West Mounted Police Post of 1887-88 nears completion, and eleven Clydesdale horses, former inmates at the Okalla Prison Farm at Burnaby, are now in minimum detention harnessed to sight-seeing wagons.

The tidal wave which was sweeping over the coastal region overflowed once again into the lower mainland. In the final days of the 1966 celebrations, a Farm Machinery Museum opened its new interpretation centre on the site of the first organized farm in the province located within a few hundred yards of the restored Fort Langley. This project is partially financed by the federal Department of Agriculture and is affiliated with the University of British Columbia. The Fort Langley settlement is unincorporated, has a population of less than one thousand and is the only community of its size in Canada with three viable museums.

The Kamloops Museum initially a product of the 1930's moved into its present building in 1957 where it displays pioneer relics, natural history specimens, and a miniature early trading post. To celebrate the 1966 centennial, a full-scale replica of the original Fort was built which included a Factor's cabin. Unfortunately a 1972 flood did irreparable damage to the Fort and the display of farm machinery, vehicles, and larger artifacts including a stage coach.

Obviously not all communities elected for historical museums when considering centennial projects. In the Okanagan Valley, Penticton embarked on the development of a civic centre in the downtown area, and in 1966 opened a cultural complex on the fringe of its residential district. Its museum collection along with its venerable curator was transferred to the new building which also provides space for the regional library, a small auditorium, activities workshops, and exhibition area.

Kelowna, forty miles to the north, had been creating a contemporary civic centre in stages since 1958 which included a regional library and art gallery facilities. In 1967 the log cabin museum was replaced by a fire resistant and well designed building within the civic square, and which citizens now affectionately refer to as "the dug-out." However, provision has been made for additional expansion to provide space for a permanent art gallery – possibly when another centennial comes around.

It is possible to conjecture that the modest demands of the Vernon Museum Society and the local art group for a cultural centre to serve as a monument to the 1966 and 1967 events led to a sequence of stormy controversies that eventually produced an urban renewal project almost overnight. In 1958 Vernon had about nine thousand inhabitants. In that year its museum was located in a derelict store building adjacent to its equally antiquated fire-hall. To visit the museum was an embarrassment, both to the out-of-town visitor and the members of the historical society who apologized for the fact that, lacking space, finances and civic co-operation, it would still collect and, to the best of its ability, preserve pioneer artifacts until such time as a miracle occurred. There was also an art society renting wall space in the Legion Hall for three-day showings of local and travelling exhibitions at infrequent intervals during the winter months.

By 1966, the population of Vernon had increased by fifteen hundred, but the city was still largely inhabited by elderly people who had found the region ideal for retirement. The city is thirty-three miles north of Kelowna and six miles from the northern extremity of Lake Okanagan. Consequently it lacks the attractions of water sports found at Kelowna and Penticton. Its economy depends heavily on fruit growing and packing although it has an extensive history of lumbering and mineral mining. A century and a half ago Vernon was serving the entire Okanagan as distributing point, but with the decline of lake transport the community had been by-passed. Through necessity its citizens had to rely largely on their own resources for entertainment and recreation.

In 1964 art and museum societies started their agitation for a museum-gallery complex. Plans were drawn up and the proposal publicized, only to meet with resistance from citizens who visualized increasing mill rates. The following year a more ambitious project was launched calling for a completely new and integrated civic complex. Soon the battle lines were drawn. Violent opposition to what was viewed as abandoned civic responsibilities and wasteful squandering of taxpayers' money descended on city hall. Stuart Fleming, then Member of Parliament for the constituency, in an article celebrating the completion of the controversial project, succinctly portrayed the political climate of the moment when he wrote, "The civic complex represents a renewed beginning. Vernon's severest critics must love it best – or one must hope so – because

305

there are so many of them. Happily, the construction of the civic centre, civic complex or whatever other term may best describe what has been done, does herald the end of negative thought in this community."

A consortium of four architects created first a philosophy followed by a generalized overall concept to blend several individual structures into one uniform design on the three and a half acre site. In a souvenir issue of *The Vernon News* (Monday, May 9, 1966), an anonymous writer states, with justification, that "The result is a complex that is unique in Canada and to the best of anyone's knowledge, no other community of comparable size has developed a site that so integrates the buildings and provides an architecturally-balanced scheme. Within the complex, there are several patterns – one is of a square with a disrupted corner – and it repeats itself in different ways throughout. Another pattern, that of the battened wall and sloping copper roofs, similarly is repeated. The layout follows the principle that the public should walk through the centre, not around it. The pedestrian malls and squares were designed to provide variety. A boulevarded Centennial Way is proposed between the Community Centre on the Harris property and the main site, thus linking all buildings. Parking is provided on the periphery of the site, with access on all four sides from the existing street pattern. Parking lots are sunken so that the beauty of the buildings and the landscaping will not be lost in a sea of cars."

The Civic Centre, as distinguished from the Community Recreational Centre, is the site for the city hall and council chamber; a "Public Safety" building, an innocent-sounding name for police station and court house, contains, among other facilities, a cell block of twenty-six air-conditioned units each painted in bright, cheerful colours and including modern sanitary equipment. It is said the pleasant environment has had "no appreciable increase in the city's crime rate." A new fire hall is relatively isolated on the square "because of the nature of its functions"; and the museum-library-art gallery occupying a total of twelve thousand square feet is located on another corner of the square. As with the other buildings, the cultural-historical complex is functionally effective, each area being self-contained.

The Community Recreational Centre two blocks away is a twin dome structure which includes a spacious auditorium with tilting equipment controlled by hydraulic jacks, making possible a sloped floor proscenium theatre to seat twelve hundred, or alternatively a dual purpose convention and banquet hall to accommodate up to thirteen hundred. A twenty-five metre swimming pool designed to meet Olympic standards and a gymnasium measuring 48 by 84 feet with a 24 foot high ceiling occupy half of the twenty-four thousand square foot site.

As to capital costs, for a city of twelve thousand a fabulous expenditure of $2,358,088 was incurred. The federal government, under what was at the time its Municipal Development Loan, provided a $357,796 write-off, and a further Winter Works indebtedness of somewhat less than $6,000 was cancelled. The sale of houses moved from the site realized an additional $33,792. Much of the balance is being carried through a sale of debentures to the tune of $750,000, all of which suggests that there are financial wizards, even in small communities of twelve thousand.

A number of satellite museums have appeared in recent years throughout the Okanagan Valley. At Salmon Arm, the local historical society opened the official centennial museum and archives in 1967. Immediately south of Kelowna at Naramata a regional library and museum is administered by the municipality, while in what is known as the Okanagan Mission district the Father Pandosy Mission, founded by the Oblate Fathers in 1859, has been restored on its two acre site on which five log buildings still exist. Adjacent to the Mission, a reconstruction of a Salish Indian encampment was recently completed. Two miles from the United States border, at Osoyoos, a small pioneer museum complex exhibits pioneer relics, paintings, and regional fauna in four buildings formerly serving as customs house, schoolhouse, church, and jail.

Having no relationship to either provincial or federal centennials but opened in 1959, the Dominion Radio Astrophysical Observatory at White Lake, a few miles out of Penticton, now attracts thousands of visitors annually for elementary instruction on Canada's explorations into outer space. Only five miles from the same city, a five hundred acre wild game farm was opened in 1967 where experimental studies are made relating to the breeding of animals brought from tropical countries.

East of the Okanagan in the Kootenay-Arrow Lakes region, the Boundary Museum at Grand Forks was opened in 1958, devoting most of its space to mining but with a small area delineating the Doukhobor way of life, which, contrary to popular belief, has for the most part been integrated. In 1967 the Castlegar and District Museum was founded which also displays artifacts relating to the Doukhobor sect, but placing greater emphasis on the Arrow Lakes' economy of the nineteenth century. A centennial museum also made its appearance at Greenwood which places emphasis on mineral mining.

Ecological imbalance caused by the diversion of watersheds currently is causing widespread concern. Historians and archaeologists have, particularly over the past twenty years, shown concern about the destruction of significant historical signposts from Egypt's Aswan Dam project to the headwaters of the Columbia River. In 1964 the Revelstoke and District Historical Association moved its collection of artifacts into the diminutive basement room of the Regional Health Centre and started agitation for the salvaging of pioneer buildings due to be submerged in another hydro development. In 1969 the provincial government turned over land for the creation of Columbia Village under the direction of the Association, and since that time with the aid of local service clubs a restoration program has commenced.

North of Dawson Creek and possibly anticipating the 1971 events, a museum was opened at Hudson's Hope, and near Fort St. John at Mile 46 on the Alaska Highway an early Roman Catholic church and an Anglican Abbey were restored as an ecumenical gesture. On the west coast, approximately seven hundred miles from Vancouver as the planes fly, a proliferation of museums came into being between 1967 and 1971 at Kitimat, Terrace, and Smithers; but possibly the most isolated institution in the province is at Tatla Lake, between the Fraser Plateau and the Coast Range, a municipal library-museum.

38

The Indians in British Columbia did not sign a treaty but were relegated to reservations following Confederation. A superintendent of Indian Affairs, with nine agencies throughout the province, attended to the elementary needs of the various tribes, sought to settle disputes, and administered the white man's code of justice. The various tribes had their own native culture; those residing in the coastal regions, the Haida, Tsimshian, Kwakiutl, and Nootka in particular were adept at wood carving and used this craft generously.

As long as the Indian worked with his craft, performed his rituals, and enjoyed his festivities all was right in the white man's world. But in the second decade of this twentieth century, the Federal government, influenced by the zeal of Christian missionaries, decided that some festivals, the Potlatch for instance, were a profligate and immoral habit resulting in the squandering of belongings and treaty money in order to impress the beneficiaries. The Potlatch was an all important ritual associated with the social life of the tribe, such as marriage, the giving of a new rank, mourning of the dead, the raising of a mortuary pole, and other ceremonial occasions.

The R.C.M.P. was given the authority to ban such rituals, confiscate the accumulated gifts and turn over the booty to the National Museum in Ottawa for safekeeping. Superficially the end results were much the same, the naive code of the Indian perceived a fine distinction between free-will offerings and what they felt was outright theft. Fifty years later the now rare and valuable articles of the Potlatch were still in the safe-keeping of the federal museum. At irregular intervals requests for their return were made but only in the fall of 1972 was positive assurance given that the disputed artifacts would be released from impoundment. The value of the exciting carvings, masks, totem poles, domestic, and other utensils as a rich art form signally failed to make an impact on the senior echelon of civil servants during the first fifty years of the century.

The Provincial Museum of British Columbia was essentially

devoted to the disciplines of natural history and the earth sciences, adding an ethnological department almost unobtrusively in 1930. It was a further ten years before the museum director announced that, having gathered important artifacts, an ethnic (Thunderbird) park would be developed to encourage active programs with the Indians for a continuation of their crafts. Lacking protective legislation, this resultant publicity accentuated alien raids with ethnologists, archaeologists, and souvenir hunters from the United States and abroad having a field day collecting trophies instead of scalps for values not more than the price of Hudson's Bay beads. In this same decade the Department of Anthropology at the University of British Columbia received a gift of a large ethnological collection that encouraged a group of dedicated academics, led by the Doctors Harry and Audrey Hawthorne, to take positive steps to preserve the Indian culture and significantly with the full co-operation of the Councils of the various Bands. Their efforts, however, were hampered due to persistent shortage of the essential finances with which to pursue collecting, research, and preservation.

These two projects at the Provincial Museum and the University were the first conscious steps taken to seek a rapport with the West Coast Indians within the common denominator of *homo sapiens*. The University museum was formally started in 1947 in a portion of the basement of the campus library.

In 1950 Mungo Martin, a Kwakiut chief and master carver, joined the museum staff as consultant and to serve in a liaison capacity between the University and the various tribes. Seven years later, Dr. Thea Koerner financed an expedition to a deserted village on Anthony Island to salvage remaining Haida poles and saw to it that a giant's handful of the massive totemic symbols were embedded in the campus grounds to form Totem Pole Park. At the same time, the Anthropological Department has extended its studies far beyond Canada and now includes artifacts drawn from Asia.

The West Coast Indian display, representing only one quarter of its collection of approximately 10,000 items, attracted international attention at the 1969 version of Man and His World. Due to its popularity the collection remained in Montreal for a second season, and undoubtedly this resulted in a federal commitment of $2,500,000 for the erection of a permanent museum at the University of British Columbia. The total museum concept required two full years of planning with construction getting under way on April 1, 1973 and a formal opening is already set for the same day two years hence.

To describe the overall impact this completed building will make on the visitor can only be done through the use of superlatives. The philosophy upon which it has been conceived as expressed by architect Arthur Erickson is "to convey the idea to all who visit (or use) the museum that at one time, on this (Pacific) coast there was a noble and great response to this land that has never been equalled since."

It is to be a museum both within and without walls – entrance galleries descending to conform with the sloping terrain to The Great Hall, towering up to forty feet in height with floor to ceiling windows providing an unobstructed view of reconstructed villages representing the three major Indian cultures of the west coast. In addition, massive carvings by contemporary artists and areas adapted for ceremonial events – even the Potlatch – carving and other activities are also included. A series of galleries will have a rooftop reflecting pool for related displays from prehistory onwards and another gallery will house the Walter and Marianne Koerner Masterwork collection.

Hazelton is one of the more isolated settlements of the province, lying north of the 55th parallel and seven hundred miles from Vancouver. As a positive and intelligent gesture toward its Indian population, a community committee in 1948 developed a realistic method for a continued use of the native skills within the tribal environment. A major step was the opening of the Skeena Treasure House, a replica of a native community house built by the habitants, to serve as a museum; this new building also provided an outlet for a new generation of craftsmen and women.

Today, and within a few hundred yards of the original museum in this still remote region 'Ksan, an authentic Gitaksan (people of the Skeena) Indian Village has been created, a project believed to be unique on the North American continent, by the 'Ksan Association in co-operation with the National Historic Sites Service and the Province of British Columbia, using funds raised locally and augmented by federal and provincial grants. 'Ksan embraces the 1960 Fireweed or Treasure House and is augmented by the Feast House, reminiscent of the potlatch days, a Stone Age or Frog House in which the story of ancient "cedar bark" culture is told, and The Wolf House with totem poles, canoes, native symbols and implements. All of these make possible the re-creation of rituals, and symbolic festivals. More important is the fact that 'Ksan is now serving as the first all-Indian vocational training centre for the youngest generation, who will develop into "artisans adept in the artistry of carving, beadwork, leather work, painting and other forms of native arts and crafts."

While 'Ksan tends to overshadow other recent developments in this same ethnological area, the Kwakiutl tribe re-created and opened an authentic community house at Alert Bay in 1966. Situated on a diminutive island at the south end of Queen Charlotte

Strait the visitor must travel by ferry in order to view the programs of Indian songs and dances and demonstrations of craftsmanship.

The Haida Indians are developing their own tribal museum at Skidegate Inlet on the Queen Charlotte Islands and will encourage full participation of tribal members and the white community as an exercise in integration. On the rugged west coast of Vancouver Island the Hesquiat Band are similarly bent on creating their own museum and to that end are reclaiming what is left of their native artifacts and conducting archaeological digs. On the lower mainland at Chilliwack the Wells Centennial Museum opened in 1971 and devotes an area to the women of the Salish tribe who have revived the ancient craft of true-loom weaving.

For tourists and scholars interested in sociology or in the study of Indian cultures, a planned Totem Circle tour covering approximately one hundred miles embraces twenty historic sites in one of the last bastions of unspoilt, unpolluted scenic wilderness. As late as 1966, the road leading into Hazelton was hazardous and navigable on its own terms. Today Highway 16 from Prince George to Prince Rupert is blacktop all the way including the short detour into Hazelton.

In Vancouver in the summer of 1964, a visiting museologist roundly condemned municipal authorities and citizens for permitting the City Museum to languish in the heart of skid row. The speaker claimed that the large and significant collections ranging from Oriental treasures to pioneer artifacts were in danger of being damaged or destroyed. The talk brought critical editorial comment and a flood of letters to the editors, the tenor being that such interlopers should mind their own business.

Six months later the Community Arts Council of Vancouver in co-operation with the Junior League invited Dr. Theodore Heinrich, one time Director of the Royal Ontario Museum, to conduct a survey of civic needs in the areas of art galleries and museums. The report was caustic but constructive. The major recommendation proposed a multi-million dollar complex to include not only museums but to serve as a civic reception centre complete with restaurants and cocktail lounges. City fathers were impressed and developed a program for submission to the taxpayers. Following the pattern of such referendums, the proposal was turned down. However, with the centennial capital grants program under review, followed by the offer of a million and a half dollars for a Planetarium from lumber tycoon Dr. H.R. MacMillan, Council ignored the adverse vote and, in co-operation with the University Endowment Lands Committee, proceeded to build its Centennial Museum and Planetarium at a total cost of $4,500,000. The complex was formally opened on October 26th, 1968.

The cultural complex is architecturally pleasing but sadly deficient in many technical areas, lacking storage space for the extensive collections of natural history, anthropology, ethnology, archaeology, geology and other miscellaneous artifacts which on moving day totalled 1,060,000 items. Three main display areas, each having four galleries, surround a sunken courtyard, with each wing dedicated to its individual discipline. A Children's Museum is located in the lower level and adjacent to the 217-seat auditorium, making possible uninterrupted programs for the younger fry without intruding into the general display wings.

Initially receiving adequate administrative finances, the complex became an outgoing, exciting, and colourful operation. A Vancouver columnist in December 1968 called the Museum-Planetarium the Success Story of the Year "shimmering away on the shores of Kitsilano [and which] had 37,852 visitors in the first full month of operation." This number had risen to 100,000 in May of the following year, 60,000 of whom attended the computer operated planetarium shows. Within the first few months of operation its forty staff members were joined by a volunteer army of 120 citizens.

Provision had been made for a new archives building to replace the oversized closet space that had been allotted to its founder, the irascible but persistent Major James Skitt Matthews since 1927. A few months prior to his death at the age of 92 in October 1970, City Council announced that a permanent archives dedicated to this legendary figure would be erected on the museum site and would provide much needed reserve storage space for the museum collection. The archives opened in 1973 and have an independent display area in addition to research and reading rooms.

On the same site and serving as an annex to the Maritime Museum, the schooner St. Roch, the history making R.C.M.P. Arctic cruiser, is on display following a complete restoration by the National Historic Sites Service. In this age of Arctic exploration and recent experiments with the reinforced tanker, the St. Roch can be viewed as the pioneer in this field having left Vancouver on June 23, 1940 and arriving in Halifax on October 11, 1942. After modifications the craft made a return journey in 82 days, the first vessel to navigate the north-west passage in both east and west directions.

The museum complex after such a spectacular beginning surprisingly again became the subject of political in-fighting at City Hall and funds were curtailed even in face of a steady attendance of about 500,000 each year. However, despite disruptions and some resignations, behind-the-scenes planning continued. With most if not all frustrations resolved in late 1972, a new and politically free Board received an annual fiscal assurance of five hundred and ninety thousand dollars from municipal coffers. A new gallery area opened in 1973 to tell the story of cultural contributions made by early immigrants of many ethnic origins.

Since its founding in 1926, the Vancouver Art Gallery has been under the jurisdiction of an independent board which to date has had seven directors. More recently the gallery has developed a new sense of direction which includes retention of large areas for the display of more traditional works while also devoting much of its energy to the contemporary art scene. Noon-day recitals and other activities have made the gallery a focal point for people of the business world in addition to the tourist. In mid-1968, while a major show of antique automobiles was held at the Pacific National Exhibition grounds, the art gallery staged its own automobile show to illustrate the more aesthetic aspects of this mechanical era. Away from all this but within the building an active program directed to school groups does its bit as an annex to the Vancouver school system.

In 1970 the gallery society opened The Race Track Centre on the exhibition grounds as a one-year pilot project designed to attract visitors from the junior set to the old timers who felt like dropping in to see what it was all about. Jean Lowndes, art critic of *The Vancouver Sun,* went into detail by reporting that "mothers can come with their children and paint with them and dance with them to establish new kinds of contact. . .an eighty year old can work beside a six year old making a xylophone from B.C. fir, foam rubber, and cardboard tubing. Or he can fashion a drum from soya barrels obtained in Chinatown and covered with sheepskin, and osterisers are on hand for making paints out of beets, onions or just plain dirt." So successful was this project that it was transferred to an abandoned east end church the following year and then to an obsolete baseball park in 1972. It continues to rove the city and environs for any usable premises.

In October 1971, the gallery introduced a unique "Art in the Schools" program throwing in a French language course as a bonus to its multi-media demonstrations and workshop while other artists and animators visited day-care centres, senior citizens' groups and correctional institutions. As if this were not enough, an all embracing program called "Art for Everyone" makes sure that no individual be left out. This project reaches into all corners of the province with a half-ton truck driven by an all-purpose staff member who "personally assembles the exhibits, presents it, discusses it with school children and adults from morning to night."

In the gallery itself a small area known as "Free Space" is set aside for seven-day one-man shows where any B.C. artist may display his wares, entrants being chosen by lot. A succession of major exhibitions of national and international importance is organized for the main gallery. One such show, "Sculpture Inuit," had its premiere in Vancouver before leaving on a tour of Europe, the Soviet Union, the British Museum, and ending up in Canada's National Gallery. With all these activities the gallery is in danger of strangulation and only within the past few months was compelled to sacrifice much needed exhibition space to find accommodation for administrative services. If all else fails the Board may even pre-empt the venerable old Court House two blocks away.

Aquaria, along with zoos and botanical gardens, are rarely associated in the public mind with museums, yet their overall functions are the same. It is one thing to kill an animal, stuff it and place it behind glass, but more mature study is possible when the creature is alive and kept in a simulated natural environment.

The Vancouver Public Aquarium is administered by a non-profit community society receiving fiscal support from the city, including rent free space in Stanley Park. Over the past few years it has developed an international reputation for its research and exploration into new areas of marine studies while continuing to encourage light-hearted showmanship in its ever expanding complex. It is one of the few museums in Canada that has in operation a laboratory where older students in the Vancouver school system can participate in scientific research with the aquarium's educational staff. Its daily performances in the summer months by dolphins, sea turtles, and tropical sharks are climaxed with the acrobatics and show-off tendencies of the two-ton "killer whale." It is not surprising that attendance figures increase each year and will shortly pass the 1,000,000 mark.

The Vancouver Zoo, which is distinguishable from the Aquarium only because no admission fee is charged, is completely administered and financed by the civic Board of Parks and Recreation. It forms part of the park museums' complex embracing a Children's Zoo, Wildlife Refuge, Botanical Gardens, and a totem pole display at Lumbermen's Arch. Here again the visitor can see both history and natural history in action. No record of attendance is kept but park officials estimate that over 1,500,000 visitors pass through the zoo each year.

The Parks Board also administers the Queen Elizabeth Botanical Garden and Arboretum in the south Cambie Street area where its famed rose garden has seasonal displays of old and modern roses planted in chronological order. At Vancouver's Exhibition Park, the Lipsett collection of historical paintings by John Innes are displayed along with a large number of Indian relics. Also in the metropolitan area the Vancouver Branch of the Ukrainian Women's Association is at 154 Tenth Avenue East and the Old Hastings Mill Store museum once part of an 1865 logging operation is on Alma Road.

The municipality of Richmond erected a cultural centre as its tribute to the 1967 centennial, while in New Westminster The Irving House, a Victorian mansion built in 1852 now serves as a municipal museum. The municipality of Cloverdale has its Surrey Centennial (1958) Museum and after some expansion attracts over 70,000 visitors annually. This institution has a historical society with a membership of over 3,000 and a junior "Beaver Club" with 2,500 enthusiastic youngsters who engage in a continuous round of activities. The Matsqui, Sumas, and Abbotsford Museum also made its debut in 1970 and Port Moody and Ladner have also added to the proliferation. At the last mentioned community the old Municipal Hall was taken over by ardent historians of the region in November 1968. Eleven months later the building was re-opened with period rooms, and display space for ethnic and community hobby groups.

In 1964 only seventeen museums and related institutions were listed on Vancouver Island but by the time the federal centennial was over an additional fifteen were in operation. Of the more recent Island openings generally associated with Canada's centennial and which have not previously been mentioned are: the Link and Pin Museum at Sayward adjacent to Kelsey Bay; a small museum at Cumberland; and the new Nanaimo Centennial Museum in Piper Park, an intriguing architectural concept taking its theme from the octagonal Bastion a few blocks away.

One mile north of Duncan, a young open-air museum that is destined to become one of the major technological institutions in Canada, is the Forest Museum and Arboretum. Opened in 1966, within two years its boundaries were extended by a further fifteen acres. The museum devotes its major exhibits to pioneer logging operations but also has visual stories of tree growth. A narrow gauge logging railway takes visitors around the perimeter of the exhibits. It is the one museum in Canada devoted to technical advances in the logging industry and in 1970 a start was made to develop a fully managed modern capsule forest with the planting of 250 seedlings. Presently emphasis is on the contribution made to Canada's economy through the exploitation of 700,000 miles of British Columbia's forest reserves, with the arboretum demonstrating the industry's reforestation policies. As the museum extends its program ecological factors could be introduced.

Within the perimeter of Greater Victoria, major developments have been seen in the past decade. The new (Centennial 1967

316

variety) museum opened in October 1968 and now dominates the down town area on what has been christened Heritage Square. The overall plan embraces the Helmcken House; Thunderbird Park; a three storey building equipped for displays of natural history, the earth sciences, archaeology, ethnology, pioneer history, and allied subjects; a fourteen storey structure for reserve collections, administration, and research; and a contemporary archival building. The entire complex costing approximately $8,000,000 is well designed and aesthetically pleasing. Unfortunately little or no thought was given to the frantic appeals of museum staff for major administrative budget increases resulting in a near-disastrous opening. Belatedly and with the impact of both professional and lay criticism additional finances have been forthcoming. Ironically approximately fifty per cent of the 1972 revenue was provided by federal sources making possible still further developments in display and education programs. The museum is now re-established as one of Canada's major institutions providing the 1,000,000 or more visitors each year with well told visual stories of man and his mixed relationship with his environment.

Accepted in 1972 as a National Museums' "associate," a five-point expansion of activities is under way in research, museum training, advisory services to the small community institutions, including assistance in display design, and an ambitious series of travelling exhibitions. This program is being aided and abetted by a new political administration whose premier announced shortly after taking office an emergency grant of three hundred and seventy thousand dollars was to be given to complete the long delayed anthropology gallery. In addition, the minuscule half million dollar grant for museum operations of 1972-73 was given an 80 per cent hike in the first budget under the new regime. As a National Museums' Associate this institution plans to establish six Exhibition Centres in strategic locations within the province and convert some obsolete railway coaches into a historical travelling museum which will be pulled by an equally antique steam locomotive purchased for the nominal sum of one dollar from the MacMillan-Bloedel lumber corporation. Historians from the museum staff have also been called in by the new Premier to plan restoration of his office to the period of the 1900's after a rich harvest of artifacts, including old beams, desks and leaded windows had been discovered in storage.

The Provincial Museum throughout its eighty years of operation has built up an international reputation for its research and continuous flow of publications. Nine of the more popular handbooks were recently reprinted producing an estimated $20,000 in revenues.

In 1945 the Victoria Art Society rented a down-at-heel store in the business area as a gallery for the exhibition of local paintings. Twelve months later the Society became a charter member of the Western Canada Art Circuit thus making possible a continuing program of travelling exhibitions. In 1951 the Spencer family, long time Victoria merchants, donated their Moss Street mansion to the Art Society for conversion into a permanent gallery and its first, professional director-curator was appointed. These events coming in rapid succession radically changed the initial philosophy of the Society. The emerging policy was designed to develop significant collections – a program which in the past twenty years saw rejections of two major benefactions that could have tended to lower standards.

In more recent years the gallery has attracted sympathetic patrons, one of whom, Mrs. Isabel Pollard of San Francisco, has consistently added to an important Japanese department. Another benefactress, Mrs. Chen King Foh and her daughter, formerly of Djakarta, donated 306 examples of rare and ancient porcelain, jade, bronze, lacquer, and *cloisonné* in addition to an extended loan of over 400 other oriental artifacts. To have this collection released from Indonesia in 1970 required substantial diplomatic and other assistance, including the use of a Canadian Forces plane for transportation of these rare pieces.

A small but growing collection of Old Masters is also on view including a portfolio of eighty drawings attributed to Goya. Contemporary works by American and Canadian artists continue to find their way into this relatively small but highly important institution. To celebrate the 1958 centennial, the Art Gallery added two contemporary galleries, and two further annexes were formally opened in November 1970 as a premature tribute to the 1971 festivities. The gallery's 1972 program involved preparation of its extensive collection of Japanese arts for showing at the Royal Ontario Museum. The gallery has also received an assurance of another bequest of "more than a million dollar collection of Renaissance and Baroque art," yet the annual grant from the province as late as 1972 remained at $10,000.

Emily Carr, Canada's legendary woman painter and author, was born in Victoria in December 1871. In her younger days she was described as wilful. Later in life she became an eccentric who preferred the discomforts of an erratic existence surrounded by animals, occasionally deserting the flesh-pots of the city to cohabit with the Indians. An impulsive and highly emotional painter, Miss Carr went to Paris to study but returned "after having learnt nothing" yet bringing back a more sophisticated technique and a new philosophy. Apart from a small coterie of friends (some of whom were not too

318

sure), Miss Carr had to wait until 1927 to be discovered by members of the Group of Seven and the late Eric Brown, first director of the National Gallery. It was only after her death at the age of seventy that her wilfulness and eccentricities were recognized as growing pains toward genius.

Over the years Emily Carr developed a bitterness toward Victoria. As a result, much of her collection went to the Vancouver Art Gallery in recognition of the encouragement she had received from that institution and one of its foremost members, Dr. Lawren Harris. The belated recognition given to Miss Carr as a painter has overshadowed her ability as author. It has yet to be recognized that she made valuable contributions to anthropology and ethnology through her interpretations of the Indian villages growing out of her complete understanding of the culture of a people who, at that time, were also viewed as eccentric and wilful.

During her lifetime Miss Carr lived in three homes, but only her birthplace at 207 Government Street has been given historical blessing. The house was restored with the aid of technical architectural advice and funds from the National Historic Sites Service, and formally opened in 1971. The main floor rooms have been furnished in the period of 1880-1900 and contain representative reproductions of paintings showing a span of ten years in her painting career, and other memorabilia. Only one provincial institution, the Public Archives, had the foresight to acquire some of Miss Carr's painting prior to her death.

The University of Victoria has its campus collection of Canadian paintings and sculpture distributed in the open corridors of the Fine Arts Department and the Library. However, in 1966, the gabled Tudor home of Mr. and Mrs. K. E. Maltwood, together with its contents, was given to the university, and now, according to the Dean of Fine Arts, is the only museum in the world entirely devoted to Art Nouveau of which William Morris was its most influential advocate and progenitor. Situated five miles from the campus at the junction of Highways 17 and 17a, it contains, in addition to fine examples of the decorative arts of the period, paintings and sculpture by Mrs. Maltwood, architectural drawings by Elmslie, and the giant Zodiacal Effigies of Glastonbury. Mrs. Maltwood's will includes a grant to the Royal Society of Arts (England) of which she was a Fellow, for archaeological research in the region of Glastonbury where relics of the pre-Roman era, probably related to the Arthurian legend, are believed to exist.

An Island restoration recently undertaken, and still to be completed by the National Historic Sites Service is Fort Rodd Hill, a coastal artillery installation built in the five year period 1895-

1900 and which includes the Fisgard Lighthouse dating from around 1880, on the small island of the same name. The original fort plan formed part of the coastal defence system designed to protect Esquimalt Harbour, established as a naval base in 1864, a battlement from which "no shot was fired in anger." The same federal agency completed the restoration of Craigflower Manor in 1967; refurbished the home and created a small farmstead annex. Also as a centennial gesture the O'Reilly family of Victoria restored the ancestral home of the Hon. Peter O'Reilly, one time magistrate, high sheriff, and member of the British Columbia Legislative Assembly.

The Dominion Astrophysical Observatory on Little Saanich Mountain north of the city, has an interesting display area on its main deck and permits public observation on its seventy-two inch telescope.

One of the smallest, most obscure, least financed but highly effective museums in Canada is the small green-painted shack known as the Francis Park Nature House, dedicated entirely to the younger population who participate in nature walks with eighty year old Freeman King. The Nature House is, in effect, an experimental station and laboratory where the youngsters, fresh from talks and hikes, return to study in the intimacy of the building, the life cycle of insects and other small creatures of the forest. This project has its parallel at Rock Forest, Quebec, where le Cercle des Jeunes Naturalistes des Pics-Dorés do their bird watching and star gazing through the summer months.

It can only be hoped that this project will be continued when its patron saint is no longer able to continue his program. In the meantime, the museum and park attracted ten thousand visitors in 1970, fifty per cent of whom were children. The Independent Order of Foresters built an addition to the existing museum; children of the group cut and marked two new hiking trails, and, says octogenarian Mr. King, classified "a lightning strike which possibly will be a blessing in disguise for now we can make a study of what might follow a fire in relation to ecological change."

The Maritime Museum of British Columbia had its genesis in the former Officer's Quarters on Esquimalt's Signal Hill in 1955, moving to the former Hudson's Bay Bastion in downtown Victoria in 1967. The museum specializes in the history of the west coast merchant marine and naval services with emphasis on British Columbia's economic growth through sea-borne development. Since occupying its new and enlarged quarters, a room has been dedicated to the work of the Hydrographic Services, a second room deals with the functions of the Marine Section of the Department of Transport, and another area is to be specifically devoted to fishing, sealing, and whaling. Despite the important contributions this museum is making in its own highly specialized field, it suffered from lack of financial support from the government at the two lower levels. An interesting footnote in relation to this subject appeared in the report of the Chairman of the Board at the sixteenth annual meeting held in May 1970, when he stated that "we had asked the provincial government for a grant of $7,000 but had received only $3,500. It was the government's opinion that we should close our doors during the winter months and they noted that we had not followed their advice."

In the spring of 1972, still confronted with a provincial administration antagonistic to subsidization of such institutions, it was officially announced that the museum would permanently close its doors and dispose of its collection. The Director of the National Museum of Science and Technology, recognizing its significance, sought first priority for the museum's contents. However, within a few weeks the National Museums' Board of Canada provided funds to keep the institution alive until such time as a permanent solution could be discovered and an approach made to the new provincial administration. Given this incentive the museum board has initiated a refurbishing program which will include new display areas relating both to the history of the West Coast merchant marine and that of the Royal Canadian Navy. The small staff that had been receiving little more than token wages for their dedication now have salaries comparable to those paid to provincial personnel just a few blocks away.

The director and staff of the Provincial Museum and Public Archives and other provincial agencies have developed a tradition of advisory services for the community institutions throughout the province. Leadership has been given for the founding and development of the British Columbia Museums' Association, the most active regional association in Canada, which holds annual three-day seminars and publishes the *B.C. Museum Round-Up,* a sixty to seventy page quarterly devoted to competently written technical papers geared to the custodians and volunteers of the small museum.

The impact of more than one hundred and fifty museums in British Columbia is making itself felt on the tourist industry and educational authorities, but until 1973 appeals to the government for financial help had fallen on deaf ears. Reflecting the philosophy of a new generation of governments of all political stripes, Premier Dave Barrett recently told an interviewer that "the rich cultural heritage of Canadians transcends all politics," and added that "progressive programs will be initiated without delay so that British Columbians and Canadians from coast to coast will be made aware of the legacy left for them by the aborigines and early pioneers."

On the horizon are two additional federal projects: one at Fort

St. James where the National Historic Sites Service in co-operation with the province is restoring the fort; and the second on Nootka Island, two hundred miles up the west coast of Vancouver Island, where Captain Cook landed in 1778.

39

The two areas designated as territories, the Yukon and the North-West, cover over a million and a half square miles, largely uninhabited with a concentration of population in about a bakers' dozen of communities. The largest of these is Whitehorse (Yukon) which had 4771 residents in 1966, followed by Yellowknife, now rapidly expanding as the new capital of the Northwest Territories and which had only 3741 inhabitants in 1966. The total population of this vast, relatively undeveloped region is about 43,000 with a density per square mile of 0.07 in the Yukon and 0.02 in the Northwest Territories, yet museums manage to be created, live, and actually flourish in this area.

Canada may not have the most northerly museum in the world but in terms of isolation Dawson City, in addition to being less than 100 miles south of the 60th parallel, is 300 air miles north of its nearest museum neighbour in Whitehorse and 800 miles northwest of the rapidly expanding museum in Yellowknife.

There is every reason to believe that more museums will be opening in this vast expanse of what was, until recently, described as wasteland. Arts and crafts centres have already appeared on Baffin Island and other Eskimo communities in the northeast. It may just be that with the recent rush northwards in the search for more natural resources to exploit, more museums should be encouraged with policies directed toward ecological research and interpretation.

The Museum of the North at Yellowknife was founded in 1957, expanded in 1963, and is now, or shortly will be, controlled and administered by the Government of the Northwest Territories. For the moment it appears to emphasize ethnology as illustrated by the native Eskimo and Indian crafts but undoubtedly it will have other departments closely allied with biology and the earth sciences. The Commissioner has indicated that but for fiscal cutback a major expansion program of the museum would already be under way.

However, in the Yukon a different form of action was launched in 1962 and has since been expanded. Here the National Historic

323

Sites Service, proposes to pour into the ghost towns of Dawson and Whitehorse, over the next few years, several million dollars for the restoration of many of the buildings and two or three of the derelict sternwheelers, relics of the now legendary gold rush of 1896.

Dawson City, on the Skeena River, with a population of 20,000 in 1899, is now reduced to a scant 500. To stimulate tourism, the federal government contributed half a million dollars to the Dawson City Festival of 1962. This was described by David Cobb in an article in *The Canadian Magazine* as a "makeshift effort, flashy surgery on a couple of limbs of a creaking torso"; an apt and highly descriptive summary of an over-ambitious project which, in terms of show-biz, just bombed. A more intelligent and certainly a more authentic approach is now under way with restoration work already started on the remnants of haphazard mining improvisations, and on buildings "faded by age and heaved over by permafrost." The Palace Grand, the Dawson City opera house and burlesque theatre of 1898, is now completely restored, as is the S.S. *Keno,* one of the historic sternwheelers which ploughed the Yukon rivers, with twelve more structures in the overall plan.

At Whitehorse, fifty miles north of the British Columbia border but 924 miles by highway from Dawson Creek, the McBride Museum has been in operation since 1951. Temporary quarters were abandoned when Canada's centennial year was celebrated with the opening of a new log cabin museum. One floor is dedicated to the history of the gold rush days, the other reserved for native birds and mammals of the north. National Historic Sites had started two years earlier on the restoration of the S.S. *Klondike,* a historic sternwheeler which had been beached on the Whiskey Flats for many years where it served as "a constant target for vandals despite a seven foot fence around it." The S.S. *Klondike* now serves as a museum dedicated to early water transportation in the Yukon.

The growth which had virtually buried the markers in the Whitehorse graveyard has been cut back to expose the names of many legendary figures. Surface buildings of abandoned mines are restored, while the wilderness area in the Skagway-Juneau region will shortly become an international park area with The Department of Northern Affairs co-operating with the United States to perpetuate the legend of 1898 that here at the Chilkoot and White Passes the Mounties always got their man.

On January 27, 1972, the Council of the Northwest Territories approved a policy to establish "an agency to collect, preserve and present artifacts, data, historical archival material. . .pertaining to the historical record of the North," and to create a central museum in Yellowknife to that end. Ted Boxer, permanent secretary to the Northwest Historical Advisory Board indicates that initially archaeology, ethnology and history will be featured and will seek to develop educational services reaching all areas and reinforcing local museum programs.

40 Conclusion

A historical awareness and cultural maturity sweeps across Canada. A new young breed of politician reflects this renaissance through legislation and government financing. Patrons, both in corporate and private sectors, appear on the horizon giving fresh incentives for museum innovations, experimentation, and development. The concept that history is viable only after it has aged in moth-balls for a century or more, and must so remain for an undefined posterity, is rapidly disappearing. History, we now accept, ends yesterday. A new posterity is born today.

Over the centuries museums under many different names have undertaken the responsibility to preserve a visual form of communication while adapting techniques to conform to prevailing social customs and philosophies so that scholars of this and future generations can interpret through the objects of nature and the works of man our somewhat unarticulated ideals, vices, and virtues, and above all, our ability not only to survive but to evolve new social mores. It must also ensure continuity of history in all spheres of human endeavour by building up an imperishable record from the beginning of time being aware that, as one writer has phrased it – "The future grows out of the present but only with the understanding of the past."

The increasing understanding of the individual in relation to his environment and of society's evolutionary trends is based on museum collections and the essential research within these institutions. Without this research the constituents making up our social structure would be chaotic, unorganized, and largely unknown.

The cultural ferment in Canada is expressed in all facets of society. One obvious symbol is the contemporary all-purpose auditoria which two decades ago were non-existent but are now found in every major city and many small communities from St. John's to Vancouver. The Stratford Festival, a noble experiment begun in 1953, has served as prototype for summer festivals from Vancouver

326

Island to "The Atlantic Provinces International Festival." Cultural councils and centres, now totalling one hundred or more, stimulate interest in arts and crafts in smaller communities while serving as catalysts and fund raisers. Professional and semi-professional symphonies and theatre companies are commonplace with at least four professional ballet and an equal number of grand opera companies also making their contributions to the nation's culture and prestige.

Professional authors, poets, playwrights and composers who were traditionally starving in their traditional garrets or basements two decades ago are gaining national and occasionally international recognition, along with actors, musicians, vocalists, painters, sculptors, and craftspeople, some of whom are becoming members of the more affluent society. Pioneer folk singer Alan Lund who made his lonely way across the country as troubadour has now been joined by folk and country singers Anne Murray, Gordon Lightfoot, and Stomping Tom Connors and at times augmented decibelly by Canadian rock groups. Over the past few years our major symphonies, ballet companies, concert artists, and theatre companies have sought recognition south of the border and overseas, culminating in 1972 with the Stratford Players taking Shakespeare, in English, to the Soviet Union and Poland. Individual painters and sculptors exhibit around the world while only recently "Sculpture Inuet," an exposition of the arts of the Eskimo, visited Paris, Copenhagen, Moscow, Leningrad, and Philadelphia. The Canadian Conference of the Arts, formally The Canadian Arts Council, which twenty years ago when lobbying for the implementation of the report of the Massey Commission represented no more than two score cultural societies, now speaks on behalf of one hundred and sixty-one organizations.

Recognizing that hockey and horses are also part of our heritage, the exploits of Hockey Canada cannot be overlooked with a nod in the direction of "Rodeo Royal" already booked for a series of European tours. In the interim the almost unknown Cultural Affairs Branch of the Department of External Affairs continues to negotiate reciprocal cultural exchange agreements with other nations.

The steadily increasing number of competent documentaries, dramas, and other forms of visual entertainment produced by Canadians for television and radio, together with the less publicized but highly significant films from the National Film Board studios, should not be overlooked, along with the increasing stream of books being run off the presses for international sale by Canadian publishers since the publishing crisis of 1970-71. In Ottawa the National Centre of the Performing Arts is playing a new and unique role as headquarters for a government sponsored booking office with branch agencies established in the five Canadian regions to provide a steady exchange of Canadian performing companies and individual artists as another step to advance the cause of national unity through the decentralization of this form of cultural resource.

The foregoing summary indicates an exciting Canadian resurgence but without public acceptance in the form of fiscal support and attendance it could be viewed as a massive luxury expenditure at a time of inflation and dollar instability. However, monetary values are being replaced by the search for a richer life for men and women who are becoming increasingly aware of their cultural heritage, whether it be in art, the humanities, a singular but troubled history, or sports.

Before the millenium is reached other problems must be resolved, relating to fissures appearing in what we call the Canadian mosaic. These are generally related to multi-cultural recognition but more specifically arise from the English-French controversy and the demands of the Indian, Métis and Eskimo peoples. In the cultural milieu beginnings are seen in the recent action of the Ontario Arts Council in creating a Franco-Ontarian branch "to serve as liaison between Council and French language artists and groups." In Quebec the Fédération des Centres Culturels has associate societies in New Brunswick, Ontario, and Manitoba. At the same time, the Montreal Museum of Fine Art, following its announcement that it would close its doors for two years to embark on a $6,000,000 rehabilitation project of its venerable Sherbrooke Street building, was loaning its collection of religious art to the neighbouring Centre de Documentation de l'Oratoire Saint-Joseph and placing another segment of its vast reservoir of fine and decorative arts on the walls of the provincially-administered Musée d'Art Contemporain at Montreal's Cité du Havre. The museum has also made available much of its mediaeval works to the National Gallery of Canada while other treasures will go on loan to all major art galleries from coast to coast.

Almost simultaneously, came a statement from the Quebec Cultural Affairs Department that, in association with the National (Federal) Museums' Board it had created "cadres à activités culturelles" to develop regional museums in the nine administrative regions of the province for the reception of travelling exhibitions and "for other means."

At least two museums have created exhibitions relating to the Indian culture as interpreted by Indian consultants with commentary in English and the native tongue, and noting the proliferation of museums initiated and administered by Indian bands across the country, the Canadian Museums' Association announced in April 1973 the introduction of training programs for Indian aspirants. More advanced courses will be available at the University of British Columbia in 1975.

328

In 1970 museums and art galleries received $21,000,000 from the three levels of governments, including Canada Council grants for art galleries. In addition the Canada Council provided an additional $8,000,000 to societies and individuals working within the performing arts. In recent years corporate and individual benefactors have been appearing but generally such gifts from these sources are for capital expansion or the purchase of accessions; such gestures represent no more than five per cent of total revenues.

Legislation to protect the environment, to preserve Canada's heritage, and encourage development of a cultural awareness, is on the statute books of the federal government and most if not all the ten provinces and the two territories, with Crown Corporations being appointed to implement the legislation. This pattern is being adopted by increasing numbers of municipal governments. In early 1973 four western governments were investigating the possibility for joint public lotteries to raise additional funds for culture, youth and recreation, and judging by current estimates for capital developments, which for the present decade has now reached $178,925,000, it is obvious that while the millenium has not yet been reached "a Rubicon has been crossed from which no retrogression to the past is possible," a prophetic quotation written in the mid-nineteenth century about another such Renaissance. Until this goal is reached Canadian museums now numbering close to eleven hundred continue to conserve our national treasures while serving as a mirror reflecting a never-ending saga of the Canadian Renaissance with one new institution opening every five days.

The proliferation of museums could be written off as massive overproduction of a tourist product by eager-beaver zealots and Chambers of Commerce were it not paralleled by rapidly changing philosophies and policies with both national and international significance.

While the 1973 western Economic Conference was heralded as a historical political happening, a much less publicized achievement went relatively unnoticed three months earlier when the Canadian Conference of the Arts organized a three day confrontation between cultural participants, the Secretary of State, the Canada Council and other federal agencies along with provincial Ministers or their Deputies from all ten provinces and the two northern territories to report on and make plans for co-ordinated developments of Canada's cultural life.

On August 20th 1973 the Glenbow-Alberta Institute of Calgary announced that it had induced eastern Canadian interests associated with the publishing field to establish a wholly independent multimedia company which will, for the moment at least, utilise the vast

archival, historical and cultural resources of that Institute to produce not only books, periodicals and a quarterly magazine but to
initiate and develop programs in the audio-visual areas such as
television, films and radio. The Institute also hopefully plans to
instal in its new building a highly sophisticated computerized research service available both to the casual visitor and visiting scholars, two innovations which will be closely watched by museums
throughout the world.

Worthy of mention at this late date is the announcement from
the family of the late Rt. Hon. Louis St. Laurent that his former
home in Quebec's Eastern Townships has been deeded to the nation
and will shortly be opened as a National Historic Monument. Again
in Calgary, The International Ceramics Show was opened in the
gallery of the newly built College of Art.

The major railways also are getting into the act. In Edmonton,
the Canadian National is providing trackage on a temporary basis
for the display of antique rolling stock donated by both transcontinental companies dating from 1877 to 1948 while rails are being
laid on an abandoned roadbed leading to a permanent site. This
museum is being administered by a community society. The C.N.R.
has also announced that it is moving freight sheds and warehouses
from a thirty-two acre site in Calgary on which the original Fort
Calgary was built, making possible an archaeological exposure of
about one third of the original foundations and the erection of an
Interpretation Centre in time for the city's 1975 centennary.

At Anse aux Meadows, Newfoundland, a replica of a Viking long-
ship approximately one thousand years old which was recently unearthed at Roskilde, Denmark, will shortly be displayed at the Viking International Park while 5,500 miles west word comes from
Dawson City that a former brothel (sans inmates) is being authentically restored "to illustrate the social mores of the Klondyke gold
rush days."

Canadian Museums and
Related Institutions

NEWFOUNDLAND

334

338

342

343

344

345

346

347

351

352

355

356

362

NORTH WEST TERRITORIES

YUKON TERRITORY

Bibliography

BOOKS

Bataille, Georges. "Birth of Art," *Historic Painting*. Skira.

Boggs, Jean Sutherland. *History of the National Gallery of Canada.* Toronto: Oxford University Press, 1971.

Brooker, Bertram. "A Canadian Art Movement," *Canadian Year Book of the Arts*. Toronto: Macmillan, 1936.

Brown, Mrs. Maud F. *Breaking Barriers at the National Gallery.* Ottawa: Society for Art Publications, 1964.

Carmichael, Leonard, and Long, J.C. *James Smithson and the Smithsonian Story.* New York: G.P. Putnam's, 1965.

Clark, Kenneth. *Civilization.* New York: Harper and Row, 1969.

Coleman, Vail L. *The American Museum Movement.* Washington: Association of American Museums, 1939.

Cook, Edward T. *Life of John Ruskin.* London: Allen, 1911.

Currelly, Charles T. "Royal Ontario Museum," *I Brought the Ages Home*. Toronto: Ryerson, 1956.

Eisley, Loren. *The Immense Journey.* New York: Random House, 1957.

————. "Francis Bacon," *The Light of the Past*. New York: Simon and Schuster (American Heritage Series), 1967.

Fairchild, Dr. D. "Alexander G. Bell," *The World Was My Garden*. New York: Charles Scribner's, 1939.

Fergusson, C. Bruce. *Mechanics' Institutes of Nova Scotia*. Halifax: —Archives of Nova Scotia, 1960.

Garneau, Francis Xavier. *Histoire du Canada,* translated by Andrew Bell. Montreal: Lovell, 1902.

Glyn, Daniel. *Lascaux and Carnac*. London: Butterworth, 1955.

Goode, George Brown. *A Memorial to George Brown Goode,* Part II of the Report of the U.S. National Museum. Washington: Government Printing Office, 1901.

Guthe, Carl E. and Grace M. *The Canadian Museum Movement*. Ottawa: Canadian Museums' Association, 1958.

Hahn, Emily. *Days at the Zoo*. London: Secker and Warburg, 1968.

Harper, J. Russell. "Canadian Art Galleries," *Painting in Canada*. Toronto: University of Toronto Press, 1966.

Heinrich, Theodore, A. *Art Treasures in the R.O.M.* Toronto: Royal Ontario Museum/University of Toronto, McClelland and Stewart, 1963.

Hubbard, Dr. R.W. *Development of Painting in Canada*. Ottawa: The Queen's Printer, 1964.

Hudson, Derek, and Luckhurst, Kenneth W. *Royal Society of Arts and Museums 1754-1954,* London: John Murray, 1954.

Katz, Herbert and Marjorie. *Museums U.S.A.* New York: Doubleday, 1965.

Kearley, Mark. *Emily Carr and Her Work*. Victoria: Federation of Canadian Artists, 1946.

Kelly, Thomas. *Early Public Libraries in Great Britain,* London: The Library Association, 1966.

———. *George Birkbeck and the Mechanics' Institutes*. Liverpool: Liverpool University, 1957.

Lamming, Annette. *Lascaux*. London: Longman (Pelican Series).

McLennan, J.S. *Louisbourg from Its Foundation to Its Fall*. London: Macmillan, 1918. Republished by Fortress Press, Sidney, Nova Scotia, 1957.

Mackenzie, Catherine. *Alexander Graham Bell*. New York: Houghton, 1928.

Malraux, André. "Museums without Walls," *The Voices of Silence*. New York: Doubleday, 1953.

Massey, Rt. Hon Vincent (chairman). "Canadian Museums and Art Galleries," *Report of the Royal Commission on Arts, Letters and Sciences*. Ottawa: The King's Printer, 1951.

———. *Royal Commission Studies*, see Neatby, Stacey, Morton, Spinks, Comfort. Ottawa: The King's Printer, 1951.

Mellart, James. "Man's First Murals," *The Light of the Past*. New York: Simon and Schuster (American Heritage Series), 1967.

Michener, James. "The Caves of Altamira," *Iberia*, pp. 522-523. New York: Random House, 1968.

Miers, Sir Henry, and Markham, S.F. *A Directory of Museums and Art Galleries, Report of a Canadian Survey*. New York: The Carnegie Corporation, 1932.

Moorehead, Alan. *Darwin and The Beagle*. London: Nelson, 1969.

Murray, David. *Museums – Their History*, three volumes. London: Unwin, 1904.

Oesher, Paul H. "Smithson and the Smithsonian," *Knowledge Among Men*. New York: Simon and Schuster, 1966.

Parkman, Francis. *Pioneers of France in the New World*. Boston: Little Brown, 1865.

———. *The Jesuits in North America*. Boston: Little Brown, 1867. (reprinted 1910).

Pincombe, A. and R. *Moncton's Free Meeting House*. Moncton: private publication, 1966.

Ripley, Dillon. "The Smithsonian," *The Sacred Grove*. New York: Simon and Schuster, 1969.

Robinson, C.A., Jr. "Two Worlds of Alexander," *The Light of the Past*. New York: Simon and Schuster (American Heritage Series), 1967.

Russell, Loris. *A Museum for Canadians*. Ottawa: The Queen's Printer, 1961.

368

Shelley, Henry C. *The British Museum – Its History and Treasures,* Boston: L.C. Page, 1911.

von Holst, Niels, *Creators, Collectors and Connoisseurs.* London: Thames and Hudson, 1967.

ARTICLES AND ESSAYS

Anon. "Catal Huyak." *Illustrated London News,* February 1 and 22, 1964.

Balcarres, Lord. "Museums of Art." *Encyclopedia Britannica,* vol. 19, pp. 60-64, 1910-11.

Bishop, Morris. "1066," (The Bayeau Tapestry). *Horizon,* Vol. VIII, No. 4, 1966, pp. 4-26, American Heritage.

——— "The Duty of the Princes Is Magnificence" (The Middle Ages). *Horizon,* Vol XII, No. 4, 1970, pp. 54-61, American Heritage.

Boggs, Jean Sutherland. "The National Gallery." *Canadian Collector,* November 1969.

Bogner, Walter, F. "Museum Architecture." *Encyclopedia Britannica* Vol. 15, pp. 1033-1037, 1970.

Brown, Eric. *National Gallery Catalogue of Paintings 1912-13.* Ottawa: The King's Printer, 1912-13.

Burrow, J.W. "Makers of Modern Thought" (Charles Darwin). *Horizon,* Vol. VII, No. 4, pp. 41-47, 1966, American Heritage.

Cobb, David. "Bright New Life for Yukon Ghosts." *Canadian Magazine,* 1968.

Collins, W.H. "History of the National Museum (Canada)." *Annual Report of the National Museum 1926,* pp. 32-70, Ottawa: The King's Printer.

Connybeare, F.C. "Iconoclasm." *Encyclopedia Britannica* Vol. 14, pp. 272-275, 1910-11.

D.S.L. "The Morgan Library," *J.P.'s Place. Newsweek,* January 12, 1970. p. 64

Flower, Sir Wm. Henry. "Museums." *Encyclopedia Britannica,* 1889.

369

Fox, Arthur. "The Athenium and the Museum." *The Book of Newfoundland,* Vol. 4, St. John's: Newfoundland Publishers, 1967.

Fox, Sir Cyril. *Report on Museums of McGill University.* Montreal: McGill University Press, 1931.

Gesner, Abraham. *Catalogue — Gesner's Museum* (New Brunswick). H. Chubb, 1842.

Holland, Wm. J. "Museums of Science." *Encyclopedia Britannica,* Vol. 19, pp. 64-69, 1910-11.

Honeyman, T. J. "Eric Harvie and Glenbow." *Scottish Field,* August 1961.

Huth, Hans. "Museums and Galleries," *Encyclopedia Britannica,* Vol. 15, pp. 1037-1053, 1970.

Judge, Joseph, and Amos, James L. "Williamsburg: City for all Seasons." *National Geographic,* Vol. 134, No. 6, Washington: National Geographic Society, December 1968.

Kermode, Francis, "Jack Fannin." *Annual Report of Provincial Museum of B.C.* 1938, Victoria.

Key, Archie F. "Canada's Museum Explosion." *Museums' Journal,* Vol. 67, No. 1, London: British Museums' Association, June 1967.

Luckhurst, Kenneth W. "The Story of Exhibitions." *The Studio* (England), 1951.

Martin, J. Lynton. *Museums in Nova Scotia.* Halifax: Nova Scotia Museum, March 1969.

Mellaart, James. "Catal Huyak 1965." *Newsletter Royal Ontario Museum,* Toronto, 1966.

Napoli, Mario. "Greek Wall Painting." *Horizon,* Vol. XII, No. 4, 1970, pp. 22-25, American Heritage.

O'Dea, W.T., and West, L.A. (Editors). "Museums of Science and Technology," *MUSEUM,* Vol. XX, No. 3, Paris: UNESCO, 1967.

Parkin, George R. "History of Canada." *Encyclopedia Britannica,* Vol. 5, pp. 156-165, 1910-11.

Parr, A.E. "Functions of Museums." *Curator* Vol. 6, No. 1, 1963.

370

Pearson, Kenneth, and Connor, Patricia. "The Strange Case of Mellaart." *Horizon,* Vol. XIV, No. 3, 1967, pp. 4-14, American Heritage.

Robbins, M.W. (Editor). *The Belmont Report.* Washington: American Association of Museums, 1969.

Rubin, Jerome S. "Art and Taxes." *Horizon,* Vol. VIII, No. 1, 1966, pp. 4-15, American Heritage.

Schouten, J.F. *Theme of the Evoluon.* Institut Voor Perceptie Onderzoek, Eindhoven, January 1967.

Setton, Kenneth M. "Bayeux Tapestry – The Norman Conquest." *National Geographic,* Vol. 130, No. 2, Washington: National Geographic Society, August 1966.

Shotwell, J.T. "The Middle Ages." *Encyclopedia Britannica* Vol. 18, pp. 409-412, 1910-11.

Simmins, Richard. "Crisis in Art Museums." *Canadian Collector,* November 1969.

Squires, W.A. "The Gesner Museum." *History and Development of the New Brunswick Museum,* New Brunswick Museum, 1945.

Stenklo, Aina. *Stora Kopparberge Museum.* The Falun Mine, Falun, Sweden.

Symonds, John A. "The Renaissance." *Encyclopedia Britannica,* Vol. 23, pp. 83-93, 1910-11.

Trevor-Roper, H.R. "The King's Prayer Factory." *Horizon,* Vol. VIII, No. 1, 1966, pp. 66-74, American Heritage.

MUSEUM PUBLICATIONS (TECHNICAL AND PROFESSIONAL)

International

MUSEUM (quarterly) multi-lingual, UNESCO, Place de Fontenoy, Paris 7e, France or Information Canada, Ottawa.

ICOM (quarterly) International Council of Museums, 1 rue Miollis, Paris 15e, France.

National:

MUSEUM NEWS (monthly) American Association of Museums, Washington, D.C.

CMA GAZETTE (quarterly) Canadian Museums' Association, Ottawa, Ontario.

MUSEUM JOURNAL (quarterly) The Museums' Association, London, England.

MUSEUM ACCREDITATION. A Report to the Profession. American Association of Museums, Washington, D.C. 1970.

Regional

MUSEUM ROUND-UP. (quarterly). British Columbia Museums' Association, Victoria, B.C.

THE GRANDE NEW DAWSON AND HIND QUARTERLY. Association of Manitoba Museums, Winnipeg, Manitoba.

QUEBEC HISTOIRE. (bi-monthly). Fédération des Sociétés d'Histoire du Québec, Montmagny, Quebec.

DIRECTORIES

Museum Directories and Statistics:

1899 *Museums – Their History, Vols. 2. and 3.* (see Murray, David) London: Unwin, 1902.

1903 Museum Bulletin No. 3. Merrill, F.J.H. (ed.). Albany: New York State Education Department, 1904.

1910 *Bulletin No. 1. Vol. 10.* Rae, Paul M. (ed.). Buffalo: Buffalo Society of Natural Sciences, 1911.

1932 *Directory of Museums and Art Galleries* (Canadian). Sir Henry Miers and S.F. Markham. New York: The Carnegie Corporation, 1933.

1937 *Education Bulletin No. 4.* Dominion Bureau of Statistics. Ottawa: The King's Printer, 1938.

1951 *Report of the Royal Commission on Arts, etc. 1949-51.* Appendix VII, pp. 485-490. Ottawa: The King's Printer, 1951.

1951-52 *Museums and Art Galleries*. Ottawa: The Queen's Printer, 1955.

1957 *Inventory of Canadian Museums* (see The Canadian Museum Movement) Guthe, Appendix, pp. 36-48. Ottawa, Canadian Museums' Association, 1958.

1961 *Directory of American and Canadian Museums*. Washington: American Association of Museums, 1962.

1964 *Directory of American and Canadian Museums*. Washington: American Association of Museums, 1965.

1964 *Museums and Art Galleries 1964*. Ottawa: Dominion Bureau of Statistics, 1966.

1965 *Statistical Survey of American and Canadian Museums*. Washington: American Association of Museums, 1966.

1968 *Canadian Museums and Related Institutions*. Archie and Marjorie Key (eds.). Ottawa: Canadian Museums' Association, 1968.

1970-71 *Official Directory of American and Canadian Museums*. New York: Crowell Collier, 1971.

1970 *Canadian Museums – Statistical Survey*. Statistics Canada. Ottawa: Information Canada, 1973.

1970-71 *Directory of Canadian Museums 1970 with Supplementary Listings 1971*. Statistics Canada. Ottawa, Information Canada, 1973.

1971 *Directory of Canadian Archival Repositories*. Ottawa: Canadian Historical Association (Archives Section), 1972.

1973 *American and Canadian Museums*. New York: Cowell Collier, 1973.

1973 *Canadian Museums and Related Institutions* compiled by Archie F. Key (see supplement *Beyond Four Walls*. Toronto: McClelland and Stewart, 1973.)

Index

NOTE: Page references to Canadian museums and related institutions currently operating or under active development will be found in the Directory.

Giovo, Paolo, 17
Goode, George Brown, 17, 62-63, 86, 91
Government Agencies, Canadian
–National
 Canada Council, 77, 184, 228-29, 239-40, 328
 Canadian Broadcasting Commission. *See* Canadian Broadcasting Corporation
 Canadian Broadcasting Corporation, 170, 327
 Canadian Centennial Commission, 16, 175-76, 188, 198, 206-7
 Canadian Film Institute, 232
 Canadian Wildlife Service, 216
 External Affairs, Dept., 327
 Geological Survey of Canada, 122-28, 162
 Heritage Canada, 238
 Indian Affairs and Northern Development, Dept., 148, 222, 237
 Interior, Dept., 127
 Local Initiatives Program, 237
 Massey Commission, 138, 172-73, 217-18, 223, 227-28
 National Centre for Performing Arts, 327
 National Conservation Laboratory, 236
 National Defence, Dept., 225-26
 National Film Board, 170, 327
 National Historic Sites. *See* National Historic Sites Service
 National Historic Sites Service, 156, 174, 177, 178-79, 181, 188, 193-94, 197, 217, 220-21, 237-38, 243-44, 268-69, 282-83, 299-300, 303, 311, 313, 319-20, 322, 324. *See also* Museums, Canadian
 National Museum. *See* Geological Survey of Canada
 National Museums Board, 224, 234-36
 National Parks Administration, 148, 222, 237
 National Parks Service, 174, 222
 National Research Council, 147
 Northern Affairs and Natural Resources, Dept., 148, 222

Resources Development, Dept., 237
 Secretary of State for Canada, Dept., 231-32
–Provincial
 Cultural Affairs, Dept. (Manitoba), 270
 Culture, Youth and Recreation, Dept. (Alberta), 299
 Historic Resources Administration (Prince Edward Is.), 186
 Historical Resources Administration (New Brunswick), 203
 Newfoundland Geological Survey, 104
 Northwest Territories Historical Advisory Board, 324
 Ontario
 –Niagara Parks Commission, 244, 252, 255
 –Ontario Heritage Foundation, 249, 251
 –Province of Ontario Council of the Arts, 253-54, 328
 –Records and Archives, Dept., 245
 –Toronto Historical Board, 248
 –University Affairs, Dept., 254
 Quebec
 –Arts Council of Montreal, 211
 –Cultural Property Commission, 211
 –Ministère des Affaires Culturelles, 207, 211
 Saskatchewan Arts Board, 276
Grand Tour, 23
Greece, ancient, 17
Gregory I (Pope), 20
Green, Nancy, 303
Gresham, Sir Thomas, 34
Grimani, Giovanni, 23
Group of Seven, 15, 146
Guast, Pierre de, 98
Guthe report, 246
Guthrie, Ossian, 90

Haliburton, Thomas C., 100, 108, 188
Harley, Robert, 1st Earl of Oxford, 36
Harris, Lawren, 319
Harris, Robert, 183